The History of the National Association of Intercollegiate Athletics

Competition • Tradition • Character

John R. M. Wilson
Vanguard University

ISBN: 1-58518-929-4
Cover design: Jeanne Hamilton
Book layout: Jeanne Hamilton

Coaches Choice
P.O. Box 1828
Monterey, CA 93942
www.coacheschoice.com

Dedication

For my late father,

John A. R. Wilson,

who was not a sports fan
but who made sure that I was.

Acknowledgments

A literary accounting of the NAIA's lengthy and celebrated history has been long overdue. Thanks to Dr. Francis Hoover and Dr. Carroll Land, two gentlemen who chose to write their doctoral dissertations on the NAIA, and the author of this book, Dr. John Wilson, fans of the Association now have the opportunity to reminisce about the "old days" and discover interesting facts and stories perhaps heretofore untold. Dr. Hoover's dissertation covered the NAIA from its inception in 1937 through 1958. Dr. Land wrote his dissertation on the years 1959 to 1977. Dr. Wilson utilized his recent sabbatical to build on the works of Drs. Hoover and Land and added the organization's more recent history from 1978 to 2004. Anyone who has ever been associated with the NAIA will be forever indebted to these three men.

John Wilson would not have been able to accurately reflect the Association's history without the gracious commitment of time and the memory of important details and dates provided by many people. Much thanks goes to the people John interviewed:

John Arnold, James Chasteen, Cedric Dempsey, Tom Feld, Jeff Farris, Cliff Hamlow, Dawn Harmon, Wayne Kraiss, Rocky Lamar, Carroll Land, Dave Olson, Bill Patterson, Ron Prettyman, Carol Putnam, Wally Schwartz, Louis Spry, Jeff Struckle, Joe Struckle, Lori Thomas, and Bob Wilson.

Many thanks to NAIA staffers Nancy Elstun, Dawn Harmon, Mindy Pinkerton, and Carol Putnam, who put many hours into locating files, documents, and stories for John's research. As always, they put in the extra work with enthusiasm and a smile. Also deserving of our gratitude is NAIA staff member Rob Miller, who acted as liaison between John, the staff, and the publisher. As usual, Rob performed his duties with the same incredible passion he brings to work every day.

Any project of this magnitude needs funding and we owe much gratitude to the Founding Members of the NAIA Alumni Association who not only determined this book was a necessary effort, but provided all the funds necessary to see the project through to completion.

The NAIA is a family—a family built on a solid base of values and a true dedication to the development of young people through education and athletics. Most of all, it is a family of individuals who care deeply for this Association. That deep, heartfelt care was evident along every step of the way as this book was created. My involvement was minimal but very rewarding as I had the good fortune to meet or reconnect with NAIA family, all the while learning more about the Association's storied past.

Thank you to all involved in making *The History of the National Association of Intercollegiate Athletics* a reality.

Steven B. Baker
NAIA President and CEO

NAIA is known as a "small college" organization. We are proud of this fact. We aim to be "small" athletically, regardless of enrollment, because of our philosophy. Naturally the majority of our members will be of moderate enrollment, but today the determining factor in athletic "smallness" or largeness depends primarily upon size of athletic budget . . . [not] enrollment. In this sense, we hope we shall always be small.

Al Duer, 1959

Contents

Preface

Until now, no one has published a history of the NAIA. However, two unpublished (and therefore largely inaccessible) doctoral dissertations treated the early years of the association. Francis Lentz Hoover produced *A History of the National Association of Intercollegiate Athletics* as his dissertation at Indiana University in 1958, and Carroll Land wrote *A History of the National Association of Intercollegiate Athletics* (note the similarity in titles), carrying the story forward another two decades, to nail down his doctorate at the University of Southern California in 1977. For almost two decades, NAIA leaders have talked of updating those works, but it was not until the new Alumni Association got off the ground in 2000 that the project became a priority. With Carroll Land himself a founding member of the alumni group, its leadership began seeking someone to make it happen. I learned of the need at the September 2002 convention, and with a sabbatical scheduled for the following fall semester, volunteered to write this book.

Because little has been published on the NAIA's history, I drew heavily on the Hoover and Land dissertations for the first seven chapters of this book—uncited material was derived from their work, and that information was supplemented by *The NAIA News*, the official publication of the NAIA until its demise in 1998. For championship results at the end of each chapter, also uncited, I have used The *NAIA News* and the excellent media guides put out by Dawn Harmon and the NAIA's Sports Information Department each fall, winter, and spring. For the years since 1998, I have also utilized the archives sections on the NAIA Web site (www.naia.org), a great treasure of a resource available to anyone. For the bulk of the work since 1977, I used the official records of the association, including correspondence, minutes of executive committee meetings, Council of Presidents minutes and agenda books, and anything else in the NAIA archives that seemed relevant. A few pertinent articles (along with Jack Falla's *NCAA: The Voice of College Sports* (Mission, KS: NCAA, 1981), whose definite article reveals perhaps more than intended about the NCAA's worldview) also provided worthwhile help and are cited in footnotes throughout the book.

Supplementing these written records, I conducted a number of interviews, both in person and on the telephone, some formal, some casual. Those interviewed were:

John Arnold, Baker student and 1940s NAIA worker
Steve Baker, NAIA CEO since 1997
James Chasteen, NAIA CEO 1991-1996
Cedric Dempsey, NCAA President, 1993-2002
Tom Feld, President, Mount Mercy College, COP leader

Jeff Farris, NAIA Executive Director, 1986-1990
Cliff Hamlow, Azusa Pacific AD, GSAC commissioner
Dawn Harmon, NAIA SID
Wayne Kraiss, Southern California College President, COP member
Rocky Lamar, MidAmerica Nazarene men's basketball coach
Carroll Land, Pt. Loma Nazarene AD, baseball coach, NAIA President, 1981-82
Dave Olson, Pacific Lutheran AD, NAIA President, 1985-86
Bill Patterson, NAIA Director of Development, 1987-97; Vice President
Ron Prettyman, AD at Southern California College, Cal State Dominguez Hills
Carol Putnam, NAIA Administrative Assistant
Wally Schwartz, NAIA staff
Louis Spry, NAIA and NCAA staff
Jeff Struckle, NAIA Director of Member Services
Joe Struckle, President of Northwest Oklahoma State, COP leader
Lori Thomas, NAIA Director of Human Resources
Bob Wilson, Vanguard AD

I have benefited from varying levels of editing for content and writing by several people, including Mary (my wife and ace editor), Bob Wilson, Carroll Land on some early chapters, historian and NAIA athlete Greg Olson, and neighbor and friend Ed Lackey. Lori Morrison provided technical expertise in setting up the typescript. Vanguard University provided me with a sabbatical leave in fall 2003, making the whole project possible. Vanguard SID Beth Renkoski shared some of her historical files with me. Finally, the NAIA staff was always helpful in supplying me with information and materials, especially Rob Miller and Jeff Struckle. The NAIA's eagerness to help, ongoing encouragement, and avoidance of attempts to influence what I wrote were exemplary. Despite all the assistance, errors of fact and interpretation have no doubt crept into the book, and for those I bear full responsibility.

John R. M. Wilson
Costa Mesa, California
June 2004

1

Beginnings
1937-1944

Nineteen thirty-seven was a long time ago. Franklin Roosevelt had just been re-elected president in a landslide win over Republican Alf Landon of Kansas, but the United States remained mired in the Great Depression; the country would not regain full prosperity until World War II stimulated a breathtaking economic boom. The president, frustrated by the Supreme Court declaring New Deal legislation unconstitutional, undermined his popularity that year by trying to pack the aging Court with like-minded supporters. Domestic legislation, stunning in its reach during FDR's first term, ground to a halt by 1938 as Southern Democrats, alarmed by Roosevelt's power grab, joined Republicans in a conservative coalition that lasted through the rest of the century.

By 1938 people were becoming increasingly concerned about foreign threats to world peace. Japan had attacked China in July 1937, in effect beginning World War II in Asia. In 1938 Adolf Hitler began adding countries to Germany's Third Reich, with Austria and Czechoslovakia falling under his sway before his attack on Poland finally provoked England and France to declare war on him in September 1939. Yet the United States, in an unusually isolationist mood, kept her distance from the war. Despite Roosevelt's desire to be the "arsenal of democracy," and his very real efforts to help England survive Hitler's juggernaut, not until December 1941, when Japan delivered an invitation that could not be refused, did Americans openly join the anti-fascist cause.

During the Depression, American people by the millions sought escape from the grim economic and foreign realities. Movies provided the most reliable refuge from life's trials. Stars like Clark Gable, Bette Davis, Shirley Temple, and Mickey Rooney shone on the big screen, along with dancers Fred Astaire and Ginger Rogers and comedy teams like the Marx Brothers. Movie quality far surpassed the economy. *Snow*

White and the Seven Dwarfs in 1937 offered the first taste of a full-length Walt Disney animated feature. Over the next five years, an astounding four of the American Film Institute's top six films of the century hit the theaters: *The Wizard of Oz* and *Gone with the Wind* in 1939, *Citizen Kane* in 1941, and *Casablanca* in 1942.

Sports offered another escape. Baseball was still the unquestioned national pastime, and the New York Yankees provided a dynasty to believe in. They won pennants every year from 1936 through 1943 except for 1940, when they lost out to the Detroit Tigers by two games. And they did it despite the legendary Babe Ruth's retirement in 1935 and the loss of the Iron Horse, Lou Gehrig, to disease in 1939. Arguably the biggest sports hero of the late thirties wasn't even a human being. An undersized West Coast horse, Seabiscuit, captured the heart of America when he upset 1937 Triple Crown winner War Admiral in their 1938 match.

Professional football had a relatively small following in those days; not until the Baltimore Colts' classic 1958 overtime win over the New York Giants did the game really connect with the American public. Still, the Chicago Bears' 73-0 walloping of the Washington Redskins in the 1940 National Football League championship game did turn the heads of those who were paying even minimal attention. The college game, on the other hand, attracted throngs of rabid fans. Minnesota, Notre Dame, and Army won multiple unofficial championships (determined in the polls, not on the playing field) between 1936 and 1949. To have the top teams actually conduct a playoff to determine the winner was an idea whose time had not yet come . . . and still hasn't as of 2004 for Division I teams in the National Collegiate Athletic Association (NCAA).

For basketball fans, professional basketball was still ten years in the future, as the National Basketball Association got off the ground in the 1946-47 season. But in 1939 the NCAA launched what would become its premier showcase, hosting a national basketball championship series in Evanston, Illinois, won by the University of Oregon. Indiana, Wisconsin, Stanford, Wyoming, Utah, and Oklahoma State would also garner top honors before World War II finally ended in 1945, with the first three of those winning their titles in Kansas City.

But the NCAA was not the first. In 1938 New York hosted the inaugural National Invitational Tournament, bringing in teams from around the country to vie for a collegiate basketball championship. Temple University won the first year, and Long Island, Colorado, Long Island again, West Virginia, St. John's twice, and De Paul took home first place trophies by the end of the war. The nation's largest city had a good thing going.

But the NIT was not the first, either. In 1937 Kansas City hosted the very first national collegiate championship tournament, and therein hangs a tale.

❖

In reality, national basketball championships in which college teams participated already existed. The Amateur Athletic Union, or AAU, sponsored one right in Kansas City in 1936. These tournaments were not limited to colleges, though; AAU teams featuring older, more experienced players (basketball "tramps" in the words of a *Kansas City Star* editorial) provided an uneven playing field for collegiate teams. It would be nice, many college coaches thought, to have a national championship limited to college teams.

The AAU helped to bring about the college tournament. Following their 1936 event, the organization announced that it was moving to Denver for 1937. Evidently the Colorado city had offered a better financial deal. What made this situation particularly troubling for Kansas City was that it had a new Works Progress Administration-financed facility under construction. President Roosevelt himself dedicated the Municipal Auditorium on October 13, 1936. This state-of-the-art building seated 9,960 for basketball but, despite a city noteworthy for its enthusiasm for basketball, it lacked a major event in that sport with the AAU having left town.

According to legend, area businessman Frank Cramer and James Naismith, the inventor of basketball, sat around the kitchen table and discussed the possibility of organizing a tournament for small colleges in Kansas City.[1] Certainly association with Naismith's name would impute prestige to the event. In November 1891, as deteriorating weather precluded outdoor sports, young Naismith, a physical education instructor at a Massachusetts YMCA school (now Springfield College), wrestled with the problem of providing healthy indoor physical activity. He sat down and wrote out thirteen rules for a new game and asked the school janitor to find two 15x15 boxes for goals. The unsung janitor instead found two half-bushel peach baskets and installed them against the balcony, where a person could retrieve the ball from the baskets and put it back into play.

The game was a smash hit in the classes, and students carried it home with them to numerous YMCAs over the Christmas holidays. Within a year basketball was being played from coast to coast. The first intercollegiate game, on February 9, 1895, saw the Minnesota State School of Agriculture top Hamline, 9-3, and immediately lay claim to the state championship.[2] In 1898 Naismith, having completed a medical degree in Denver, moved to the University of Kansas, which would become a basketball power for the next century.[3] It is certainly plausible that the elderly Naismith might have discussed the idea of a new tournament with his friend Cramer. No doubt basketball enthusiasts in the area spent a great deal of their social time lamenting the void in the local sports calendar.

Something had to be done. According to Francis Hoover, the most reliable source on early NAIA history, Dr. J. A. Reilly of the Kansas City Athletic Club, a man who had actively promoted AAU tournaments in town, approached *Kansas City Star* sports editor C. E. McBride, wondering if a college-only event could be developed to replace the AAU's format.[4] McBride referred him to Emil S. Liston, the athletic director of Baker University, a small college in Baldwin City, about 50 miles southwest of Kansas City and 15 miles south of Lawrence, home of the University of Kansas. Liston was a close personal friend of Naismith, so it is not unlikely that they had been among those throwing around ideas for a new basketball competition. When Dr. Reilly approached the Baker coach, his inquiry found fertile ground. Liston assisted Reilly that first year, but the latter faded from sight as Liston seized the initiative and, in essence, became the father of the NAIA. It is interesting to note the parallels between the origins of the NCAA and NAIA: both emerged as answers to particular problems (football violence, a basketball void) and eventually grew into major organizations with broad responsibilities.

Emil Liston, born in Stockton, Missouri, on August 21, 1890, grew up in Baldwin City, graduated from the local high school, and compiled a very impressive record as an athlete at Baker, winning eleven letters in football, basketball, and baseball. After graduating from Baker, he spent seven years coaching and directing athletics in Kansas, Missouri, Michigan, and Connecticut, and he also attended graduate school at Harvard University for two summers and received a Master's degree in 1930. He returned to Baker in 1920 to serve as athletic director, a post he held until 1945—along with coaching football (till 1937), basketball, and baseball. His coaching record was studded with accomplishments: four Kansas Conference football titles and two in basketball. He was also a builder, spearheading construction of the Baker University Stadium and field house.[5]

As a coach, the staunchly Methodist Liston strictly disciplined his players, insisting that they conduct themselves in a way that would bring credit to Baker and themselves. He established a Department of Physical Education with an accredited major by 1927. He was a key figure in organizing the Kansas Conference Coaches Association, serving as that body's president for two years. In other words, Liston was a can-do guy. When Reilly asked for his help, he was unleashing a powerful force.

The 1937 tournament was an invitational affair, and until almost the last minute the size of the field was unclear. Ultimately, it seems, venue availability forced Liston and Reilly to limit the entries to eight, despite newspaper assurances in late February and early March that sixteen schools would compete. On March 8 the *Kansas City Star* reported that eight teams would play on March 9, 10, and 11 for the championship. The paper, presumably with McBride calling the shots, waxed eloquent about the possibilities for the new collegiate tournament, which could "preclude any chance of the National AAU tournament ever returning to this city." On March 8, in its finest booster mode, the paper suggested that "No particularly vivid imagination is required to visualize this 8-team tourney as the forefather of an immense college tournament of national scope."

Reilly and Liston faced two key problems. First, how should participating teams be selected? Liston sought conference champions or high finishers from six nearby states, and the two organizers sent out questionnaires to area colleges soliciting feedback and support for the tournament. A positive response heartened Liston. Many respondents expressed hopes that a tournament champion might gain recognition from Olympic officials in 1940, only the second Olympic Games to include basketball.

Financing was the second problem. The tournament, like the organization that grew out of it, ran on a shoestring. The AAU had run the previous tourney, and no fund was available to tap for the proposed collegiate gathering. As a result, Liston and Reilly approached the manager of the Municipal Auditorium, George Goldman, and convinced him to make the auditorium available at no charge, with many attendants also volunteering their services. Participating colleges would cover their own travel costs, with tourney proceeds to cover food and lodging in Kansas City. Goldman underwrote the local costs until the revenue had been generated.

On the court, Southwestern College (Winfield, Kansas) blew out Dakota Wesleyan, 54-26, in the first game. Central Missouri Teachers College (Warrensburg) handled Luther (Iowa), 56-38. Morningside (Sioux City, Iowa) topped Liston's Baker squad, 29-21. Arkansas State Teachers College (Conway) nipped St. Benedict's (Atchison, Kansas), 34-33, in the only close game of the eight played. In the semifinals, Central Missouri took care of Southwestern, 38-24, while Morningside outscored Arkansas State, 40-33. Southwestern won the third place game, the playing of which becoming a tradition that would last fifty years. In the championship game, Central Missouri's Mules downed Morningside, 35-24, to become the first champion in a list that has stretched well beyond sixty over the decades since.

Though the first National Intercollegiate Basketball Tournament took in a disappointing $700 in gate receipts, Liston's enthusiasm and determination were unflagging. He met with participating coaches on the second day to capitalize on the inaugural momentum and lay plans for a 1938 tournament, one that would be truly nation-wide in scope and produce a winner that could justly be proclaimed a national intercollegiate champion. The group named Liston chairman of the board of managers, or board of management as it was also called, and charged him with selecting board members to plan and operate the upcoming tourney. Liston told the newspaper that he had already reserved Municipal Auditorium for the week before the national AAU tournament in 1938, and asserted his belief that at least thirty-two teams could be brought in for Kansas City's newest attraction.

The following week Liston headed off to Denver and the AAU competition to talk with college coaches there and try to get them on board. Ironically, the AAU had placed colleges in a separate bracket in 1937, responding to long-time demands by the college coaches and, in fact, vitiating a major argument for the new Kansas City tournament. Too late! Liston had concluded that small colleges had no future in the AAU tourney, and providing them with a venue to gain wider recognition spurred his efforts to establish the new athletic event. He held firm to his rationale even after the NCAA launched its first tournament in 1939—small colleges would not get much of a chance in the NCAA or the AAU, so they needed the Kansas City gathering to display their talents to the nation.

Significantly, Liston named a board entirely made up of athletic directors and basketball coaches, both positions he held himself. These men, career athletics people, would run the organization until 1986, when college presidents seized power in a momentous change in direction. The first board was comprised of the following men from colleges and universities of varying sizes: Eugene Eberhardt, Oregon State Normal University; John Bunn, Stanford; Forrest Cox, University of Colorado; S. M. Clark, New Mexico Normal University; Al Baggett, West Texas State Teachers College; Henry P. Iba, Oklahoma A&M; Pat Mason, Rockhurst College, Kansas City; R. G. Rogers, Morningside College; W. B. Woodson, Arkansas State Teachers College; Arthur "Dutch" Lonborg, Northwestern University; Roy E. Tillotson, Franklin College, Indiana; A. F. Rupp, University of Kentucky; Roy Clifford, Western Reserve University; Max E. Hennum, Carnegie Institute of Technology; and Clair F. Bee, Long Island University. Liston had recruited an impressive collection of talent. Even the casual basketball fan can recognize luminaries like Hank Iba, Adolph Rupp, and Clair Bee.

Clearly, Liston himself ran the show. He informed board members that no one was to make money from the tournament. George Goldman underwrote the tournament so that teams would continue to be guaranteed room and board in Kansas City, including 24 hours beyond a team's elimination. Any receipts beyond covering those costs, should they develop, would be moved into a reserve fund under the board's control. Liston hoped to build up a reserve fund for more independent operation once the underwriting ceased. He wrote to the board on the eve of the 1938 tournament that it was "sponsored by no individual and no organization, but by the colleges and universities interested; this is an attempt to establish a national clearing house for university basketball."

The 1938 tournament expanded to its standard long-term format of 32 teams, though Western Kentucky could not make it and had to forfeit their game. The tourney had indeed gone national, with teams from Oregon to Virginia, and from Texas to the Dakotas. Though Baker University did not play, Topeka's Washburn University provided a local favorite, ultimately losing in the third-place game to Murray State, Kentucky, 33-

24. For the second year in a row, Central Missouri took home the title, beating Roanoke, Virginia, handily, 45-30.

In 1939, the Mules were knocked out in their bid for a third consecutive triumph, losing in the quarterfinals to Peru State of Nebraska, 45-31. Peru State wound up fourth, losing the third place game to Glenville State, West Virginia, 73-49. For the title game, 7,000 fans turned out to see the crowd favorite, Milky Phelps of San Diego State, take on Southwestern, Kansas. Phelps had an unorthodox one-handed jump shot that entranced the fans, and he took San Diego State to the brink of victory before they lost a cliff-hanger, 32-31, the only title game ever decided by one point.[6] Southwestern took home the first Maude Naismith Trophy, funded and presented personally by basketball's founder and named in honor of his wife. Although Naismith apparently planned to award the trophy on a regular basis, he died on November 26, 1939, and left no written proviso to that effect. As a result, the association has since provided the trophy as part of the routine tournament expenses.

Liston had evidently been working on the idea of taking the tournament beyond its early state for some time. In the fall of 1939 he published a circular entitled *Intercollegiate Basketball* as the official publication of the National Association of Intercollegiate Basketball, an organization that did not yet exist. He apparently set forth the objectives of the proposed body in that pamphlet.

On Sunday morning, March 10, 1940, the men attending the national tournament met in the Phillips Hotel in Kansas City. At that meeting Liston was chosen as temporary chairman. A Constitution Committee had already been at work before the gathering, and it presented its proposal. Following discussion, a new committee was named to revise the draft and bring it to an afternoon meeting. Further modification took place at that point, awaiting final approval the next morning. Meanwhile, a Nominating Committee was charged with drawing up a slate of four Executive Committee members and six officers.

The March attendees adopted the National Association of Intercollegiate Basketball constitution and chose Liston as executive secretary-treasurer, though the office would be commonly called simply executive secretary. The other five officers of the NAIB were all athletic directors: President Morris H. Gross, San Diego State; First Vice President E. F. Kimbrell, Westminster College (MO); Second Vice President Louis E. Means, Beloit College (WI); Third Vice President Flucie L. Stewart, Appalachian State College (NC); and Fourth Vice President C. E. Miller, Baltimore University. The four members of the Executive Committee were athletic directors Al Baggett, West Texas State College, and Raymond W. Hanson, Western Illinois State Teachers College, and basketball coaches Charles Dee Errickson, Washburn College (KS), and Charles R. Davies, Duquesne University (PA).

The leadership became something of a "good old boys" club, as the practice developed immediately of Executive Committee members simply moving up through the ranks until they became president, and even staying on the committee another year as immediate past president. Changing the guard was a very slow process, which on the one hand provided lots of continuity and knowledge of the committee's workings, but on the other discouraged new ideas and innovation. Ultimately, in the 1980s, this structure helped precipitate the presidential takeover.

Liston, confident in the way things were moving and not wanting to wait until the organizational meeting, had filed application to register the trademark of National Association of Intercollegiate Basketball in his own name on February 19, 1940. The rights to the name were formally transferred to the NAIB on December 1, 1941.

At that first annual meeting in 1940, the founders of the NAIB set forth four purposes and a rationale for the new organization:

1. To foster an appreciation of intercollegiate basketball and an acceptance of the responsibility for its growth and development.
2. To establish uniformity in the game through district meetings and intersectional play culminating in a national championship tournament.
3. To encourage district organizations, to foster clinics and other similar meetings for the good of the game.
4. To serve member institutions through the office of the Executive Secretary-Treasurer, which office shall act as a clearing house for helpful information and service.

   Fundamentally, the National Association of Intercollegiate Basketball believes in the socializing values of intersectional and national competition. In the development of such a program . . . the responsibility for the management and control rests with the administrators of college basketball. NAIB believes that such a program is compatible with a well-rounded, sound, educational program. Such a program administered through the NAIB organization is without the dangers of commercialization by private promotion.[7]

While the movers and shakers were upgrading the organization in their meetings, the players were providing Kansas City's basketball fans with the fourth annual display of athletic prowess. After Delta State, Mississippi, beat Hamline College, Minnesota, for third place, 45-26, Milky Phelps led his San Diego State team back for another title match. For the second consecutive year, the Aztecs had put on a grand show, pulling out four last-minute victories. In the end, though, they fell short, losing to the fourth straight area college to win the tournament. This time Tarkio College, just about 115 miles north of Municipal Auditorium, won the big game, 52-42.

❖

At this point it might be wise to take stock of what the competitors of the new NAIB organization were doing. According to a detailed analysis of the emergence of athletics at Indiana State Teachers College in the late nineteenth century, students had taken the initiative in organizing teams and competition. Fairly early on, however, the faculty and administration had taken over control, providing continuity, stability, and financial viability through allocations of student fees.[8] Just as some medieval universities had been student organized, so had some sports programs. But who would manage relations between different institutions? For most of its history, the NAIB/NAIA defined itself at least in part by its similarities to and differences from the National Collegiate Athletic Association, or NCAA.[9]

The NCAA had been born in late 1905, partly in response to football mayhem in college games that took many lives each season. President Theodore Roosevelt, a fan of the game, pushed for reform of the rules in order to prevent the abolition of the game, which he saw as the likely alternative. By 1910 some sanity had been brought to football, and by 1919 over 400,000 students in 170 colleges were part of the NCAA. According to the organization's constitution, its object was "the regulation and supervision of college athletics throughout the United States." To that end, the NCAA tried to educate colleges to the right ideals. By 1919, the two key issues facing that body were eligibility and amateurism.[10]

Rivaling the NCAA was the Amateur Athletic Union, organized way back in 1888 and claiming control over all amateur athletics. By 1926, it was clear that while the NCAA sought to make athletics an integrated part of the whole collegiate educational program, the AAU was not interested in that vision of sports. In addition, the AAU favored a top-down governance ideal while the NCAA argued for a looser model based on local autonomy as colleges strove to realize the ideals promoted by the NCAA. The relationship between those two organizations had its ups and downs for most of the twentieth century, with their roles in selecting Olympic athletes one of the most contentious areas.[11]

Two studies of the early NCAA have suggested that its most significant achievement was the codification and printing of rules for sports. The Spalding sports equipment company had published rules into the twenties, but their rulebooks implied that only Spalding gear was official. In order to permit easy reprinting of rulebooks and to negate the favoritism toward Spalding equipment, the NCAA began publishing rulebooks.

A key issue in the thinking of Emil Liston was the place of the small college in the collegiate sports scheme of things. Within the NCAA small colleges began agitating for more recognition in the 1930s, and in 1937 a committee was established to develop a program for the smaller schools. Even defining a small college led to confusion. A college might be small in size or it might be small in the ambitiousness of its athletic program—either one could lead it to be designated "small."

In his study of the NCAA, Theodore Forbes argued for a special role for small colleges:

> Unlike the powerful "big time" universities, they are relatively free from pressure of bowl games, highly competitive schedules, and other external forces. Freedom from these obligations should permit the small colleges to take the leadership toward improving intercollegiate sports and point out the philosophic concepts in relation to general education, if they would but acknowledge and act upon their convictions.[12]

Yet another twenty years would pass before the NCAA would establish a College Division to handle such institutions. Meanwhile, Liston had made clear his view that small colleges had little future in the AAU basketball tournament, one rationale for going ahead with the new Kansas City program. He appears to have believed that the neither the NCAA nor the AAU recognized the unique characteristics of small colleges, and the emerging NAIB sought to fill that void and realize the ideals that the pressures of big-time sports were corrupting in many NCAA institutions.

While regulation was one aspect of the NCAA's mission, another started to take off in the late 1930s: national championships. In 1921 outdoor track and field became the first NCAA-sponsored national event. Wrestling followed in 1928, thirty years before the NAIA added the sport. Then came the explosion: boxing and swimming in 1937, gymnastics, tennis, and cross country in 1938, and golf and basketball in 1939, the latter two years after the Kansas City predecessor of the NAIB tourney was launched. The NCAA went on to add fencing in 1941, baseball in 1947, and hockey in 1948. Thus, in terms of possible competition for national championships, the NAIB, by definition, was not remotely competitive in the 1940s.

The NAIB was, however, starting to develop its own traditions. At the 1941 tournament, the Kansas City Jaycees sponsored the first "Tip-Off" banquet for around 125 NAIB members and guests. This inaugural affair gradually expanded to include all 32 teams in the tournament, their coaches and managers, and other guests, and became one of the highlights of the week.

That year the annual meeting featured discussion about strengthening the 32 districts and their organization; the districts would long be the key building blocks of the NAIA structure and in those early years the leadership sought to find the best way to enhance the functioning of those key elements. The old boys took care of their own that year as well; the Executive Committee agreed that the retiring president would remain for another year on the body.

Another problem troubled the delegates in both 1941 and 1942—how to prorate travel money among participating teams. This issue, and the more critical one of not having enough money to pay all the travel costs, would bedevil the NAIA for the rest of the century. In 1942, the 32 teams from 21 states averaged almost 1500 miles round trip to come to Kansas City. Sentiment favored providing more funds to teams traveling the greatest distance, but just how to best distribute the funds continued to elude the Executive Committee during the war years. The amount of monies available for use had already expanded considerably beyond the meager levels of the first year or two. The 1942 tournament generated gross income of $12,797, of which $2787 went to Municipal Auditorium (George Goldman's early subsidizing of the tournament as auditorium manager had paid off for the facility), leaving a balance of $10,000 for use by the Association. That was the biggest chunk of income for the NAIB, with only annual dues of $10 from each of the 110 member institutions adding any significant further funds.

The annual meeting in those early years had decision-making ability beyond what would later evolve. It appears that the delegates to the meetings reached decisions, and if a school did not send a representative, it was bound by the decisions of those who did. In one instance in 1942, a constitutional change was passed and went into effect immediately. In another development, the 1942 gathering established a method to choose district chairmen. Those districts with at least six members would elect the chairman from among themselves by late spring. If there were fewer than six members in a district, the NAIB president would appoint the leader.

The tenuous existence of the young organization, and an indicator of how it was, in fact, more or less operating out of a suitcase, was brought home in 1943. On January 3, a fire destroyed the gymnasium at Baker University, where Executive Secretary Liston hung his two hats as athletic director and NAIB leader. Most of the organization's records perished in the conflagration. In another record-keeping mishap, in 1957 movers lost a file cabinet of NAIA papers while moving headquarters from Los Angeles to Kansas City.

On the court, the NAIB tournament flourished. In 1941, Milky Phelps returned for a third run with San Diego State. Sitting out the early part of the opener with an injured knee, he saw his team fall behind Western Montana. Phelps had his knee taped, entered the game, hit his first shot, and the Aztecs were off and running. Phelps hit a key game-winner in the quarterfinals to beat Texas Wesleyan, then, after West Texas

State knocked off Santa Barbara in the third place game, led San Diego State to their lone NAIB title, 36-34, over Murray State of Kentucky. The fans went home happy that night.[13]

In 1941, Northwest Missouri State, a quarterfinal loser, had been the last area team to survive in the tourney, but in 1942 two regional teams reached the semi-finals. Hamline's Pipers crushed Central Missouri, 45-27, and then Pittsburg State (Kansas) lost a tough 37-36 contest to Southeastern Oklahoma. In the final, Joe Hutton's Hamline squad won a hard fought 33-31 victory, showing a much-improved offense since their 1895 three-point output in the first college game.

By early 1943, World War II had engulfed Americans, and even for those not in the service, life had been disrupted profoundly. Symbolizing that impact, the opponents in the 1943 tournament's opening game agreed that the losing team would donate blood to support the war effort. Southeast Missouri State beat Dakota Wesleyan, 50-30, prompting the media to allege that the team was "out for blood." One of the happy stories of the tournament was tiny York (Nebraska), enrollment 50, upsetting Akron University, 53-49, before being eliminated by only two points by North Texas State. In a happy final match-up for area fans, that Southeast Missouri team edged Northwest Missouri, 34-32, for the tournament title.[14]

The war cut into intercollegiate athletics dramatically. Manpower, scheduling, coaching, and travel all suffered seriously—gas rationing made non-essential travel such as team trips very difficult to manage. Most of the NAIB member schools discontinued their active membership, and there was not much reward for those who stuck it out. The 1944 tournament was canceled due to travel restrictions and other factors that militated against such "frivolity." The war consumed lesser matters, sometimes literally. Fans mourned when they heard that the first big tournament celebrity, Milky Phelps, had been killed in battle.

2

The NAIB Pioneers Desegregation 1945-1951

By the spring of 1945, the outcome of World War II had become clear. It was just a matter of time before the United States, Great Britain, the Soviet Union, and their allies completed their victory over the fascist forces of Germany and Japan. Accordingly, life began to return to normal, even before the German surrender in May and the Japanese capitulation in August. Things were not totally normal—the St. Louis Browns, who had taken advantage of the watered down quality of major league baseball in 1944 to win their only American League pennant ever, played a one-armed outfielder, Pete Gray . . . and he hit .218! But big league stars began trickling back to the United States during 1945, and a large number of other returning GIs took advantage of the GI Bill of Rights and launched government-subsidized college careers. Higher education began a boom that would last into the 1970s as first the GIs, then increasing numbers of women, then the baby boomers caused record growth in enrollments. The times were good.

The NAIB happily participated in the good times. In March 1945, the national basketball tournament resumed, although with only sixteen teams the first year back. Travel restrictions had been only partially lifted, and most schools had not revitalized their athletic programs to the point of being able to participate. Area teams did not find the late war environment very rewarding, but some new faces did. Eastern Kentucky knocked off Southern Illinois in the third place game, and unheralded Loyola of New Orleans roared to a convincing 49-35 triumph over Al Duer's Pepperdine Waves in the title game.

At the 1945 convention, held concurrently with the tournament, delegates focused on how to get the NAIB back to normal. During the war many schools had let their memberships lapse and had paid no dues. The convention opted for the carrot rather than the stick, seeking to educate the delinquent schools about their obligations and to urge them to reestablish their active membership rather than punishing them. Attending members recognized the extraordinary conditions produced by the war and refused to allow those circumstances to negate the body's growth and positive approach.

As happens in all organizations that survive and thrive, after the war the NAIB began to manifest signs of professionalization, or perhaps one might say bureaucratization. In contrast to the mushrooming of government agencies and their explosive growth during the war, the NAIB's institutionalization barely registered on the scales. Nevertheless, up until 1945 volunteers had run the organization. Beginning in 1945-46, Liston earned $500 to serve as executive secretary, a relatively modest addition to his Baker University athletic director salary. The next year the NAIB stepped up his role, giving him an expanded position as half-time executive secretary with his salary jumping to $2000.

Liston's openness to an expanded NAIB role stemmed from a series of health problems. He had broken his leg in the autumn of 1945, and this incapacity was compounded when he contracted hepatitis while in the hospital; later he added blood clots to his list of physical woes. Though he was only 55 years old at that point, he seemed caught in a downward spiral, and in 1946, while vacationing in Colorado, he suffered a heart attack. All of this misfortune led him to cut back on coaching, freeing him to spend more time on NAIB business. Because he was receiving disability payments from insurance policies, Liston felt financially secure enough to decline his salary, helping the very modestly endowed organization to have a little monetary breathing room. Impressed with his generosity, the Executive Committee in May 1947 bought him an easily operated car, one he could drive even with his leg problems.

At that point Liston resigned his position at Baker and the NAIB rewarded him with a 10-year term of office as full-time executive secretary at $4000 per year, a sum hiked to $4500 in 1948 and $6000 in 1949. Baker generously provided him with office space so he continued to run the NAIB from the college; this practice of, in essence, operating out of a suitcase, would continue until 1957.

Some enduring traditions were launched in those early post-war years. In December 1945, pre-season four-team tournaments, later to be known as "tip-off tournaments," began in Kansas City. The first year, teams from Pepperdine, West Texas State Teachers College, Loyola of New Orleans, and Valparaiso, Indiana, played in the initial "tip-off" affair, and Valparaiso trounced West Texas, 51-34, for the title. The NAIB continued to sponsor such events in succeeding years as they moved off to member campuses.

At the 1946 tournament, two area businessmen launched another popular and enduring event, the Cramer breakfast. Frank Cramer had been one of the figures who played a part in launching the first tourney in 1937. He and his brother Chuck produced sports treatment products like tape and balm, and their Cramer Products business in Gardner, Kansas, about 25 miles southwest of Kansas City, grew into a major supplier for athletic teams across the nation. On Tuesday, March 12, they held the first Cramer breakfast, an opportunity for coaches and officials and guests to informally get together and socialize. Since by Tuesday morning eight teams would have already lost games in Monday's opening competition, the Cramers featured a "mourners' bench" for coaches of teams that had lost the preceding day.

For the second consecutive year, the tourney did not prove fruitful for area teams. In the semi-final games, the top two teams from 1945 both lost, which permitted Pepperdine to crush Loyola, 82-55, in the third-place game to gain a measure of revenge for their defeat the previous year. In the 1946 title game, Southern Illinois, a fourth place finisher in 1945 in the midst of four straight appearances in Kansas City, beat out Indiana State, 49-40, for the championship.

In 1947 the Kansas City Junior Chamber of Commerce, big boosters of the basketball tournament, launched a program that would in due course evolve into the "honorary coaches" tradition. In 1946 the Jaycees had begun helping promote the tournament and selling tickets to the week's games. In return they received ten percent of the sales they made. The following year members of the Jaycees were assigned to each visiting team to take responsibility for entertaining them while they were in the city. These local citizens would eat with the team, host them at the tip-off banquet when that tradition was established, and sit with them at their games. This program proved to be a very popular public relations gesture, enduring to this day.

After two years without a regional representative in the four semi-finalists, the 1947 tourney featured nearby Emporia State. The area favorites lost a nail-biting 56-55 overtime semi-final game to The Thundering Herd (Marshall of West Virginia), and then fell in the third-place game to Arizona State-Flagstaff (now Northern Arizona University), 47-38. In the opening round Marshall had outgunned River Falls (WI), 113-80, despite the losers' Nate DeLong firing in 56 points, a tourney record that would last until 1972. In the final, Marshall knocked off Mankato (MN) State, 73-59, to lay claim to the championship trophy.

During the war, trophies had been unavailable, and in 1947 Liston opened negotiations with the family of James Naismith, who had initiated the Maude Naismith Trophy for the winning school in honor of his wife. The Naismith family continued its interest in the tournament, but wanted to rename the title trophy the James Naismith Trophy. Once the details were worked out, in 1948 trophies were awarded under that name to winners going back to 1943.

One question that plagued the NAIB was just who should play in the national tournament. District committees were charged with the responsibility of determining what team or teams would come to Kansas City. As had been the case in earlier years, a school did not even have to belong to the NAIB in order to solicit an invitation. If a team did want to come, it had to pay a $25 fee to play (and also win the district committee's endorsement). In 1946 that modest amount (still more than the $10 annual dues for membership) was doubled to $50, and a proposal to redouble it the next year was tabled. As might be expected, the idea of outside schools coming in to play in their national tournament began to irritate members. What was the point of belonging if outsiders could come in and steal the show? Logic won out and in 1950 outsiders were barred from participation.

Just how the NAIB tournament teams were to be selected led to some friction early on. District playoffs to determine a representative began in some districts after the war, but some districts had far more teams than others while others had strong conferences whose champion should logically represent the district. Another complication was that some districts were far removed from Kansas City. The organization wrestled annually with finding an equitable means to determine recompense to teams traveling to Kansas City for the national tournament. One argument for district playoffs was that they would provide revenue to help defray the costs of a trip to the nationals for the winner. For 1947 district playoff earnings were split, with 50 percent going to the participating teams, 20 percent to the district treasury, another 20 percent to the district champion's expenses for the Kansas City trip, and 10 percent to the national office. The bottom line, however, is that there has never been enough money to cover all the costs for teams, meaning that for a college's financial officer, winning a district championship was a mixed blessing. It sure felt good, but it also meant that he had to come up with funds to make the trip to Kansas City happen.

The NAIB, despite presenting a major event in the biggest city in western Missouri, was in reality a tiny part of one sport among many in a nation whose attention was mostly focused elsewhere. The anticipated peace and harmony after the war had not appeared. Instead, the United States had plunged from World War II into the Cold War, and, with the advent of atomic weapons, the security that had seemed a birthright before 1941 had been forever compromised. After fighting a war against a racist Adolf Hitler, many black Americans and a few thoughtful white citizens looked askance at the wretched state of race relations in their own country.

In 1946, Jackie Robinson played baseball for the Montreal Royals, the Triple-A farm club of the Brooklyn Dodgers. Playing in International League cities drove a much-publicized wedge in the wall of segregation. His debut with the Dodgers in April 1947 cracked the wall in sports and captured the imagination, both admiring and horrified, of sports fans and the general citizenry. Though considerably less visible to the public at large, the NAIB played a significant and admirable role in desegregating college basketball and sports in general.

Keep in mind that in the late 1940s the United States still had legal segregation in most Southern states, and Missouri, with its heritage of slavery, fit that mold. Thus the NAIB functioned in an environment that was at best indifferent and at worst actively hostile to racial integration. Besides that, a substantial proportion of the NAIB colleges were in the South, making any progressive racial ideas very difficult to voice even if one subscribed to them.

The race issue first arose in the 1946 tournament. Morningside College of Iowa brought a black forward named Rosamond Wilson with its team. Theoretically, the NAIB was open to any team good enough to qualify, but in fact, as Francis Hoover put it, "the organization preferred that the participants be white only." The NAIB by-laws did not include any discriminatory provision, but the tournament committee had essentially implemented an informal rule against black participation when the organization was established. When Wilson appeared in Kansas City, he was forced to stay on the bench and serve as his team's manager as Morningside went down to defeat on his 19th birthday.[1]

In January 1947 the president of the NAIB, Pepperdine athletic director Al Duer, wrote to Liston condemning the discrimination policy as shameful and undemocratic and calling for its abolition. In Los Angeles, Duer lived in a much more progressive racial environment, a fact that no doubt encouraged him to take the lead in challenging the system. Liston responded supportively to Duer's letter, but noted the obstacles in the way of changing. Perhaps Duer could talk with some of the Southern leaders of the organization at the 1947 tournament. Duer did so, but made little headway against the region's well-entrenched attitudes.[2]

The next year two factors combined to force action on the issue. First, Manhattan College of New York, invited to the 1948 tournament, told officials it would not attend because of the bar against black players. Even though Manhattan had no black players, the school refused to condone segregation. Liston immediately asked the school to reconsider, saying the NAIB Executive Committee was going to deal with the issue during the tournament. Manhattan did in fact go to Kansas City and won two games before being eliminated in the quarterfinals.

The second impetus for change came in the form of a letter from Louis G. Wilke, chair of the 1948 Olympic Basketball Committee. He also protested exclusion of black players from the NAIB tournament, and said that such a policy jeopardized NAIB participation in the Olympic basketball trials that were so important to the association. This last letter arrived just two days before the tournament, moving Liston to poll the Executive Committee by wire about changing the policy. The urgency of the situation, coupled with an intense desire to see the NAIB gain recognition by participating in the Olympic trials, led to a 7-2 vote in favor of lifting the ban.[3]

The first black player to play in the tournament was Clarence Walker, a reserve guard for Indiana State. His team had placed second in 1946, wound up second again in 1948, slipped to fourth in 1949, and won the tourney in 1950. Coaching Indiana State was a promising young coach named John Wooden. Wooden was already well recognized, and his teams were noteworthy for their excellent deportment and for always wearing coats and ties when they traveled.[4] When Walker first entered a game, he shook so hard he was almost paralyzed, but a favorable response from the crowd loosened him up and turned a potentially ugly moment into a positive one. The event also set a precedent. The next year, despite a few angry letters to Liston from critics of the change, black players came with their teams from San Jose State, Portland University, and Lawrence Tech of Detroit.[5] One major battle for equality had been won.

The next fight took longer to wage and win. Black colleges and their representatives began agitating in 1950 for their admission to national tournaments. Eddie Jackson of Howard University, Harry Jefferson of Virginia State College, and John McLendon of North Carolina College attended the annual convention of the National Association of Basketball Coaches, an umbrella organization with NCAA and NAIB coaches participating. The NABC president, John Lawther of Penn State, agreed to put the issue before his executive committee, and reported that the committee had unanimously approved the petition and supported the long overdue integration. Unfortunately, the NABC did not put on the national tournaments.

The black leaders then moved to the NCAA and NAIB to seek their approval. The NCAA dealt them a quick blow, however, when that association announced that it would hold its spring 1951 convention in Dallas, a bastion of segregation. The hotel there would not even permit black members to participate as full members of the organization. Black coaches and athletic directors, unwilling to suffer the indignities of supplicants in a hostile environment, boycotted the convention. Despite an impassioned letter from Mack Greene, athletic director at Central State University in Ohio, to top NCAA officials, the matter of discrimination never even came up at the convention.[6]

On August 15, 1951, twenty-one representatives from black colleges met in Chicago and organized the National Athletic Steering Committee (NASC) to study and overcome discrimination in intercollegiate athletics. Their primary goal as an organization, with President Harry Jefferson and Executive Secretary Mack Greene leading the way, was to get a black team into either the NAIB or NCAA championship tournaments. The NCAA quickly dashed any hopes for immediate relief, demonstrating several ways that defenders of the status quo could undermine efforts at change. The NCAA told NASC that its "championship apparatus" could not fit in black colleges. The association had no way to include "small" colleges at all, and it had arbitrarily defined black colleges as small. Besides, McLendon wrote, "the NCAA voiced the fear that fans may not accept or appreciate the kind of game you play," and "your coaches may not be competent enough."[7] Fortunately, the NAIB proved more open and receptive, though that is a story for the next chapter.

With the integrated Indiana State team participating (along with such future NCAA Division I schools as Arizona State, Brigham Young, San Jose State, and Louisville), the 1948 tournament unfolded without incident. Wooden's lads won a tense 66-65 overtime semi-final game over Hamline while Louisville eliminated Xavier of Ohio, 56-49, in the other Friday game. In the finals, Wooden's last game before moving on to UCLA and lasting fame in the national coaching spotlight, Indiana State fell to Louisville, 82-70.

As for the Olympic trials that had been such a motivating force for the NAIB, the agreed-upon format was carried out. The two NCAA finalists, the National Invitational Tournament (NIT) winner, and the NAIB champion Louisville were placed in one bracket, and three AAU teams and the YMCA champion made up the other. In the event, Louisville was eliminated in the first round.

❖

Nineteen forty-nine turned out to be another eventful year for the still-young organization. Pursuant to a change promulgated in 1948, past presidents became ex-officio members of the Executive Committee as long as they represented member schools, providing the old boys club one more means of on-going solidarity.

The annual meeting was historic because, for the first recorded time, someone suggested that the NAIB broaden the scope of its mission to add other sports than basketball. This proposal, to which Liston responded favorably, led to the formation of a committee to explore the possibilities.

Another committee was established to work up a simple code for individual athlete eligibility for the national tournament. It is worth noting that early attempts to set such standards limited the issue to post-season action, something the NCAA retained for many years after the NAIA shifted to a more stringent, every-semester eligibility test to take part in any intercollegiate athletic contest.

Yet another issue raised at the convention concerned the naming of an All-America basketball team. The NAIB had been naming All-American teams since 1940, but in reality they were all-tournament teams. To actually name a national team posed some tough questions. Whereas one could watch all the players in the tournament and have first-hand impressions (and statistics), selecting a national team meant relying on the observations of others. The committee developed a procedure whereby players would select an all-opponent team with the proviso that players selected had to play for member colleges and universities. The NAIB began naming the All-Americans in 1951.

The 1949 tournament provided an added incentive for the winner: a four-game, ten-day trip to Hawaii at the start of the 1949-50 season. A nice mixture of young blood and perennial NAIB powers reached the semifinals. Hamline knocked out Beloit, Wisconsin, 52-43, stalling the last eight minutes after their big star Vern Mikkelson fouled out, and Regis, Colorado, eked out a 48-45 double-overtime win over Indiana State in the other semifinal. Then Hamline, the 1942 tournament winner, picked up its second title with a 57-46 win over Regis.

While in retrospect the desegregation of the national tournament stands out as the pivotal 1948 event in the association's history, 1949 brought another critical transition. Emil Liston's health woes since his 1946 heart attack had eased enough that he had actively directed the NAIB's affairs as executive secretary. But on October 26, 1949, "Lis," as he was known to his friends, suffered a second, fatal attack and died at his home in Baldwin City, leaving the organization bereft of its most important leader.

Two days later the Executive Committee met in Kansas City and charged Gus Miller, the current president, with handling Liston's duties until a new executive secretary could be selected. Rather than launching a national search, Miller and four other committee members sought a successor among college men who were already familiar with the organization. The committee screened applications and suggestions with a target date of November 27 for the next full Executive Committee meeting in Kansas City. At that meeting, the search committee recommended A. O. Duer to take over operating the NAIB. After extensive discussion, Duer accepted, with the provision that no major new projects be undertaken until he had gotten his feet firmly on the ground.

Al Duer, 44, had served as athletic director and basketball coach at Pepperdine University in Los Angeles since 1939, and he continued in those positions until 1957, running the association out of his Pepperdine office as Liston had done at Baker. The new leader had already been very active in the NAIB. From 1940 to 1943 he had served as the first district chairman in California, and in 1942 he drove his Pepperdine team to the national tournament in a two-car caravan, barely making it back to Los Angeles after worn out tires stranded him in Colorado's mountains en route home.[8] In 1943 he won election to the Executive Committee, taking his turn as president during the 1946-47 school year; from that position he had catalyzed the integration of the NAIB tournament in 1948.[9]

The 6-foot-2-inch cigar-smoking Duer had demonstrated some ambition akin to Liston's by organizing his own basketball tournament in Los Angeles, a National College Invitational Basketball Tournament for December 1947. With the Helms Athletic Foundation underwriting $25,000 in costs, Duer brought in Arkansas, Idaho, BYU, Loyola, Marshall, Pepperdine, Syracuse, and West Texas State to play, with Marshall edging Syracuse, 46-44, in the final. USC and UCLA, the local powers, had already been booked for the tourney dates, but said they would play in 1948, so the Helms Foundation pledged support for another year. Unfortunately, the Pacific Coast Conference decided to establish its own tournament, so USC and UCLA were again no-shows. Hamline's team, which wound up its season the NAIB winner, clobbered Pepperdine, 62-38, in the final. The bottom line was grim; the tournament again lost $5000 and, with no prospect of the big Los Angeles universities participating, Helms pulled the plug.[10]

In many ways, Duer reflected the attitudes of the church-related liberal arts college at which he worked. A former colleague and dean at Pepperdine, Earl V. Pullias, set forth his vision of the goals of such a college at a 1971 commencement address at Pasadena College (now Point Loma Nazarene University). Duer's leadership of the association clearly reflects these points. The college should be increasingly Christian in all aspects of its work, recognizing that the general spirit of the campus educates more significantly than any individual part. One should do well whatever one undertakes, including a good balance between work and play, body, mind, and spirit. Duer constantly sought to promote an integration of education and sport in the NAIA, reflecting this ideal balance. One should live within one's income, a trait that Duer applied overzealously in his new position. He was the proverbial man who threw nickels around like manhole covers, counting paper clips and requiring staff to turn in a pencil stub when they needed a new pencil, creating a slight aura of paranoia in the office.[11] (That frugality well suited him as Liston's successor. The NAIB founder, who was accused of loving basketball only just ahead of stretching the dollar, famously told officials when he sent them their checks, "If you don't need it, send it back.")[12] Small was beautiful—it was important to preserve the personal touch in an increasingly impersonal world. A Christian liberal arts college, or a national sports association of small colleges, should provide freedom with responsibility—the NAIA should not have a large staff of regulators, but encourage a healthy degree of self-regulation. One should not be dismayed by the complexity and difficulty of the urgent problems of modern life, but face up to them and the dark side of human nature, realizing that negative experiences could be a source of growth.[13] Thus Duer managed to lead the NAIA for twenty-six years and remain optimistic through all the trials of that tumultuous time. This Christian understanding of life led him to continually focus on (and pontificate on) the ties between ethics and sports, a focus that helped distinguish the NAIA from the NCAA.

One ethical issue that troubled the NAIB was gambling. In 1946, the NAIB had passed a resolution against organized gambling. In 1949-50 Gus Fish, basketball coach at Kansas State Teachers College in Emporia, began providing a statistical service for NAIB schools. Since the wire services did not carry such material at that time, the new service dispensed some valuable information, though it was limited to basketball in its early years. The association, however, was concerned that organized gamblers could use such information, if improperly handled. This fear of gambling prompted the unprecedented exclusion of a member institution, the University of Nevada, from the national tournament in 1950. Because the school could not afford to make the trip (again the financial limitations of the NAIB manifest themselves), a gambler had offered to finance it for them, and the team had accepted. This troubling connection led to the exclusion.

The following year, the potential for a gambling scandal was realized, though in the NCAA. CCNY and Kentucky were among seven NCAA schools from which 32 players had reputedly fixed 86 games. CCNY had just become the first team to win the NIT and NCAA titles in the same year and was a major basketball power; the scandals were instrumental in the college de-emphasizing the sport. It may be that the NAIB's great sensitivity on the issue helped avert such a disaster in its own ranks.

The NCAA was wrestling with other ethical issues at the same time. In 1946 delegates to a Conference of Conferences drafted "Principles for the Conduct of Intercollegiate Athletics." They related to definitions of amateurism, requiring athletes to meet the same academic standards as non-athletes, not using financial aid for athletic ability (!), and not offering athletes financial inducements to attend one's school. These principles were adopted in 1948 as the Sanity Code to restore sanity to intercollegiate athletics. It added investigation to regulation and enforcement as NCAA functions. However, the one penalty for violations was expulsion from the NCAA, a drastic step. When seven schools were found to be in violation of the code in January 1950, the Convention could not muster the required two-thirds majority to expel the violators. That lack of will proved fatal to enforcement, and in 1951 the Sanity Code was repealed.[14]

An NAIB literary milestone occurred in January 1950 when a new monthly magazine, the *NAIB News*, made its debut. It eventually grew into an impressive publication, but the early issues were neither timely nor comprehensive. Though it was supposed to be a monthly for all NAIB members, only five issues appeared in 1950. In September 1952 the name became *NAIA News*, though the quality did not appreciably improve. Over the years the publication appeared monthly, quarterly, fortnightly, and finally, in late 1998, not at all. Regular features included championship events calendars, violation reports, lists of NAIA coaches' associations, a film library, financial reports, rulings on cases, newsmakers, and a sports information directors

(SID) column. In addition, as the years went by thorough coverage of championship tournaments became a major feature, though in those early years coverage of the one, then few, championships was skimpy to the point of invisibility. Interestingly, though the NAIA did not sponsor football championships until 1956, *NAIA News* began carrying extensive post-season football statistics in 1953, something not even provided for the association's flagship basketball programs.

In 1950, some of the issues raised in 1949 were resolved at the annual convention. The Executive Committee would henceforth have *two* past presidents, a current president, and four vice-presidents, along with five members serving staggered five-year terms. This arrangement meant that first-year members would fill only two of twelve positions, giving the "old boys" a solid edge. In addition, non-member schools and member institutions delinquent in paying their dues would no longer be eligible for the post-season championship tournament. And, just as the NCAA was wrestling with eligibility issues, the NAIB ruled that transfer students had to be in residence 18 weeks at their new schools to be eligible for playoffs and the national tournament, which meant, in effect, that they had to begin the fall quarter or semester at the new school to be able to play basketball in March. As earlier noted, this first eligibility legislation pertained only to post-season activity.

In what would be the first of several annual awards, the NAIB launched the NAIB-E. S. Liston Memorial in the form of a plaque and a $300 scholarship to the outstanding junior student to participate in the national tournament. Qualification was to be based on scholarship (minimum 3.5 grade point average), citizenship, character, and playing ability. John Wilson of Eastern Illinois State Teachers College won the first award in 1950.

The 1950 basketball tournament included Al Duer's Pepperdine team, which made appearances in 1942, 1943, 1945, 1946, 1950, 1951, and 1952, with a second-place finish in 1945 representing their finest showing. Emil Liston's Baker squad had appeared in 1937 and 1941, been eliminated in the first round each year, and did not reappear in the nationals until 1996, when they lost a first-round game in the Division II tournament. This time Pepperdine got by American University (DC), 54-50, but fell in the second round to Tampa, 69-61. Tampa wound up losing the consolation game to Central Methodist (MO), 80-67. Taking the title after several close calls, Indiana State upended East Central (OK), 61-57, appropriating the Sycamores' only championship in twelve appearances in the tournament.

In 1951, the association approved the most momentous transition since it had been established back in 1940. Just as the original tournament had reflected the fruits of much informal discussion and concrete action, expanding the NAIB beyond basketball to other sports grew out of spontaneous letters from member schools and a groundswell of enthusiasm at the 1951 convention. The level of support became evident when the delegates asked Duer to poll the entire membership by mail, and before that survey had even begun, told the Executive Committee to go ahead and expand as soon as it seemed feasible.

Track and field seemed the sport with the greatest support. It had been the very first NCAA national championship way back in 1921. Fortuitously, District 10 had already planned to hold a track meet at Kansas State Teachers College in Emporia in the spring of 1951. That event became in effect a trial run for a possible national championship, and Duer and the Executive Committee watched the nearby meet with keen interest, even subsidizing it to the tune of $400. The Emporia meet was a big success in terms of participation, interest, and finance, and helped to stimulate the widening of the association's offerings. Duer's questionnaire to the membership on the heels of this successful event elicited a high proportion of positive responses. Thus, the Executive Committee agreed that on June 6 and 7, 1952, national championships would be held in Abilene, Texas, for track and field—and golf and tennis.

Two other items of business highlighted the last year of the organization as a strictly basketball association. First, district playoffs were made mandatory in order for a district to be represented in the national tournament. Revenues from those playoffs were henceforth to be split with five percent to the competing teams, 30 percent to the district treasuries, and the remaining 65 percent to offset travel costs to Kansas City for the nationals.

Second, the Helms Foundation worked with the Executive Committee to establish an NAIB Hall of Fame as part of the Helms Athletic Foundation Hall of Fame building already established in Los Angeles. Recipients had to win approval of both the Executive Committee and the Helms Hall of Fame Board. Those persons selected to the Hall of Fame fell into three categories: contributors, coaches, and players. Criteria for selection were:

Contributor—(1) Must be one who has made a major contribution worthy of national honor. (2) Must have made a contribution in the area of NAIB institutions over a period of years in coaching, publicity, etc. (3) His character and leadership in the field must be of the best.

Coach—(1) Have coached for 25 years, with a majority of this time in NAIB schools. High school coaching can count on the 25 years. (2) Must possess high athletic and moral qualities. (3) Must have been loyal to the NAIB organization.

Player—(1) Must have been out of competition at least 5 years. (2) Must have been highly skilled in his sport. (3) His moral qualities and sportsmanship must be in harmony with those of NAIB.[15]

It is noteworthy that athletic or coaching skill in itself is not sufficient to merit selection. The NAIB's emphasis on character, stressed by both Liston and Duer as early leaders and maintained as a key element of NAIA distinctiveness down to the present day, shines through in these criteria to honor the best of the best.

The last basketball tournament under the NAIB name took place in March 1951. Baldwin-Wallace of Ohio, playing in its second consecutive (and last) nationals, knocked off Regis in the third place game, 82-78. In the title game, Millikin of Illinois, making its first appearance in the tournament and led by national scoring leader Scotty Steagall, fell just short of upsetting a perennial power, but the Hamline Pipers prevailed, 69-61, for their second championship in three years and third in a decade.

3

The National Association of Intercollegiate *Athletics* 1952-1958

The wheels had been set in motion at the 1951 meeting, propelling the NAIB to its multi-sport future. At the 1952 gathering, a logical question arose: what should be the name of the broadened organization? The National Association of Intercollegiate *Basketball* was clearly no longer appropriate. At the general meeting, many ideas surfaced, but two fairly quickly outdistanced the others. One was the National Association of Intercollegiate Athletics. The other was the National Association of Intercollegiate Sports, whose abbreviation NAIS would rather neatly comprise the first four letters of Naismith, the founder of basketball. Though this acronym seemed a rather cute play on letters, Naismith's son Jack argued against it, maintaining that the organization was not for the sport but for the athlete, and thus that NAIA was a more fitting name. The convention then agreed to send out the top two choices to the membership for a vote. The result was a landslide victory: the organization would henceforth be known as the National Association for Intercollegiate Athletics.

Harry Scott, a professor of physical education at Columbia University, served as a consultant and helped to formulate the basic philosophy of the new organization, one that remained intact well into the 1980s.[1] The 1952 meeting also changed the way votes were handled. At the earliest gatherings everyone present had voted. This practice had given way to voting on the basis of the number of persons on district committees, assuming they were at the meeting. In 1952 each district got one vote, which simplified the tallying if not the overall process.

One other order of business modified a long-standing practice. Instead of assessing each member institution a $10 membership fee annually, the NAIA would charge a sliding scale from $10 to $50 based on enrollment. With the organization broadening its sports offerings and coping with overall cost increases, this move to enhance revenues seemed a long overdue one.

Beyond the renaming of the organization, by far the most important business of the 1952 convention concerned the question of black colleges. The issue arose on June 5, 1951, when Central State College of Ohio applied for admission to the NAIB. Al Duer responded positively, welcoming the new school on board. Then, in October, the embarrassed Duer wrote again, more cautiously. He admitted that he had not been aware that "yours was a colored college." Desegregation had barely begun in the nation, and Missouri, a former slave state, had barriers up to prevent racial mixing. Because of the potentially explosive response that might greet attempts to bring a "colored" team into Kansas City, Duer wanted to take the matter up with his Executive Committee.[2]

Mack Greene, the athletic director at Central State, had heard that sort of waffling before. He emotionally called on Duer to apply the NAIB code of ethics, which included a clause against all prejudice. Duer, who had been a catalyst in getting integrated teams into the tournament back in 1948, had his heart in the right place, but he still needed a push to tackle the potentially divisive issue head on. Besides Kansas City being a Southern city, many of the association's member institutions were situated in the former Confederacy. In 1951, Duer found himself called upon to challenge strongly-held beliefs and practices that today may seem impossibly alien, but that were a well-entrenched part of the fabric of society then.[3]

The NAIB head met with Greene in Cincinnati in January 1952 at the NCAA meeting, which was being held concurrently with the National Athletic Steering Committee's (NASC) first meeting. That black organization had just been launched the previous August to fight segregation in college athletics and win admission to either the NCAA or NAIB tournament. Duer was encouraging, telling Greene that Central State had been accepted as a full member of the NAIB and would be eligible for the Ohio District play-offs two months later. When he learned that NASC was sponsoring a national tournament of black colleges at Fisk University in Nashville, Duer proposed that the NAIB sponsor the new event, with the winner going to Kansas City to play in the NAIB tournament. Greene was delighted, but Duer cautioned him that the Executive Committee would need to confirm the arrangement. That turned out to be more of a challenge than Duer expected. Though NAIB leaders unanimously backed admitting the black colleges, two of them questioned sponsoring the NASC tournament, and Duer confessed to Greene that the arrangement simply was not going to happen in 1952.[4]

As happened so often in the fight against segregation, an unexpected roadblock to Central State appearing in the Ohio District playoffs emerged. The new district chair, Don Renninger of Findlay College, claimed he had no record of Central State being approved to participate, and therefore ruled the black school ineligible. When Duer confirmed Central State's membership, Renninger said he would resign if he were not upheld. Duer backed off for the moment, but took up the matter at the convention, and there carried the day, though not for another year. On March 12, 1952, the Executive Committee unanimously endorsed a program for the upcoming 1952-53 school year that would admit all eligible black colleges to the NAIB, provide NAIB sponsorship of the NASC tournament and invite the winner to Kansas City, and make Central State eligible for the 1953 Ohio District playoffs, and therefore ineligible for the NASC tournament. As other districts integrated, further black colleges would be eligible to reach Kansas City through district playoffs rather than the NASC route. The Executive Committee then established a "District at-large" (District 29) for all NASC members in the NAIA, thus making the NASC tournament in essence a district playoff. The general membership at the convention enthusiastically approved the measures.[5]

Over the course of the next year, 36 black institutions joined what had become the NAIA, and those in segregated areas of the country had their own tournament as a route to Kansas City. Duer successfully put pressure on the city to open up to black teams, in essence telling local officials that if they wanted to keep the national tournament, which had become a major local sporting event in those days before Kansas City had major league baseball, football, or basketball, they would have to integrate local accommodations. Branch Rickey has been rightly celebrated for signing Jackie Robinson to integrate major league baseball in 1947, but baseball failed until the social upheavals of the sixties to challenge segregated lodging in its southern cities like St. Louis and its Florida spring training sites. John McLendon, a chronicler of black basketball's evolution, called Duer "the most single influential force in providing upward mobility and athletic opportunities for Black athletes during the 1950-1960 period."[6]

From a historical perspective, these off-the-court events far surpass the games with which they were concerned. Nevertheless, the games went on, and in 1952, the last year without representation by black colleges, fans were treated to some nail-biting thrillers before a champion was finally crowned. In one semi-final game, Southwest Missouri had to play two overtime periods before finally eking out a 70-67 win over Southwest Texas State. Then Murray State won a cliffhanger from Portland (OR), 58-57, to advance to the title game. Southwest Missouri then captured the Naismith Trophy with a comparatively easy 73-64 triumph.

In 1953, the black schools of District 29 played off for the honor of being the first to compete in the national tournament. Tennessee A&I State University (later known simply as Tennessee State) hosted the district playoff in late February and upset favored North Carolina College. When the team took the floor in Kansas City, Mack Greene was in the stands, apprehensively gauging the crowd's response. Mindful that Duer had warned him two years earlier that the NASC leader did not know Kansas City fans, Greene was relieved and delighted that the crowd welcomed the Tennessee team as warmly as any other, despite their "extra protective cutaneous pigmentation."[7]

On the court, the blacks acquitted themselves well, which is less surprising to fans today, when over 80 percent of the National Basketball Association's players are black, than it was then to both blacks and whites—little basis for determining black abilities relative to whites existed since they did not compete with each other. Tennessee State won a thrilling opening game, 89-88, over Geneva College (PA), then followed that up with a convincing 79-56 triumph over nearby St. Benedict's. They finally met their match in the quarterfinals, falling to East Texas State, 72-67. The Texans wound up fourth, losing in the consolation game to Indiana State, while Southwest Missouri successfully defended its title, beating perennial power Hamline, 79-71.

Duer was unaware at the time that a potentially devastating blow to the integrated tournament had been averted. The chair of the Alabama-Mississippi District, John Ricks, told Tennessee State athletic director Henry Kean that if both Mississippi Southern and Tennessee State got by the first three rounds, the white school might cancel their semi-final match. Both teams won their first two games, putting them on a collision course, but both lost in the third round. Before those losses, though, Ricks told Kean that the Mississippi Southern coach and players had said they would play, and that it was fine with Ricks.[8] The tournament, and Tennessee State players' deportment, had peacefully improved race relations in a way that was not often evident in other contexts during the turbulent decade that followed.

Seizing the moment and perhaps seeing an opportunity to further the cause of civil rights, a number of NAIA schools scheduled interracial games the following season, including Peru State (NE), Eastern New Mexico, Southwest Missouri State, and Culver-Stockton on the white side and Kentucky State, Fisk, and Central State among the black schools. Tennessee State was invited to the St. Paul, Minnesota, Christmas Tournament as well. Everything was going so well that NAIA President A. G. Wheeler appointed a Select Committee on Integration to spur the acceptance of the District 29 teams into their regional districts.[9]

The following spring Tennessee State was back in Kansas City as District 29 champion, coached again by Clarence Cash. This time the team was eliminated in the first round by Regis (Colorado). (Eventually St. Benedict's beat Western Illinois, 62-56, for the title. The big draw in that 1954 tournament was Rio Grande (Ohio), whose Bevo Francis had set the all-time collegiate single-game scoring record of 113 points that season. He helped beat Arizona State with a meager 28 points, but his 27 were not enough to get by Southeastern Louisiana in the second round.) But Tennessee State had impressed sufficiently that they were invited to Kansas City to play in the Tip-Off Invitational Tournament the following Christmas, an honor generally offered to the top two finishers in the spring tournament and six other schools of basketball distinction. John McLendon had replaced Cash as coach for the 1954-55 season and was delighted with the invitation. But things were not as rosy off the court as on it.

McLendon recognized that Cash had been forced to house his teams in rather shabby hotels in Kansas City. He told Duer that he would happily accept, but only on the condition that Tennessee State's team could stay downtown with the other teams. Duer conferred with the Executive Committee and the Kansas City Chamber of Commerce, and, with their endorsement, called McLendon back to agree to his terms. Integrating the tournament continued its ripple effect on the community.[10] To cap the story, Tennessee State upset top-seeded Southwest Missouri State in the opening round and went on to win the Christmas tournament, crushing local favorite Rockhurst by 22 points in the final.

The task of integrating the Southern districts did not go smoothly or swiftly. As a result, with growing numbers of black institutions in District 29, it had become more than twice as large as any other district. McLendon, whose team had lost the district title in 1955 to Texas Southern, joined others in asking for more representation in Kansas City, and in 1956 a new District 6 was created to double black representation. By 1958 District 6 was split into District 6A and 6B, assuring three black schools of a trip to the nationals. In fact, in 1956 Central State of Ohio won its district, so that school, Tennessee State, and Texas Southern all played, with Texas Southern, led by 6-foot-10-inch center Benny Swain, going all the way to the championship game before falling to McNeese State, 60-55, in an almost-successful upset bid.[11]

The 1956 tournament, despite the successful integration of the previous three years, generated more racial tension than any other. Two days before the start of competition, Delta State College (MS) withdrew because it could not get "protection" from playing against blacks. The college wanted assurances that it would not have to play against black players, a request unanimously rejected by the Executive Committee, to its credit. The Committee issued a tactful press release noting that race relations in the district were such that it would not be wise for a team from there to play in the tournament.

Eventual champion McNeese State, a Louisiana institution, was the focus of the other tournament tension. The team resolutely resisted pressure not to compete, but Governor Robert F. Kennon accompanied the squad to Kansas City and appeared to be looking for a racial incident to legitimize yanking it from the competition. As it happened, McNeese State defeated all three of the black colleges on the way to its championship, and no racial problems arose. Ironically, one of the Louisianans' best players was Frank Glen. According to the well-preserved self-serving logic of slave owners, the very light-skinned Glen was black even though he was obviously racially mixed. McNeese claimed that Glen was Jamaican, and thus acceptable, pointing up another absurdity of racism: racially mixed foreigners were somehow acceptable, but not Americans.[12]

In March 1957, Tennessee State was back in the thick of NAIA news. Again coached by John McLendon and starring future professional players Dick Barnett and John Barnhill, the unseeded Tigers survived scares in the quarterfinals (90-88 over previously-unbeaten Western Illinois) and semifinals (71-70 over Pacific Lutheran). They then blitzed Southeastern Oklahoma in the title game, 92-73, garnering the first-ever NAIA championship by a black college.

While all of this pioneering integrated basketball action was taking place at Municipal Auditorium, the NAIA members continued to deal with other issues at their annual meetings. In 1953, the association addressed an issue of institutional legitimacy when it agreed that any new school joining the NAIA must maintain accreditation with its regional accrediting agency. To make this academic upgrade more palatable it was not made retroactive, so shaky current members were able to continue their active roles.

The 1953 gathering also established a professionalism rule that placed it in conflict with the United States Olympic Committee and the Amateur Athletic Union and led to tensions with such organizations. Professionalism had long been a matter of great debate in amateur athletic circles—it would be decades before professional athletes could compete in the Olympics. The NAIA decided that if a player became a professional in one sport, he would still be considered an amateur in all other sports, presumably feeling that a professional career in one sport was like an outside job and did not logically affect any other sport. The NCAA quickly followed suit—in 1974.

Duer also launched a campaign that bore fruit two years later. He called for the application of standards of eligibility for all competition rather than simply limiting those standards to post-season playoffs and national tournaments. This proposal, adopted in 1955, gave the NAIA a decided edge on the NCAA in assuring that the term student-athlete was not an oxymoron. In 1951 the NCAA had approved an advisory (that is, without any enforcement mechanism) policy that athletes should be making normal academic progress toward a degree. Once certified in the fall, students were eligible for the entire year, which in practice made possible up to a year of competing without even attending a class.[13]

The NAIA passed another milestone in its professionalization in 1953 by establishing the National Association of Intercollegiate Athletic Coaches to discuss problems peculiar to the NAIA. Various coaches' organizations for particular sports already existed across the lines of governing bodies, as for example basketball coaches from the NAIA, NCAA, NJCAA, and high schools met to deal with basketball issues. NAIA coaches often wore more than one hat (remember Emil Liston coaching football, basketball, and baseball along with being athletic director at Baker) and thus encountered problems and experiences quite different in many ways from those of more specialized coaches at large universities. Volney Ashford, Missouri Valley College athletic director, became the first chair of the National Coaches Advisory Committee. The NAIAC met annually during the basketball tournament in Kansas City as a spin-off from the larger convention that assembled at the same time.

Little substantive action characterized the 1954 convention. In 1955, two moves already mentioned took place: the application of eligibility standards to all competition, and the increase to two black college districts. The number of NAIA member institutions had taken off with the addition of new sports to its agenda. In 1950-51, the number of NAIA schools had been 314, or about ten for each of the 32 districts. By 1954-55 the number had jumped by more than a third to 435, or close to fourteen per district, an overall membership that stabilized for the next decade. Though District 29 was by far the largest, growing pains affected the entire association. In other action at the 1955 annual meeting, the number of non-officers on the Executive Committee was reduced from five to four. Further, district basketball playoff games were to be held on the home courts of participants, presumably to reduce the possible costs of outside gym rental and thus enhance the proceeds available to send teams on to the nationals.

In the new sports introduced when the association first broadened its national competitions, the track and field scene can best be summed up by the name Abilene Christian. The Texas college won the initial meet in 1952 over San Diego State, finished second to South Dakota State in 1953, won again in 1954 and 1955 (with Texas Southern and Emporia State trailing in those two meets), then slipped to second in 1956 and 1957 as Occidental (CA) won its first two of three consecutive championships. Aside from South Dakota State and Emporia State, all of those top finishers were from warm weather states.

Tennis also produced a remarkable pattern of consistently winning teams following three years of early competitiveness. In 1952 Pepperdine, Al Duer's school, won the first NAIA title, followed the next two years by Hardin-Simmons (TX) and Redlands (CA), a college that would dominate in the late sixties and early seventies. In 1955 Lamar State launched a dynasty that lasted six years, with the Texans successfully taking on all comers over that period.

The third expansion sport, golf, joined tennis and track and field in a spring sports festival the first five years of the broadened menu, with Abilene, Texas, serving as the host city the first four. The local track and field program seemed to benefit from a home field advantage, and other Texans fought off all out-of-state competition to monopolize the golf matches. North Texas State won in 1952, 1954, and 1955, losing narrowly to Hardin-Simmons in 1953. Then Lamar State showed that Texans could win on the road as well, winning the 1956 match in San Diego. They followed that up with consecutive wins in Beaumont, Texas, in 1957 and 1958.

At the 1956 convention, delegates enthusiastically voted to expand the NAIA's sports offerings beginning that fall. The year saw participation in post-season playoffs reach new heights, and not just because of the increased number of sports. Out of 437 teams playing NAIA basketball, one-fourth (110) took part in district and national tournaments. But opportunities widened dramatically when the NAIA added national championships in wrestling, swimming, football, cross-country, and baseball. More cities stood to host national playoffs, too, as the association voted to separate the golf, tennis, and track and field events beginning in 1957. Plans were already set for San Diego to host the three sports in 1956, but that would be the last spring sports festival until the idea resurfaced in the 1990s.

Omaha, Nebraska, hosted the first cross-country meet and established an early tradition by providing the home course for every meet through 1967. South Dakota State established some instant credibility in the sport by winning the first year over Fort Hays State (KS) and finishing second to Howard Payne (TX) in 1957. Ray Mation of Redlands was the inaugural individual winner.

The NAIA had demonstrated its interest in football by publishing detailed statistics for the sport even before launching a national championship. Choosing to dub the title match the Aluminum Bowl, the NAIA became the first association to directly sponsor a bowl game. The game took place in Little Rock, Arkansas, and featured Montana State and St. Joseph's (IN). After a big buildup, the game itself was something of a letdown. Playing before a national CBS television audience, the teams were hampered by rain and a muddy field and slogged their way to a 0-0 tie. The wider effects were significant, however. Adding football to its championships appreciably augmented both costs and revenues to the association; now basketball had a second revenue sport for company. Unfortunately, Little Rock was rocked by racial problems in 1957. That was the year the army forcefully integrated Little Rock Central High School at bayonet point, and racial tensions in the city necessitated moving the football game to St. Petersburg, Florida, where it was renamed the Holiday Bowl. Pittsburg State (KS) edged Hillsdale (MI), 27-26, in a much more satisfying contest to become the first clear-cut NAIA national football champion.

The first national swimming meet was held at Southern Illinois University on March 23, 1957. The host team finished second to East Carolina, 54-50. The following year North Central (IL) splashed its way past the competition and won handily, with Central Michigan a distant second.

Baseball debuted as an NAIA national championship event in June 1957. Sul Ross State College (TX) hosted the event, which featured eight teams in a single-elimination format. In the final game, Sul Ross edged Rollins (FL), 8-7, to capture the first NAIA title. In 1958 twelve teams competed, this time utilizing a double-elimination approach. Casual fans could be excused if they thought champion San Diego State had brought its football team instead of baseball, as the Aztecs slugged their way to 11-1, 17-0, and, in the final against Southwestern Oklahoma, 23-9 victories.

The new wrestling championships did not debut until March 1958, when Mankato State (MN) hosted the meet and defeated second place Illinois Teachers College to win the title.

Beyond expanding the championships open to NAIA schools, the 1956 convention took several other steps to improve the organization's operations. District committees were expanded so that each member institution was represented at district meetings. Catastrophic insurance coverage had been made available in 1954. In 1956, three different levels of broader coverage were offered to association colleges, with injury-prone football a big variable. The executive secretary's salary jumped again, to $10,000, as his responsibilities widened.

Finally, the membership directed that a special meeting of selected college presidents, faculty athletic representatives, coaches, and Executive Committee members convene in June to develop a list of Aims and Objectives for the broader organization. After great deliberation, that special committee sent its proposal to the members for their feedback. It reconvened at the 1957 convention and incorporated those comments into a revised proposal, which was adopted by the membership there. Because they reflect a well-considered assessment of the organization's rationale at this crucial state in its development, they are included here.

The National Association of Intercollegiate Athletics believes:
- That one of the purposes of higher education is to develop each individual to the fullest extent of his capabilities both as an individual and as an athlete.
- That everything which takes place in a college must be evaluated in terms of the educational purposes of higher education.
- That a broadly based program of physical education for all students should include prescribed physical education courses, intramural and extramural activities, and intercollegiate athletics.
- That intercollegiate athletics should be an integral part of the total physical education offering of a college and not a separate organization with different principles, aims, and objectives.

- That the program of intercollegiate athletics offers the participants valuable educational experiences not provided in other phases of the physical education program.
- That the major emphasis of the program of athletics should be instrumental in educating participants and other students in moral and ethical values inherent in the program.
- That the program of intercollegiate athletics in all its phases should be so conducted that the educational and ethical status of the college will be enhanced.
- That the program of intercollegiate athletics should be controlled   absolutely and completely by those responsible for the administration of the college.
- That the department of physical education, of which intercollegiate athletics is a part, should have a place in the institutional structure comparable to that of any other department; that it should be subject to the same institutional policies, budgetary provisions and controls, as are all other departments of the college, and that members of the faculty of the department should be selected in the same manner and have the same rights, privileges, and responsibilities as other faculty members of comparable rank.
- That colleges should compete with other colleges having similar educational philosophies, policies, and practices.
- That all students participating in intercollegiate athletics should be admitted to the college in the same manner as other students and should be regularly enrolled students making normal progress, both quantitatively and qualitatively, toward a degree.
- That all financial aid to any student in money or in kind, except that which comes from members of his immediate family or from those upon whom he is legally dependents, should be administered by the college under policies and procedures established by the college for administration of scholarships and grants-in-aid to students having special abilities.
- That member colleges of the association and individual members therein have the obligation to strive toward the attainment of the purposes of the organization and to work co-operatively with others in improving programs of intercollegiate athletics.
- That the role of the association is that of working co-operatively with and providing leadership to member institutions, toward the realization of these basic beliefs.

The 1957 meeting saw the emergence of Faculty Athletic Chairs (what are now known as Faculty Athletic Representatives, or FARs) as a significant force in the NAIA. Under the leadership of Perry Mitchell of Central Washington State, chair of the Faculty

Athletic Chairmen Committee, these faculty members worked on eligibility issues, academic standards, and organization. Their presence provided a deterrent to any temptation the athletic directors might have had to water down academic standards.

Delegates also took a major step toward a more democratic decision-making process. They changed procedures to slow down the implementation of new rules and standards to ensure more time for deliberation and broad input. Instead of instantaneous application of new rules, a two-year process would henceforth be used. If the Executive Committee and convention delegates agreed upon a piece of legislation, it would be mailed to the membership along with explanation to facilitate widespread discussion at the local and conference levels. Then representatives would vote on the matter at the next convention. If approved, it would go by mail to the membership for a mail vote. Even if approved at that point, it would become effective one year after adoption.

A related change toughened the standards for passage of changes in rules and standards. Prior to this time, a simple majority had been sufficient to move legislation. Due to the importance of rules and standards, henceforth it would take at least 51 percent of member schools voting, and 75 percent of those voting in favor, to pass a measure dealing with rules and standards. Both of these measures, appropriately, were sent to all members by mail ballot and subsequently approved.

The NAIA appeared to be thriving. During the summer of 1957 the Executive Committee met in Kansas City to begin preparing handbooks for member schools, district chairs, and committees of various NAIA constituencies such as Faculty Athletic Chairmen. The project was designed to incorporate "records, policies and practices, rules and standards of participation, constitution, aims and objectives" and other information not hitherto organized in a usable fashion. Yet for a couple of years Duer and the NAIA felt they were under siege as the NCAA sought to snatch their very existence from them.

At the NCAA's annual meeting in Los Angeles in early 1956, the rival group decided to launch a small college tournament beginning in 1957. The College Division championship, to be held in Evansville, Indiana, offered 32 smaller NCAA schools their first chance at a national title. The NAIA's success at integrating the Negro colleges into their tournament seemed to spark a concerted response; keep in mind that the NCAA defined the black schools as small colleges. Duer attended the NCAA gathering and made a strong pitch to save the NAIA, but by unanimous vote the delegates proceeded. Duer wrote to a friend that "everyone here knew for sure that the aim of this move of the NCAA was to put us out of business. . . . My good friend, Mr. [Walter] Byers [NCAA president] has put us Number 1 on his wanted list and makes no secret he is after our scalp."[14] This suspicion seemed borne out when the NCAA set up a black regional tournament, the victor of which would qualify for the Evansville event. Some in the NAIA feared that despite their pioneering efforts both in national basketball tournaments and in including black schools, they might be upstaged by the more prestigious NCAA.

Duer was upset that some black schools did not share his concern. Mack Greene urged black colleges to maintain dual membership so they could attend the national tournament of their choice. Duer felt this recommendation showed appalling disloyalty after what he had gone through to integrate his organization. Still, strong black voices from John McLendon and Texas Southern's Alexander Durley called for a loyalty pledge and most small colleges, black and white, remained loyal for years to come.[15] As their leaders argued, the NAIA had done great things for black colleges in the past five years. It had given them the opportunity to compete on an equal basis, including having a black on all of its committees. With powerful and grateful voices like that paving the way, the black colleges did stick with their benefactors. It does seem likely, though, that by establishing a competing small-college tournament the NCAA contributed to halting the numerical growth of its rival for a decade.

Relations with other athletic organizations continued to be an important component of NAIA life. In the summer of 1957 members of the Executive Committee met with their NCAA counterparts in Denver to try to establish more amicable relations. Evidence, or lack thereof, suggests that they accomplished little to nothing beyond clearing the air of some of the acrimony that had developed. In 1958 the NAIA affiliated with the National Federation of State High School Athletic Associations and the National Junior College Athletic Association; together the three termed themselves the National Alliance of Athletic Associations. The NAIAC (coaches' association) voted to make NAAA rules official for NAIA (optional during the season, mandatory for the Holiday Bowl). Since NCAA rules had previously been standard, one senses a bit of payback in this move.

One more sign of the professionalization of the NAIA came in the summer of 1957 when the organization moved its executive offices from Los Angeles to Kansas City. Emil Liston had operated out of his Baker University office until his death, and Al Duer had used his Pepperdine base since 1949. With the association having survived the NCAA assault and having a fairly secure future, it seemed a good idea to relocate to a more central location. The NAIA rented a suite of offices in the Aladdin Hotel, close to the Municipal Auditorium, its essential birthplace. Duer liked the idea of working in a hotel, for it facilitated putting up guests in Kansas City.[16] Along with the new facilities, Duer added a full-time Publicity Director and other office workers. The NAIA had a home of its own at last.

4

At Home in Kansas City
1958-1962

With its move to Kansas City, the NAIA had taken a significant step toward professionalization. No longer would it operate out of the corner of an athletic director's office, its leader subject to the conflicting demands of his other position. In a real sense the move meant progress. Yet the advances came at a cost. The NAIA during its first years in its new home found itself caught up in unanticipated and unwelcome new conflicts, ones that threatened the whole concept of amateur sports as Liston and Duer had promoted them. The NCAA's new College Division, as intended, launched a concerted effort to lure away smaller colleges from the NAIA—those lesser institutions now had a choice to make, and the struggle with the NCAA grew increasingly bitter in the years that followed. That battle was, in fact, part of a broader movement that the NAIA resisted, but was in the long run unable to hold back—the evolution of "big-time" college athletics as a major force on the American scene.

Al Duer recognized that the NAIA was involved in a fight for the very soul of college athletics. The nation was becoming more and more captivated by the glamour of "big-time" programs, and in his speeches, articles, and policies, Duer sought to resist the trend by focusing on the concept of an "educationally integrated athletic program." Writing in the newly expanded *NAIA News* in March 1958, he argued for that integration as opposed to an athletic program being a "separate commercial or promotional adjunct." This approach, he contended, "must continue to be the distinguishing quality of our program and its test of membership." For the rest of his lengthy tenure as NAIA Executive Secretary, Duer fought tenaciously to uphold this ideal.[1]

In the late fifties, the association struggled with growing pains. As new sports were added to the NAIA menu, administering the organization became increasingly complex. Much of the work was done through standing committees, with Executive

Committee members being given responsibility to supervise two or three committees and particular sports. Duer spent a great deal of his time, mostly by mail, ensuring that these chairmen kept on top of their assignments. The Awards Committee, for example, coordinated balloting for election to the Hall of Fame, and they petitioned Duer to overturn the regulation that prohibited honoring sitting members of the Executive Committee. Their reasoning was that members might serve for ten years as senior figures in the athletic profession, and thus could be passed by for well-deserved recognition.

The NAIAC, established in 1953, played an increasingly important role in running sports events. Prior to its existence, appointed sports advisory committees that had grown out of NAIA districts and areas ran sports activities. By 1959 the NAIAC was establishing "sections" for individual sports, so that coaches would belong both to the broader body and to their specific sport's section, with its own officers and some responsibilities for their national championships. Sections had been established for football, basketball, track, and baseball. At the 1960 annual meeting the NAIAC was restructured into ten sections; each would report to the NAIAC board, which in turn would report to the Executive Committee.

The NAIA's financial health has always been a concern. By 1958, it was already established policy that teams in non-income-producing sports (tennis, golf, and track and field in the early additions) had to cover their own expenses. This policy often produced serious hardship for cash-strapped colleges, and it meant that determining the sites for the national championships could have a significant impact on participating institutions.

The precarious overall financial condition of the NAIA necessitated a careful balancing of income and expenditures. For 1958-59 the total projected income was estimated at around $40,000. Of that amount, $18,000 derived from the dues of 465 member colleges, roughly $14,000 from national basketball tournament revenues, about $3,000 from the football program's receipts, and an estimated $5000 from district basketball playoffs. With only 44 percent of the year's $42,000 budget deriving from stable and reliable dues, the NAIA depended far too much on the fluctuating and uncertain revenues from tournaments. The 1959 convention accordingly voted to raise dues from an enrollment-based range of $25 to $70 to a heftier $35 to $100, anticipating that this hike would move the organization closer to covering 75 percent of its operating expenses from predictable dues payments. A year later dues were boosted another 50 percent as operating a multi-sport association proved to be an expensive proposition.[2]

If internal matters such as finance had been the worst of the NAIA's problems, Duer would have felt much less pressure. But "foreign relations" caused so many stresses that the executive secretary might have been tempted to create a State Department to deal with them. One enduring pressure point dating from the organization's beginnings in the late 1930s concerned the association's desire to have a chance to represent the United States in the Olympic games. This pressure forced Liston and then Duer to navigate the rough water between the United States Olympic Committee, the AAU, and the NCAA, and it sometimes prevented them from maintaining policies they felt were best for their member colleges and athletes. At the March 1959 meeting the Executive Committee succumbed to the outside pressure and voted to conform to the AAU and Olympic definition of "amateur," which held that becoming a professional in one sport made you a professional in all. The rule was to be phased in by 1962, permitting current students to finish their eligibility without having the rules shifted under them.

The Olympic tension, though it involved very few athletes and hit the nation's radar screen only quadrennially, disproportionately affected the NAIA's self-conception and prestige. More persistent and critical to the association's health, the "conflicting events" issue had become a major flash point after the NCAA created its College Division in 1957. Many schools held dual membership in the NCAA and NAIA, and since rules and competitive levels varied, they often waited until the last minute to decide which playoffs to favor with their presence. This procrastination frustrated the NAIA since it weakened their tournament's competition and wreaked havoc with planning, publicity, and revenues. At the March 1959 meeting the NAIA adopted a policy that assumed an NAIA institution (whether or not a dual member) would play in the post-season unless it informed the district chairman well in advance of the selection process that it was opting out. To opt out was acceptable, but to do so and play in an NCAA tournament would lead to suspension from all district and national events, loss of the right to vote on district or national issues, and loss of the right to serve on committees during the suspension. Suspensions, to be meted out by the Executive Committee, would normally be for one year.

Yet again the NAIA could not simply act on its own. Sometimes an NAIA member institution's entire conference might belong to the NCAA, with a requirement that its champion participate in the NCAA playoffs. With both organizations putting pressure on a college, dual membership looked less appealing, and Duer recognized that the conflicting playoff issue could catalyze the NCAA's intent, namely to spirit away NAIA members. That year the Executive Committee did suspend Belmont-Abbey (North Carolina) for playing in the NCAA tourney instead that of the NAIA.

The racial integration issue continued to haunt the nation and the NAIA. Though the organization had pioneered the inclusion of black athletes in its national basketball tournament in 1948 and black colleges had been added in 1953, those Negro institutions had not been integrated into their districts yet. In the South, certainly, and in the North, less adamantly, resistance to equal treatment of such colleges continued.

The Executive Committee discussed the integration issue at the 1959 meeting. The committee reasoned that some border and northern states could probably absorb the black colleges into their geographical districts, and that it would be desirable for the national office rather than the colleges to take the initiative. Duer proposed that the national office develop a plan to absorb those schools and also help them to schedule games against "white" colleges. NASC, the organization of black colleges' athletic directors, conference commissioners, and other representatives, was strongest in three major conferences. The Southern Intercollegiate Athletic Conference functioned in South Carolina, Florida, Georgia, Alabama, and Tennessee. The Southwestern Athletic Conference operated in Louisiana and Mississippi. The Central Intercollegiate Athletic Association included schools in Virginia and North Carolina. Those areas made up Districts 6 and 29 in the NAIA, the only ones not carefully defined by geography.

Despite significant opposition to the desegregation proposal, over the next eight years 17 black institutions were moved into their geographical districts. Missouri, Oklahoma, Texas, Arkansas, Kentucky, Tennessee, West Virginia, the District of Columbia, Maryland, Delaware, Ohio, and Pennsylvania witnessed this progress, which took place against the explosive backdrop of the civil rights movement of the sixties. In spite of these advances, as late as 1967, 53 NAIA member institutions remained segregated in their three "at-large" districts in the Deep South.[3] The long, slow process would not be rushed to completion.

Fortunately for the sanity of those running the NAIA, on-field competition—the *raison d'être* of the organization—continued to take place in 1959-60, and the number of sports with national championships further increased. In 1959 one of the nation's major growth sports, soccer, became the tenth sport added to the NAIA championship repertoire. Within a year the soccer coaches had organized their committee, aligned teams into areas, and appointed area chairmen, and they planned to select their first All-America team in 1960.

Baseball people celebrated a move to Sioux City, Iowa, in the spring, the first time outside Alpine, Texas. Incentives for the switch included lights to permit night games, easier transportation, room and board provided by Morningside College, and a $5,000 subsidy from the Sioux City Jaycees to help cover the teams' traveling expenses. It also landed the NAIA just an hour north of the NCAA baseball tournament, well established in Omaha, Nebraska.

Football featured playoffs in 1959 for the second time, with four teams competing for the national title, prompting a not-too-subtle dig at the NCAA in an *NAIA News* back-page advertisement. The NAIA, trumpeted the ad, required those seeking national titles to "prove their claims on the playing field" in all ten of its championships.[4] Despite the virtue of such a competition, the NAIA suffered a major blow to its prestige and visibility when CBS, which had televised the first four championship games, announced that it was dropping that coverage. Citing a policy change to cut back on football bowl coverage and, more critically, a lack of sponsors, the network dealt a powerful setback to the NAIA in its attempt to compete with the NCAA.

As part of the association's professionalization, the NAIA launched its workshop program in February 1960, hosting administrators representing 28 colleges and providing them with insights into the NAIA's operations and their responsibilities as member institutions. From this modest beginning, workshops grew over the years to be a major educational component of the organization.

Two days prior to the NAIA's March annual meeting, district chairmen gathered to discuss various issues, a pre-meeting that proved so helpful that it became a fixed part of the annual calendar. In 1960 the chairmen focused on amateurism, rules interpretation, relations with the Olympic Committee, organizational finances, running the various national sports championships, athlete subsidies, and the growing threat (promise?) of outside booster clubs helping finance athletic programs.

The highlight of the gathering came with the unveiling of the new NAIA Handbook. Mutual of Omaha Insurance Company, the company that wrote insurance policies for NAIA schools, printed this publication. The book defined standards for competition and administration, adjusting differences in some sixty conferences to develop uniformity. Though Duer admitted that policy disputes and interpretive differences would always be an issue, he believed the handbook represented real progress for the increasingly professional association.

Foreshadowing a major shift in organizational management a quarter century down the road, the Presidents Advisory Committee began to assert itself as a force with which to be reckoned. The presidents gathered for meetings of the Association of American Colleges and the American Association of College Teacher Education, both much broader than the NAIA's membership, and while at those meetings broke off to discuss their NAIA issues. Not surprisingly, they shared great concern over the intrusion of money into college athletics. Gate income was declining as financial aid to athletes increased along with other expenses. Two increasingly common responses to this problem had surfaced. One was to emphasize one or two sports (usually football and basketball) that generated gate receipts and publicity while cutting back on funding, or eliminating entirely, non-revenue-producing sports. As they noted, this approach hardly squared with policies followed in other departments at colleges. The second response was to permit increased funding from booster clubs and alumni groups, with the attendant loss of control such outside money could bring. The Presidents Advisory Committee joined with the Executive Committee to warn against such practices.

The war with the NCAA continued to escalate. In 1958 Al Duer had been removed from the Olympic Basketball Committee after serving on it for eight years. He was told that his had not been an NAIA seat, but an NCAA slot. NAIA representation, Olympic officials said, would not be possible until the association had brought its amateur rule into conformity with Olympic standards. With no voice on the Olympic Committee and no right to participate in the Olympic trials in 1960, Duer argued that the NAIA needed to accelerate its rule change to be effective September 1, 1960, rather than 1962 as had been planned.

The Olympic Basketball Committee met twice to consider permitting the NAIA to participate in the Olympic trials. The NCAA bitterly opposed the idea, but the NAIA's pledge to change its amateur rule, coupled with its alliance with the AAU, fended off the NCAA's aggression. At first the committee proposed two AAU teams, two NCAA teams, one armed forces team, and an NAIA team. The NCAA objected, arguing that it too should have small college representation, suggesting one small college team with six NCAA and six NAIA players. The NAIA frowned on that mixing, leading to a compromise. Eight teams would take part in the upcoming trials: three from NCAA (two university, one college division), three from AAU, one from the armed forces, and one for the NAIA. *The NAIA News* gleefully noted that of the 36 players thus allotted to the NCAA, only five were drawn from its college division. It appeared clear which association best represented small college players.[5] When this decision was made public, a second meeting was convened., during which NCAA executive officer Walter Byers exploded and walked out, saying that if the NAIA was allowed to participate the NCAA would not. He evidently calmed down and backed off that threat. To avoid potential opportunities for NCAA mischief, the AAU advised the NAIA to assure that they could not be blocked by their amateur rule being out of conformity. Faced with that scenario, the membership voted 256-11 to change their rule by June 15, 1960.

The Olympic trials took place from March 31 to April 2 in Denver, where the NAIA exacted a large measure of revenge against the proud NCAA. In the first game, an NAIA all-star team, trailing 42-39 at the half, rallied to defeat recently crowned NCAA champion Ohio State, 76-69. They shut down Jerry Lucas, holding him to one point in the second half, and he and his fellow future professional stars John Havlicek and Larry Siegfried could not turn the tide. Charlie Sharp of Southwest Texas with 17 points and Jack Moreland of Louisiana Tech with 14 paced the NAIA squad. The joy of that huge upset could not be dispelled by the subsequent events in the trials. The NAIA cagers lost their second game to the AAU's Peoria Caterpillars, 89-68, then fell in the third-place game to the Goodyear Wingfoots, 88-77. On top of that, no NAIA player was selected for the 12-man Olympic team. Nevertheless, the sweetness of the upset of Ohio State was a long time dissipating.[6]

The following school year saw the same issues dominate the NAIA's agenda. In an article in *The NAIA News*, Willamette University President Herbert Smith presciently forecast: "The decade of the 60s is destined to be a time of evaluation and reevaluation of educational practices the like of which we have not experienced in a comparable period in the educational history of America."[7] This upheaval applied not only to the athletic scene but also to the entire nature of higher education as the sixties indeed proved to be a decade of unprecedented campus turmoil. Among the trends that thoughtful educators were resisting was the movement toward college and high school athletic programs rampaging out of control. Harvard's James Conant quoted a colleague saying, "American intercollegiate athletics have gotten out of hand. They have become infested with commercialism and professionalism, sapping . . . the fine ideals they exemplify."[8] Further exacerbating the problem, the Soviet Union had "won" the 1960 Olympics by winning the most medals, and in those tense Cold War years, that propaganda coup stimulated the "win-at-any-cost" sports fanatics as though Olympic victories actually decided whether communism or capitalism was a better system.

The NAIA's Presidents Advisory Committee, reorganized in 1959 and increased from nine members to 32, one per district, continued to expand its role in the association. Duer, a self-described confirmed idealist, believed that their increased involvement showed that the NAIA was going to resist the evils of unfettered athletic programs. He also thought their heightened activity was the most important development of the year. Their committee endorsed a three-year study to try to determine solutions to the problems of intercollegiate athletics, a research project they estimated would cost $50,000 and sought to fund from foundation grants. They also suggested that a president be included as a member on the NAIA Executive Committee, a proposal fulfilled when their leader, Morton Cunningham of Fort Hays State (KS) was elected. Further, they recommended workshops around the country to identify and address the problems faced by intercollegiate sports. Four workshops were held in 1960-61 in Montana, Oregon, West Virginia, and Kansas; another two in Kansas and Washington followed the next year, the decline a function of overextended national staff.

At the 1961 meeting the NAIA took a large step to tighten eligibility standards and apply them more uniformly. Prior to that time, teams had prepared eligibility lists, but they were only forwarded to the national office when a team became eligible for district or national competition. This decentralized system understandably led to uneven administration. The National Eligibility Committee had not, before 1960, ruled on eligibility cases, but had confined itself to writing and interpreting rules. The 1961 changes required institutions to file eligibility certificates with the district eligibility chairman by a fixed date. If questions arose, they should be handled at the district level if possible, or passed along to the executive secretary if not; he would refer them to the Eligibility Committee. Once again the NAIA had beaten the NCAA to the punch.

Unequal districts presented recurring problems in the NAIA. In places like Montana, travel time between far-flung colleges was exceedingly great. No satisfactory solution has ever been developed for this problem in sparsely settled areas of the country. In addition, some more populous districts had far fewer members than others, forcing scattered schools to face similar long road trips. Meanwhile, the black college districts, 6A, 6B, and 29, were swamped with schools. Ironically, some problems could have cancelled each other out had all parties been willing. District 19 (Mississippi and Alabama) had only six members, of which but half were able to participate. Integrating those states' black institutions into District 19 would have raised it to a healthy size, but no records suggest that such drastic action was even considered. Segregation affected the football championship game as well—St. Petersburg, Florida, site of the Holiday Bowl, proved unwilling or unable to integrate lodging and grandstand seating, leading the NAIA to vote to move the 1961 title match to Sacramento, California, where it would be known as the Camellia Bowl.

The district chairmen continued their practice of meeting just in advance of the national convention to discuss vital issues. Their most pressing problems all seemed to relate to the NAIA's ongoing rivalry with the NCAA: the lack of NAIA prestige, the dual membership complication, and the stresses of conflicting events. The latter led to the suspension for a year of Prairie View College (TX) and MacMurray College (IL) for participating in the NCAA's college division tournament instead of the NAIA event in Kansas City. Unfortunately, justice was not always meted out evenhandedly. Four other schools had committed the same violation, but their districts had not recommended punishing them. Though grass roots governance by district has been a highly-touted strength of the NAIA, it does occasionally lead to such inequities.

The national meeting gave delegates an opportunity to celebrate. The Hall of Fame inducted Al Duer as a "contributor," to widespread acclaim. The reason for allowing currently serving NAIA leaders to be voted in became clear in this surprise move. Duer had indeed earned his accolade. As athletic director and basketball coach at Pepperdine, he had taken his team four times to the national tournament and earned a second, third, and fourth place finish. He had worked closely with NAIB founder Emil Liston and had served as district chairman before taking over the executive secretary position in 1949.

Duer's vision for the NAIA may well have been his greatest contribution. He strongly believed in integrating education and athletics, and he appealed to the better nature of institutional leaders by arguing for as few rules as possible while trying to keep members focused on the NAIA mission. He constantly repeated his warnings against succumbing to the siren song of big-time university athletics and compromising one's principles to compete with schools lacking the sound philosophical commitment of the NAIA. And he felt, with some justice, that he had led the organization to a level of maturity at which the rules and standards had been established. Now it was a case of understanding them, accepting them, and implementing them uniformly. His associates recognized how vital Duer had been in bringing the NAIA to that level of excellence and delighted in honoring his achievement.

In 1961 a vigorous, youthful new president took the nation's helm. John F. Kennedy promoted physical fitness as an important national goal and appointed former Oklahoma football coach Bud Wilkinson to spearhead the effort. Wilkinson called on the NAIA to join in encouraging physical fitness at its member institutions, a goal the NAIA membership endorsed and promoted.

While it was difficult for anyone to oppose physical fitness, the unity of purpose in Kennedy's program did not spill over into the organizational war between the nation's athletic associations. In 1962 a national crisis flared up over who would control amateur sports in the United States, with the NCAA and the AAU slugging it out for supremacy. Even though United States Olympic Committee President Avery Brundage warned that the international body would not certify a coaches' organization or collegiate group, the NCAA refused to back down. A February meeting between NCAA and AAU representatives failed to resolve the organizations' differences, and the NCAA vowed to push ahead and form coaches' federations in track and field, basketball, baseball, and gymnastics to try to displace the AAU. At its annual meeting in March 1962 the NAIA, still concerned about ensuring its members representation in international competition, endorsed the AAU. As they told Brundage, they wanted to do what would benefit amateur athletes, and that would best be served by supporting legally constituted organizations recognized by international bodies—i.e., the AAU.

Prior to the quadrennial USOC meeting in Washington, D.C., Duer had been invited to testify on behalf of the NAIA's right to membership in the USOC. The NCAA had directly challenged that right, but Duer's testimony swayed the organization to support greater representation at the meeting. At the gathering the NCAA executive director argued that no other collegiate organization could have representation except through the NCAA. He tried to entice the NFSHSAA (National Federation of State High School Athletic Associations) to support his position by promising it full representation in several key Olympic bodies while denying it to the NAIA. The NAIA and AAU allied their forces in support of the status quo, which carried the day.

A week later a representative of the Federation for International Basketball, Lou Wilky, called a meeting of interested parties to settle the issue for that sport. Delegates argued angrily for their positions and failed to resolve their differences, so Wilky came up with a proportional representation that did not please anyone, but resolved the issue for the moment. The AAU and NCAA got seven representatives apiece, the NAIA and YMCA each got three, the NFSHSAA and Jewish Welfare Organization got two, and the National Junior College Athletic Association, Army, Navy, and Marines one apiece.

The Presidents Advisory Committee, having established a Research Committee under Dr. Harry Fritz to study the matter of controlling athletics, made four recommendations to the Executive Committee:
- That all financial aid including grants, loans and work, controlled by the institution be granted on the basis of established need of the individual to attend the institution of his choice.
- That all financial aid to students participating in athletics be administered and controlled by a regular faculty committee which administers assistance to other students in the institution.
- That the maximum amount of assistance, in form of scholarship or grants, not exceed the tuition fees charged by the institution in which the student is registered. (This should be interpreted to exclude grants for board, room, and training tables, books, and incidental expenses.)
- That funds from outside sources be administered through the regular channels and established policies of the institution and shall not be used, in any way, to transcend the above policies.[9]

The presidents saw the dangers of increased aid, and their recommendations would have limited the maximum amount of aid to tuition, allotted it on the basis of need, and kept control of it in the hands of non-athletic people. That was a lot for athletic directors and coaches to swallow, and the Executive Committee balked, tabling the proposal for a year after lengthy discussion. It never did win over the membership.

The NAIAC, concerned that a small coaches' association would be weak, ruled that in order to have its own sport committee, fifty coaches would have to have joined from that sport. They would then have to draw up a constitution to be approved by the NAIAC and the Executive Committee. Until their numbers reached fifty, a sport would continue to be run through an advisory committee under the Executive Committee as they had in the past. Membership in the NAIAC boomed, however, with an additional 73 new coaches joining during the year and running the total to 564. (A school could belong to the NAIA without its coaches joining the NAIAC.)

A hint of things to come emerged with the beginning of an affiliated conference program. Much more modest than the automatic qualifying that accompanied the concept in the nineties, this first step provided that conferences with at least fifty percent of their members in the NAIA would be eligible for the following services: the chance to report conference news in *The NAIA News*; all statistical services; copies of *The NAIA News*; all mailings about rules, standards, and the like; reports of research studies; recommendation of conference personnel for NAIA honors; and representation at annual meetings through a national conference committee.

The spring 1962 issue of *The NAIA News* published an illuminating look at the size of NAIA member institutions. Almost 90 percent of the schools had enrollments smaller than 2,500 students, with a median around 1,000. The average size had increased by 110 over the previous year, reaching 1,289. The largest university in the association was American University in DC at 8,276.

Enrollment	Number of Schools
Over 4000	12
3000 – 3999	23
2500 – 2999	13
2000 – 2499	30
1500 – 1999	49
1000 – 1499	95
750 – 999	75
600 – 749	42
400 – 599	89

As the 1958-59 school year began, the NAIA sponsored nine national championships, with soccer added as a tenth in the fall of 1959 and bowling an eleventh in the spring of 1962. On the football field, four-team playoffs began in 1958 with one team representing each area of the country, which meant that sixteen teams played over the four-year period. Only Lenoir-Rhyne (NC) took up more than one of those slots. In 1958, Northeast Oklahoma beat St. Benedict's (KS), 19-14, in one semi-final, while Northern Arizona pounded Gustavus Adolphus (MN), 41-12, in the other. The Oklahomans then decisioned Northern Arizona, 19-13, to take the title. The following year a whole new cast of teams took the field. Texas A&I topped Hillsdale (MI), 20-10, while Lenoir-Rhyne stomped Southern Connecticut, 47-20. Lenoir-Rhyne had used up most of its offense in the semi-final, and Texas A&I took home the championship, 20-7. In 1960, Humboldt State (CA) topped Whitworth (WA), 13-6. The other semi-final had a curious outcome. Lenoir-Rhyne and Northern Michigan played to a 20-20 tie, with the former declared the winner on the basis of penetrations beyond the opponent's 20-yard line! Having survived by so narrow a margin in their first game, Lenoir-Rhyne pulled out all the stops in the final with a decisive 15-14 victory over Humboldt State. In 1961, with the championship redubbed the Camellia Bowl and moved from St. Petersburg to Sacramento, Linfield (OR) wrapped up one of the final slots by knocking off Whittier (CA), 18-7. Meanwhile, Pittsburg State (KS) forced out Northern (SD), 28-14, to grab the other opening. The Kansans then beat Linfield for top honors, 12-7.

Soccer made its debut in 1959, and thrilling matches characterized the first three finals. That first year Pratt Institute (NY) edged Elizabethtown (PA), 4-3, in two overtimes. Elizabethtown could not quite get the job done for a second straight year in 1960 when the team played to a 2-2 tie with Newark Engineering, the game called after four overtimes. Newark returned the next year, and like Elizabethtown, could not quite prevail in their two final tries. This time Howard (DC) scored with 18 seconds remaining to win the soccer title, 3-2.

Cross-country competition, run on Omaha's four-mile course, saw Emporia State establish the first powerhouse in the sport with victories in 1958, 1959, and 1961. Only an overwhelming win in 1960 by Southern Illinois, led by individual champion Joe Thomas, interrupted the Hornets' string.

The basketball tournament had one of very few racial incidents in 1959. Two-time defending champion Tennessee State, coached by local star John McLendon, heard the Illinois Normal College band playing and cheerleaders singing "Bye-Bye Blackbird" before the game. McLendon took the team off the floor while officials stopped the performance. The incident apparently motivated the black players, for they set a new tournament scoring record with a 131-74 trouncing of their antagonists. Led by All-American Dick Barnett, who won his second straight tournament MVP award, Tennessee State became the only NAIA team to capture three straight basketball titles, whipping Pacific Lutheran, 97-87, for the crown.[10]

In 1960, despite losing Barnett to the NBA and McLendon to the pros (the first black coach at that level), Tennessee State looked like a good bet for a fourth title in a row when they ran into Westminster (PA) in the semi-finals. The wily underdogs played a delay game and then gambled at the end. Trailing 38-37 with 2:49 to play, they went for an all-or-nothing last shot try for the win. With nine seconds left, Ron Galbreath took the shot, which bounced off the rim, but Don McCaig tipped in the rebound and Westminster had their 39-38 upset win. Tennessee State's 18-game win streak was history, along with its three-year run as national champions. Exhausted by that effort, Westminster fell to Southwest Texas and its star Charlie Sharp, 66-44, in the championship.

The following year the top-seeded Westminster Titans tried the same strategy against Grambling (LA) in the semi-finals, but this time the shot did not go in and they wound up on the short end of a 45-44 score. Georgetown (KY) roared through the competition in the other bracket to set up the title game, but Grambling peaked at the right time and pulled out a solid 95-75 triumph for the crown.

Westminster was back in 1962, cutting through five rivals, including Southeastern Oklahoma in the semi-finals. Prairie View A&M (TX) survived an overtime test by Ashland (OR) in the first round, and then trounced their competition on the way to the final game. For the second time in three years, Westminster came up short in the title game, losing to Prairie View, 62-53.

For some reason, swimming seems more prone to dynasties than most sports. North Central (IL) finished second in 1959 and 1960, and then won the team championship the next three years, led by free-style ace Richard Blick. East Carolina splashed to the title in 1959 and Southern Illinois in 1960 before North Central began its run.

The other winter sport, wrestling, saw Mankato State (MN) repeat as champion in 1959, edging Southern Illinois, which wound up second in both 1959 and 1960. Their second runner-up finish came at the hands of Bloomsburg State (PA), which won in 1960 and again in 1962, with Lock Haven State taking the title in 1961 and giving Pennsylvania three straight titles.

Baseball featured four different winners in the four-year period. In 1959, Southern University (LA) flattened Nebraska-Omaha, 10-2, to cop top honors. The next year they slipped to third place as Whitworth (WA) edged Georgia Southern, 4-0, for the title. In 1961 East Carolina bounced back from a 14-5 shellacking at the hands of Sacramento State to beat out the Californians, 13-7, in the final game, a route permitted by the double-elimination format. In 1962 Georgia Southern, runner-up in 1960, nipped Portland State, 2-0, to grab their championship. As a non-revenue sport, baseball was especially pleased when Pepsi Cola began subsidizing the travel expenses of both golf and baseball in 1961.

Track and field, like swimming, pitted men against the clock or measuring chains as well as each other. Outstanding athletes could more often perform to expectation than was possible in team sports, where luck or caprice could play a decisive role in close games. Thus Winston-Salem (NC) beat out East Texas State in both 1959 and 1960, by only one point the first time. Then Texas Southern grabbed the crown the next two years, nipping Tennessee State by only two points in 1961.

Lamar State (TX) racked up its fifth and sixth consecutive tennis titles in 1959 and 1960 before falling off the NAIA roster. Then a new champion sallied forth from the Lone Star state. Pan American won in 1961 and 1962, the first two of five straight titles. Something must have seemed awry, for the NAIA Executive Committee ruled in 1962 that no more than two non-citizens could play on a tennis team. Here the NAIA was doing its best Canada imitation, though of course Canada sought to restrict American domination of its cultural life.

In golf, Western Illinois, led by individual champion Jim King, edged Lamar State by six strokes in 1959. Lamar, winner of the previous three titles, bounced back to win in

1960 and 1961, giving the Texas school five crowns in six years; their star Bill Levely also copped the individual title in 1961. Western Illinois, however, was not finished—in 1962 they captured their second title in four seasons.

Finally, buoyed by a $25,000 per year subsidy from the Bowling Proprietors of America, the NAIA launched bowling as an eleventh sport in April 1962. Gannon College (PA) toppled the opposition to win the first bowling championship.

5

Battling the NCAA
1962-1966

During the years 1962 to 1966 the United States slid into war in Vietnam, a war that would reshape the contours of American politics and stimulate the baby boom generation hitting college age in 1964 to attack many basic social practices and assumptions. Amid this general setting, the assassination of President John F. Kennedy on November 22, 1963, triggered the end of a long era of political stability and, as John Brooks wrote a few years later, caused "a clean break with the past."[1] Old values and beliefs came under fire, and the world of sports did not escape the turmoil. Al Duer and his colleagues in the NAIA faced up to the challenge to the traditional ideals they held dear and urged the association to fight to move college athletics back to "sportsmanship and high-level intellectual experience" rather than the "win at any cost" philosophy they saw gaining ground in America.[2] To preserve that vision of sports meant, as they saw it, continuing the ongoing domestic war with the NCAA.

Olympic representation had been an important consideration in forming the NAIB back in 1940, and it continued to be a focal point in the NAIA's struggle with the NCAA, which in fact was merely a subset of the all-out war between the NCAA and the AAU to dominate American amateur athletics. The crux of the fight was the International Olympic Committee rule stating that any Olympic competitor had to be "a member of the organization in his own country affiliated to the International Federation recognized by the International Olympic Committee."[3] The NAIA had long supported the AAU in the battle to be that organization, and the AAU had reciprocated by endorsing NAIA claims for a voice in the ruling councils of American amateur athletics.

In 1952, when the NAIB membership voted to add more sports to its basketball offering and change its name to the NAIA, NCAA executive director Walter Byers had written an inflammatory letter to Duer arguing that the NAIA had no right to establish their organization because the NCAA was already the governing body for intercollegiate athletics. The NCAA approached the AAU to ask their support in denying rights of representation or participation to the "upstart" organization. The AAU refused, making a permanent positive impression on the NAIA leaders. Then, adding injury to insult, in 1957 the NCAA organized its college division for smaller colleges, exactly the constituency that the NAIA had been serving for twenty years. Over a quarter of the NAIA's institutions soon held dual memberships, weakening their support for NAIA events. In addition, the NAIA seat on the USOC was taken away and given to a representative of the NCAA's new college division.

In 1960 Byers walked out of a USOC meeting to protest the NAIA being allowed to participate in the Olympic trials. The NAIA's upset of NCAA champion Ohio State poured salt on the wound and appeared to earn the undying enmity of the NCAA chief. In 1962 the Department of State asked the NAIA to form an all-star team to play the Russian national basketball team in a series of exhibition games. The NCAA petulantly denied five athletes from dual-affiliation colleges the right to play, threatening them with ineligibility.

Relations between the AAU and NCAA were not much warmer than those between the US and the Soviet Union at that point. Fearing disruption of the American Olympic effort in 1964, and keeping in mind that the Russians had "won" the 1960 Olympics, Attorney General Robert Kennedy called meetings in October and November 1962 (sandwiched around the Cuban missile crisis, which suggested a rather higher level of importance to the international dispute) to try to work out a truce among the two antagonists and other sports associations. As the NCAA saw it, the groups worked out an agreement at each of the meetings, only to see the AAU repudiate each one a few weeks afterward.[4] While the NAIA saw the NCAA as the big bully trying to get its way, the NCAA depicted the AAU as a power-hungry organization more interested in winning organizational battles than in serving athletes. The public, fed up with the constant bickering, was inclined to say "a plague on both your houses."

With the collapse of the Robert Kennedy plans, President Kennedy called in General Douglas MacArthur to arbitrate the dispute. MacArthur had brokered an earlier détente back in 1928 as head of the American Olympic Committee, so he was familiar with the history of the antagonism. While MacArthur worked, the NAIA petitioned the USOC for greater representation, and in November 1963 the association's efforts were rewarded by the addition of three representatives to the USOC board: Duer plus the 1963-64 and 1964-65 NAIA presidents. At the same time, the NAIA's voice on the full USOC was increased from one vote to five, a splendid triumph. The NAIA enthusiastically celebrated this recognition as a great advance.

By January 1964 MacArthur had worked out a deal by which amnesty would be granted to athletes disqualified for competing in unsanctioned events; the AAU and the U.S. Track and Field Federation, an NCAA body, would each get three members on an

Olympic Eligibility Board to make eligibility determinations; and an "athletic congress" would be called with representatives from all amateur athletic bodies to work out a permanent plan. The compromise gave the USTFF authority over meets involving high school and college athletes and the AAU authority over non-students.[5]

For the 1964 Olympic basketball trials, the USOC awarded the NCAA three team slots, the AAU two, the armed forces two, and the NAIA one. Duer noted that once again the NCAA's claim to represent athletes at smaller colleges was revealed to be a lie; the designated "college division" NCAA team chose only one player of its 12 from a small college. Following the trials, NAIA-member Pan American University's Lucius Jackson was selected for the Olympic team and played a key role in the American gold-medal performance; however, NCAA members succeeded in keeping Grambling's Willis Reed from joining Jackson as a second NAIA athlete on the squad. Reed recovered from the slight and became the National Basketball Association rookie of the year the ensuing season. Also at the games, Florida A&M's Bob Hayes cemented his title as the "world's fastest human" by winning the 100-meter dash in an Olympic-record 10 seconds flat.

In the spring of 1965 the USOC board stunned the NCAA by approving an amendment to its constitution. The new law required that the *majority* of the votes on each Olympic games committee (one committee for each sport in which the United States participated) be reserved for the internationally-recognized governing body of that sport—i.e., the AAU. The AAU bloc on the USOC had pushed this policy through, presumably with the warm support of the NAIA. Frustrated by their stinging defeat, the NCAA came very close to withdrawing from the USOC altogether, though they were narrowly dissuaded from doing so.

Congress, like much of the public, decried the internecine fighting between the AAU and the NCAA, and in the summer of 1965 Senator Warren Magnuson (D-WA) convened a Commerce Committee hearing to get to the bottom of the dispute. He invited Duer to testify, soliciting an objective perspective. Duer took full advantage of the opportunity to establish the NAIA as a legitimate and relevant voice in matters of amateur athletics. He noted that he had taken part in more than 20 meetings over the preceding four years trying to work out a solution to the two bodies' differences, and had attended every USOC meeting since 1946. In particular, he argued for the right of the NAIA to have representatives on international bodies and for its athletes to be fairly represented in Olympic and Pan American game trials. He supported his position by noting the Olympic gold medals won by such NAIA athletes as Ralph Boston, Lee Calhoun, Bob Hayes, Bobby Morrow, and Dick Stebbins. He concluded by denouncing as unsound and unnecessary the dual sanctioning sought by the NCAA.

Duer wrapped up his testimony by listing five recommendations to solve the ongoing controversy. First, a body composed of all amateur organizations sponsoring national programs should handle the administration of amateur athletics. Second, increasing offsetting representation to other worthy organizations such as the NAIA could ease the AAU-NCAA power tension. Third, only one "sanctioning" body for national and international competition should be established, as Olympic rules dictated. Fourth, the USOC should exercise more positive leadership in promoting amateur athletics in the United States and resolving differences between constituent organizations. Finally, he suggested establishing an arbitration board of men of the highest prestige in the country to resolve differences that could not be handled among rival organizations or the USOC.[6]

NAIA leaders and other supporters felt that Duer's testimony had brought great positive publicity to the organization, getting its philosophy out to the public in a way that had never been managed before. Further, the NAIA head's testimony apparently had a positive impact on the issue of the NAIA's international role. A year later, the long and bitter dispute finally reached its climax at the October 1966 meeting of the USOC. There, for the first time, the USOC board of directors voted for NAIA representation on all Olympic game committees for which the organization held national championships. In addition, the NAIA won nominal representation on committees for a number of other sports sponsored by member institutions though they were not part of the association's national title plans, including bobsled, boxing, women's gymnastics, judo, shooting, women's swimming, women's track and field, water polo, and weightlifting. Happy with this long-overdue recognition of the NAIA's clout, the Executive Committee launched a drive to raise $40,000 for the Olympic fund, calling on each member institution to come up with $100 per year.

The tension between the NAIA and the NCAA would not ease for another three decades, however. Though one might argue that only so many possible dates existed for season-ending district and national events, the NAIA suspected the NCAA of deliberately scheduling championships to conflict with theirs. The college division had established championships in basketball, cross-country, golf, tennis, track and field, and wrestling. In 1962 they announced that several would be held simultaneously with already-scheduled NAIA events, ratcheting up the tension between the rivals.

In March 1963 the Executive Committee took two steps to try to keep NAIA members from straying. First, they ruled that any conference with over 50 percent NAIA membership that pledged its champion to a conflicting event could not have another member participate in district or national NAIA playoffs in that sport. Further, to sponsor a conflicting event would earn a school a two-year suspension from the NAIA; apparently, however, the severity of this punishment limited its use. Because NAIA eligibility rules were more stringent than those of the NCAA, dual member schools sometimes contended that they only needed to follow the tougher guidelines in sports in which they wished to qualify in NAIA national playoffs. In September 1963 the Executive Committee explicitly rejected this argument, saying that all NAIA institutions had to abide by all NAIA eligibility rules for every sport they sponsored. Violations would render a college ineligible for *all* district and national NAIA events.

Enforcing such rules fell to the Executive Committee. District eligibility committees were to report any violations to Duer, who would take them to the Executive Committee for interpretation of violations, assessment of penalties, and possibly asking the National Eligibility Committee to further investigate allegations. The Executive Committee also took steps in 1963 to enhance the academic legitimacy of the association by giving colleges not accredited by their regional accreditation bodies two years to start seeking approval, placing them in a probationary status until they had won that symbol of legitimacy.

The NAIA passed another milestone in its movement toward integration when Executive Committee member A. W. Mumford died. Alex Durley of Texas Southern University, the first committee member from a black college, was appointed to fill out the rest of the year. Then at the annual meeting in March 1963, he won election to serve out the balance of Mumford's term.

The NAIAC, the association's coaches' organization, developed a great plan to build its membership. They asked the Executive Committee to approve a dues increase along with the inclusion of coaches' dues in institutional dues billing. The proposal won approval at the annual meeting, with implementation during the 1963-64 school year. The number of coaches in the NAIAC jumped from 693 in 1962-63 to 1,122 the following year and up to 2,089 by the fall of 1966. Tripling the membership certainly strengthened the mandate of the group and opened the way to add sections beyond the six that existed in 1963: baseball, basketball, football, track and field, golf, and wrestling.

Nevertheless, the NAIAC suffered a setback at the 1964 meeting when its budget proposal included funds for its president to attend the national meetings. The Executive Committee denied this request, citing an unwritten policy to provide no travel expenses to the annual meeting to anyone beyond the Executive Committee. Widening this coverage could open the door to further requests for subsidy by worthy applicants; the rather precarious NAIA budget might be seriously endangered once that door was opened. Even more pertinent to the nature of the association, the NAIA had thrived on a spirit of volunteerism, with the officials' institutions picking up their travel costs as well as smiling on their time off campus as an "in-kind" contribution to the NAIA's health. (In 1966, when the NAIA's coffers were a bit more flush, the request was granted.)

Aside from the ongoing NCAA wars, in 1963-64 the association faced other issues. Duer, who had dedicated his life to the NAIA, had difficulty understanding representatives of member institutions who did not share his single-minded dedication to doing whatever it took to enhance the organization's quality and prestige. In fact, he found such "vacillation" among members the most serious problem confronting the NAIA. Dual membership was anathema to him for it weakened the association and bespoke a disturbing lack of loyalty. The black institutions for which Duer had expended so much of his energy and moral capital particularly offended him. In 1964, Districts 6A and 29, two of the three southern black districts, trying to have their cake and eat it, too, had pledged their regular-season champion to the NAIA and their post-season tournament champion to the NCAA.

Of course, the three black districts were different from the others, which were organized geographically instead of racially. Somehow the different nature of the black districts seemed a factor in their lukewarm commitment, and following the advice of the Research Committee set up to resolve the problem, the NAIA began to move on actually integrating the black school into the already-established districts where feasible. They began in 1964 with Ohio, Pennsylvania, and Virginia.

Eligibility questions continued to plague the NAIA. The new handbook seemed dated almost before it was printed, as numerous cases too tricky to handle on the district level made it to Kansas City for interpretation. Mimeographed sheets from the national office attempted to fill the interpretive gap. Many issues concerned the 24-hour rule, which mandated a student to have completed 24 units in the previous year. How did night classes, correspondence courses, extension courses, and summer school impact that requirement? A related issue concerned what exactly constituted a term of attendance. A clarified policy defined that as being enrolled in six hours for college credit.

Another prickly area concerned hardship cases. "Hardship" came to mean injury or other acts of God not within the player or coach's control. The clarified policy provided that a player who had appeared in no more than one game or contest could appeal to the Eligibility Committee to be allowed an addition year of competition.

The 1964-65 school year did not present any significant new problems, but several old ones continued to demand attention. Integrating black colleges into their geographic districts continued, with Le Moyne College, Lane College, Fisk University, and Knoxville College smoothly added to District 24 (Tennessee), and Arkansas A&M and Kentucky State joining District 17 and District 24, respectively.

Duer's bugaboo, the conflict between the NAIA and the NCAA's college division, forced more measures to try to keep control of the membership. The NCAA scheduled events on the same dates as NAIA national championships in basketball, football, swimming, and wrestling, and regional meets in golf and tennis. Even more aggravating to Duer, the NCAA arranged to hold its swim meet at Illinois State Normal University and the wrestling match at Colorado School of Mines, both of which were NAIA schools.

The NCAA escalated the conflict, vowing to boycott any track and field meet that did not seek its sanction and threatened serious penalties on NCAA institutions that were so brazen as to take part in events not sanctioned by the NCAA. The continual battle was taking its toll on Duer and the Executive Committee since they needed to make decisions on dual member issues, which seemed to be increasing in number. Out of 455 NAIA members, fully 30 percent, or 138 held dual membership. More disturbing, 40 percent of the district chairmen represented dual-membership institutions, suggesting an alarmingly ambiguous organizational leadership. It was time to get tough. The Executive Committee promulgated a new policy based on the NAIA by-law stating that "each member institution shall . . . be assumed to be in full support of the total program of NAIA." Henceforth, any NAIA member institution whose personnel played a part in organizing a competing event would forfeit its right to have its people serve on any NAIA committees. Those leaders in conflict with the new policy could serve out their terms, but would be ineligible for any further election or appointment until their conflict of interest was resolved. Further, institutions should take care not to elect leaders whose loyalty might be in question. The policy did leave a bit of wriggle room by allowing for exceptions in cases of significant financial differences or loss of school time . . . if application was made in a timely fashion.

The NAIA walked a tightrope between allowing member colleges to thumb their noses at the championships it had developed, and pressuring the members so much that they decided to simply opt out and join the NCAA. The Executive Committee dealt with 13 dual membership issues at the 1965 meeting, placing several schools on one or two-year suspension, warning others, and issuing ultimatums to still others. Early indications supported the hard line, as the number of colleges needing such discipline declined the following year. But the battle for the allegiance of member colleges was far from over.

The NAIAC continued to flourish as a component of the NAIA. Membership, sparked by the new system of institutional dues, was skyrocketing. On the other hand, much work still needed to be done. Many coaches still did not belong, including those of seven of the 32 teams playing in the 1965 basketball tournament. As it grew, the NAIAC broadened its activities. Many of the sections began holding clinics to coincide with their national tournaments and coaches' meetings. In addition, they began planning a new semiannual magazine entitled *The NAIA Coach*. The publication would publicize matters of interest to coaches, and from their ranks would be drawn authors to write the articles. The NAIA national office would split the costs of publication with the NAIAC.

With the growth of the NAIA in general, the Executive Committee kept working at ways to effectively decentralize as much of the association's operations as possible, in keeping with the traditional emphasis on grass-roots control rather than overly centralized management. In practice, that meant devolving more control to the districts. At the 1965 annual meeting, the District Chairmen's Committee noted that for the first time, after coming very close on a number of occasions, all of the 32 district chairs were in attendance. After discussion with the district chairs, the Executive Committee ranked district needs in order of priority: more funds, more service events, better administration, and more workshops.

During the 1965-66 school year, national office employees from Duer on down enjoyed a physical change. The preceding spring's basketball tournament, the most lucrative ever held, had left the association with a surplus of $33,500 for the year, and a rare feeling of wealth may have infected even the frugal Duer. After eight years in the Aladdin Hotel in downtown Kansas City, years during which the NAIA had dramatically increased both its numbers of member institutions and sports offered, the NAIA needed more space. In keeping with Duer's appreciation of the convenience of working in a hotel, they moved just a block to the Hotel Phillips, but the new facility more than doubled the square footage at the staff's disposal to over 1,600 square feet, including a reception area, a conference room, and a mail/supply room in addition to four private offices.

The growth had not stopped. During the preceding year, 26 new colleges had joined the NAIA, boosting membership to a new record high of 470. Well over half, or 269 different schools, participated in post-season playoffs in at least one sport, providing a measure of athletic fulfillment for 3,836 athletes. With the increased numbers, in both the 1965 and 1966 conventions members had raised from the floor the suggestion that it might be time to subdivide the NAIA into two competitive divisions, following the example of the NCAA. The Executive Committee turned the matter over to its Research Committee to poll members on their response to the idea. Later experience would show that, true to the bureaucratic model, establishing two divisions in some sports as membership grew proved much more realizable than the flip side, reducing the number of divisions as numbers declined.

Another symptom of organizational growth concerned eligibility issues. According to the new procedures, eligibility forms were to be filed with the district chairman in each of the NAIA's 32 districts. But with that many districts and so many member institutions, the level of understanding and competence varied widely. The five most-asked questions dealt with defining the "term of attendance" (six hours), applying the 18-week transfer rule to summer school, how to incorporate junior college transfers into four-year programs, amateurism, and individuals seeking exemption from rules. For the first time, the procedure was spelled out with precision. By October 12, December

14, and March 8 (or corresponding dates in future years), each member institution was to submit its official eligibility forms for any sports it sponsored to the district eligibility chairman to review, approve, and file.

Coaches increasingly joined NAIAC, along with their particular sport's coaching association, which brought together NCAA, NAIA, junior college, and high school coaches. In a parallel move, athletic directors launched their own trans-organizational association, NACDA (National Association of College Directors of Athletics). The Executive Committee encouraged athletic directors to join and add their voices to national discussions of intercollegiate athletics while learning from their counterparts in other associations.

Of course, all of this growing overhead was being developed to better serve the athletes playing NAIA-sponsored sports. In 1962-63 those sports numbered eleven. In the fall cross-country, football, and soccer had national competitions. In the winter, basketball, swimming, and wrestling took center stage. Then came the deluge, with five sports on tap in the spring: baseball, bowling, golf, tennis, and track and field. By 1966, though, winter had caught up to spring, at least in the number of sports featured that time of year. Gymnastics made its national debut in the winter of 1964 and indoor track and field in 1966, bringing the NAIA's total number of sports to thirteen.

Kansas continued its domination in cross-country. Emporia State took its fourth title in five years in 1962, but slipped behind Fort Hays State the next year despite the Hornets' John Camien winning his first of two consecutive individual crowns. In 1964 Howard Payne of Texas, the 1957 winner, temporarily broke the Kansans' lock on the sport, though Fort Hays finished second, foreshadowing their rebounding to take top honors again in 1965. That year the NAIA determined that the top 15 finishers at the nationals would be designated All-Americans.

In football action, top-ranked Central Oklahoma State played to expectations, knocking off Lenoir-Rhyne, 28-13, in the 1962 Camellia Bowl. The Broncos earned their way into the championship by squashing Emporia State, 20-0, while Lenoir-Rhyne's Bears downed Northern State (SD), 20-7, in the other semi-final. A new record crowd of 13,260 saw 15 NAIA records smashed in the course of the championship game.

In 1963, St. John's (MN) annihilated Emporia State, 54-0, in the semi-final game, winning it a spot in the third and last Camellia Bowl in Sacramento against unbeaten Prairie View A&M. Billy Nicks, whose Panthers had won the National Negro championship four times, was named NAIA football coach of the year, but could not get his team past St. John's, who won a wide-open title game, 33-27.

The next year, Concordia (MN) whipped Linfield (OR), 28-6, to gain a shot at Sam Houston State, 32-21 winners over Findlay (OH). Playing in Augusta, Georgia, neither team was able to master the other and they wound up in a 7-7 tie.

In 1965 St. John's returned to the title game with a convincing 28-7 semifinal win over Fairmont State (WV). Linfield, coming off a tough 30-27 triumph over Sul Ross State (TX), made it one round farther than the previous year, but Bob Gagliardi's Johnnies crushed them, 33-0, in the championship game. St. John's thus capped a perfect 11-0 season in which they had yielded only 29 ground yards per game through their entire schedule. Gagliardi earned coach of the year honors, but he was just beginning. When St. John's later moved to the NCAA Division 3, he continued coaching the team and in 2003 passed Grambling's Eddie Robinson as the winningest college coach in American history when he bagged his 409th. The downside of the 1965 game was that a rainy day in Augusta slashed the crowd's size and the NAIA lost $10,000 on what was becoming a wandering championship.

East Stroudsburg (PA), one-goal loser in a 1961 semi-final soccer game, came back in 1962 and beat Pratt Institute convincingly, 4-0, for the title. The next year they lost by a goal again in the semi-finals of a sport that had become a near-monopoly of northeastern teams. Then the hazards of late autumn weather caught up with the tournament. A snowstorm forced cancellation of the championship game, leaving Earlham (IN) and Castleton State (VT) as co-champions. In 1964 and 1965 another team from the region, Trenton State, produced back-to-back wins, beating Lincoln (PA), 3-0, and then Earlham, 6-2, behind Wayne Huston's four goals, in the two finals.

Basketball continued to be the NAIA's flagship sport, as well as the most visible of the winter competitions. In 1963, twelfth-seed Pan American University (TX) blew out the competition in early rounds, then beat Grambling, 90-83, in a semifinal game and topped Western Carolina, 73-62, to win its sole NAIA basketball title. The next year the defending champions could not sneak in under opponents' radar, for they were the top seed. But their early victories were less decisive than in 1963, and in the semi-final they barely got past Carson-Newman, 56-54. The other semi-final game had a strong regional flavor, as Kansas City's Rockhurst College edged nearby Emporia State, 66-61, to reach the finals for the only time in their eight total appearances in the national tournament. It was a good year for the tenth-seeded locals, as they outgunned Pan American for the title, 66-56.

In 1965 Central State (OH), one of the early black schools to mainstream in the NAIA, totally dominated the competition. Coming into the tournament as the top seed, they did nothing to dispel that ranking, winning by 21, 14, 9, and 16 points on their way to the final game. Their opponent, Oklahoma Baptist, meanwhile, befitting its fifteenth seeding, squeaked by opponents by less convincing margins, then ran into an Ohio buzz saw; Central totally dominated the title match in a romp, 85-51.

Central State returned in 1966 as the top seed, but Norfolk State knocked them out in the quarterfinals. Meanwhile, Oklahoma Baptist, seeded eleventh, rode the hot shooting of 6-foot-8-inch Al Tucker into the finals against fourth-seeded Georgia Southern, who had won overtime and one-point squeakers on their way to the final. At that point, Tucker, the tournament MVP, took over and poured in 41 points in an 88-59 blowout win for the Bison, giving the Oklahomans their sole NAIA title in six final appearances.

In swimming competition, North Central (IL) finished their run as an NAIA power with their third straight national championship in 1963, and their fifth consecutive top-two finish. In 1964, however, Macalester (MN), runners-up in 1963, launched their own claim to swimming fame, winning the first of their three consecutive titles, edging Eastern New Mexico in all three years.

Pennsylvania continued to dominate NAIA wrestling. Lock Haven State won the title in 1963 and 1966, while finishing second in the two intervening years. The 1966 team was led by four-time champion Jerry Swope, whose coach, Gray Simon, was the only other four-time winner. In 1964 Moorhead State continued the pattern of a Minnesota school taking the championship whenever Pennsylvania faltered, but the next year Pennsylvania's Bloomsburg State captured its third crown in six years, edging out Lock Haven for state bragging rights and national honors.

Gymnastics made its initial appearance on the scene in 1964, with Western Illinois winning that debut title match, and then coming right back to win again in 1965. The next year Northwestern Louisiana State stopped Western Illinois' string by taking the title down south, though the defending champs did capture the runner-up position.

In January 1966 the thirteenth NAIA national championship made its debut at Kansas City's Municipal Auditorium. It was there Southern University showed that prowess in outdoor track and field readily moved indoors and captured the first indoor track and field meet over Fort Hays State, with sprinter George Anderson of Southern winning honors as the top meet athlete.

Baseball featured a different champion each season. In 1963, fireballing right-hander Fred Beene led Sam Houston State past Grambling, 2-1, in the final game, fanning twelve and driving in the game-winning run. It was the first appearance for both schools in the finals. The 1964 titlist, West Liberty State (WV), came up through the losers' bracket and beat Grambling, 6-4, to reach the final game, and then 3-2 to win top honors, leaving Grambling frustrated for the second straight season. The following year, Carson-Newman (TN) rode strong pitching right through to the title, edging Nebraska-Omaha, 3-2, in the last game. Hitting was back in fashion in 1966 as Lewis (IL) beat up on everyone but Oregon's slugging Linfield, which derailed Lewis 8-2 early on and then dismantled them, 15-4, in the final game.

Bowling passed around the honors for three years, as the University of Southwestern Louisiana won in 1963, Kearney State (NE) in 1964, and Omaha in 1965. In 1966 the Bowling Proprietors of America cut back their subsidy for the bowling competition, forcing a reduction in the national field from 32 teams to eight. Omaha showed it could handle a small field as well as a large one, repeating as champion.

Four different schools captured golf titles. The Eastern New Mexico Greyhounds, led by Steve Spray, took top honors in 1963. In 1964 Texas Wesleyan returned the crown to the Lone Star state where Lamar State had held it for so long, and East Texas State continued that tradition with a victory in 1965. But the University of Southwestern Louisiana snuck the crown across the state line a few miles with a triumph in 1966.

Pan American University continued its domination of tennis. The two-time defending champions racked up three more titles in 1963, 1964, and 1965, with Ken Lang a singles and doubles champ in 1963 and George Kon a singles winner for the team in 1965. In 1966, however, a new dynasty was born, one that would become one of the most dominant in any NAIA sport. Redlands (CA), led by singles and doubles winner John Yeomans, captured the first of six consecutive national championships, and went on to win nine in ten years.

In track and field, Maryland State captured the 1963 title, beating out Nebraska-Omaha. The following year Emporia State edged two-time runner-up North Carolina College to capture first place. Then in 1965, Southern University-Baton Rouge (LA), led by top meet performer Theron Lewis, won its first top honors. The Southern squad repeated in 1966, and made it three in a row in 1967, one of several black schools to find great success competing in the NAIA.

6

Fine Tuning a Mature NAIA
1966-1971

The United States seemed to be unraveling in 1966. The country was torn between increasingly bitter supporters and critics of the Vietnam War, emotionally wrung out by the civil rights movement and the emerging black power component that alienated many moderate supporters, and bemused by the counterculture's challenges to the traditions and mores of the past.

The NAIA, by contrast, had just concluded the best year in its history. It had gained more members than any year since it expanded beyond basketball in 1952 (47), pushing its numbers beyond 500 institutions. Receipts from its basketball tournament had jumped 10 percent. An NAIA all-star team had competed in the Pan American Game trials and landed four players on the 12-man squad representing the United States. Ice hockey had been tabbed as the fourteenth sport to enjoy an NAIA national championship competition. The NAIAC continued to mature as a component of the parent organization and had become capable of carrying most of the load in putting on those national tournaments. The number of affiliated conferences (those with more than half NAIA schools) rose from 36 to 41. Talk now turned to making the NAIA an *inter*national association, as the issue of Canadian colleges joining the growing numbers reached flash point in 1967. With a lessening of tensions with the NCAA, the NAIA could focus on improving its own operations with less distraction than had been the case in the past.

The Canadian issue was a bit tricky. After lengthy discussion at the 1967 March meeting, delegates concluded that if the northern institutions could meet NAIA criteria and demonstrate the integrity of their programs, they should be eligible to become part of the association. Canadian academic programs differed from their American counterparts, however. In most of Canada, according to the physical education director at United College in Winnipeg, degree-granting institutions offered three-year programs plus an honors year. They did not operate on a quarter or semester system, but rather courses ran for an entire year. Thus eligibility derived from passing one set of exams at the end of the academic year; a student was either eligible or ineligible for the whole next year. To further complicate matters, Canada did not have accreditation agencies like those in the States. Nevertheless, the American institutions recognized that the similarities between themselves and their Canadian counterparts were much more significant than their differences, and they reached northward by sending invitational letters to 26 schools that seemed most similar to themselves. Lakehead University of Port Arthur, Ontario, became the first Canadian institution admitted when the Nor'Westers joined up in the summer of 1967. Within two years, Simon Fraser University in Burnaby, British Columbia, was well on its way to becoming a major force in NAIA athletics, making a big splash in swimming competitions.

The NAIA's Research Committee, directed by Harry Fritz of Western Illinois, undertook several projects during the 1966-67 school year. A survey on financial aid turned up such diverse practices that the committee was unable to formulate any policy recommendations. Dealing with the ongoing redistricting issue proved more amenable to resolution. Because institutions were continually joining the NAIA, while a lesser number were departing, and given that Districts 6A, 6B, and 29 were made up of Southern black institutions not integrated into their geographical areas, there clearly existed an ongoing need to recalibrate the boundaries of the districts.

The committee met three times in the course of the year, and it sought to bring districts as close as possible to the optimum number of members (15), move some schools into different districts that they more commonly scheduled, and integrate as many as possible of District 29's black colleges into their geographic districts. This overhaul of the districts was the most ambitious attempted to that time, and the committee sent letters to all the affected athletic directors explaining the rationale for the changes. The letters noted that the basic policies governing changes were:
- Requests of individual institutions and districts
- An attempt to keep districts from reaching too high or too low a membership total as compared to the current national district membership average of 15.
- Strengthening of districts.
- Integration of predominantly Negro schools into previously all-white districts wherever and whenever possible.[1]

The new arrangements roused relatively little controversy. At the spring 1967 meeting, the executive committee listened to complaints about the operation of the new districts during the school year, and the small number of objections heartened the members.

At the 1967 meeting, a milestone of sorts occurred when Morton Cunningham, president of Fort Hays State College in Kansas, became the first college president to ascend to the presidency of the NAIA. He had broken the athletic directors' Executive Committee stronghold a few years earlier and worked his way to the top of the ladder. Though in a couple of decades presidents would seize control of the organization, their time had not yet come; no other president had been elected to the governing committee since Cunningham in 1960. Still, the NCAA trailed far behind the NAIA in this regard; not until James Frank in 1981 would a college president head the rival organization.

The NAIAC established some ethical guidelines for contacts with players at other schools, clarifying and codifying potentially disruptive situations. Should an athlete initiate contact with the athletic director or coach at an institution other than that at which he had matriculated, the contacted school was obligated to notify the athlete's current college in writing within ten days. Athletes had the right to explore other opportunities, but the penalty for tampering was severe. If a coach should initiate contact with another institution's player, he would be publicly reprimanded and his school would be barred from all NAIA events for a full year.

The coaches' organization continued to mushroom in growth, with another 346 coaches added to the rolls during the year. In order to give more members an opportunity to take part in a leadership role, the NAIAC reduced the term of office for board members from two to one year, doubling the opportunities for service.

The NAIA dealt with a more period-specific issue, military service, in an appropriate manner. Because of the draft and the war in Vietnam, many students faced crucial decisions about their future. Some saw their patriotic duty as joining up, and it seemed that such commitment should be rewarded, not penalized. As a result, students whose college careers were interrupted by a year or more of continuous active military service were deemed to be immediately eligible for athletics upon registering at any college, exempting them from the transfer rule and the 24-hour rule.

Meanwhile, athletic directors formed a new committee for themselves, though it took a more outward orientation, focusing on NAIA leaders playing a more active role in NACDA, the broad multi-association body of athletic directors. Some 30 percent of NACDA members represented NAIA colleges, and this seemed a good, and hitherto non-political, forum for improving members' administrative skills.

The Executive Committee approved a new honor, the A. O. Duer Scholarship Award, which would be presented annually to a junior with a grade point average of 3.75 or higher and significant athletic achievement. They also standardized awards for teams, which would henceforth honor first through fourth places in each sport, and individuals, who would receive a uniform ceramic tile plaque.

The Development Committee, aware that the NAIA had always sought recognition in international sports events, recommended that the association contribute $50,000 to the Olympics, $20,000 for the Pan American trials, $10,000 for the development of sports, and another $10,000 for the Federation of International Sports Union games, along with $5,000 to administer these areas. The Executive Committee demurred at such a broad commitment, but did set a goal of $50,000 for the Olympics, asking each member school to contribute $100. With tight budgets and more pressing priorities, colleges found such an optional obligation easy to slight; a year later Duer reminded them that along with Olympic opportunities NAIA members needed to participate in fundraising.

The 1967-68 school year marked the penultimate stage in the NAIA's integration project that had begun back in 1948, when Indiana State reserve Clarence Walker became the first black athlete to play in the national tournament. Black colleges had been admitted to the tournament in 1953, and some had been integrated into their geographical districts since that time. Nevertheless, 53 schools were still segregated in "separate but equal" black districts 6A, 6B, and 29. It was time to complete the pioneering NAIA mission.

On August 25, 1967, a crucial planning meeting convened in Kansas City. Duer, his capable assistant executive secretary Joe Axelson, Harry Fritz and the Research Committee, and others met with the commissioners of two of the three Negro conferences and the chairman of NASC. They reviewed the history of the NAIA's actions to include the black institutions in the association and, after much discussion, agreed to finally fully integrate for the 1968-69 school year. During the intervening months, the Executive Committee and the Research Committee devoted hours to hammering out the details of the integration, writing letters, making phone calls, or meeting personally with all the affected institutions, black and white. In the end, over 100 member institutions in eight districts were affected by the moves.

As the fall of 1968 approached, the NAIA scheduled a series of key meetings on September 8 and 9, inviting athletic directors from the affected districts to attend. At the same time, NASC chairman Eddie Jackson wrote to each of the Negro colleges to invite their attendance as well. The meetings, held at Presbyterian College (SC), Catawba College (NC), and Atlantic Christian College (NC), seemed to serve their purpose. Few complaints surfaced during the year of transition and the integration went smoothly. Al Duer proudly saluted his organization in the winter 1968 issue of *The NAIA News*, noting incorrectly that black schools had been granted their first opportunity to compete for the national title in 1947, and properly taking pride in his personal and institutional role in making integration a success. Thus concluded one of the NAIA's most significant and positive contributions to the sports world.

Though the decibels of the dispute had dropped dramatically, the NCAA-AAU feud continued to simmer. Senator Magnuson held further meetings probing relevant track and field organizations, but opted to delay any final action until after the 1968 Olympic Games. At that point, he felt, a committee with one representative from each affected organization, plus an unbiased at-large figure, would be able to work out a solution. Duer, numbed by years of fruitless efforts to bring reason to bear on the dispute, said that the NAIA would accept any arbitrator's decision, but that it was impossible for the combatants to work out a final resolution to the struggle. He urged Senator Magnuson to have his committee make the tough call and impose it on the bitter rivals.

The NAIAC continued its remarkable growth, reaching 2,231 coaches. Each of them received a membership card granting him admission to district and national playoffs. The organization also clarified its terminology, though one still heard people who should have known better demonstrating that they did not:

Association: A coaches' group representing a sport which has a national championship and which has a membership of 50 or more and which has an approved constitution;

Sports section: A coaches' group representing a sport which has a national championship, but which has a membership of less than 50;

Advisory Committee: A group of coaches representing a sport which has not been approved for competition at the national championship level. This is the beginning step toward becoming a sports section.[2]

The NAIA made a significant hiring decision for the national office in 1967. Wallace Schwartz took a position as assistant to the executive secretary, where he would coordinate various committees and help administer national championship events. He would leave a significant stamp on the organization during his tenure, which ran more than a quarter century. In another shift in the Kansas City office, Tom Reno left after five years in charge of public relations, with Michael Kleinman taking over his post. The timing was good for the newcomers: the executive secretary was awarded a $1000 salary increase and his subordinates a $600 hike.

Despite the relative peace between the NCAA and the NAIA, conflicting events continued to put pressure on both member institutions and the association itself. During the year the NAIA hit five institutions with two-year suspensions for violating the organization's policy: Ashland College, Northern Michigan University, Norfolk State College, Bethune-Cookman College, and McNeese State University. As long as dual membership was a popular option for colleges, the tension would continue.

The 1968-69 school year brought an innovation to the management of the NAIA. For the first time, the Executive Committee held a formal interim meeting in Kansas City in November. At this gathering, though only six of the ten members were present, a number of issues were resolved, including placing New Mexico Highlands University on probation for canceling four contracted basketball games; supporters of the institution were especially aggrieved because their highly-regarded football team was thus barred from post-season competition.

That fall, the NAIA's development program was assigned to Wally Schwartz. He sought to stimulate voluntary contributions to the Olympic Fund and the International Development Sports Program. One stimulus to giving was the publication of contributors' names on the back page of *The NAIA News*. Schwartz got good marks for his work, but only 55 percent of schools were contributing anything. Given the voluntary nature of the contributions, that is not a figure to take lightly.

Honors awarded generally elicit less resistance than monies assessed, and so it was that a new NAIA group, the Distinguished Athlete Association, proved popular. It invited members of the NAIA Hall of Fame, all-America or all-tournament players in various sports, players on any championship teams, and recipients of the E. L. Liston, Gene Waldren, or A. O. Duer awards to join. Duer felt that with increased staff on board, it was finally feasible to get such an organization off the ground. Even though membership was a rather pricey $10 per year, over 200 athletes joined that first year, getting the DAA off to a rousing start.

At the annual meeting, for the first time the Athletic Directors' Association (ADA) met and hashed out various topics in panel discussions. Members, most of them also active in the more broad-based NACDA, were pleased with the results of their new meeting and agreed to make it a regular part of the annual convention. Conference commissioners also gathered to deal with issues they held in common, and their newly-established committee laid plans to regularly convene at the convention. It is one of the truisms of bureaucratic politics that once a body is established, it lives on even after its initial purpose has been fulfilled. Contradicting that norm, the Sanctioning Committee recommended that it be dissolved, and the Executive Committee complied. (The following year, the Professional Relations and Education Committee also deactivated itself until such time as it was needed. If in no other way, the NAIA was different by resisting the "bureaucratic imperative.")

Dual membership issues continued to plague the association, but as the numbers seemed to be holding constant while NAIA membership increased, the relative impact of the problem declined, or at least did not motivate the Executive Committee to make any change in policy. Only two sanctions were handed out: a one-year probation to Texas Southern University, and two years to Alcorn A&M.

Duer frequently cited tougher academic standards as an NAIA distinctive in contrasting the association with the NCAA. One troubling flaw in the NAIA's academic rigor concerned accreditation: 46 member institutions were not accredited by their regional accrediting associations. Of those, 13 had been admitted to the NAIA on the understanding that they would soon achieve that goal. The Executive Committee, recognizing the weakness, ruled that all active members must be accredited by 1972 or they would be demoted to associate member status. Further, associate members were to be accredited by 1975 or, presumably, be expelled. These moves reflected the increased stature and maturity of the organization and its ongoing desire to raise its standards.

The NAIAC continued its rise in influence and clout within the association. Membership approached 2,500, and the group won approval of a constitution during the year. Drawing upon its subordinate associations and sections related to individual sports, the NAIAC processed recommendations through an executive board and passed them along to the NAIA Executive Committee.

Periodically the NAIA has focused attention on developing character, seeing that emphasis as a way to distinguish itself from the NCAA. During the 1968-69 school year, the association launched its "Conduct of Athletics" program, designed to promote sportsmanship on the part of players, coaches, and fans. Articles in *The NAIA News* and *NAIA Coach*, mailings, speeches, and program inserts were used to stimulate awareness of the drive, and Duer claimed it had gotten off to "a fine start."[3]

As the NAIA grew and its staff increased, the potential for turnover likewise grew. In 1969 Joe Axelson, who had capably served as public relations director from 1961 to 1963 and assistant executive director the ensuing six years, resigned to become general manager of the NBA's Cincinnati Royals. To fill the void he left, Duer brought on Dr. Charles Morris, the High Point College athletic director; a man with a wealth of pertinent experience, he had coached five sports at David Lipscomb College, headed the physical education department there, and served as District 26 chairman. An additional assistant, Glen Davies, with 19 years of experience working with YMCA programs in various cities, joined Morris, Wally Schwartz, and Mike Kleinman in the growing national office.

One rather odd abortive initiative marked the year. Duer announced that water polo had become the 15th national championship sport, with host Western Illinois defeating Hendrix College (Arkansas) in the title match-up. The next year, the sport was cut back from a national invitational tournament, a lesser commitment than a national championship, to an area invitational. Although 41 schools were reportedly planning to add the sport, only 11 actually sponsored it in 1969. How that marginal a sport got approved as a national competition is a mystery. Less controversially, volleyball joined the galaxy of NAIA sports in the spring of 1969. In addition, the decathlon made a rather strange entrance on the scene with a competition at Westmont College (CA) being retroactively determined to be the first NAIA championship, and a second then planned for spring 1970. Not only was the timing puzzling, but considering the decathlon a separate event from the association's track and field competition seems curious. In fact, listings of decathlon champions are included in the track and field section of NAIA record books, so this artificial division apparently had a short life.

Duer kicked off the 1969-70 sports year with a challenge to the association to make the "Conduct of Athletics" program an even greater success in its second year.[4] His lead article in the fall issue of *The NAIA News*, reflecting Duer's constant commitment to integrating character and sports, condemned the win-at-any-cost approach that diverted attention from good sportsmanship, high ethical standards, and fair play. He did not oppose fighting to win, but argued that the pursuit of victory should not detract from the character-building aspects of sports.

A survey of the membership had pinpointed the three most serious problems in the pursuit of character in athletics: the conduct of the coach, conduct involving officials, and fan behavior. Duer spelled out just what sorts of areas coaches needed to work on, telling them that they were unquestionably the most influential figures in the sports programs, and that their relationships with their players, officials, fans, and others set the tone for behavior. Schools also needed to select good officials, treat them well before, during, and after the games, and maintain a solid professional relationship with them. Crowd control involved preventive measures such as educating the college community to proper behavior and developing a code of behavior for all concerned in athletic events to prevent touchy situations from arising. It also meant keeping alcohol away from games, curbing rowdy-ism and improper language, and firmly handling any misconduct. Duer unquestionably believed in the positive possibilities of sport for building character and to have the NAIA leading the way in this direction reflected his deepest desires.

The NAIA launched a development program under the direction of Glen Davies, seeking to raise $330,000 over two years to help members with travel, housing, and other expenses in non-revenue-producing sports tournaments. Davies first went after local leaders to develop a "500 Club" of donors putting up that amount of money. As with many of the association's small, private colleges, the NAIA as an organization had no endowment to speak of, and Duer believed that attracting some significant contributors was vital to the NAIA's future health.

The Executive Committee gave special attention to eligibility problems during the year, with amateurism, transcript falsification, and transfer issues addressed. A dozen schools were reprimanded for laxity and seven others placed on probation. Trying to promote familiarity with eligibility rules, which were not always perfectly clear, the committee generated a chart, "Seven Easy Steps to Eligibility Compliance," and published it in many venues over the course of the year.

Charlie Morris, one of Duer's new assistants, took responsibility for revitalizing the workshop program that had, after a promising start, fallen into disuse. Morris set as a goal hosting a workshop in each district every four years, which would mean eight per year. The Executive Committee put some teeth into the workshops by setting aside $3,500 to fund their reintroduction.

The NAIA was near its zenith at this point in history. Over the previous two years another fifty member institutions had joined, running membership to 550. During the preceding year, 1,078 institutions (counting multiple sports separately) had participated in post-season playoff games, with 7,189 students involved. Only 87 schools did not participate in any district or national action, less than 20 percent of membership, and a grand total of 65,815 athletes took part in intercollegiate athletics under the auspices of the NAIA. Growth, of course, creates problems as well as engendering celebration. The New England area (District 32) had grown so large that it had to be divided into a northern and southern area, with 14 and 19 members respectively.

In a more dramatic growth-related development, the membership voted to move to two football divisions for the fall of 1970. After considering the proposed change for several years, the association made the move, soliciting opinions from schools about which division suited their football program. Fully 97 percent wound up in the division they preferred, with the NAIA Football Coaches Association making the final decisions. The two divisions were both divided into four roughly equal areas to generate four teams to play off for a national title. The wandering football bowl problem seemed to have found a resolution as well. The semifinal games would be played on the campus of one of the teams, and the championship game somewhere near one of the finalists' home fans, a practice that had been producing good crowds and gate receipts for a few years.

The association made two general policy decisions of some importance. First, all-American honors would be accorded to the first three finishers in indoor and outdoor track and field, swimming, wrestling, and (in its curious detached condition) the decathlon. Second, providing some sense of an overall national sports winner, the NAIA would begin naming as all-sports champion the school that racked up the most points in championship competition. The initial winner in the big Eastern year of 1969-1970 was Eastern Michigan University, trailed by Eastern New Mexico in second and Eastern Illinois in third place.

By the fall of 1970, the NAIA had reached a degree of stability in its staff, with Al Duer ably assisted by Wally Schwartz, Charlie Morris, Glen Davies, and Mike Kleinman, all with at least a year's experience under their belts. Once again the association moved, and again it was a short, block-long move from Hotel Phillips to the Dixon Inn Hotel. The nearby President Hotel was reserved for national convention functions, which could thus have all functions under one roof for the whole week.

A bit disturbed by the overwhelming numbers of athletes turning up for open national competitions, the Executive Committee took action at the spring 1971 meeting. Within a year each coaches' association within the NAIAC was to develop a plan to qualify athletes for their particular national championships if they did not already have one in place. This, in effect, put a stop to open entries at the national events.

In what many church-related institutions no doubt saw as the start of a "slippery slope" to losing their distinctiveness, the NAIA bent without revoking its long-standing rule against Sunday competition. Since many member institutions had principles and policies prohibiting such activity, this was a sensitive subject. The waiver permitted the ice hockey and baseball championships to include Sunday games for 1971 only, but established a precedent that others would seek to expand. At this time in history, almost no college, high school, or kids' athletic programs included a Sunday component, but the sacredness of the Sabbath was one of the traditional values challenged by the cultural revolution of the 1960s. The country would never be the same again.

Relations with black colleges may already have been on their own slippery slope. The NASC, representing such institutions regardless of their NAIA or NCAA affiliations, actively sought to play a role on NCAA committees as its members already did in the NAIA. Duer wrote to NASC chairman Vanette W. Johnson on October 30, 1970, that he was shocked by this disloyalty to the NAIA after it had taken such pioneering action to integrate. More specifically, he noted that Article VIII, Section II of the NAIA by-laws stated that member institutions who were part of any "committee for organizing or administering any part of the NCAA program shall thereby disqualify all members of their administration or athletic staff from serving on any NAIA committee."[5]

Johnson responded that he had no intention of undermining his group's warm relations with the NAIA and suggested a meeting to hash out their differences. At the March 1971 NAIA convention in Kansas City, the Executive Committees for both the NAIA and the NASC met together and discussed the issue at length. The upshot was a victory for the NASC. The NAIA agreed to remove the by-law section prohibiting dual members from participating on NCAA committees. The NASC's self-interested policy of trying to play both sides of the street had effectively weakened the NAIA's equally self-interested attempt to force its own members to declare their allegiance either to it or the NCAA. Partly because of this decision, the dual membership challenge would haunt the NAIA for the rest of the century.

At least the two dominant organizations were talking to each other. In May 1971, three representatives of the NAIA's Executive Committee met with three NCAA representatives in Washington, D.C., to initiate a dialog about issues such as conflicting meeting and game dates. Perhaps peaceful coexistence could be extended from the Cold War's geopolitical realm to the American sports world.

Eligibility issues continued to be a primary NAIA focus. Clarifications of issues, including limiting the war service exemption to the first two terms following release from active duty, were a regular feature in *The NAIA News*, and Duer wrote editorials hammering home his strong belief that eligibility compliance is not a platitude. Athletes were to be making normal progress toward a recognized degree, carrying 12 units, and have completed 24 units in the past two terms of attendance. Duer continued to emphasize that this deliberate integration of athletics and education was a critical distinguishing characteristic of the NAIA, and one of which members should be proud, not grudging.

The spring tournament, the 35th in the organization's history, brought together many of the famous names from its past with the naming of an all-time NAIB tournament team and the top NAIB and NAIA coaches to date. Joe Hutton of Hamline won top honors as NAIB coach, compiling a 591-208 (.738) record from 1929 to 1965. He won 19 Minnesota Intercollegiate Athletic Conference titles and three NAIB trophies, in 1942, 1949, and 1951. His 36 tournament wins had not been matched to that time. The NAIA coach was Ralph Nolan of little St. Benedict's College. He won two titles by very different routes, unseeded in 1954 (the only winner ever to begin unseeded) and top-seeded in 1967. The all-time NAIB tournament team, selected by a committee that had seen all of the players in action, included Milky Phelps (San Diego State), Hal Haskins and Verne Mikkelsen (Hamline), Gene James and Andy Tonkovich (Marshall), Earl Keth (Central Missouri State), Duane Klueth (Indiana State), Johnny Orr (Beloit), Scotty Steagall (Millikin), and Lloyd Tucker (Southwestern of Kansas).[6]

Fall sports underwent some significant changes over these five years. Cross country moved from four to five mile courses, football split into two divisions, and soccer discovered a dynasty.

Cross-country had only two winning schools during the 1966-70 seasons. Eastern Michigan took the title in 1966 and 1967, then again in 1970. The two intervening years saw Fort Hays (KS) State come out on top. Swamped with entries as an open competition, the cross-country coaches agreed in 1966 to limit schools to a maximum of six athletes and hold their national meet on the Saturday before Thanksgiving. Two fine runners set records within three years. Pat McMahon of Oklahoma Baptist successfully defended his crown in 1966 with a four-mile record time of 19:53.6. The next year John Mason of Fort Hays State won in four miles, only to see the race lengthened an additional mile the following year. Undeterred, he won again, leading his school to the team title, setting a five-mile mark of 23:40.0 that was never surpassed; with the NAIA going to an 8000-meter length in 1996, his record should stand forever.

The 1966 football title game matched two unbeaten teams, Wisconsin-Whitewater and Waynesburg (PA), in Tulsa on a blustery 24-degree day that kept the number of fans down and the game in the red. Waynesburg, sparked by the running and passing of halfback Rich Dahar, won going away, 42-21.

Another battle of unbeatens in 1967 matched Eastern Washington State and Fairmont (WV) State in Morgantown, West Virginia. The venue's proximity to one of the competing schools stimulated attendance, as 12,250 turned out to make a financial as well as artistic success of the game. The happy business outcome suggested a solution to the monetary losses the association had been suffering at neutral sites, one that would be implemented thenceforth. Not only that, but the local fans went home happy as Fairmont State's Falcons came from behind to claim a 28-21 victory in the game.

The next year Troy State (AL), behind a five-touchdown passing assault by Sim Byrd, captured a 43-35 scoring marathon over Texas A&I. The Red Wave, playing before a friendly record crowd of 15,000 in Montgomery, stopped A&I from capturing their first title since 1959. In 1969, however, the Javelinas were not to be denied. In Kingsville, Texas, Coach Gil Steinke copped his second championship, riding junior quarterback Karl Douglas to a 32-7 triumph over Concordia (MN). Douglas passed for 305 yards and three touchdowns, ran for a fourth, and kicked two conversions to dominate the game. In 1970, Douglas repeated as game MVP when he led Texas A&I to a second consecutive crown, blowing out Wofford (SC), 48-7.

In 1970 the NAIA split its nearly 300 football schools into two divisions. In the inaugural Division II playoff, Anderson (IN) beat Minot State (ND), 20-14, and Westminster (PA) beat in-state rival Edinboro State, 20-7, in the semifinals, and then Westminster claimed the first D II title, 21-16, over Anderson.

Soccer fans saw the beginning of a dynasty at Quincy College (IL), but Davis and Elkins (WV) contested that dynasty's claim to supremacy through the 1970s. Quincy blew out defending champion Trenton State (NJ), 6-1, in the 1966 final, decisively signaling the passing of the torch to a new team with four goals from freshman Edmundo Camacho. The undefeated Hawks, in only their third year as a varsity program, heralded a westward shift in NAIA soccer, one that became even clearer the following season as Quincy downed Rockhurst (MO), 3-1, in an all-Midwest final featuring many players on both teams from the St. Louis soccer hotbed. Westmont (CA) lost to Rockhurst early on, but was the first school from west of the Rockies to play in the nationals. Al Duer proclaimed soccer the fastest-growing NAIA sport, with 145 teams participating.

In 1968, Quincy sought its third straight title. For the first time, the eight area soccer champions came to the same site for the nationals, making this the biggest collegiate soccer tournament in the country. Quincy, however, fell to Davis and Elkins in the final, 2-1, in five overtimes. The Senators focused on defense and pulled out the upset win despite being outshot 40-11. The next year, the low-scoring defense-minded team from West Virginia beat Ottawa (KS) and Spring Arbor (MI), each by a 1-0 score, to return to the final game. This time they faced Eastern Illinois, who had run up 4-0 and 6-0 wins to reach the title game. For the second straight year, the final could not be decided in regulation time, and this time Davis and Elkins came out on the short end of the match, losing 1-0 in two overtimes to Eastern Illinois. In 1970, Davis and Elkins again took two 1-0 wins into the final, and this time they matched up with Quincy in another battle of the dynasties. The Senators uncharacteristically went on a scoring spree and downed Quincy's Hawks in the deciding game, 2-0, for their second championship in three years—and their last, as it turned out.

Kansas City area fans turned out in record numbers (69,743) to follow St. Benedict's (KS) nearby team in the NAIA's basketball tournament in 1967. The top-ranked and number-one seeded Ravens displayed a well-balanced attack to overcome Oklahoma Baptist's Al Tucker, who hit 47 points in the final and 471 over three years to eclipse Dick Barnett's career record of 451. Despite Tucker's performance, St. Benedict's won, 71-65, and took home their first title since their unseeded 1954 team surprised everyone.

NAIA basketball exploits were not limited to the national tournament. In April 1967, the NAIA all-stars won the Pan American trials and placed four men on the 12-man team. In April 1968, rewarding Duer's long fight to get respect, the NAIA won the Olympic basketball trials and placed Don Dee and Glynn Saulters on the Olympic team. As for the tournament, 1965 champion Central State (OH) fought its way back to the title game with a tenacious zone defense. Facing them in the final was Fairmont State (WV), a school that had captured the football championship just months earlier. Trying to match their football team, the Falcons fell just short. Central State took the title, 51-48.

In 1969, the Eastern New Mexico Greyhounds, well-coached and playing near-perfect team basketball, won the final game, 99-76, over unseeded Maryland State. The next year, the teams matched up again in the semifinals, and the Greyhounds won again, 76-74. A very strong field, tense games, and some exceptional players contributed to a record attendance for the 1970 tournament, 69,255, despite the lack of a local team staying the distance. In the end, seven foot Elmore Smith and six-foot-seven-inch Travis Grant led their Kentucky State team to the championship, prevailing over Central Washington State, 79-71. That same duo led the Thorobreds to a repeat title the next year as Grant repeated as scoring leader and Smith as rebounding leader. The top-seeded Kentucky State squad overwhelmed Eastern Michigan, 102-82, in the final.

Eastern Michigan was, however, the top swimming power of the period, edging Claremont-Mudd (CA) as the top pool power. Claremont-Mudd took the title in 1967, but then finished second three straight years to Eastern Michigan before slipping from the top two, replaced in second place in 1971 by Simon Fraser (B.C.), the overwhelming power of the seventies.

In wrestling, Lock Haven (PA) won its fourth and final title in 1967, edging Adams State (CO), then gave way to Adams State, who won in both 1968 and 1969 before slipping back to second place in 1970. In 1970, Nebraska-Omaha took home top honors, and then in 1971 the crown passed to Central Washington. Of all those schools, Adams State would prove to have the most impressive long-term record in wrestling.

The relatively new indoor track and field competition had a repeat champion in 1967—Southern University of Baton Rouge (LA)—and a new winner the following year, Prairie View A&M (TX). Both of those teams also won the outdoor track and field competitions, Prairie View under the guidance of Hall of Fame coach Hoover Wright. In 1969 Eastern Michigan, the all-sport winners in 1970 and 1971, showed that they were already highly competitive in 1969, launching a three-year run as indoor champions to go with their swimming titles.

Gymnastics competition was minimal. After Western Illinois had won the first two national competitions in 1964 and 1965, Northwestern Louisiana State had won in 1966, and it reeled off another five consecutive titles through 1971, undeterred by the establishment of qualifying competitions in 1967.

Ice hockey, introduced as a new NAIA championship in 1968, also lacked much competitive excitement. Bemidji State (MN) iced the first title and went on to control the sport each season through 1971.

Spring sports also had some dominant repeat winners. In tennis, Doug Verdieck won four straight national singles titles, playing a key role in his father's Redlands teams winning championships every spring from 1967 through 1971. In bowling, Wisconsin-La Crosse took the 1967, 1968, and 1969 honors, with Harding (AR) then taking over for 1970 and 1971.

Golf was a different story, as five different institutions won over the five-year period: Southwest Louisiana, Indiana State (PA) in 1968 when qualifying reduced the numbers of entrants, then Texas Wesleyan, Campbell College (NC), and St. Bernard College (AL). Volleyball, launched as a national competition in 1969, had three winners in its first three seasons: Earlham (IN), UC San Diego, and Church College of Hawaii.

Track and field had two repeat winners. In 1967, Southern-Baton Rouge took top honors, though Texas Southern sprinter Jim Hines was named top performer. Prairie View A&M captured the overall team title in 1968 and 1969, but Eastern Michigan, showing remarkable ability in a variety of sports, won in 1970 and again in 1971. Jeff Bennett of Oklahoma Christian won the first two decathlons those last two years, though on different sites than the track and field competition as the ten-event sport sought to establish its identity.

Aside from volleyball, baseball was the only actual team sport on the spring menu, for all other team winners were simply accumulations of individual performances. New Mexico Highlands University captured the 1967 title by defeating Glassboro State (NJ) twice, 5-4 and then 6-1 in the title game. The tournament was played with speed-up rules that eliminated much of the sport's down time; the final game took only 1:40 to complete. In 1968, Cinderella favorite William Jewell (MO) won its first national championship in any sport with a dramatic 13-inning 4-3 win over Georgia Southern on a Larry Libeer leadoff homer. In 1969, William Carey (MS) and LaVerne (CA), two first-time entries in the national tournament and also the two smallest of the field of eight at 750 and 800 students, respectively, traded early victories before matching up in the final game, where William Carey pulled out a 5-3 triumph.

The 1970 final culminated in a dramatic moment. Northeast Louisiana's Indians had edged Eastern Michigan, 7-6, to force a final game in the double-elimination tourney. Pitching dominated that match-up, with neither team scoring for eight innings. In the bottom of the ninth, with two on and two out and two strikes on Huron catcher Dave Smigielski, he smacked a single to center to drive in the game's only run and sew up yet another crown for Eastern Michigan. In 1971, an equally thrilling finish unfolded. The Linfield (OR) Wildcats took a 7-2 lead into the seventh inning of the final game, only to have David Lipscomb (TN) fight back to tie the game at 7-all in the ninth. Two Wildcat runs in the tenth were barely enough as Lipscomb's Bisons, who had pulled out three earlier tournament wins with dramatic ninth-inning rallies, came back with one and had the tying run on base before Linfield could nail down the final out.

7

The NAIA at Its Peak
1971-1975

By 1971, the NAIA could look back on almost twenty years of existence as a multi-sport intercollegiate association and thirty-five as a basketball operation. In his history of the middle years of the NAIA, Carroll Land characterized the institution at this point in its history:

> After more than 30 years of existence, the NAIA had attained a more mature state. The embryonic and adolescent stages of the organization had naturally been accompanied by growing pains; having survived the developmental stages, however, the NAIA had arrived as a national sports organization of recognized quality whose maturity was evidenced by its philosophical stability, financial solvency, proof of quality athletics and athletes, stable membership of more than 500 institutions, the athletic liberation of the black schools, its influence on amateur and international athletic competition, and the fulfilling of genuine needs for hundreds of colleges and thousands of athletes. The thrust of the organization had now changed from a struggle for existence—and the justification of that existence—to the concentration on improvement that characterizes a mature organization.[1]

Al Duer had been part of that operation since 1940, and at the 1971 convention the 66-year old Kansas native was honored at a testimonial dinner celebrating his accomplishments with the association. Though he was already a year past the normal retirement age, the Executive Committee had asked him to remain until he reached 70, and to take it on a year-to-year basis after that. As he recalled, Duer had somewhat lightly accepted the invitation to take charge of the NAIB after Emil Liston's death in 1949, but had to wrestle with making it a full-time job and moving from Los Angeles to Kansas City in 1957. "I enjoyed teaching, there were very few pressures as athletic director and in my position in the Pepperdine administration, and just serving on an N.A.I.A. committee. I was moving into a developing organization with very little assured income to run it. So the move was not only a psychological decision, it was a financial gamble."[2]

In helping build the NAIA to its healthy status in 1971, Duer consistently stressed the philosophical foundation of the small-college organization, and the basis of that philosophy was that the NAIA must be self-supporting. Member institutions were to build a solid program not dependent on gate receipts but on the school's regular educational budget, for only football and basketball produced income sufficient to cover expenses. Though the NAIA had lost a number of members to the NCAA as they sought major college status, he reflected that those remaining in the NAIA were in a healthier position because they had kept a sense of proportion in running their athletic programs.

Within the national office, Duer had created a healthy environment (penny pinching aside). He was available for his staff at all times, and insisted that they stay "in the loop" on organizational business. Everyone was to put a blue copy of correspondence in a reading file, and each Friday the file was circulated around the office so each administrator was current on what his colleagues were doing. In addition, he convened a meeting at 10 sharp each morning in the hotel coffee shop for a 30-minute sharing time. One would have had to make a concerted effort in order to be uninformed.[3] Of course, as the staff grew in size, some of the procedures that had served Duer as a one-man operation were modified. Wally Schwartz was rather appalled at the simple behavior Duer had showed in his business operations. Reflecting his fatherly tendency to look for the good in people, Duer tended to trust them. "We shook hands over the telephone," he would say after making arrangements for a championship tournament. Part of the process of bureaucratization is that such honor-based personal transactions give way to more formal, written arrangements befitting a larger organization, an evolution often evoking regret at losing "the good old ways."[4]

Each year, the NAIA sponsored a number of special events, and administering them necessitated a process for approval and operation. An event should be "socially and educationally significant and sound," include at least 50 percent NAIA participants, submit to supervision of all financial transactions, and include restrictions on advertising of alcohol, tobacco, or drugs. Among the events approved for the fall of 1971, a fairly typical year, were four football games: the Black All-Star Classic in Houston, the Boothill Bowl in Dodge City, Kansas, the Cowboy Bowl in Loughton, Oklahoma, and the Mineral Water Bowl in Excelsior Springs, Missouri. In addition, the Baker Invitational Basketball Tournament in Kansas and the Top of Texas Basketball Tournament merited NAIA approval. Such non-championship events represented a simple extension of the tip-off basketball tournaments begun back in the mid-1940s.

Another NAIA initiative, reinvigorated in March 1969 by the Executive Committee, was the workshop program. The committee had mandated that each district have a workshop each four years, and after two years the program was almost on schedule, with 14 workshops having taken place. Workshop administrator Charlie Morris contended that they afforded an effective means to help athletic directors, coaches, faculty athletic representatives, and sports information directors better grasp the NAIA's values and procedures, and that the constituents were responding enthusiastically.[5]

The permissive approach to behavioral problems that emerged from the sixties began to affect NAIA operations by the early seventies. Standards of conduct at sporting events had declined, and NAIA schools found themselves trying to control players and fans who no longer felt constrained by traditional standards. At several games, fights had broken out among fans and, sometimes, players. At the national basketball tournament, undesirable behavior included "people sleeping in the halls of hotels, immoral acts in and around the hotels, too many people in hotel rooms, and beer can littering."[6] The Executive Committee directed member institutions to clarify responsibility for prevention of incidents and crowd control, to take strong disciplinary action against offenders, and to institute rewards for good behavior. As the membership affirmed by their vote at the 1972 annual meeting, the NAIA would not ignore, condone, or tolerate conduct that was detrimental to their athletic programs. Unfortunately, the NAIA was but a tiny piece of a national fabric that was unraveling, and it could not turn back history on its own. It could try, however; perhaps reflecting a sense that the coasts were more radical than the heartland, the Executive Committee ruled that all future national championship events were to be held in the central belt of the nation, a limitation that proved short-lived.

Member institutions continued to violate NAIA policy, although sometimes a school's transgression grew out of an innocent mistake. Still, Southern Colorado State drew a two-year probation in all sports and six other colleges drew basketball-only suspensions for violating the conflicting-event policy. In addition, eleven members merited one-year suspensions for violations of eligibility policy.

The struggle with the NCAA for member loyalty led the NAIA to hire Haskell Cohen, a New York publicist, to increase the association's national exposure. Cohen was to release some NAIA news from his office, on the assumption that news from New York was somehow more noteworthy. In the eyes of some observers, Cohen did little to earn his hefty $12,000 fee, since in general he just said that "the NAIA should do . . . ," with predictably negligible results. The Executive Committee debated heatedly over whether he should be retained for another year. No doubt many small college, often small-town athletic directors harbored suspicions about slick New York operators, but they lost the battle and Cohen was given another year. In a related story, Mike Kleinman, who was supposed to be running public relations for the NAIA, resigned. Don L. Powers, a Butler

University graduate in journalism with several years experience as a small-town sportswriter, replaced Kleinman on the NAIA staff.

Between intramural and intercollegiate sports there fell a third category, one that was poorly defined and very modestly regulated—club sports. The Research Committee had solicited responses on the issue in an October 1970 questionnaire that produced a solid 60 percent return, and had then recommended that the Executive Committee draw up guidelines for club sports. That body defined a club as one affiliated with an educational institution and composed of officially enrolled undergraduate or graduate students of the school. Guidelines were minimal: don't sacrifice the quality of existing intercollegiate, intramural, or physical education programs, and administer a club sport through the department of athletics and physical education. Otherwise, local discretion should be the rule.[7]

For about twenty years after 1947, racial integration was a hot issue in the NAIA, and indeed in the whole sports world. The NAIA had, as we have seen, played a positive and activist role in bringing racial equity into college sports. The next major frontier in sports had to do with integrating women into the male-dominated athletic scene. Women's intercollegiate competition had flourished at elite women's colleges around the turn of the century, but physical educators had become convinced that women were too delicate to handle such activity. In the 1920s, as women were gaining the freedom to vote and winning grudging acceptance in the white collar work force, they found their athletic options ironically limited to "play days" and intramural sports. The new women's movement growing out of the sixties led women to push for legal equality with men. With the passage of the Educational Amendments Act of 1972 with its famous Title IX, the question of women's place in intercollegiate sports was back on the table.[8]

The act said that "no person in the United States shall, on the basis of sex, be excluded from participation in, be denied the benefits of, or be subjected to discrimination under any education program or activity receiving Federal financial assistance." Title IX mandated "that all schools receiving Federal funds must provide equal opportunity for male and female athletes." The act was not to take effect until 1978, but it provoked a major scramble by colleges to try to bring their institutions into compliance before they were hit by lawsuits. Not surprisingly, it also provoked fevered efforts to sidetrack the athletic provisions before they could take effect, most notably a 1974 NCAA plea to the Department of Health, Education, and Welfare that men's sports would suffer if equal funding took place.[9]

In 1972, women did participate in intercollegiate athletics, but made up only 15 percent of college athletes. More ominous for athletic programs, they received only about two percent of athletic funding. Since women made up approximately half of college student bodies, it was clear that both their opportunities and their claim for proportionate funding needed major attention. Title IX, in essence, said that women should not have to resort to bake sales and car washes to fund their team trips, but that they should be included in athletic budgets equally with men. The act caused an uproar as men argued that women were not as interested as men in sports competition, and that non-revenue-producing men's sports would need to be sacrificed to bring women's funding up to men's levels. Whatever the merits of such arguments, the American intercollegiate sporting scene would never be the same again.

Leaping into the fight for women, a new organization was born in 1972. As the NAIA had been born out of a basketball tournament for small college men's teams in 1937, so was the Association for Intercollegiate Athletics for Women (AIAW) launched with a national basketball championship for women's teams.[10] Thus began a ten-year odyssey for women's sports with the NCAA, NAIA, and AIAW all playing active roles in the drama. Early in 1972, Al Duer met with AIAW representatives to get a sense of their ambitions, and with the approval of the Executive Committee issued a statement supporting the new body's claim to be a sports governing body for women and complimenting their work.

Within the NAIA, the NAIAC established a coach of the year award in each sport section. The athletic directors, in turn, formally established the Athletic Directors' Association (ADA) and included a two-day workshop at the national convention as an opportunity for their members to share insights with each other.

The problem of violence continued to grow in society as a whole and within the collegiate sports world as well. Athletics people grew increasingly frustrated because a significant part of their ethos centered on the authority of the coach, who was much like a military general in his absolute control over his subordinates. That control, which could be exercised arbitrarily and unfairly, attracted the scorn and criticism of proponents of individual freedom and autonomy whose attitudes Tom Wolfe captured in his catch phrase "the me decade." The authoritarian coach did not fit in the emerging mentality of the times. Nor did top-down, arbitrary administration of athletics generally.

Duer ran smack into this new way of thinking at the spring 1973 convention. He told the delegates, "Athletics should be a privilege not a right of the athlete."[11] But things were not as simple as they had been. The NAIA had established a Conduct of Athletics Committee, and in 1972-73 it fell under the Executive Committee's Paul Pierce. The committee, which had been operating for several years, had begun running into problems of "due process," leading to increased roles for lawyers as the NAIA and member institutions had to consider the legal aspects of any disciplinary actions they took. Pierce's committee, with legal advice, came up with five guidelines for monitoring the conduct of athletics, the first of which directly contradicted Duer's argument that athletes were a privilege, not a right.

- An athlete has a personal and property right in so far as competing for an institution is concerned, and he cannot be deprived of this right without due process.
- The personal and property right is guaranteed by the 14th Amendment of the Constitution of the USA.
- If it is felt that the athlete is guilty of misconduct, he must be given written notice of the hearing date, time and place.
- The hearing must be in the area of the school or near where the athlete lives.
- The district executive committee could be the group conducting the original hearing.[12]

The committee followed up with specific guidelines for assuring the rights of the athlete in any disciplinary action. While the athlete's rights were thus protected, the administration of athletics became much more complicated, and often exasperating. It must have been especially frustrating to Duer, who had always tried to do the "right" thing, even if it might not have been exactly in compliance with the rules. For example, he had bought shoes and paid the way for an impecunious Bob Hayes to attend the Olympic trials in 1964, seeing such action more as a good Christian helping someone in need than a nefarious circumvention of the rules to benefit one's own team. The new way of considering legal technicalities ahead of doing right had to strike Duer as a serious loss of freedom.[13]

The Conduct of Athletics Committee dealt with many other matters. The fall 1972 issue of *The NAIA News* published a list of 24 preventive ideas to control athlete and fan behavior. Some were new and some were tried and true, but athletic administrators facing increasing problems were grateful for the help. They also set forth appropriate procedures for investigating incidents that might merit punishment. Though legal red tape had greatly complicated the NAIA's administrative functions, the organization kept working at solving its problems.

The NAIA continued to participate in international sports events, which were highly popular at the time. Several athletes and coaches participated in the World Student University Games in Moscow again in 1973, while an all-star basketball team played a series of games in Israel and the Quincy soccer team toured the People's Republic of China, just beginning to open up after President Richard Nixon's visit. In a personal as well as an organizational coup, Al Duer was elected as third vice-president of the USOC, a source of great pride to him.

The Athletic Directors Association pushed a membership drive, as the new association tried to garner input from as many institutions as possible. At the 1973 annual meeting, Harry Fritz conducted a workshop on approaches to solving the financial crisis in college athletics, tackling one of the pressing issues of the day head on. A select group of athletic directors formed another new organization, the Past Presidents Committee, which gave the most experienced and expert NAIA veterans a forum for exercising influence and sharing their expertise. One immediate role was making them the Nominating Committee for candidates for the Executive Committee, searching for candidates offering geographical balance, proven leadership ability, high ethical and moral standards, the respect of his district, and some degree of national recognition.

Redistricting issues showed the difficulty of promoting the good of the NAIA as a whole. Earlier plans to split District 32 (New England) while combining Districts 1 and 5 in the northwest were temporarily shelved when the latter resisted being combined. So District 32 became Districts 32A and 32B and District 1 and 5 retained their independence. But there were now 33 districts seeking 32 playoff spots at the national tournament, and a committee of small district chairmen at the national convention determined that for 1974, Districts 1 and 5 would have to conduct a bi-district playoff rather than 32A and 32B. A year later, District 5 members were moved into a geographically vast District 12 (Montana, Wyoming, and the Dakotas) and 32A, northern New England, became the new District 5.

Four schools were disciplined in one sport for playing in conflicting NCAA contests, and three others were penalized for athlete and student fan misconduct. Those three—Birmingham Southern, Jacksonville State, and Oregon College of Education—included two black colleges and precipitated a visit from NASC's C. D. Henry to express his concern about "due process." The Executive Committee met with him and reviewed the standards recently established by the conduct of athletics committee, noting the NAIA's attempts to provide fair and legally defensible treatment for all colleges and athletes.

At the August 1973 interim meeting of the Executive Committee, Al Duer maintained that the challenges had never been greater for the NAIA, but that the opportunities were likewise unprecedented. As the association wrestled with all the issues before it, Duer urged the Executive Committee to hold fast to its aims, objectives, and philosophy, and to continue to work hard to build character, citizenship, and leadership while emphasizing conduct.

A special committee in the House of Representatives had begun an investigation of the ongoing struggle for the soul of amateur athletics in the country, and was especially annoyed that some organizations (the NCAA) had refused to allow their players to play on an American all-star team against a visiting Russian squad. Duer testified to his support for the AAU as the legitimate body representing the United States in the international arena.

Violence was not the only "seventies" problem. The culture of the sixties had made the use of drugs a common rite of passage by the next decade, and drugs in athletics had become a significant problem. Duer had been invited to go to Washington to testify at a hearing on the subject. The NAIA became the first organization, amateur or professional, to voluntarily involve itself in the government's inquiry, no doubt stimulated by Duer's straight-arrow persona.

The Executive Committee again sought to ease tensions with the NCAA, initiating meetings between representatives of both bodies to discuss conflicting dates, NCAA divisions, women's athletics, differing philosophies, and international competition. The long-standing conflict between the two organizations continued to take a toll on both sets of members. In particular, the NCAA had developed a proposal in March 1973 to move from a major college/small college split to *three* divisions, with the 664 NCAA member schools having great opportunity to determine their own placement. The possibility of different sports in the same institution competing in different divisions complicated the accounting process, but in August the membership voted at a special convention in Chicago in favor of the new three-division lineup. Forty-one championships would be on the line, 17 in Division I, 13 in Division II, and 11 in Division III. More schools opted for Division I (237) than Division II (194) or Division III (233), and no two of the NCAA's divisions matched the NAIA's membership of 558. Yet the more specialized appeal of the NCAA's three divisions must have piqued the interest of many NAIA schools, for in 1974-75 the NAIA could muster only 513 members, the lowest total since 1965-66. Membership would remain fairly constant, between 509 and 527, through 1984 before the next big dip came.[14]

Signs that the NAIA was bearing the heaviest costs in the battle for schools with divided allegiance began to appear along with the defections. The NAIA established a special committee to study the issue of dual participation in light of the handbook's prohibition of such behavior. In what appears to be a sign recognizing NAIA weakness, the convention approved a proposal to allow an institution to participate in one conflicting event, not to include football or basketball, the two revenue-producing NAIA sports. Even that concession provoked a motion from the floor to up the limit to two events; though the substitute motion failed, it suggests that member loyalty had some serious limitations. A second indication of NAIA weakness involved the special events program. To add to their appeal, the fee for approval of such an event was dropped from $100 to $25, and the requirement for financial accounting was eliminated. It appeared that the NAIA was running scared.

The NAIA invited an AIAW representative to the spring 1974 annual meeting to further coordinate the two associations' work. The AIAW had moved swiftly and already offered national championships in 11 sports for four-year schools and another three for junior colleges. Having both the NCAA and NAIA as models of what to do, and what not to do, in building a national sports association gave the AIAW a big advantage as it quickly forged ahead. The AIAW and NAIA agreed to continue to meet in the future and developed a joint questionnaire for NAIA schools to ascertain the stage of their development of women's sports programs.

Three major events dominated NAIA news during the 1974-1975 year: the moving of the basketball tournament from Municipal Auditorium to the new Crosby Kemper Arena, the retirement of Al Duer, and the search for Duer's successor.

The relocation issue had been brewing for a couple of years, and the Executive Committee had gone back and forth on whether moving was a good idea or not. Kemper Arena would seat 16,284 as opposed to Municipal Auditorium's 9,960, but more was not necessarily better. Especially for the day games, small crowds would be lost at the new venue, which lacked the intimacy of the smaller traditional location. More critical, the new facility was four miles from downtown, where the hotels for teams, fans, and other participants were located. Duer was especially concerned that, no matter what convenient transportation might be arranged, businessmen in the downtown area, who could casually drop in on an 11 a.m. or 1 p.m. game as a break in their work day, would not bother to go four miles for the privilege. There were very few eateries in the Kemper area, either.

Despite the serious reservations, at their August 1974 interim meeting the Executive Committee voted to move the tournament to Kemper. The terms of the deal were a maximum rent of $20,000, a five-year contract with a one-year clause renewable annually, and no other similar events to be scheduled at Municipal Auditorium in conflict with the tournament. In addition, the city agreed to provide shuttle bus service from downtown to Kemper every ten minutes. One observer accused the city of, in essence, blackmailing the NAIA into agreeing to the move to justify the construction of the new structure. If the NAIA didn't move, the city implied, competitive scheduling at Kemper would undermine their attendance at Municipal Auditorium. Attendance did decline at Kemper, though evolving social practice may well have contributed to that; working wives proved less enthusiastic about going out for basketball than when they had been home all day, and as NCAA basketball playoffs became a major phenomenon in the eighties, it was much easier to sit at home and watch on television than to venture forth to Kemper.[15] Whatever the case, the move from Municipal Auditorium was the first step in the gradual estrangement between the city and the NAIA.

The retirement of Al Duer after 26 years at the helm of the organization created a rift in continuity that came at a critical time in the NAIA's history. Duer had major surgery in July 1974 and missed the August meeting while convalescing, but bounced back to run the organization full time until his retirement. The surgery may have affected the

1971 idea of taking Duer's post-70 years one at a time, for there does not seem to have been any discussion of keeping him on board beyond 1975, and the aged leader declined a proffered emeritus status. His departure was formally announced at the spring 1975 convention and understandably brought forth tributes there, in *The NAIA News*, and in the *Kansas City Star*, along with his designation by the Kansas City Sports Commission as the Man of the Year for 1975. He had indeed overseen a remarkable growth in the organization. When he took charge of the NAIB in 1949, it hosted one national championship and had a goal of establishing some committees. When he retired, 32 district committees, 16 sports committees, 20 general committees, and numerous special committees helped provide the superstructure for 16 national championships. Attendance at the national convention, barely over 200 in his early years, was over 1200 in 1974.[16] Duer's final day in the saddle was July 31, 1975.

Finding a replacement for Duer as executive secretary proved complicated and convoluted. At the August 1974 interim meeting, President Arnold Kilpatrick, First Vice-President Robert Livingston, and Executive Committee member W. C. Myers became the Search Committee. Letters went out to past presidents and current Executive Committee members to solicit nominations of likely prospects for the job. They should be no older than 57, have national and international stature, a pleasant personality, career preparation, speaking ability, credibility, character, integrity, enthusiasm, and good health. The committee sifted through the nominations in Dallas on September 5, and then worked out a secret agreement with their chosen candidate, who insisted that his name be kept quiet because of the sensitivity of his current position. For half a year, the parties in the know managed to keep the deal secret.

At the 1975 convention, Joe Axelson signed a contract to take the helm of the NAIA—another year down the road. He was to take over on April 15, 1976, though he held out a slight hope that he might become available earlier. On the prearranged date, his obligation as president and general manager of the NBA's Kansas City Kings would conclude. Given the sensitive local nature of his ongoing employment, it was understandable that he insisted that his name continue to be a secret. Axelson had been a top aide to Duer during the 1960s and seemed a splendid choice for the job, though the eight-and-a-half month gap between Duer's retirement and Axelson's availability caused major concern in the NAIA. Who would run things in the interim? The new president, Robert Livingston of the Oregon College of Education, volunteered to fill the breach and serve simultaneously as president and acting executive secretary if necessary. Interestingly, there seems to have been no suggestion that Duer remain in charge until his successor became available. Not until May 7, 1975, did Livingston send a letter to NAIA member institutions informing them that a secret selection had been made. He expressed some hope that the unnamed Axelson would be available on August 1, but explained his plan to do double duty as long as needed. And there the matter rested when Duer retired on July 31.

At the spring 1975 gathering, Livingston cited three serious problems facing the NAIA now that the succession question had been settled. The first was the challenge presented by the NCAA's new Division III, a direct competitor for smaller colleges wishing to have an athletic program offering competitive opportunities without allowing it to distort the institution's educational priorities—in other words, the sort of college that comprised a majority of the NAIA's membership. The decline in NAIA membership following the 1973 establishment of Division III set off alarm bells in the NAIA's Kansas City headquarters. The second (and related) problem was the ongoing issue of dual membership in the NAIA and NCAA. The NAIA's leverage in dealing with conflicting events for dual members had suffered with the establishment of Division III, and already the association had had to make concessions to keep its members from bailing out. Symptomatic of its sense of wavering support, the Executive Committee ducked on disciplining three direct violations of the policy. Alcorn A&M, Grambling, and Slippery Rock had all played NCAA instead of NAIA football playoff games in 1974, but the Executive Committee agreed to take no punitive action and reconsider its policy. The third problem had to do with the pro-amateur rule. The NAIA had changed its rule in 1960, agreeing to the Olympic standard that being a professional in one sport made an athlete a professional in all sports. Now the NCAA had reneged and was allowing professional athletes to compete in other sports as amateurs. It was just one more example of the ongoing stresses the NAIA faced in its rivalry with the NCAA.

One bright spot in "foreign relations" concerned the women's sports issue. NAIA representatives met with AIAW leaders on at least two separate occasions, and warm relations continued between them. Duer was sufficiently impressed with the quality and worth of the AIAW's efforts that with the Executive Committee's approval, he wrote to the presidents of all NAIA member institutions recommending that they affiliate with the AIAW if they conducted women's intercollegiate programs.

More confusing, the international amateur scene had been upset in 1973 when FIBA, the international basketball association, had taken the American franchise away from the AAU. In 1974, it was awarded to the Amateur Basketball Association of the United States of America (ABAUSA). The NAIA then joined the ABAUSA, only to find that it would have no representation on the new body's council. It was one more instance of the NAIA struggling to get the respect due it in the broader world of sports.

Frustrated by its lack of publicity, the NAIA was heartened by a tentative agreement for the Hughes Television Network to carry NAIA sports events and pay the association $40,000. The deal, negotiated by Haskell Cohen as part of his controversial $12,000 contract, fell through after months of anticipation, and that was the last straw. Cohen was sacked in March, but fell between the cracks at the end of the Duer regime— Livingston finally followed through the decision with a letter in September. Trying a less expensive alternate publicity boost, the NAIA hired someone to work on Sunday evenings compiling the weekend's statistical reports for Monday dissemination. It was a more modest approach befitting the organization.

With the NAIA facing major challenges to its prestige, and even existence, Al Duer stepped down at the end of July. He had taken great pride in his role with the USOC, and the highlight of his retirement came when he served as a flag bearer at the 1976 Olympics in Montreal. His retirement beyond that was not terribly happy. He lived in Los Angeles with his daughter, but he had never had much in the way of hobbies and without his work, he felt rather lost, a feeling exacerbated by continual health problems. Though the NAIA invited him to the annual meetings and other events, he increasingly felt irrelevant up until his death in 1987.[17]

Eastern New Mexico dominated cross-country competition over this four-year period, finishing second to Adams State in 1971, losing out to Malone (OH) in 1972, then clobbering Malone in 1973 to gain a measure of revenge, and finally setting a record in 1974. In that meet, all five Eastern entries finished in the top dozen to rack up a record low point total of 28. In a major technological breakthrough, the 1972 meet, held in Liberty, Missouri, saw the results calculated by computer for the first time, permitting team awards to be made at the banquet the same evening.

Division I football featured four different winners. In 1971, second-seeded Livingston (AL) nipped top seed Arkansas Tech, 14-12, for the title. The following year a paltry 4,539 saw East Texas State's Lions, fresh off a 54-0 demolishing of Central Oklahoma in the semi-finals, edge Carson-Newman (TN), 21-18, in another close final. In 1973 Clint Longley quarterbacked Abilene Christian's Wildcats to a convincing 42-14 win over undefeated Elon (NC). Texas A&I, already three times a winner, copped its fourth in 1974, capping a 13-0 season by coming from a 17-7 deficit and topping Henderson State (AR), 34-23, before over 12,000 fans in their home stadium.

There were also four new schools atop the Division II football heap during this period. Unbeaten Cal Lutheran upset top-seeded Westminster (PA), 30-14, for the 1971 title. The next year, Missouri Southern got by Northwestern (IA), 21-14, leading the losers' coach, Larry Korner, to pledge to go all the way the next season. He kept his vow—the Red Raiders reeled off a perfect 12-0 season, culminating in a 10-3 championship victory over Glenville State (WV) that earned Korner coach-of-the-year honors. In 1974, yet another new winner emerged, and decisively: Texas Lutheran crushed Missouri Valley in the final game, 42-0, a portent of things to come.

Soccer power was not as evenly distributed as football power. In 1971, Quincy (IL) racked up its first title under Jack McKenzie and third overall with a 1-0 triumph over arch rival Davis & Elkins (WV) in bone-chilling 33-degree weather. The next year the far west's top team, Westmont, won its first title, edging perennial bridesmaid Davis & Elkins, 2-1, in two overtimes, led by goalie Gary Allison. But in 1973 and 1974, Quincy established itself as the dynasty of the '70s, beating Rockhurst, 3-0, then Davis & Elkins, 6-0, for its second and third titles in the decade.

Basketball continued to be the flagship sport of the NAIA. In 1972, Kansas City fans witnessed the climax of Kentucky State's run at the top as the Thorobreds whipped top-seeded Wisconsin-Eau Claire, 71-62, in the final game to tie Tennessee State's record of three straight titles. Travis Grant set a new single game record with 60 points against Minot State in the opener, broke the career tournament record with 518 points (34.5 per game), established an NAIA career record with 4,045 points, and took home his second straight tournament MVP trophy. With Grant's graduation, though, parity returned. Guilford (NC), led by Lloyd Free and M. L. Carr, edged Maryland-Eastern Shore, 99-96, in 1973. Then, in the final Municipal Auditorium tournament before the move to Kemper, 72,082 watched through the week, and Clarence "Foots" Walker led West Georgia College, the 14th-seeded team, over Alcorn State (MS), 97-79, for top honors. The next year, despite a heavy snowfall early in the week, 69,555 attended games at Kemper, and Grand Canyon College (AZ), with MVP Bayard Forrest keying their efforts, beat Midwestern State (TX), 65-54, to win the championship.

A measure of competitiveness arrived in ice hockey as well. Bemidji's domination gave way to Lake Superior State (MI), which won in 1972 and 1974. Bemidji did win in 1973, but the Soo Lakers' 4-1 win over the Bemidji in 1974 earned them a measure of revenge for three straight seconds to the Beavers from 1968 to 1970. In 1975, the College of St. Scholastica (MN) clobbered top-seeded Gustavus-Adolphus (MN), 7-1, to take home their first trophy in only their third year playing ice hockey.

After Eastern Illinois broke Northwestern Louisiana's string of six gymnastics victories in1972, Wisconsin established a monopoly on the sport. In 1973 and 1974, Wisconsin-Oshkosh took top honors, and in 1975 Wisconsin-LaCrosse nipped Oshkosh by 0.4 points. Wisconsin-Stout was third, and Platteville, Parkside, and Stevens Point also represented the state system in the top dozen finishers.

Indoor track titles all went to Sun Belt teams. Dallas Baptist College won in 1972, and then Jackson State (MS) took team honors in 1973 despite Olympic gold medalist Rod Milburn's stellar performance for Southern University (LA). Texas Southern, led by Tony Fulton's two wins, took the top spot in 1974. At this point, in an attempt to level the playing field, the Executive Committee limited teams to a maximum of three foreigners. In 1975, the indoor meet moved from Kansas City, where it had taken place since its inception in 1966, to Greensboro, NC, with a $10,000 subsidy from the state enriching the NAIA pot. Jackson State recaptured first place and Mike Boit of Eastern New Mexico was named top athlete of the meet.

Simon Fraser (BC) dominated swimming more convincingly than any team in any NAIA sport for the decade. Following a second-place finish in 1971, in 1972 they rode Peter Harrower's three meet records and one more mundane win to a 332-217 thrashing of Claremont-Mudd. The Clansmen repeated in 1973, then cracked the 400-point barrier for the first time in 1974, with John Van Buren managing six wins, including two individual and three relay records. By 1975, murmurings against the dynasty were becoming more open as Simon Fraser garnered 515 points, won 14 of 18 events, and set 13 new records. In a sign of things to come, the first woman to compete as a swimmer did so in 1975. Anne-Marie McCaffrey finished 20th in the 1650-yard freestyle, joining two divers in the competition; divers had been competing for a couple of years already.

Adams State (CO) swept wrestling competition through the period, winning in 1972, 1973, and 1975. Only in 1974, when they slipped to 11th place behind Central Washington State, did the Indians fail to take top honors.

Baseball took spring headlines. In 1972, LaVerne (CA), led by hurler Ben Ochoa, beat David Lipscomb, 4-1, in the final to leave the Bisons runners-up for the second straight year. In 1973, with the designated hitter in place in all playoff games, United States International University (CA) swept five games for the title, including a complete-game 7-2 win by Ken Koskie in the championship game despite 105 degree heat in Phoenix. Tom Brennan stopped a Sam Houston rally in the ninth inning, then drove in the winning run in the bottom of the inning to give Lewis (IL) a 3-2 victory in 1974, then Lewis frustrated the Texas team again in 1975 with a 2-1 win in the final game to take back-to-back titles. During that 1975 season, NAIA baseball teams also saved a bundle of money by switching from wood to aluminum bats.

Harding College (AR) won two out of four bowling titles, taking top honors in 1972 and 1975. The College of Great Falls (MT) won in 1973 and Clarion State (PA) triumphed in 1974, breaking up the Harding wins. Meanwhile, USIU (CA) shot the best golf games in 1972 and 1974, with Wofford (SC) in 1973 and Texas Wesleyan in 1975 grabbing the other golf titles. In tennis, East Texas State nipped Redlands in 1972, but the Californians came back strong and won their eighth, ninth, and tenth tennis crowns under Coach Jim Verdieck. Redlands dominated tennis as Adams State ruled wrestling, though not as overwhelmingly as Simon Fraser controlled the swimming world. Church College of Hawaii rebounded from a 14-11 deficit in the final game to top Graceland College (IA) and repeat as volleyball winners. In 1973, Graceland had its turn at the top, and in 1974 perennial threat George Williams College (IL) finally captured the elusive title. To wrap up the volleyball winners, California State-Dominguez Hills edged BYU-Hawaii for the 1975 crown.

Track and field passed its title around to four schools in four years. In 1972 North Carolina Central, led by coach-of-the-year LeRoy Walker and sparked by the meet's top performer, Larry Black, were the class of the meet. The following year Tommy Fulton of Texas Southern ran the first NAIA sub-four-minute mile to lead his team to the track championship. In 1974 Eastern New Mexico, paced by Kenyan double winners Phillip Ndoo and Olympian Mike Boit, edged Southern California College. Boit ran for MVP honors in 1975 although Southeastern Louisiana State won the team title. NAIA supporters were delighted to learn that spring that LeRoy Walker, the North Carolina Central coach, had been tabbed as the head coach for the 1976 Olympic track team, just the sort of recognition that Duer had fought for over his long career.

All-sports winners, the schools with the most successful, well-rounded athletic programs, showed some consistent leaders. Eastern Illinois led the way in 1971-72, with Adams State, USIU, and Eastern New Mexico trailing. USIU moved to the top in 1972-73, squeaking past Eastern New Mexico and leaving Wisconsin-Oshkosh and Nebraska-Omaha back in the pack. Eastern New Mexico kept improving and led the way in 1973-74, with Fort Hays State second and Wisconsin-Parkside and Bemidji Sate tied for third. In 1974-75 the Greyhounds successfully defended their crown, but Wisconsin was making its move: LaCrosse, Parkside, and Oshkosh ranked second through fourth, and possibly began looking for new worlds to conquer.

8

The NAIA A.D. (After Duer)
1975-1979

With the retirement of Al Duer, it would be a good time to take stock of the health of the NAIA. Membership for 1974-75 comprised 513 institutions, down from a peak of 561 just three years earlier. Anxiety underlay surface optimism as the possibility of more and more defections to the NCAA's new Division III loomed on the horizon. Yet the NAIA had jumped out to a 20-year lead over the NCAA in providing small college competition on a national level. Further, in the two decades or so since the NCAA *had* established its rival College Division in 1957, in an average year the NAIA had lost 22 members, but gained 27. The smaller association had some saleable history and distinctives, and if it could market those effectively, it could anticipate a long and healthy future.

One strength was a democratic form of administration. Duer had preached democracy continually, even though he tended to run things rather autocratically. The NAIA was divided into 32 districts, grouped into eight areas, and each district had its own elected chairman, Executive Committee, and various other committees. These district bodies had considerable autonomy in running their own affairs, and many NAIA insiders believed that this district structure was the key to NAIA success.

Eligibility standards were solid, but minimal, leaving responsibility largely in the hands of institutions. They, in turn, had to certify that all athletes were eligible for all athletic contests during the year. Most issues related to running the colleges' sports programs, including length of seasons, team and staff size, and financial aid limitations, likewise fell under the control of the member institutions, or perhaps their conferences. Beyond that, the NAIA provided an extensive system of awards at the district, area, and national levels, with all sixteen national championship sports honoring top athletes and coaches with a fairly consistent program.

Perhaps most appealing to the membership, the NAIA was run largely by coaches and athletic directors, whose practical policies reflected their years in the trenches tempered by the organization's ideal of integrating athletics and education. These men—and at that point they were still virtually all men—embodied the ideals and perspective of small colleges and worked to make a success of their carefully controlled programs.[1]

Dave Olson, athletic director at Pacific Lutheran College in Tacoma, Washington, elected to the Executive Committee in 1978, explained just how that integration played out at his institution. Pacific Lutheran was "first and foremost an institution of higher education," providing "Quality Education in a Christian Context." The school's athletic program was co-curricular, not extra-curricular, meaning that it was "a legitimate aspect of the educational thrust." One key to this approach was hiring competent, qualified educators to coach the players, ones who saw athletics as "a means to an end, rather than an end in itself." The program was inclusive: designating sports as major or minor was forbidden, intramural sports incorporated a vast majority of the student body, and the institution developed a full-fledged women's program long before Title IX mandated it. Critically, the department was funded like the rest of the college—gate receipts went into the general fund, so winning (with attendant higher revenues) did not affect the conduct of the overall athletic program, further encouragement to focus on the participant. Though the program was highly competitive, coaches stressed competing against the individual's "best self" rather than just beating the opponent. Such an approach permits an athlete to be a "winner" more often and for a longer time than the usual winner/loser dichotomy in sporting events. Membership in a conference with similar educational and philosophical convictions encouraged an atmosphere of trust and a level playing field in terms of academic and financial aid rules. Quoting Admiral Richard Byrd, defending the cost and risks of an Antarctic expedition, Olson concluded, "It is not just getting there that is important—but what you learn along the way." He thus articulately summed up how one college sought to implement the ideals endorsed by the NAIA.[2]

❖

At the national office, incoming President Robert Livingston acknowledged in a letter to the office staff dated July 10, 1975, that his hopes that the mysterious new executive secretary might be able to take over on August 1 did not appear likely to be fulfilled. He therefore set forth his plans to fill both positions until the anticipated April 1976 transfer of power, assisted by a half sabbatical from his home institution.

Almost immediately, that plan fell apart. The Executive Committee held its annual interim meeting in Kansas City from August 7 to 10. At that point, members learned that Joe Axelson not only had not been released from his existing contractual commitments to the Kansas City Kings to permit an August 1 transition, but that he was not going to take the NAIA position at all. Speculation abounded within the tight circle, but not beyond—Axelson's identity continued to be a closely guarded secret. At least one observer later recalled that Axelson had simply wanted more money than the NAIA was prepared to commit to the position. Another blamed Livingston, saying that an ill-advised press release pointed so clearly in Axelson's direction that he was forced to withdraw his name to mollify his current employer.[3] Whatever Axelson's motivation, following the meeting Livingston sent word to all member institutions that the search for a new executive secretary had been reopened. He, past President Arnold Kilpatrick, First Vice-President Steven Senko, and Fourth Vice-President W. C. Myers would serve as the Search Committee. Nominations should be sent in by October 1 for the committee to evaluate.

In late October, the Search Committee met and narrowed the suggested names down to five for the full Executive Committee to consider. The broader body met in Dallas in mid-November and over the next month sifted through the five to come up with their man. On December 15, 1975, Livingston held a news conference in Kansas City to announce that Dr. Harry G. Fritz had been selected and would take over his duties on April 12, 1976, leaving Livingston in his dual role for another four months.

The 55-year-old Fritz had for the previous five years been athletic director and dean of the School of Health Education at the State University of New York at Buffalo. He had earned his bachelor's degree from Transylvania College (KY) in 1946, his M.A. from Kentucky, and his doctorate from Indiana in 1954. He had a broad athletic background that equipped him to relate to student athletes, coaches, athletic directors, officials, and leaders in other organizations. The burly six-footer had earned four varsity football letters, four in basketball, and two in baseball. He had coached football for a year during a 1948-1953 sojourn at Central Missouri State, had been an official, and had wide experience as an author and consultant. He spent 1954 to 1964 at Bemidji State, serving as athletic director, department chairman, basketball coach (four years), and assistant football coach (eight years). He moved on to Western Illinois to direct the athletic and physical education programs there until his move to SUNY Buffalo in 1970.

Besides a long and active association with the NAIA, Fritz was well plugged in to the wider sports world, a strength that he utilized astutely as NAIA executive secretary. At the time of his selection, he was serving as president of the National Association for Sport and Physical Education (NASPE) with its 33,000 members. He had also put in two terms on the Board of Governors of the American Alliance for Health, Physical Education and Recreation (AAHPER), representing it on the United States Collegiate Sports Council and the Amateur Basketball Association of the United States. In addition, he had joined the National Association of Collegiate Directors of Athletics (NACDA) when it was born in 1965 and been part of its Executive Committee from 1968 to

1972. He had demonstrated leadership skills at every step of his career, and he appeared to be an outstanding choice to take charge of the NAIA.[4]

Even before Fritz took over, encouraging signs signaled a thaw in relations between the NAIA and the NCAA. By an overwhelming vote at the 1975 convention, delegates approved a resolution permitting institutions to opt out of NAIA playoffs, including football and basketball (the major problem sports), if they chose. They had to file declarations of intent to participate fairly early in the season, and if they filed and then did *not* compete, they would incur significant penalties. But the thrust was clear: the NAIA dramatically reduced the tension between the two associations over conflicting events and gave their member institutions increased autonomy. In a separate resolution, limitations on the number of games an NAIA school could schedule against NCAA opponents were also eliminated.[5]

Not that NAIA leaders shrank from distinguishing their organization from their larger rival. At the 1976 convention, President Bob Livingston noted that the NCAA employed eight full-time staff to do nothing but investigate and enforce NCAA rules; he was glad that the NAIA, without the resources to commit to such an enforcement arm, had little need of it, either. The NAIA processed 27 constitutional and by-law proposals, and handled them efficiently with appropriate discussion in a morning session. The NCAA, Livingston noted, had treated over 200 items, often in wholesale fashion. The joys of modest size were not to be denied.[6]

Defections did concern the leadership. The Iowa Intercollegiate Athletic Conference, eight schools strong, announced that in the fall of 1976 they would operate under NCAA rules and regulations, while retaining their NAIA membership. This pattern of schools or conferences holding dual memberships in a transitional period between the NAIA and NCAA would prove troubling over the next two decades. Fritz wrote and telephoned school officials at the eight institutions to try to avoid a total defection, and staved off such an eventuality for the time being. However, it was disconcerting to learn that the NCAA had committed $150,000 to subsidize Division II and III national championships. Money talks, and tempted NAIA schools were listening.[7] Livingston mouthed what would become an NAIA mantra over the next quarter century: perhaps the association was better off without lukewarm members.

Fritz put his considerable negotiating skills to work on the NCAA issue. On December 1, 1976, a new NAIA-NCAA Joint Committee met for the first time and focused on their common mission to promote intercollegiate sports. At subsequent meetings the committee examined topics like recognizing each other's national championships, common "declaration of intent to participate" dates (building on the NAIA's spring 1975 cease-fire), dual representation on rules committees, and other topics.[8] Fritz believed that relations were good, as he reported in 1978, and cited their cooperation in 1979, when he restated his goal of servicing NAIA members so well that they were not tempted to bolt. Nevertheless, he recognized graciously that sometimes it would be in an institution's best interests to leave the NAIA for the NCAA, and he did not begrudge it that decision. His upbeat stance shone through in his 1979 address to the convention when he spoke of the NAIA as having over 500 institutions "and growing."[9] If a positive outlook had power to shape an organizational mood, Fritz assuredly was capitalizing on that predisposition.

Fritz's optimism and diplomatic skills shone through in other areas of "foreign relations." President Gerald Ford, dismayed by the constant bickering between the amateur sports organizations, had appointed another Commission on Olympic Sports in 1976. The NAIA again played a vital role in testifying before the commission, and also in Senate hearings in 1977 and 1978 designed to generate legislation to clean up the mess. In 1978 Congress finally passed the Amateur Sports Act, establishing the USOC as the "overall coordinating body for amateur sports" in the United States. While other bodies had been hostile or neutral toward this move, the NAIA had been highly and actively supportive. In fact, Fritz reported, the "NAIA has rightfully been credited as the major reason for the successful passage" of the legislation. Fritz, named to the newly reorganized USOC, believed the NAIA was uniquely positioned to play a major part in healing the differences between different organizations.[10]

The new executive secretary took an activist role in other relationships as well. He told the 1979 convention that considerable time and energy had been expended over the past two years to increase the NAIA role in intercollegiate and amateur sports. He cited the Commission on Competitive Safeguards and Medical Aspects of Sports, the National Operating Committee for Safety in Athletic Equipment, and the United States Collegiate Sports Council as three groups in which the NAIA was playing an increasing role. He cited the latter, sponsor of the World University Games, as a particularly strategic spot for the NAIA to wield its influence, saying that the World University Games were second only to the Olympic Games in worldwide prestige.[11]

As it had under Al Duer, the NAIA under Harry Fritz participated in a wide variety of international competitions. Fritz noted that the NAIA had been the first and for many years the only opportunity for college teams to take part in international competition in the United States and abroad.[12] The new executive secretary concluded an agreement with the National Institute of Sports in Mexico that would take representatives of seven sports to Mexico in the fall of 1978. In addition, an NAIA basketball team was to represent the United States in an international tournament in April 1979. The value of the NAIA's contribution to international good will was attested by a State Department grant of $12,000 to support the association's efforts.[13]

Defining an amateur, and relating that definition to other organizations' definitions, provoked extensive debate at the conventions in 1976, when it was finally tabled, and

1977, when the issue was resolved. Up until 1960, the NAIA had ruled that being a professional in one sport did not make one a professional in any other sport. Under pressure from the USOC, and seeking to ensure that NAIA athletes would not be excluded from Olympic consideration, the association had changed the rule to read that a professional in one sport was a professional in all. Then, prior to the 1976 Olympics the NCAA had adopted the old, more permissive NAIA position, and still been able to take part in the Montreal games that year. What should the NAIA do?

The issue illustrates the democratic nature of the organization. Both the International Competition Relations Committee (unanimously) and the Executive Committee opposed going back to the original NAIA position. They noted that prior to 1960 the NAIA had been regarded as a bit of a renegade organization, citing the example of Howie Schultz playing first base for the Brooklyn Dodgers and basketball at Hamline at the same time. The 1976 motion had been tabled to seek USOC guidance, and the NAIA public relations department suggested that no one had been denied access to the Olympics in 1976 and so, presumably, changing to the NCAA position would be alright. NAIA leaders, who had worked hard establishing close ties with the USOC, called for the defeat of the resolution to change. Clark Swisher, an Executive Committee member who had worked with the USOC, noted in particular that there was virtually no chance that body would change its position on the issue, even if it was not enforcing its policy.

Dave Olson argued from the NAIA's philosophical base in favor of the change. He noted that the organization was committed to the athlete, to the student, to the participant. Many athletes (five out of 2500 Pacific Lutheran students) had thought they could make it professionally in a sport only to find they were not that good; they subsequently enrolled in college to try an alternative career path. There were far more athletes who fell into that category than would lose their Olympic eligibility should the USOC enforce its ban. To deny them the opportunity to play in other sports seemed to be yielding to the strictures of the USOC rather than looking out for the best interest of the student. It also, in the litigious mood of the times, could be construed as denying an individual's right to participate.

The district chairmen unanimously supported the proposal. Then a former NCAA member contrasted the NAIA to his old association, noting that the NCAA was interested in punishing dishonest coaches, where the NAIA claimed to be out for the welfare of the student. He eloquently challenged his colleagues to put their votes where their hearts were. They responded, voting 49-34 in favor of doing what the NAIA had believed correct before succumbing to USOC pressure in 1960, allowing a professional in one sport to compete as an amateur in other sports. The measure then went to the entire membership for a mail vote, and that democratic expression also strongly favored the proposal.[14] The NAIA had returned to its original conception of amateurism.

Several governance issues surfaced during these four years. In 1977, the title of the executive secretary-treasurer was changed to executive director and he was no longer to be an officer on the Executive Committee, though he would continue to be a member. That 1977 convention also elected Dr. John Visser, president of Emporia State University, as the new member of the Executive Committee. Visser took seriously the active participation of member presidents in governing the body—15 of them had just taken part in a long Presidents Advisory Committee meeting the day before, and with Visser's election, their inclination to play a larger role in NAIA matters took a leap forward.

Visser addressed the convention and directly avowed the presidents' interest in playing a more active role in running intercollegiate athletics. He spoke in favor of a proposal on the floor to limit athletic scholarships to tuition, with any further aid to be need-based with athletes treated just like other students. This proposal had stemmed from a meeting of the American Association of State Colleges and Universities, an organization of institutional presidents numbering over 300, about half of which were NAIA schools. Visser recounted four pertinent resolutions those presidents had passed. First, they affirmed the NAIA position that athletics were an integral part of higher education. Second, they affirmed the principles of Title IX, no matter what the courts or HEW ruled. Third, they recognized the AIAW as the proper organization to administer women's sports championships. Finally, they pledged to participate actively in their particular athletic associations. Despite Visser's eloquent plea, the delegates voted down the proposal, 61-33, with the strongest argument contending that it would hamper local, conference, and regional autonomy and thus violate the NAIA's decentralized structure.[15]

In an effort to ensure more accountability in governance, the Executive Committee imposed some specific controls. In 1976, following up on an audit at the time of the Duer-Fritz transition, they mandated an audit every three years, just to ensure good business practices. In 1978, citing a desire to ensure the democratic operation of the NAIA (even when they didn't get their way), they solicited a continual study of association operations to achieve that end.

Several notable policy changes passed during these four years. In an ongoing effort to give more clout to affiliated conferences, the 1978 convention provided them each with one vote on the floor. That same year, the 18-week transfer-waiting period was cut to 16 weeks, which coincided more accurately with the length of a semester. In 1979, the six-hour term of attendance definition was upped to 12, with the telling argument being that it was unfair to count as a term of attendance for eligibility purposes a load that did not make a player actually eligible. In addition, that 1979 convention eased the wording of the by-law ban on advertising alcoholic beverages at NAIA venues—the fact that Kemper Arena, site of the national basketball tournament, had them embedded in the scoreboard made for an embarrassing inconsistency.

Finally, President John Strahl and Executive Committee member Carroll Land wrote a letter to *The NAIA News* concerning the question of Sunday competition. Aside from hockey, which had somehow bypassed the NAIA screening process (did any church-related schools play hockey?), the association had historically taken a conservative position on the matter, allowing only emergency use of the Sabbath (for example, to make up a rained-out game at a playoff). The 1977 soccer final, however, had been set for a Sunday, raising Strahl and Land's concern. Institutions had had autonomy in season length scheduling and off-season activities, but Sundays had never been a planned part of the NAIA program. The national temptation to overemphasize sports, including the NCAA moving increasingly toward seven-days-a-week scheduling, seemed a dangerous precedent to the writers, and one that the NAIA needed to resist. The Executive Committee had discussed the issue and, it appears, concluded that the association would continue to oppose the "wholesale use" of Sundays for athletic competition. So the writers wound up their letter by urging church-related colleges to continue to support the NAIA as best serving their athletic interests.[16]

In 1978, the NAIA Baseball Coaches Association began naming Academic All-Americans, a practice that rapidly spread to other sports offered by the association. Honoring student-athletes who achieved at least a 3.0 or 3.5 grade point average, depending on the sport, the awards further emphasized the importance the NAIA placed on the combination of athletics and scholarship. Later the nomenclature was changed to Scholar-Athletes due to a copyright issue with the All-American term.[17]

Administrative advances helped the NAIA office service its member institutions more effectively. In the fall of 1976, with the hotel-favoring Duer no longer in charge, the NAIA offices moved to the entire second floor of the Midland Building, providing 4,200 square feet of space. After two decades in the Aladdin, Phillips, and Dixon Inn hotels, the NAIA for the first time had a permanent and spacious headquarters. The addition of a WATS (wide area telephone service) line to permit toll-free phone calls was welcomed by the staff, as was Charlie Morris assigning an Executive Committee or staff member as a specific representative to each district, providing a higher degree of accountability. One further boost to the staff came with the establishment of an intern program through Western Illinois, providing half-year internships to help ease the regular staff workload while providing the students with valuable experience. In the fall of 1977 Charlie Eppler joined the staff as the new public relations director; one significant outgrowth of that came a year later when *The NAIA News* moved from a quarterly publication to a bi-monthly magazine incorporating *The NAIA Coach* and providing upgraded coverage of the whole NAIA sports scene.

To pay for upgraded facilities and ever-increasing costs in the inflation-wracked seventies, the spring 1977 convention endorsed a hike in member institution fees. They had stayed at a nominal $10 per school during the Liston years and then moved to a sliding scale based on institutional size in the fifties. After that, they had increased every three to four years as their reliable, fixed amount diminished as a share of the whole NAIA budget, forcing reliance on highly variable tournament revenue to run the association. The possibility of television revenues supplementing income, or at least signaling higher NAIA visibility, annually raised NAIA hopes, only to dash them on the rock of commercial reality. The new dues scale, running from $300 to $550 per year, passed by a 3-2 margin despite a floor contention that smaller schools were being asked to bear a disproportionate share of the increase.[18]

The question of the place of women in college sports, raised unavoidably by the passage of Title IX in 1972, increasingly occupied the time and thoughts of NAIA leaders. They met at least twice a year with AIAW representatives and worked through that organization as the route to promoting women's championships. Some schools, like Pacific Lutheran, had already developed full women's programs before Title IX forced the issue. Others, like Point Loma College in San Diego, responded quickly to the legislation and established women's programs to parallel men's. Yet working with the AIAW proved frustrating. That body mixed two- and four-year schools, provided for no divisions, and had difficulty showing how a team could qualify for national championship competition. Their national conventions were not well managed, as leaders tried to handle too many too complex issues in too little time.[19]

At the spring 1976 NAIA convention, the Executive Committee met with six presidents to map out the route to compliance with Title IX. The NAIA had surveyed its members about their women's programs the previous year, and continued to press members to work with the AIAW toward national competition. Nevertheless, it was inevitable that both the NCAA and NAIA would ponder establishing their own women's divisions if the AIAW approach did not live up to expectations. At the 1976 gathering, President Bob Livingston offered his personal opinion that eventually both national men's organizations would offer parallel women's athletic programs. But that was in the future. Through most of the seventies, the NAIA maintained excellent relations with the AIAW and seemed reasonably optimistic that the new organization offered the best route to full women's participation on a national level.

But the NAIA did not passively allow the AIAW to dictate its agenda. In 1978 it established a Task Force on Women's Athletics to determine how the NAIA might develop women's programs within its own organization. Chaired by Point Loma College athletic director Carroll Land, the task force had been assessing the existing women's programs within the NAIA and soliciting feedback about women's sports with a goal of presenting a proposal to the 1979 convention. The group developed a five-point statement of goals for an NAIA women's program.

- To develop commonality of rules and guidelines for sports competition for men and women.
- To achieve equitable and proportionate representation by men and women at all levels of governance in the NAIA.

- To make available institutional membership in the NAIA in the Men's Division, Women's Division, or both.
- To expand the NAIA program to include competitive opportunities and championship events for women and to provide for selected district/national sports championships beginning in 1979-80.
- To explore the sponsorship of co-educational intercollegiate sports and establish co-educational programs that will reflect membership preferences.[20]

The bulk of floor discussion at the 1979 convention concerned the task force's proposal to launch the NAIA women's championships program. Although Fritz claimed that "consideration of questions concerning women's competition by the NAIA . . . should not be interpreted as any lessening of . . . support [for the AIAW]," it is hard to see any other valid interpretation.[21] Land argued that the issue was not really for the convention to establish a women's division, but to allow the entire membership to make that decision democratically on their own campuses and reflective of their own needs and priorities. John Visser noted that his Emporia State campus had fully integrated women and had an assistant athletic director for men and another for women, and that his whole Central States Intercollegiate Conference had achieved such integration. Moving to the national level seemed the logical next step. It would also simplify matters, he argued, for Emporia State to work with only one national organization in times of budget cutting.

Kay Wilkins, a delegate from Bradford State College, presciently expressed concern that, while most delegates to the national convention had become well informed on the issue of women's sports, many of their colleagues back on their own campuses did not share that level of expertise and thus would not likely make as informed a decision.[22] She also noted that Joan Warrington of Pittsburg State (KS) was slated for election to the Executive Committee later that morning. She wondered what the first woman on that body would do for the next eight years if the measure failed to pass. She also challenged the men that they might not know enough women to be able to select good representatives of their perspective in the future. Representatives from different districts reported that their districts supported the proposal (as was the case with men, it would enable women enrolled in small colleges to compete against like institutions), or opposed it (they were loyal to the AIAW as the legitimate representative for women).

When the vote was taken, the measure to establish a women's division passed overwhelmingly, 109-20. In due course, Joan Warrington, director of women's athletics at Pittsburg State, did win election to the Executive Committee. She earned a Ph.D. from Michigan and had spent 1977-1978 as Executive Secretary of the AIAW.[23] The women's division measure went to the membership, and as Kay Wilkins had forecast, met a narrow defeat there. Needing 66.7 percent to pass, it stalled at 66.0 percent. But the women would be back.

Out in the arena, fall sports included cross-country, and the competition was still fierce, whereas during the eighties and nineties a few teams totally dominated the sport. In 1975 and 1976 Edinboro State (PA) raced to back-to-back crowns in its only two appearances ever in the NAIA's top two cross-country teams. In 1977 Adams State (CO) took its second crown ever, foreshadowing its overwhelming domination in the 1980s. In 1978, Pembroke State (NC) won its sole crown.

In Division I football, Texas A&I defended its 1974 crown in 1975 with convincing 37-0 wins over Oregon College and Salem (WV) in the semifinals and title game. The Javelinas extended their consecutive-game winning streak to 39 the next season when they rolled to a record third straight title, wowing home field fans with a 26-0 trouncing of Central Arkansas. Led by quarterback Richard Ritchie through the entire streak, Texas A&I's trifecta is unmatched in NAIA football history. In 1977, both of their strings ended. Their win streak stopped at 46, just one short of Oklahoma's college record, in a 7-6 loss to East Texas State. Their three-year run at the top of the national heap also ended when Lone Star Conference rival Abilene Christian fought past all rivals, topping Southwestern Oklahoma in the national championship game, 24-7. The next season the conference racked up its seventh Division I title in a row and ninth in ten years, as Angelo State went 14-0 and swamped Elon (NC) in the final game, 34-14. Following a dismal experience in Seattle in 1977, the 1978 game in McAllen, Texas, not only brought the game to the perennial winning conference's home state, but also proved a financial winner.

Texas Lutheran also defended its 1974 crown in 1975 as the Division II football champs hammered denominational rival Cal Lutheran, 34-8, in the title match. In 1976, though, a non-Texas team, Westminster (PA), eliminated Texas Lutheran decisively in the semifinals, 31-0, and followed that win up with a 20-13 triumph over Redlands (CA) for the championship. The Titans came right back in 1977, dropping Cal Lutheran, 17-9, after both teams squeaked by semifinal rivals by one point. In 1978, Concordia (MN) picked up its only football crown, edging Findlay (OH), 7-0, to sweep the first eight-team playoff.

Soccer produced some thrillers, with perennial contenders evenly matched in many key games. In 1975, Quincy edged Simon Fraser, 1-0, on a clutch goal by Emilio John with only 30 seconds left on the clock. The two teams clashed again in the semifinals in 1976 and the Clansmen won a measure of revenge when they edged the defending champions, 2-1, in *fourteen* overtimes. The game started at 8:30 p.m. and didn't end until 12:55 a.m., when Brad Mason, a reserve back, scored the winner. The Canadians then nipped Rockhurst in the final game of a very rough series, 1-0. In 1977 Nigerian Emilio John once again led Quincy to the top with a 3-0 win over Keene

State (NH). The Hawks returned in 1978 with a bit of a cushion. Dr. Pepper put up $25,000 to sponsor the tourney, covering a chunk of teams' costs. This time Quincy outshot Alabama-Huntsville, 29-6, en route to a 2-0 victory, giving coach Jack Mackenzie six championships in his ten-year career as head coach at the Illinois college.

Basketball produced four different champions in four years, indicating the greater degree of difficulty in keeping a dynasty on top in a five-man sport. In 1976 ninth-seeded Coppin State (MD) knocked off Henderson State (AR), 96-91, to take home the trophy. The next season, Texas Southern, seeded fifth, survived early scares and peaked in the championship game, blowing out the tournament's unseeded Cinderella team, Campbell (NC), 71-44. In 1978, Grand Canyon (AZ) notched its second win in four years as the 1975 winners took a precarious route to the top. In the quarterfinals, they took five overtimes to beat Central State (OH), 88-82, riding Richard Bacon's eight points in the fifth overtime to the victory. In the final, Grand Canyon's Antelopes knocked off Kearney State, 79-75, preventing the unseeded Nebraskans from pulling off a major upset. In 1979, third-seeded Drury (MO) took home top honors by beating Henderson State, 60-54, in the final game. By this time, NAIA schools in the northwest were installing a new slam-dunk rim developed by Western Washington coach Chuck Randall. This NAIA innovation won widespread support in the wake of backboard-shattering power dunks, and is standard equipment today.

Simon Fraser splashed to four consecutive swimming titles, and though regional rival Central Washington finished second in the first two, no team came anywhere close to matching coach Paul Savage's Canadians.

Wrestling proved much more competitive. In 1976, Adams State won its second straight title, but Mike Reed led Eastern Washington to a very tight win over Grand Valley State (MI) in 1977, ending that mini-dynasty. Southern Oregon took top honors in 1978, with Grand Valley again frustrated after losing by less than three points for the second straight year. Central Oklahoma won its first title in 1979, foreshadowing its dominance in the sport during the eighties.

Jackson State (MS) totally dominated indoor track and field. The 1975 winners were back on top in 1976, 1977, tied Abilene Christian in 1978, and won outright again in 1979.

Wisconsin schools continued to rule gymnastics, with LaCrosse garnering top honors in 1976 and 1977 and then giving way the next two years to perennial power Oshkosh, paced by Casey Edwards.

Early automatic ice hockey winner Bemidji State skated on thin ice during this four-year stretch. In 1976 Wisconsin-Superior beat St. Scholastica (MN), 8-5, in the title game. The losers made it all the way to the top in 1977, beating Gustavus-Adolphus (MN), 3-2, in a thrilling final. By 1978, Bemidji was back on track, but they lost the final game to Augsburg (Minnesota), 4-3. The Beavers finally regained their accustomed spot at the top of the ice heap in 1979, skating past Concordia (MN), 5-1, in the final.

In spring sports, baseball had a mini-dynasty in place after Lewis (IL) won its third consecutive crown in 1976, knocking off Lewis-Clark State (ID), 16-8, in the final game. Their shot at four straight fell short in 1977, when upstart David Lipscomb (TN) rebounded from an 11-1 opening game pounding to fight its way through the losers' bracket, then made two first-inning runs stand up for a 2-1 victory over Southeastern Oklahoma, the team that had eliminated Lewis earlier. In 1978, Emporia State (KS) also rebounded from an opening game loss, a 4-0 shutout at the hands of Missouri Southern. The Hornets, behind the first nine-inning no-hitter in NAIA playoff history from series MVP Kevin Mendon, evened the score, 2-0, then won the rubber match between the two teams, 8-6, for the championship in a rainy week. The 1979 series moved to Nashville, encouraged by underwriting from the Nashville Sounds Double-A Southern League team, and there set attendance records for the championship game (8,779) and the week (29,006, or almost double the 1975 record of 15,621 in St Joseph). Helping to fuel the fans' interest was the presence of local David Lipscomb College, invited to replace Grand Canyon when the Area 2 winner withdrew. In a series marked by tight games, the local favorites won their second title in three years with a 5-4 final game win over High Point (NC), who had earlier twice rallied in the ninth inning of games to stay alive in the tourney.

Track and field competition began with runner Mike Boit of Eastern New Mexico repeating as top performer and leading his school to a first place finish in 1976. Jackson State, led by sprinter Earl Thomas, took top honors in 1977. In 1978 and 1979 Texas Southern, paced by sprinter Fred Taylor, won back-to-back championships, the Tigers' fourth and fifth track and field titles going back to 1961.

The orderly world of tennis unraveled in 1976. After Redlands had won nine of ten titles, and finished second the other year, they hit a dry spell. Mercyhurst (PA) beat the perennial champs in 1976, then Flagler (FL) netted the top spot in 1977 behind ace player Gordon Jones. East Texas State provided yet another new winner in 1978, and Atlantic Christian (NC), runner-up in 1978, moved up a notch to first place in 1979.

Gardner-Webb (NC) edged Elon (NC) by one stroke to capture in 1976 golf title, then repeated more easily over Sam Houston State the following year. The Texans were just getting warmed up, though, for they took top honors in 1978 and 1979, beating out second-place finishers Elon and Gardner-Webb, respectively—those three schools pretty much dominated the sport over the four-year stretch.

Two teams dominated volleyball, with Graceland (IA) edging Rutgers-Newark in 1976, then finishing second to George Williams (IL) in 1977 and 1978. Graceland grabbed the top spot again in 1979, topping George Williams in the final match. It was also the final match in another way. Following the 1979 season, ignoring the pleas of George Williams' coach and NAIAC volleyball chairman Jerry Angle, the NAIA terminated the sport. Though volleyball was a spring sport and thus did not interfere with most indoor sports, and though Angle argued that more and more schools were adding volleyball, its meager participation level among member institutions led the NAIA to discontinue it after eleven years as a championship sport. Over that span George Williams and Graceland each won three championships.

Bowling also felt the knife. Glenville State (WV), West Liberty State (WV), and St. Vincent (PA) won titles in 1976, 1977, and 1978, but interest in the sport had declined drastically. First offered as a national championship competition in 1962, bowling had attracted over 100 competing schools during the sixties, but the number had dwindled to a meager 31 colleges by its last season. Loss of its earlier subsidy from the National Bowling Council contributed to the Executive Committee's decision to pull the plug at its 1978 summer meeting. With the elimination of the sport, Arkansas' Harding College, winner of four titles, had a secure place in history as the association's top bowling school.[24]

Eastern New Mexico completed its three-peat as all-sports champion in 1975-76, but gave way in 1976-77 to Wisconsin-La Crosse as the new standard-bearer, trailed by Adams State and Simon Fraser. Adams State moved up to the top spot in 1977-78, with Eastern Washington, La Crosse, and Abilene Christian (TX) also in the hunt. Wisconsin-La Crosse reclaimed first place in 1978-79, dropping Adams State back into second.

9

Women Have Their Day
1979-1983

When last we left our heroines, they had been denied their bid to be a part of the NAIA championships program. Despite an overwhelming affirmation by the better-informed delegates to the national meeting in March 1979, the women's measure failed by an excruciatingly narrow margin in the ensuing mail vote by all members. But the NAIA did not operate in a vacuum, and the world of women's sports was changing even as the NAIA's advocates for women prepared their second effort to sway the membership.

The AIAW had included junior colleges under its mantle when it was organized in 1971, but during the seventies the two-year schools had seen their other champion, the NJCAA, challenge the AIAW's right to speak for its members. Junior college presidents had concluded that it would be better for their institutions to have men's and women's athletics under the same umbrella, and they ultimately convinced the AIAW that they would give junior college women a fair deal under the NJCAA. So, the AIAW let the junior colleges depart their organization with their blessing.[1]

The NAIA's relations with the AIAW followed a different path. While the women's organization remained part of the AAHPERD until late in the seventies, relations with the NAIA were good. Duer and Fritz both promoted warm ties with the AIAW, and it appeared for a while that they might combine efforts to offer compatible programs for both genders. Around 1976 some women were even working on logos that would show the interdependence of the two organizations. But the AIAW broke away from the AAHPERD and went in a different direction.

The change was subtle, but had profound effects. Instead of being primarily interested in the development of women's sports, the AIAW increasingly sought the development of women through athletics. More and more, a self-perpetuating radical minority controlled the AIAW and worked openly with the broader feminist movement to advance their agenda. The growing hostility toward men and men's organizations that characterized radical feminism came to dominate the AIAW. Working hand-in-hand with men and their organization came to be viewed as selling women out, and talk of a merger or of a close and cooperative relationship evaporated.

Under those circumstances, NAIA presidents came to the same realization as their junior college counterparts—the best answer to Title IX and the advancement of women's sports was to integrate women into the NAIA. One step that helped to build a measure of trust toward the NAIA was the election of Joan Warrington to the Executive Committee in 1979 before the membership had even approved creation of a women's division. The AIAW, however, perceived the NAIA as a threat to their dominance and also to women controlling their own destiny. AIAW leaders clearly were not interested in working in any arrangement they did not control.[2]

The NCAA had responded to the establishment of the AIAW in 1971 with a declaration that they had no interest in contesting the new group, promising they would keep their hands off women's new-found aspirations for a vital national sports program. Unenthusiastic and inconsistent, the NCAA fought against Title IX in court, tried an abortive coup in the mid-seventies to take over women's sports, supported the Tower Amendment to exclude revenue-producing sports from Title IX's provisions, then accommodated women's efforts while their court battles continued in the late seventies, arguing in *NCAA v. Califano* that Title IX imposed an unconstitutional quota system.[3] At their January 1980 convention, the NCAA, recognizing their legal vulnerability under Title IX, approved a proposal to hold women's championships in five sports (basketball, field hockey, swimming, tennis, and volleyball), but only in Divisions II and III, beginning in 1981-82. Thus, with the NAIA membership having narrowly rejected instituting women's championships in the 1979 vote, the NCAA beat them to the punch. The larger organization went even farther at their 1981 convention, voting to hold national championships in nine sports (basketball, cross country, field hockey, gymnastics, softball, swimming and diving, tennis, outdoor track, and volleyball) in Division I, and adding fencing, golf, and lacrosse for all three divisions, launching the entire program in 1981-82. They also appointed a director of women's championships to coordinate the new activities.[4]

So when the NAIA convened its annual meeting in March 1980, it did so knowing that the NCAA was proceeding to institute its first women's championships about 18 months down the road. Noting that he had heard criticism that the 1978-79 task force had not included enough women, and realizing that he had not fought aggressively enough in the mistaken impression that the measure would sail through on its merits, Carroll Land introduced the Committee on Women's Athletics that had been preparing to submit a new women's sports proposal. Charlie Morris of the national staff and Land provided experienced NAIA voices, and three women did the heavy lifting: Jessie Banks of the University of Southern Colorado, Joan Warrington of Emporia State, and Margaret Waters of East Texas State University. No doubt reflecting both Title IX imperatives and the NCAA's vote two months earlier, Land argued that establishing the NAIA program was not an option, but a must. He gently chastised opponents for misrepresentations and untruths, and for trying to hold off the inevitable end to the NAIA as an old boys' club.[5]

The AIAW did not support dual membership for its members. In early 1980, it called for a five-year moratorium on NCAA (and NAIA?) championships for women, though the NCAA had already approved its Division II and III programs. It sought to avoid some of the corruption that had marred men's sports programs, so those women had established their own rules. Among them were bans on off-campus recruiting and athletic scholarships, as well as permitting women to transfer and play the same year. Adherence to NAIA rules would violate those provisions, making peaceful coexistence impossible. Land did say his committee favored waiving eligibility restrictions for two years to permit dual membership, but given AIAW's reluctance to cooperate, that seemed unlikely.

F. L. Cassen of Southwestern University sought to delay the start of the women's program, slated for the fall of 1980, for a year, ostensibly to permit careful selection of sites, formats, and other considerations. He contended that it would be a big mistake to launch such a major initiative and then do it poorly. Besides, the NCAA was catching flak for its program and, he suggested, the NAIA didn't want to make the same mistake the NCAA had. Warrington countered that NAIA institutions had in fact already had a year to make preparations for a women's program—the events of 1979 had indicated the path to the future, and the committee had established the fall 1980 target as a way to get the NAIA out in front in women's programming, and also to give the AIAW a chance to rethink its opposition to accommodation with the NAIA. Besides, as another delegate argued, the NCAA had not made a mistake instituting a women's program. Waiting simply did not make sense. The delegates concurred; they rejected the amendment.

Two floor arguments in favor of moving forward with women's championships followed. Bob Moorman contended that the AIAW was segregated, with its black schools placed in a separate group reminiscent of the NAIA's old District 29. Black women, he argued, should have the opportunity to partake of the NAIA's well-integrated structure. The Park College indoor track coach said that, although the AIAW contended it had different divisions, his small college team had had to compete against the likes of Ohio State and the University of Missouri, rather limiting their chances of being competitive. The NAIA's focus on small colleges offered a more balanced alternative.

Arguing against the proposal, Ricky Grundin of Ohio Dominican College noted that the AIAW had championships in 17 sports, not the mere nine the NAIA planned. She also felt that because women's programs were so wildly unequal, to move women's teams right into the same conferences that men had created would produce some competitively disastrous inequities.

As the star witness against the NAIA commencing a women's championship program, AIAW President Christine Grant was permitted a guest appearance on the floor to argue her case. She expanded on the Grundin remarks, observing that the 971 AIAW member institutions would in a year be sponsoring 39 national championships in 17 sports on three divisional levels, with schools able to choose their divisional level by sport. NBC had just signed a four-year one-million-dollar television contract to carry AIAW events, money that would be divided among all three divisions, a coup that had to pain the underexposed NAIA's delegates. Finally, she said, at the just-concluded AIAW national convention, with the exception of one free-thinking delegate, the assembly had unanimously opposed the NCAA and NAIA staging women's championships.

Despite the eloquent, and in retrospect rather desperate, arguments to preserve the AIAW's exclusivity, the delegates, as they had in 1979, voted decisively in favor of commencing NAIA women's championships in the fall. The tally was 113-12, an overwhelming endorsement of this significant step for the association. Land accurately observed that, although the NCAA had voted to proceed with some women's championships two months earlier, the NAIA had been moving in that direction for considerably longer than their rival. If the membership approved the convention's recommendation this time, the NAIA would still beat the NCAA into action by a year. Before sending the recommendation out to the members, the delegate also resolved to achieve "equitable participation of women at all levels of governance," and set up a committee on women's athletics to monitor carrying out that mandate.[6]

This time the members came through for women. Seventy-nine percent of eligible institutions voted, far surpassing the minimum of 51 percent, and they supported the measure, 267-119, a close but clear 69 percent. The NAIA was once again out in front on a breakthrough integration measure. In response, an ad hoc Committee on Implementation, chaired by Joan Warrington, met in Kansas City to plan the inaugural events. The five members of the Committee on Women's Athletics were all on board, along with Phyllis Holmes of Greenville College, LaVerne Sweat of Hampton Institute, and Wally Schwartz from the NAIA staff. The ad hoc committee worked up sites, dates, and formats for each of ten championships to take place during 1980-81 and presented their recommendation to the Executive Committee's summer meeting for confirmation. The NAIA had become a two-gender organization.[7]

At its annual meeting in January 1981, the NCAA, now trailing in the women's athletics game, addressed the issue head on. By a narrow margin they mustered the required two-thirds vote to approve adding four women to the 18-member Council that made policy decisions between conventions and two to an expanded 12-person Executive Committee charged with running the business and championship side of the organization. It then stalled in an effort to institute playoffs for Division I women. With only Division I delegates able to participate, a tie vote, then a one-vote defeat left the NCAA in the awkward position of approving Division II and III women's championships (reaffirmed overwhelmingly) but denying them to Division I schools. Finally, a third vote passed the measure, 137-117, and the NCAA had fully committed itself to women's sports.[8]

Despite both the NAIA and NCAA now offering championships for women, the AIAW held on for two more years. Some of the key members of the NAIA women's committees met with AIAW representatives in March 1981 to explore possibilities for cooperation and to propose developing an Athletes' Bill of Rights, but the future looked bleak for the women-only group. The NAIA women's division mushroomed from 285 members in 1981-82 to 460 institutions in 1982-83, and Harry Fritz forecast that it would likely surpass the men's membership within another two years.[9] The association had made such impressive strides that when a woman, Veronica Harris, was named coach of the *men's* cross country team at Chicago State in the fall of 1981, the breakthrough appointment got only minor notice in the back pages of *The NAIA News*.[10] But the *coup de grace* for the AIAW came in the winter of 1981-82 when the NCAA ran its first Division I women's basketball tournament, with undefeated Louisiana Tech taking the title. For the first time, the big schools had to choose, and while the AIAW did run its tournament, with Rutgers coming out on top, it was in effect the last gasp of that body. It had served its purpose and faded into history.

With the demise of the AIAW, a number of colleges with NCAA Division I men's basketball programs, among them Gonzaga, Hardin-Simmons, Marquette, Pan American, and William and Mary, joined the NAIA to provide a more low-key women's alternative. The NAIA had barred Division I schools from participating in NAIA national championships. To have such a rule for men and not women, lawyers advised, would violate sex-discrimination laws, so the rule was extended to women's sports. Because it seemed desirable to encourage opportunities for women to be active in the NAIA, delegates to the 1983 convention devised a procedure to process exemptions to the rule. The sports world had become a complicated maze compared to the ways things had been back in 1952 when the NAIA began.[11]

Women had their programs and were being mainstreamed in the two major athletic associations. The next question the NAIA faced was to upgrade the quality of those programs. Harry Fritz told the March 1983 attendees that there remained much room for improvement. Women needed to develop their skills, realize their potential, and fulfill the promise of equal opportunity. Men had been programmed to be competitive and think athletically and identify themselves through their athletic achievements. To get women to do so would require some significant social engineering. More women needed to get into athletic training, sports information, and sports administration. Officiating needed to be upgraded, workshops needed to be expanded, and in general women needed to seize the opportunities before them. When only 20 to 25 women coaches showed up for their sport association meeting out of over 300 possible, there clearly existed room for a substantial improvement in commitment to athletics. That was to be the next big step.[12]

❖

While the integration of women into the NAIA was just getting started, after almost a quarter century of progress it was possible to evaluate the success of the integration of black athletes into the organization. Richard Fowler, the LeTourneau College director of social research, explored one aspect in "Portrait of a Winning Team." He compared minorities on winning basketball teams in the NJCAA, NCAA, and NAIA. The junior college teams had 52 percent minorities, the NCAA 44 percent, and the NAIA 36 percent. In the four-year programs, the black athletes tended to be starters (75 percent of them), while substitutes were more likely to be white. NAIA coaches imposed the most discipline, holding on to old ways of running teams in the face of a general decline in team orientation growing out of sixties individualism. Fowler's most striking conclusion suggested a source for NAIA pride. NCAA minorities made sports their top priority, hoping to become professional athletes or go into some form of athletic work after graduation; they saw their academic pursuits as a means to an end. NAIA athletes better recognized their limitations (possibly because the NCAA siphoned off the most talented athletes) and were more focused on their academic achievement and the possibilities of future employment outside of sports. In other words, NAIA schools were more fully integrating black athletes into the ethos of academic life.[13] Since only about one in 195 college football players, to cite one example, succeeded in winning a roster spot in the NFL, the NAIA was doing a better job of preparing its athletes for life than the NCAA was.[14]

But racial integration was old hat—the development of opportunities for women dominated the period. Still, other matters also demanded attention. Concern about establishing divisions of play in sports other than football, potential changes in governance, administrative adjustments, and the challenge of defining and maintaining NAIA distinctives also occupied the association's leadership and members.

With over 500 member institutions, the NAIA encompassed a wide range of sizes and types of school. Two sources of inequality were enrollment and financial aid, and with institutional, or at least conference, autonomy on the latter, it had become increasingly difficult for some schools to compete effectively. At the 1981 convention, two proposals to create two divisions within the NAIA were presented, and then withdrawn in favor of a Research Committee subcommittee undertaking a thorough exploration of the idea, including a detailed survey to go out to the membership. Chaired by William Jordan of Black Hills State, the subcommittee met in Kansas City during that summer, sent out surveys, and then met in October to analyze the results and develop a proposal for the 1982 convention to consider. Two criteria reduced the number of sports affected: 60 percent of surveys needed to designate a sport and only sports with at least 100 participating schools would be considered.[15]

The number of institutions sponsoring each sport merits tabular presentation.

Men's sports (1981-82)		Women's sports (1981-82)	
Baseball	384	Basketball	248
Basketball	496	Cross Country	75
Cross Country	282	Golf	28
Football (2 div.)	222	Gymnastics	13
Golf	303	Softball	130
Gymnastics	11	Swimming	17
Ice hockey	30	Tennis	164
Soccer	208	Indoor track	70
Swimming	73	Outdoor track	100
Tennis	365	Volleyball	207
Indoor track	163		
Outdoor track	278		
Wrestling	130		

One survey result leaps out at a reader: by almost a three-to-one margin, awarding athletic grants in aid trumped institutional enrollment as the key factor that should determine placement in a division. Financial aid, by a 2-1 vote, meant aid awarded for athletic ability regardless of need, not aid in excess of need and based on athletic ability. The survey also revealed serious concerns about the viability of districts if the number of schools offering a sport was split by establishing divisions. Another survey result that boded ill for men's gymnastics and ice hockey was that by an almost four to one margin respondents felt national championships should be limited to sports with a minimum of 25 sponsoring institutions. The newness of the women's division made smaller women's sports less clearly vulnerable.

The March 1982 convention approved a resolution to follow football's example and "develop and initiate divisions of competition in selected sports" for the 1983-84 school year.[16] Three new sports each for men and women emerged as prospects to divide: men's soccer, basketball, and baseball, and women's basketball, volleyball, and softball. In the spring of 1982, schools chose their preferred divisions for competition, and their selections eliminated softball and soccer; either fewer than 100 schools opted for one of the prospective divisions or geographical distribution was poor, creating undue costs.

The NAIA News ran arguments for and against moving to divisions just prior to the March 1983 convention. District 5 chair Dick Costello of Southern Maine favored the proposal, noting that his schools had never won a basketball game in the Kansas City tournament and that their no-athletic scholarship policy was much like that of NCAA Division III schools. Wayne Dannehl of Wisconsin-Parkside opposed the proposed change, arguing that it would increase playoff costs, hurt traditional rivalries, and weaken the key district structure of the NAIA. Large institutions like the Wisconsin state universities could opt for NAIA Division II status, which would make it difficult for smaller schools to compete anyway.[17] Though the concept would remain alive and eventually pass for basketball, the convention smacked down the idea, overwhelmingly rejecting divisions for each of the four sports. In due course, schools on the losing end of the vote, like Southern Maine, as Costello had hinted, opted to move to NCAA Division III. Ironically, most of the Wisconsin schools like Dannehl's are also now in Division III.

Governance issues began to surface during this period and with the establishment of women's programs accomplished, they moved to the top of the list of crucial matters for the NAIA. When LeRoy Walker assumed the mantle of NAIA president at the 1980 convention, he immediately noted a clearly-recognized need to change the NAIA's governing structure "to be consistent with the times and the NAIA constitution and by-laws." He appointed a task force to consider changes in governance, along with developing a long-range plan for the association.[18]

Profile: Dr. LeRoy Walker
The new NAIA president in 1980 became the first African-American to hold the post, one year before James Frank matched that achievement in the NCAA. The last of 13 children growing up in Harlem, Walker attended Benedict College in South Carolina and earned a degree in three and a half years along with 12 letters in football, basketball, and track and field. He began coaching football and basketball at the NAIA's North Carolina Central University in Durham, struggled with segregation in the south, and rose through the ranks of the NAIA to become president. His horizons broadened beyond that, however, and he moved on to be president of the U.S. Olympic Committee from 1992 to 1996.

The rising power within the governance structure of the NAIA was the Presidents Advisory Committee, or PAC. It had been established in 1977 with one president from each of the 32 districts and provided a valuable resource for the Executive Committee, with which it met each spring to exchange views and recommendations on association matters. As a standing committee, it had the power to place legislative proposals (constitutional or by-law changes) before the delegates. The establishment of the women's division and championships owed a great deal to the initiative of the PAC.[19]

Addressing the 1983 convention, Harry Fritz made his pitch for modernizing the governing structure, calling for greater opportunities for "both men and women presidents, athletic directors, faculty athletic representatives, coaches, and others [to be] significantly expanded." After 35 years with the present arrangement, it had become "somewhat stifling" for ambitious people committed to the NAIA program. There needed to be more room available at the top and fewer bottlenecks.[20] Carroll Land, the 1981-82 president, had pushed through one reform, removing the second-year outgoing president from the Executive Committee (beginning with himself) to open up another slot for new blood. For the first time at the 1983 meeting, the general membership had nominated candidates for the Executive Committee, and after the Executive Committee screened the nominees, they had presented three to the delegates for a vote: Gordon Kingsley of William Jewell College, Wayne Dannehl of Wisconsin-Parkside, and President Leonard Campbell of Southwest Oklahoma State. Dannehl came out on top.

The membership also took care of some administrivia. In 1979 they had changed the six-hour rule for terms of attendance to 12 hours, reasoning that it was hardly fair to charge a term of attendance for a load that wouldn't even make one eligible to play. A year later, they had realized that junior colleges counted 10 hours as a full load. They were faced with the awkward possibility that a young man could play two seasons of junior college football, spend two full years there, and then come in to an NAIA school as a beginning freshman, though with only two years of eligibility remaining. So the delegates compromised and made nine hours the minimum to count as a term of attendance. They also reversed their earlier rejection of a proposal to allow 14 days rather than seven to get grades recorded after the fall term and determine continued eligibility. Christmas holidays and slow faculty graders made this a highly desirable change.[21] By 1983, the membership was so restive that it rejected 10 of 15 by-law changes presented to them, along with voting down the proposed divisional split. When leaders spoke of the need for governmental change, they may well have perceived frustration among the ranks, as well as in the pressures from college presidents for a more active role in the association.

The whole collegiate sports scene was roiled by scandal as the permissiveness and contempt for tradition and standards fostered by the sixties permeated society.

Academic foul play, with ghost courses, forged transcripts, and gift grades being exposed on a regular basis, combined with the hyper-commercialism of "big-time" sports to give a black eye to all college sports. How could the NAIA retain its sanity and preserve its distinctiveness from the semi-professional collegians? The organization's leaders wrestled with the problem and exhorted their members to resist the temptation to try to win at any cost.

In 1981, Harry Fritz voiced his frustration at the way the NAIA and other small colleges seemed invisible to the media. *Sports Illustrated* in its annual football and basketball preview gave voluminous coverage to the top 20 teams, then dismissed all the rest in a throwaway paragraph or two—a condition that persists to the present day. Over the previous 20 years, Fritz said, about 25 major colleges had received over 90 percent of the network television coverage. He called for smart marketing of NAIA contests and urged association members not to be discouraged by the commercial imperatives.[22]

President LeRoy Walker shared his thoughts on the topic in November 1980 with the American Association of State College and Universities, hearkening back to the early days of athletics in the nation, when they were supposed to develop fitness and be fun for the participant. By the late nineteenth century, Harvard President Charles Eliot was already warning that collegiate sports "present the colleges to the public, educated and uneducated alike, as places of mere physical sport, and not of educational training." Walker called on academe's leaders—boards of trustees, presidents, and chancellors— to take their rightful role in restoring sanity to collegiate athletics, to mandate that athletic programs be run financially consistently with other institutional operations, and to apply academic standards to athletes as they were applied to non-athletes. As long as football coaches earned far more money than either the president or any tenured faculty member, as at one school recently exposed in a sports magazine, commerce would dictate institutional behavior. At least NAIA presidents were listening.[23]

But was the NAIA, too, succumbing to its need for corporate underwriting, one of Harry Fritz's constant quests? *The NAIA News* of December-January 1981-82 featured a full-page article about how the Miller Brewing Company had worked out an arrangement with LeRoy Walker, providing a grant to help cover track and field costs and the first women's basketball tournament. Considering that NAIA by-laws had prohibited advertising or sale of any alcoholic beverages at sanctioned events (with a slight easing of the strictures a few years earlier to accommodate Kemper Arena's scoreboard and other "minor" deviations), this blatant change of policy is shocking. Carroll Land tells of some of his Point Loma College baseball players coming home from a national tournament with Miller-emblazoned awards jackets. Since his school prohibited consumption of alcohol, Land had them return the jackets. This whole episode suggests an erosion of principle that would have appalled Emil Liston or Al Duer.[24]

Land himself, at that point president of the NAIA, wrote a strongly worded article for the association's journal, addressing the general sports malaise that gripped the land. He decried college athletics' failure to heed the warnings of the Carnegie Foundation a half century earlier to avoid commercialism, improperly putting higher education in the entertainment business, and condoning unethical practices. On a more positive note, he cited the AAPHERD's 1976 Collegiate Sports Manifesto as stating well his ideals:

- Absolute necessity for university and collegiate autonomy in decision making
- Moral responsibility of ethical people involved in sports
- Welfare of student athletes as a basis for all decisions
- The conduct of athletics as educational in orientation
- Fairness must undergird the ethical code and governance of sport
- Finance of athletics must be similar to that of the other institutional components
- All who are involved in sports programs must assume responsibility for societal welfare, individual integrity, and a moral subscription to the betterment of sports[25]

Land recognized that the task of cleaning up college sports seemed so vast and doomed to failure that people were inclined simply to throw up their hands and give up. But, quoting Edward Everett Hale's poem "Lend a Hand," he offered an inspiration for all to do their parts and stay the course:

> I am only one,
> But I am still one.
> I cannot do everything
> But I can do something
> And that which I ought to do
> By the grace of God I shall do.

The struggle continues.

All of this bureaucratic and political effort took place to ensure student athletes their opportunities to compete for athletic glory. Cross-country led the way in men's sports in the fall, with Adams State quickly establishing itself as the dominant power in the sport. Coach Joe Vigil attributed his success to bringing Native Americans in from around Colorado to compete for the aptly-named Adams State Indians and training them well; he did not feel that the school's high altitude contributed significantly to his success, though it seems that geographical fact could give some aerobic advantage to the team.[26] Whatever the cause, Vigil's team took top honors in 1979, 1980, and 1981 before stumbling and finishing back in the pack behind Simon Fraser (BC) in 1982.

In Division I football, sparked by a game-turning 100-yard interception return by Emmuel Thompson, in 1979 Texas A&I capped the Lone Star Conference's decade of dominance by beating Central State (OH), 20-14, on ESPN television. Within four years, the entire conference had abandoned the NAIA for the NCAA. Elon (NC) didn't mourn its pending departure, but captured back-to-back titles in 1980 and 1981. In the first, they knocked off Northeastern Oklahoma, 17-10, in the renamed Champion Bowl. They came back in 1981 to edge Pittsburg State (KS), 3-0. In 1982, Central State (OK) held off Mesa (CO), 14-11, to capture its lone football title.

Division II football saw four different teams win championships in four years. In 1979, Findlay (OH) trampled a strong Northwestern (IA) team, 51-6, to take their first football crown. The next year Pacific Lutheran (WA) overwhelmed Wilmington (OH) in another blowout, 38-10, for the first of its three football titles. The by-word in 1981 was balance. The playoffs were filled with tight games, and the final carried that to an extreme; Austin College (TX) and Concordia (MN) played to a 24-24 tie. In 1982, Linfield (OR) took its first of three titles in five years with a convincing 33-15 triumph over William Jewell (MO).

Quincy (IL) continued to dominate the soccer world, capturing its third, fourth, and fifth straight championships from 1979 through 1981. The first two were nail-biters, 1-0 over perennial rival Rockhurst (MO) on a penalty kick and 1-0 over Simon Fraser, but the last was a comparative blowout, a 4-1 triumph over Alderson-Broadus (WV). That 1981 tournament expanded to 12 teams for the first time, placing three teams in each of four pools to determine the four semifinalists. In 1982 Belhaven (MS) knocked Quincy out in pool play, but couldn't parlay that win into a title. Simon Fraser, with a 17-1 edge in goals through the four games, knocked off Midwestern State (TX), 4-0, to win it all.

Basketball featured some great stories over these four years. In 1980, Cameron (OK) knocked off Alabama State in the final, 84-77. The next year saw the first overtime championship game in the tournament's history. Southern Nazarene (OK) nipped Alabama-Huntsville, 86-85, behind sophomore Todd Thurman's 39-point performance. In 1982 Biola (CA) took a 39-0 record into the final and bid to be the first 40-game winner in college basketball history, only to be upset by 14th-seeded South Carolina-Spartansburg, 51-38, to spoil their perfect season. Charleston (SC) edged West Virginia Wesleyan, 57-53, to take top honors in 1983.

Gymnastics suffered from a shortage of participating schools. Wisconsin-Oshkosh took the title all four years, giving the school eight out of the 21 championships awarded in the sport. In 1983, the NAIA voted to abolish the sport following the 1984 season, with Wisconsin-Stout capturing its only title in that last year. By the end, only 11 NAIA schools were sponsoring the sport.

Ice hockey met a similar fate. Bemidji State (MN) edged Michigan-Dearborn for first place in 1980, the last of their record seven titles in the seventeen years hockey merited NAIA championship status. The next year, Augsburg (MN) won the final, 8-3, over Wisconsin-Superior, and the Auggies were back in 1982 for their third and last trophy, beating out Bemidji State, 6-3. Wisconsin-River Falls blew out Michigan-Dearborn, 12-5, for the 1983 title, and in the final year of competition, 1984, Wisconsin-Eau Claire left Michigan-Dearborn in the runner-up slot for the third time in five years. The Wolves never did take the title. The number of schools playing NAIA hockey had diminished to only 19 by 1983-84, and it was falling fast, to a predicted seven or eight in 1984-85. It was clearly time to pull the plug on ice hockey.

Wrestling spotlighted two major powers during this period. Central Oklahoma State had edged Adams State in 1979, but the Indians took their measure in 1980, only to finish second to the Oklahomans in 1981 and 1982. Curiously, the two powers both slipped in 1983, with Southern Oregon taking down Simon Fraser for the title that year.

The indoor track and field competition got off to a rocky start. Jackson State took the 1980 title, but months later the NAIA learned that the school had run an ineligible winning athlete under another's name. Confronted with the evidence and a two-year probation, Jackson State returned their winner's hardware and bolted to the NCAA.[27] The title remained vacant with Prairie View A&M (TX) in the runner-up spot. After that, Texas Southern won in 1981 and finished second the next two years to Saginaw Valley (MI). In 1982 Billy Olson of Abilene Christian (TX) set the NAIA pole vault mark with an 18'10" record that won him the outstanding performer award.

When Simon Fraser won its ninth consecutive swimming championship in 1980, their dominance sparked an ugly revolt at the convention that March. Some Americans argued that the hoped-for influx of Canadian schools had not happened after the door was opened to them in 1967, and that Simon Fraser was the only one to join. Since Lakehead University of Ontario was the first Canadian member and remained one from 1967 to 1978, this showed that by not making waves they had remained below the chauvinists' radar. The exclusionist argument held that the Canadian athletic association did not permit athletic scholarships, so SFU had joined the NAIA and attracted all the swimmers to their institution, depriving deserving Americans of their all-American status. A motion to exclude Canadian schools (the discussion also hinted ominously that Puerto Rican and Mexican colleges might be next) was amended to not exclude members in good standing (i.e., Simon Fraser). The amendment passed, 110-16. By then it was clear that the swimming coaches in the northwest, Simon Fraser's biggest rivals, opposed the motion and that it was widely seen as nonsense.[28] When the vote to exclude Canadians finally took place, it was soundly defeated, 90-35.

Ironically, Drury College (MO), the runner up to SFU in 1980, splashed to the next two championships before the Canadians rebounded to win in 1983. Drury, it turned out, launched its own dynasty, taking first or second every year from 1980 to 1994. There is no record of any motion to exclude schools from Missouri from the championship meets.

In 1980, baseball increased the number of participants from eight to ten, one from each area plus the top-ranked remaining team and the host institution. Grand Canyon College (AZ) seemed to like the new format and took three straight baseball titles from 1980 to 1982. The first year they fashioned a dramatic 10-inning 5-4 win over Lewis (IL), easing some of the loss they had felt the previous year when they had not been permitted to participate in the nationals despite winning their area title. The next year the Antelopes returned with their bats on fire, averaging 10 runs per game and clobbering Winthrop (SC), 11-4, in the final game. Then, in 1982, Grand Canyon matched Lewis's three-consecutive titles (1974-6) with a 10-6 win over Lewis-Clark State (ID), with slugging catcher Pete Bethea winning MVP honors for the second straight year. In 1983 top-ranked Lewis-Clark defeated Lubbock Christian, 18-17 in ten innings, but the host Chaps edged the Idaho team, 4-3, to force a final game, which they won, 12-9, for the title in front of an enthusiastic home crowd.

The outdoor track and field competition found Mississippi Valley State taking top honors in 1980 and 1981. The following year Abilene Christian took first, but coming up fast was Azusa Pacific (CA), which finished second. The next year, the Cougars moved up to first place, where they remained through 1989, establishing overwhelming dominance in the sport. Nigerian sprinter Innocent Egbunike won the first of three consecutive awards as top meet performer with wins in the 100 and 200 meter dashes.

Perennial tennis power Redlands copped top honors in 1980, then slipped to second place behind Southwest Texas State the next two years. Then Belhaven (MS) nipped Lander (SC) by a point to take first place in 1983, beginning a stretch of solid teams for the South Carolina school.

Sam Houston State captured its third and fourth straight golf titles in 1980 and 1981, each year beating out Texas Wesleyan for first place. In 1982 and 1983, Wesleyan wound up in the runner-up spot again, trailing Elon (NC) the first year and Cameron (OK) the second. Over the years, Texas Wesleyan has won six titles and finished second seven times, making them probably the most impressively consistent golf program.

The all-sports award for NAIA men went to Adams State in both 1980 and 1981, giving the Colorado school three titles in four years, then to Saginaw Valley (MI) in 1982 and Simon Fraser in 1983.

❖

With women emerging from the shadows in the fall of 1980, cross-country became the first sport to crown a distaff champion. Wendy Burman led Wisconsin-Parkside to first place at that first meet, held in Salina, Kansas. In 1981, Mary Jaqua took first place and led the Adams State Indians to first place as the meet moved to Kenosha, Wisconsin, for the rest of the decade. Staying close to home, Kate Webb led Marquette (WI) to the title in 1982, as the string of first place finishers determining the winning team remained intact.

The other fall sport for women at that point was volleyball, abandoned by the men in 1979. The first championship went to Azusa Pacific (CA), paced by tournament MVP Stephanie Alphenia. Then in 1982 Hawaii-Hilo began a four-year run at the top, led in 1982 and 1983 by Edie Manzano as the islanders beat Southwestern (TX) and Texas Wesleyan for the trophy.

Basketball headlined the winter sports program for women. The first three years eight teams convened at Kemper Arena and played during the final three days of the men's tournament. In 1984, the tournament opened up to 16 teams and moved to Cedar Rapids, Iowa, before returning to Kansas City in 1986. In 1981, seventh-seeded Kentucky State survived by one point in the opening round, then beat Azusa Pacific in the semifinals and knocked off top-seed Texas Southern, 73-67, for the title. The next year top-ranked Southwestern Oklahoma cut through the competition like butter, winning by 34, 14, and 35 points (over Missouri Southern) to take home the championship. In 1983 the defending champions again rolled to the title, eliminating their last challenger, Alabama-Huntsville, 80-68, in the final game behind repeating MVP Kelli Litsch.

The swimming results looked suspiciously similar to the men's, as Simon Fraser swam to first place handily in both 1981 and 1982 behind star Judy Baker's performances. In 1983, however, Wisconsin-Eau Claire won as Americans showed they were not without the means of beating their northern neighbors.

Indoor track and field championships were held in Kansas City from 1981 until 1994. In the first meet, Jackson State (MS) steamrollered the opposition, led by Radious Jacobs. The next two years saw Texas Southern beat out Prairie View A&M each time, though Saginaw Valley distance runner Cathy Schmidt was named outstanding performer both years.

The fourth winter sport for women, gymnastics, held its championships in Georgia the first two years, and Georgia College seized the home-mat advantage and took the titles, over Gustavus Adolphus in 1981 and Southern Colorado in 1982. The meet moved to Colorado in 1983, but William and Mary (VA) proved that gymnasts could win on the road, edging Centenary (Louisiana) for first place.

In the spring, young women's hearts turned to thoughts of softball, and in 1981 fourteen teams assembled in Conroe, Texas, where Sam Houston State and Emporia State (KS) each defeated the other, 1-0, to set up a final game. Sam Houston State won the rubber match, as pitching dominated the series, by another 1-0 score. In 1982 sixteen teams took part in Kearney, Nebraska, and Missouri Western, led by Cheri Kempf, beat St. Francis (IL) in the final game, 5-0. Emporia State finally got its title in 1983, blowing out host Kearney State, 9-2, to cap a great season.

Tennis provided a second spring sport for women, and for the first fourteen years of the tournament, it was held in Overland Park, Kansas, just outside Kansas City. In 1981, the sport named two winners, as Grand Canyon and Guilford (NC) tied for the top spot. The next season, Westmont stormed in from California and beat out Guilford for the title, and in 1983 Charleston (SC) took home bragging rights with a win over Centenary (LA).

Outdoor track and field found one of the NAIA's most impressive dynasties get off to a slow start. In 1981, Prairie View A&M finished second to Texas Southern, but they would not let that happen again, reeling off nine straight championships for the rest of the decade as outstanding coach Barbara Jacket guided her team to total dominance.

Kearney State won the first women's all-sports award for 1980-81. The next year Adams State's women brought home the trophy following two straight years of the school's men doing so. In 1983, Wisconsin-Eau Claire had the most successful program in the women's division. More important, the NAIA's women's championships had been underway for three years and had been a rousing success.

The History of the NAIA

A Photo Essay

Featuring Some of the People that Have Made the History of the NAIA Come to Life

A. O. Duer, NAIB/NAIA Executive Secretary, 1949-1975

A. O. Duer, NAIB and NAIA Executive Secretary 1949-75 and John McLendon, Men's Basketball Coach of the NAIA National Champions 1957-59

Emil S. Liston, NAIA Executive Secretary 1940-49 and Baker College Athletic Director

Sheila Stearns, President, Western Montana College; first woman to chair the COP, 1996

Harry Fritz, NAIA Executive Director
1975-86

Harry Statham, McKendree College
Basketball Coach and All-Time Win Leader
at the four-year intercollegiate level

James Chasteen, NAIA President and CEO
1991-96

Jefferson D. Ferris, NAIA Executive Director
1986-90

Steve Baker, NAIA President and CEO 1997-present

Wally Schwartz, Vice President for Administration, 1968-95

NAIA Championship Sponsor Hallmark Cards

Dick Barnett, three-time basketball All-American at Tennessee State, led team to three straight national titles, 1957-59

Municipal Auditorium, home of the NAIA Men's Basketball Championship starting in 1937

Leroy T. Walker, NAIA President 1980, the first African-American to hold the post; longtime football and basketball coach at North Carolina Central

Morton C. Cunningham, President, Fort Hays State; NAIA President, 1967-68; first college president on NEC

The traditional NAIA honorary coach drawing for the participating teams

From left to right: Harry Fritz, NAIA Executive Director 1975-86; Phyllis Holmes, NAIA President 1988-89; Bob "Ish" Smith, President of the United States Baseball Federation and President of the NAIA Baseball Coaches Association (will later become President of the International Baseball Federation); John Strahl, NAIA President 1977-78; and Carroll Land, NAIA President 1981-82 (and author of the History of the National Association of Intercollegiate Athletics)

Eddie Robinson, legendary Grambling football coach, 1941-97; NAIA President 1971-72

Francis Hoover, author of Indiana University dissertation, the first NAIA history up to 1958

John McLendon and his Tennessee State team, which won the National Championship from 1957-59

John Visser, Emporia State President; NAIA President, 1984-85

David Olson, longtime Pacific Lutheran A.D., NEC leader from 1978 into the mid-1990s

John McLendon, coach of Tennessee State's 1957-59 national champs in basketball, congratulates Cameron University

Miriam Walker-Samuels, Claflin women's basketball star, lost in finals in 1988 and 1989, despite scoring 48 and 49 points, respectively

Travis Grant, Kentucky State basketball star, set tournament basketball record with 60 points against Minot State in 1972

Phyllis Holmes, Greenville College; first woman NAIA President, 1988-89

Morris Gross, coached San Diego State's 1941 national basketball champions

Phil Hutcheson, 4.0 student, broke all-time career scoring record for men's basketball in 1990 at David Lipscomb

The 1967 National Championship Team, Saint Benedict's College (KS)

10

The Great Proxy Battle
1983-1986

In the early 1980s, both President LeRoy Walker and Executive Director Harry Fritz signaled growing discontent with the governing structure of the NAIA. When the demand for change reached flash point, the new look turned out to be very different than either had envisaged—or wanted.

Fritz kicked off the concerted push for change on June 21, 1983, when he sent a memo to the Executive Committee proposing creation of a "Task Force on NAIA Governance." Citing record "frustration and ineffectiveness" at the March meeting and rampant apathy induced by a lack of meaningful opportunities for leadership within the NAIA, the executive director listed four possible changes for such a task force to consider. First, the annual meeting, where decisions were subject to a mail vote by all members, could become an annual "convention" with final decision-making authority. Second, a much more broad-based executive board, modeled on similar bodies in organizations like the NCAA, could bring legislation to the convention and function as the key decision-making organ of the association. Fritz envisioned 40-60 members, including district chairs and representatives from coaches associations, institutional presidents, and various committees. Third, he suggested cutting back the size and role of the Executive Committee and turning it into an administrative committee overseeing the NAIA's daily operations and implementing decisions of the board and convention. Finally, he suggested an overhaul of the district organization of the association, calling it both the NAIA's strength and weakness.[1]

Following the 1984 meeting, Fritz circulated his ideas to the general membership with an article in The NAIA News. In that article, he also challenged readers who believed in the NAIA's mission to become missionaries preaching the gospel of integrating athletics with institutions' educational purpose. He proudly cited higher education organizations that had praised the NAIA as a model of such integration, citing the 24-hour rule, the 12-hour rule for in-season competition, and the "continuing progress" rule. The 1984 convention had reaffirmed the association's commitment to high academic standards. Therein lay a problem. Fritz on many occasions observed that most institutions leaving the NAIA did so because they felt the association's rules were too stringent for them. The membership, he noted, created those rules, not the national staff or the Executive Committee or the Eligibility Committee. Therefore, the members needed to support them openly and enthusiastically and encourage the disaffected not to bolt from the organization.[2]

NAIA presidents provided one solid base of support for those high standards. In 1983, the temporary Presidents' Committee on Academic Qualifications and Admissions Standards had been made a standing committee. All five of its recommendations to the 1984 meeting had been approved, including requiring faculty athletic representatives to be regular, non-athletics-connected faculty members appointed by the president, not the athletic director. The Presidents Advisory Committee wanted more, suggesting changes in the governing structure to increase the role of institutional presidents in running the NAIA.[3] This desire suggested a different direction for governmental reforms than Fritz had envisioned and precipitated two years of contentious debate on the NAIA's future.

In the fall of 1984, the Presidents' Committee on Academic Qualifications and Admissions Standards showed that it planned to hold the line against those who might want to weaken the NAIA's academic standards. Responding to a request from the NAIA Football Coaches Association, they rejected eliminating the 16-week residency requirement for transfers, affirmed the policy of requiring eligibility evaluation each term, and disallowed the use of correspondence or extension courses to fulfill the "normal progress" requirement. They did, however, recommend allowing a student to take only nine hours in his first term of attendance, though the 24-hours per year requirement would still be in effect.[4]

That same fall, Fritz's task force finally met and drew up a proposed new governing structure for the NAIA. Since it followed the general suggestions Fritz had made the year before, he expressed enthusiasm for the new approach. The NAIA News devoted six full pages to spelling out the details of the proposal, including full-page diagrams of the new structure. Four main bodies would share power: a Delegate Assembly that would vote on proposed changes in the Constitution and by-laws, with each institution having one vote; a large NAIA Council with responsibility for all sports programming (what Fritz had called an executive board); a transformation of the Executive Committee into an Executive Board with revised responsibilities; and a shift from the Presidents Advisory Committee to a Council of Presidents (COP). Committees would be assigned to the appropriate body among those four. Curiously, the executive director is nowhere to be found on the elaborate organizational chart, though his position was clearly expected to continue.[5]

The proposal as diagrammed in *The NAIA News* must have confused readers. It appeared that the four key bodies were more or less on a par, with no coherent lines of authority. Members' comments and general confusion raised enough red flags that when the Executive Committee convened at the March 1985 convention, they voted 7-2 to withdraw the proposal from consideration at that time. At that gathering, Arleigh Dodson of the Eligibility Committee expressed his enthusiasm for the current arrangement, arguing that he knew where the power lay (with the Executive Committee) and felt comfortable approaching that body with an idea, or (if necessary) taking it right to the convention floor. He felt that if the presidents, district chairs, faculty athletic representatives, athletic directors, and other groups feeling left out would just recognize how readily they could share in the power, they would be content as well. There seemed to be a general sense that members didn't grasp the process, didn't know where to direct questions about governance, and as a result were frustrated. In the end, the Executive Committee (or NEC, for National Executive Committee, as it was coming to be known) requested that the task force not be reconvened until after the summer meeting to allow time for committee members to further study the proposal and the reaction to it.[6]

More revealing, the Executive Committee minutes exposed a seriously negative attitude toward the presidents. As NEC members saw it, the CEOs developed sloppy proposals longer on philosophy than practical considerations, didn't use their advisors (like district chairs) effectively, and didn't appreciate the ability and hard work of the people working down in the trenches, like the athletic directors. Carroll Land contended that an increased presidential role would be a detriment to the NAIA, for a great strength of the organization lay in it being, essentially, an athletic directors' body. Presidents should not be doing things like limiting the length of teams' seasons; if they wanted to do that, they should exercise their authority on their own campuses and dialogue with the athletic department, not try to impose uniform national standards on widely diverse schools. Land did concede that some of the problems faced by the NEC in 1985 stemmed from ineffective operating policies established a few years earlier, when he had been in charge. But it was clear that the athletic directors on the Executive Committee did not want their power taken over by the presidents.[7]

Jeff Farris, part of the Presidents Advisory Committee, recalled that when he met with the NEC at the convention, they arrived late to the meeting, left early, and essentially said come to "our" convention anytime. However flawed the task force proposal may have been, to the presidents the clear message of its withdrawal was that the Executive Committee did not want to share their power with anyone else. But the presidents were no longer willing to acquiesce in the NEC's dominance.

In the fall of 1984, a number of dissatisfied PAC members from the Arkansas and Oklahoma area had met at Fort Smith to reinforce each other's frustrations. As an example of the sort of issue that provoked presidents to action, consider the case of the University of Central Arkansas, Farris's school. In 1981, UCA had lost a first round Division I football playoff game at home to Cameron (OK), 48-27. Immediately after the game, Cameron was disqualified for using several ineligible players. To Farris and UCA fans, it seemed obvious that UCA should play the other quarterfinal winner in the area, Pittsburg State, in the semi-finals. Instead, Pittsburg State drew a bye and went directly to finals, where they fell to Elon, 3-0. Farris was unable to get any satisfaction from the NAIA office as to why this bizarre decision had been made, and found himself unable to answer the questions of angry fans. That incident triggered Farris's interest in re-evaluating the NAIA's leadership. The following spring, Texas schools joined the insurrection in a Dallas meeting.[8] The group discussed their concerns further and concluded that they needed to organize their fellow presidents to more effectively pursue power.

Three different forces vied for increased clout within the NAIA: Fritz, the NEC, and the PAC. The Executive Committee was growing increasingly exasperated that they were unable to get a coherent, audited budget out of Fritz, and at the spring 1985 meeting they voted 9-0 to review the status of his contract before the end of their summer meeting. In May, Fritz, feeling the heat, forwarded copies of his responses to earlier NEC requests for lists of his accomplishments during his tenure, objectives for the NAIA, and a self-assessment. The NEC's view of Fritz had been declining for several years, in large part because of a decline in his performance as Executive Director, which may have resulted from extenuating circumstances in his personal life.

The feeling of antipathy was mutual. Fritz seized the opportunity in his report to blister the NEC for its shortcomings. Members were too beholden to local and/or denominational interests to make a strong commitment to the well being of the NAIA as a whole. Much of the problem was not the fault of the committee, for it served too many functions for a small group of ten to handle effectively: administrative committee, executive board, and council, and because so many pressing items reached it, it became a bottleneck for NAIA action. Fritz thus supported the aborted governance change, which he had hoped would eliminate the bottleneck. Worse, aside from adding the women's program and some fundraising efforts from LeRoy Walker, "there has been very little substantial leadership from within the Committee." It should take a much more active role in proposing and pushing legislation at the annual meetings. The very nature of the committee's selecting its own members until 1983 bred popular distrust of the NEC as a powerful inner circle closed off to most members. Fritz decried the athletic director mentality Carroll Land had praised, calling it narrow and generally reflective of the parochialism of smaller institutions without a grasp of the big picture. Finally, he called on the NEC members to be more active spokesmen for the national organization. Overall, his critique in the guise of self-assessment reflected a common frustration of administrators trying to manage departments that had little knowledge of or interest in the organization's overall operation.[9]

When the NEC held its summer meeting in July 1985, Farris attended and sought to reduce the level of tension. He shared the story of the Fort Smith meeting and the CEOs' realization that they knew little about how the NAIA operated. They had come to the spring 1985 convention hoping to learn about and discuss the proposed governance change, and they had been frustrated when the topic did not come up. Executive Committee members pointed out that they had gotten the plan in the mail from the task force like everyone else, and that they had tabled the proposal in order to better understand it, an explanation that seemed to mollify Farris. He observed that the presidents needed the NAIA and the NAIA needed the presidents and implied that they should all work together, while recognizing that it was the president who oversaw all the interests of a university and thus grasped the big picture at that level better than, say, an athletic director. Bill Jordan questioned whether CEOs really did grasp the big picture and suggested giving more leeway to the athletic directors to act for the good of the institution and its program.

Farris expressed frustration about the presidents' lack of involvement. The Presidents Advisory Committee was simply advisory, and college presidents weren't used to having their desires disregarded, as their advice often was. Ironically, some of the athletic directors at the meeting may have put ideas in Farris's head. With one vote per institution at the national convention, the CEOs could have that vote if they wanted it—they appointed the delegates and could appoint themselves rather than their athletic directors, as was normally done. The CEOs also forwarded nominations for the NEC itself—if they wished, they could nominate only presidents to the committee.

Farris admitted that he did not speak for all the presidents—there was no consensus among them—but for the group of 25 to 30 who had met in Dallas. They wanted the NAIA to enhance the role of the presidents in order to improve the association, and said that if the NEC did come forth with a restructuring proposal, it might solve the problem without any conflict. He concluded, "The CEOs must not try to re-work the NAIA."[10] That forbearance did not last long.

The NEC recognized that some restructuring had to take place and formed a nine-member ad hoc committee on governance to develop a new proposal with a target date of action at the 1987 convention. They anticipated consulting with the Presidents' Advisory Committee to get their input, and though they got to work immediately, they clearly underestimated the urgency of their task. President David Olson hoped to have a preliminary proposal to begin circulating among the membership by December 15, 1985, but the possibility of taking a year-and-a-half to thoroughly analyze and refine such a plan turned out to be an illusion.

The NEC met again in mid-September, perhaps recognizing the validity of Fritz's description of them as a bottleneck. They agreed to add a third annual meeting, probably in late fall, to their regular March and summer get-togethers. At the start of their September gathering, the committee met in executive session to discuss Fritz's contract. Olson explained that the legal ramifications of sacking Fritz were still under study and that they might be on shaky ground doing so. Back on the record, they approved a motion to conduct a thorough annual evaluation of the executive director, and made it seem less personal by instructing him to do the same for his staff over the academic year just beginning. Fritz's evaluation was to be completed no later than March 1, in advance of the annual convention. In what appears to be an attempt to defuse some of the tension between Fritz and the NEC, the group unanimously voted to extend his contract a year to July 31, 1987. Nevertheless, NEC meetings with Fritz present were strained, and when John Visser wound up his presidency in March 1985 to be replaced by Olson, relations became even frostier. Visser had been far more supportive of Fritz than was Olson.[11]

The Executive Committee also reached out to the presidents. Roger Webb of Northeastern Oklahoma brought some presidential concerns to the meeting: criteria for NAIA membership, season length and number of contests, district inconsistencies toward infractions, failure to communicate with the CEOs, and the need for change in the NAIA's structure. The NEC responded immediately by changing the Presidents Advisory Committee to the Council of Presidents and making its chair an ex-officio member of the executive committee. The COP's functions were to include proposing changes to the NAIA constitution and by-laws, advising the NEC, reviewing NAIA academic and admissions standards, reviewing NAIA sports programs, including number of contests and length of sports seasons and financial aid. It must have appeared to the NEC that they had responded positively to the presidents' concerns and that the tension between the bodies would diminish with the executive committee still in control.[12]

That hope began unraveling almost immediately. Insurrectionist presidents met at the Holiday Inn in Oklahoma City. There, Tom Feld, president of Mount Mercy College in Iowa, listened to the discussion and sketched out on a napkin a proposal for a COP takeover of the NAIA. The others read what he had written, made a few revisions, and scheduled a meeting in Kansas City on November 12 for the presidents' organization to consider it. David Olson and Roger Jenkinson attended, representing the NEC. At the meeting, Jeff Farris was elected chair of the COP, and the newly empowered group moved quickly to approve Feld's plan to affect a peaceful revolution in the NAIA. As Olson reported back to the NEC after the meeting, in essence the annual assembly would be the legislative branch, the NEC would be the administrative branch, and the COP would become the governing body. NEC power would be diminished, and Olson wondered if the COP "takeover" would demoralize athletic directors, district chairs, and others in the trenches. Further, he wondered if the COP had the time or the knowledge to run the NAIA; after all, presidents had an awful lot on their plates besides athletics and they might tire of trying to manage the association.[13] He himself was obviously not enchanted with the change, even though NAIA presidents were to continue to come from the regular executive committee rotation under the new structure.

At the same time, Olson and the NEC were trying to exercise more effective control over Harry Fritz. Olson reminded the committee members to have their evaluations of the Executive Director in by December 1, and that Fritz was supposed to have in a coherent budget by November 18. If one of the criticisms of the executive committee's rule had been that they had not exercised sufficient control over Fritz, they were moving to dispel that notion. Fritz did not satisfy their request for complete financial information, and in late January, Olson was still trying to get him to more fully respond to the NEC's demands.[14]

The COP proposals generated appropriate press coverage. *The NAIA News* led off the new year with an article explaining the new plan, whose simplicity meant there was less need for extensive analysis. The Governing Assembly (the annual meeting) stood at the top of the chart. Beneath it was the COP, which would have an Administrative Committee drawn from its members to transact business between council meetings, with the executive director advising it. The executive director and the Executive Committee fell beneath the COP and reported to it, with the various committees reporting to one of them or directly to the COP. The COP would meet twice a year, in March and September. The proposal followed logically from the NAIA's mission:

> It has long been the philosophy of the NAIA that intercollegiate athletic programs be an integral part of the total educational mission of member institutions. To maintain credibility, athletic programs must be subject to the same policies and objectives as are other institutional programs.
>
> The chief executive officer is both responsible and accountable for all educational programs. It is, therefore, appropriate that NAIA university and college presidents assume a more active posture in the administration of the national association governing intercollegiate athletic programs.

The arrangement would strengthen the position of executive director, who would be accountable to the COP. The executive committee would retain its present duties except those specifically assigned to the COP or the executive director.[15]

Tom Feld told reporters that possible restructuring to enhance the presidents' power had been considered for years, but that the turmoil in athletics had prompted the proposal. The role of the COP had been like that of the NCAA's presidents commission—advisory—and that simply wasn't good enough, as their advice was not always followed. Not only would the proposed changes give the presidents on the COP more say in NAIA affairs, but Feld hoped it would encourage chancellors and presidents throughout the membership to be more actively involved.[16] It would certainly require a whole new level of engagement on the part of the presidents; up until that time, meetings of the presidents' advisory committee had been more social than policy-driven.[17]

The presidents knew how to play hardball. They needed a two-thirds vote at the 1986 convention in March to push through their proposal, and athletic directors were hardly enthusiastic in their support. So the presidents, perhaps drawing on the NEC's comments to Farris back in September, began marshalling votes. Joe Struckle, president of Northwestern Oklahoma State, took charge of the vote count, and Farris sent letters to COP members encouraging them to contact each of the CEOs in their district and do what they could to win their votes. Farris also urged the presidents to talk with their athletic staffs and assure them that the change would not be a hostile takeover, but merely a way for the presidents to work cooperatively with those already doing yeoman work. Farris consistently repeated that the change was not a take-over, which was how many athletic directors interpreted it. The national staff also suffered from shattered morale as the winds of change whipped around them and many felt indicted by criticisms of NAIA operations. In January, Farris sent a memo to each of the staff stressing his belief that involving the presidents in the NAIA's operations would strengthen the organization and give it a better sense of direction. The future of the NAIA, he said, was very bright.[18]

Many presidents appointed themselves as their institutional delegate to the convention, as they were entitled to do. Others gathered proxies from presidents who would be unable to attend. In what was styled by some as the "great proxy battle" of 1986, the chief executives packed the convention floor with their supporters. Carroll Land denounced the ploy as undermining the democratic nature of the NAIA, saying, "if you presidents keep on with such proxy votes you'll be able to have the convention in a phone booth," to the applause of athletic directors and boos from presidents. But the presidents had planned well: the restructuring measure passed overwhelmingly, 319-55. Effective August 1, 1986, presidential rule had come to the NAIA.[19]

At the same time, the NEC, drawing on its annual review of Harry Fritz, decided to sack the Executive Director. Fritz felt he was being punished for shoddy executive committee work, which had provoked the COP takeover. He had committed no wrongs against the NAIA, but he appeared incapable of changing, and the structure of the association was definitely changing. Colleagues said that Fritz was hard working and pleasant company, often wandering around the office looking for someone to talk to. But the office was in disarray and badly needed reorganization—one president thought, "the right hand knew not what the left hand was doing." Fritz was likable, but afforded too little direction.[20] Perhaps more critical to his survival, the staff's respect for him was eroding as his personal problems affected his performance.[21]

Fritz certainly found a sense of direction when the NEC tried to fire him. When Olson told him he was being let go, he said, "I'm tough as hell. I'm going to get you."[22] He said he had a contract and would sue if it were violated, refused to vacate his office, and had to be forcibly ousted by changing the locks on his door. Maybe the tough stance served its purpose. COP chair Jeff Farris remembers finally getting Fritz to accept the changes over lunch, a task no doubt made easier when the NEC announced that Fritz would become a senior consultant to the COP on the budget, staff evaluation, assessing NAIA goals and purposes, and in helping to recruit, select, and orient his successor, along with helping to plan the upcoming golden anniversary celebration. He would be able to fulfill his contract performing his new tasks, though working from home rather than in the office.[23]

During the transition period until the naming of a new executive director, Wally Schwartz, who had been working in the office since 1968, took over as chief operating officer. By May 6, he had analyzed the NAIA budget and concluded that the association had around $160,000 in its checking account and $315,000 in accounts payable. He expressed amazement that the organization hadn't gone bankrupt years ago. Though he stated that the NAIA was financially solvent, he had many ideas of how to get its financial house in better order. Fritz had piled bills in a desk drawer and paid them off, somewhat arbitrarily, as money became available. His budget statements were merely snapshots at a given moment, as he moved funds from the NAIA and the coaches associations back and forth to keep some semblance of solvency. NEC pressure for better accounting practices had led him to the presidents for support, triggering the entire governance revolution. Finally, the Fritz era was over.[24]

The NAIA had made some of its most significant contributions to the sports world by providing athletic opportunities for students who had been prevented from taking part in intercollegiate sports, notably black and female students. The NEC recommended that graduate students gain similar opportunities, proposing in 1983 that if a student attended the same graduate school as undergraduate, up to two years of the normal four years of eligibility could be used at the higher level. Hawaii also got some benefits from NAIA membership. District 29 had been established in Maryland and Virginia in 1982, but dual membership conflicts and small membership led to the dissolution of the district in 1983, returning the association to 31 districts. Hawaii, geographically the most isolated state, applied for district status in 1984 and was denied. But the five schools—Brigham Young-Hawaii, Chaminade, Hawaii-Hilo, Hawaii Loa, and Hawaii Pacific—were named the new District 29 in 1985.

At the 1984 convention, delegates elected two members to fill vacancies on the executive committee. Women reacted indignantly when all of the eight candidates on the ballot were men, making a mockery of the association's 1980 resolution to achieve "equitable participation of women at all levels of governance." Parliamentary rules prevented floor nominations, so the women were shut out. But in response to the uproar, the convention strongly affirmed its commitment to elevating women's role and passed a resolution to provide that in alternate years all nominees would be women, thus providing an automatic mechanism to bring them to parity over the next decade.[25] To ensure that women's voices were heard and potential leaders identified, in the summer of 1985 President Olson began setting up a new Women's Sports Development Committee, assuring a formalized process to focus attention on women's issues.[26]

In 1984, the NEC discussed *The NAIA News*, which constituted a noticeable drain on association funds. Over the previous year the bi-monthly magazine had cost around $43,000 to print and mail but had generated a meager $11,000 in advertising. The committee considered the desirability of a monthly publication, theorizing that more timely magazines could eliminate much of the other informational mail that went to member institutions. The questionable cost benefit of such a move was undermined by the need to bring on another staff person to handle a monthly publication.[27] What finally happened was that the new regime in 1986 changed the format from a colorful, attractive magazine to a much less expensive, utilitarian, almost photo-free publication. Aside from lower production costs, the new look had the news advantage of appearing every two weeks, thus eliminating many of those extra mailings. Still, even though it was a news magazine, it defined news selectively. New NAIA member institutions were proudly listed each year, but departing schools went unnoticed, providing subscribers a misleadingly rosy view of the association's health.

Harry Fritz was beginning to argue for a separation of the national convention and the men's basketball tournament. Back in the NAIB days, the timing was a no-brainer, but with the vast array of sports now provided by the NAIA, there was no logical reason to combine the two events. The idea would continue to percolate, but for 1984 the NEC instituted a more minor change. Hitherto the 32-team tourney had run from Monday through Saturday, with eight games Monday and eight Tuesday cutting the field to 16 teams. After that, each team played every day until the final two faced off Saturday night. To reduce the missed class time of most of the teams, the 1984 tournament would begin on Thursday and cut the field to eight by Saturday night, take Sunday off, then play three straight days to finish on Wednesday. It would give the teams a bit of a rest, though at the expense of the conceptually tidy one-week format. The convention would convene on Sunday and wrap up on Wednesday, enabling participants to take in some of the action when not in meetings.

Part of the NAIA's ongoing effort to "do the right thing," the NEC announced its cooperation with the USOC in 1984 to conduct a drug-testing program. The random testing of wrestling, men's basketball, and men's and women's indoor track athletes would not result in disqualification but allow athletes to become acquainted with the testing program, similar to the USOC program for the Los Angeles Olympics that summer. It would also help to determine if there was a drug problem in the NAIA, which would receive only aggregate results, and assist USOC research in this increasingly serious area. In 1986, the NEC introduced a more rigorous procedure, with tests of selected athletes that could lead to disqualification. The NAIA took a very cooperative approach to meeting the drug challenge, in essence saying that if there was a drug problem, the association wanted to root it out, not cover it up.[28]

Returning to an NAIB concern of the late 1940s, Harry Fritz addressed the threat of gambling to sports integrity in 1984. The basketball gambling scandals of the early 1950s were ripe for recurrence as point spreads appeared daily in the papers and with money being billed by society as the be all and end all, it was difficult for big-time sports to avoid the temptation to make a quick buck. Fritz, as he so frequently did, contrasted big-time money-ridden sports with the more modest NAIA programs and appeared to stress at least one way in which small was indeed more beautiful than large. The NAIA likely flew beneath the radar of most gamblers, but he reemphasized the critical role the association played in developing character in its athletes to help them stay above the declining moral and ethical standards of the broader society. As he keenly felt, the coaches and athletic directors played a key part in trying to improve society.[29]

Maintaining high academic standards also fell under that mandate. Fritz pointed with pride to the American Council on Education endorsement of the NAIA's standards for eligibility and participation as a model to ensure normal academic progress. Unfortunately, athletics, like so much of life, tended to level downward. The executive director noted with some frustration that the less stringent eligibility and academic progress provisions in NCAA Divisions II and III were enticing some strong schools to leave, causing a decline in NAIA membership in 1983-84. Especially noteworthy at that point were the defections of Gustavus-Adolphus, Augsburg, Hamline, Macalester, and Bethel in Minnesota in 1983 and 1984. The presidents' committee was to look at a possible easing of standards to ease the losses, but wound up affirming NAIA distinctives instead.[30]

NAIA leaders, along with those coaching young athletes, wrestled with defining success in athletics. They frequently decried focusing too much attention on the bottom line—the won-lost record—to the exclusion of other considerations. James Vickrey, president of the University of Montevallo, Alabama, called for making explicit some of the implicit criteria for determining success in athletic programs. He argued that the educational success of participating athletes should be a big factor. Further, to what degree did those in the know, including the athletes, perceive their program to be successful beyond the simple won-lost calculus? Finally, he argued that cost-effectiveness should be considered: how many athletes participated, what was the cost of the sport, and what revenues did it generate?[31]

NAIA President David Olson of Pacific Lutheran also reflected on defining success. Wins and losses made up an inescapable component of such a definition, but he contended that focusing on that alone would surely lead to unacceptable activities such as drugs, gambling, and violation of regulations that, if unchecked, could destroy sports. A better definition of success included components such as number of participants, reaching one's potential, pleasure in participation (and being a spectator), and academic achievement. He also made a significant point by noting that the "big-time" should be where you are, arguing against the bigger-is-better syndrome whereby success was measured by television revenues, large budgets, bigger facilities, greater attendance. To escape that broader societal fixation would enable athletes to gain satisfaction and happiness from the sheer joy of fair competition.[32]

And many athletes experienced that joy at the NAIA level of competition during the 1983-1986 period, including the sheer exaltation of victory for some. Adams State totally dominated cross-country in the 1980s, and the Indians swept the 1983-85 titles by wide margins, followed each year by Wisconsin-La Crosse. In 1985 Robbie Hipwood also captured the individual title for Adams State.

Division I football featured a first-time champion in 1983 as underdog Carson-Newman College (TN) beat undefeated Mesa College (CO), 36-28, handing the Mavericks their second straight setback in the Champion Bowl. In 1984 Central Arkansas, whose top-ranked team had been ousted by Mesa the year before, made it to the final game against defending champion Carson-Newman. Playing on their home field, the Central Arkansas squad had to settle for a 19-19 tie. In 1985 they wound up with the same result: playing in Conway, Arkansas, again, Central Arkansas was forced to acquiesce in a second consecutive tie, this time 10-10 with Hillsdale (MI).

Northwestern College (IA) capped a perfect 14-0 season with a thrilling come-from-behind 25-21 win over Pacific Lutheran (WA) in the 1983 Division II football championship game held in Tacoma. Local sportswriters were impressed by the sportsmanship shown by both teams during and after the game, when the two teams prayed together at midfield. Lute coach Frosty Westering commented that "How a man plays the game shows some of his character; how he loses a game shows all of his character."[33] The game was a sparkling example of NAIA ideals put into practice. In 1984, Northwestern returned to the title match, but this time finished on the short end of a 33-22 score to Linfield College (OR). The Red Raiders tried for three straight the next year, but fell in the semifinals to Wisconsin-La Crosse in three overtimes, and the winners then beat Pacific Lutheran, 24-7, to capture their sole football title.

Simon Fraser successfully defended its soccer title in 1983, nipping Midwestern State (TX), 1-0, behind the stellar goalkeeping of All-American Jerry Vick, who did not allow a goal in the five tournament games. The next two seasons found almost identical results. In 1984, West Virginia Wesleyan edged Fresno Pacific, 3-2, in two overtimes. The same two teams matched up again in the 1985 final, and they continued to be evenly matched—this time it took Wesleyan four overtimes to eke out a 4-3 win.

The basketball competition had fans on the edge of their seats. In 1984 Fort Hays State spent a lot of time on the court, having to go to overtime to edge Chicago State, 86-84, in the semifinals, then repeating the feat in a slow-down game, grabbing a 48-46 overtime championship over Wisconsin-Stevens Point. The next season, the top-seeded Tigers successfully defended their title, as Coach Bill Morse saw his son Ron, a reserve guard, hit a shot at the buzzer to edge Wayland Baptist (TX), 82-80, again in overtime. Fort Hays apparently liked the close games—they won their quarterfinal by four points and their semifinal by a single point. In 1986, 11th-seeded David Lipscomb (TN) disdained the tight games and beat Arkansas-Monticello, 67-54, to take the title.

The swimming meets, with Simon Fraser in an extended low period, featured a heated rivalry between Drury (MO) and Central Washington. In 1984, Central Washington just barely took first place over the Panthers, but Drury returned the favor, edging the Wildcats in another cat-fight. In 1986, Central Washington bounced back to nip Drury again, with Stan Vela sparking his team with a second straight outstanding swimmer award.

Indoor track and field also highlighted a few strong teams. In 1984, Texas Southern beat out Wayland Baptist for top honors, but John Creer's Baptists won in 1985 over Texas Southern and hung on to first place through 1989, decisively trouncing runner-up Adams State in 1986.

Wrestling lacked even a two-team struggle for the top spot. Central State (OK) wrapped up three consecutive crowns, beating out runners-up Jamestown (ND), Southern Colorado, and Southern Oregon, the latter the only one to come close.

Lewis-Clark State, hosting the baseball tournament in Idaho, finally kicked the second-place habit of 1982 and 1983 and slugged their way up through the losers' bracket to capture the championship with a convincing 15-2 thrashing of Azusa Pacific in the rain. The next year the Warriors lost one game, but fought back in the final from a 5-0 deficit to whip Dallas Baptist, 10-6, and delight the home crowd. In 1986, Lewis-Clark came within an eyelash of winning three straight, but Grand Canyon nabbed their fourth title in seven years, beating Lewis-Clark 12-3 in an early game, then nipping the Warriors, 6-5 in 10 innings, to return the championship to Arizona. That year, the NAIA waived its no-Sunday strictures and allowed Lewis-Clark to schedule Sunday afternoon games for teams that had not declared their opposition to that practice.

The track and field story, as was the case throughout the decade, revolved around Azusa Pacific and its Nigerian connection. Innocent Egbunike was saluted as top athlete three years in a row through 1985 and wound up with seven sprint titles. In 1986 Christian Okoye took top honors and wound up his career with six titles in discus, hammer throw, and shot put. Trailing APU in the rankings were Saginaw State in 1984 and perennial indoor champion Wayland Baptist in 1985 and 1986.

Profile: Terry Franson
From 1982 through 1991, Azusa Pacific's track and field coach Terry Franson was honored as the NAIA's top coach in his field. When Nigeria's Innocent Egbunike wanted to come to a Christian university in the United States, APU won out. Egbunike's success as a sprinter won him top national meet honors in 1983-85 and opened the Nigerian connection that brought in Christian Okoye, the award-winner in 1986 and subsequent star running back for Kansas City. Franson consistently had two or three Nigerians on his teams as they won national titles nine out of ten years, with a narrow loss to Oklahoma Baptist in 1990 the only blemish on that record. To Franson, that was his finest hour, as three key athletes were released for disciplinary reasons just before the meet. That action represented a victory for integrity and earns Franson credit for exemplifying the spirit of the NAIA.

In 1984, the only tie for first place in tennis tournament history occurred as Atlantic Christian (NC) and Southwest Baptist (MO) shared the championship. The next year, Lander (SC) won its first title, followed in 1986 by Flagler (FL), which narrowly prevented a Lander repeat behind the stellar play of Tobias Svantesson.

A new power emerged in golf competition. Following a victory for Limestone (SC) in 1984, Huntingdon (AL) captured the crown in 1985 and 1986 on their way to four straight championships and a long, illustrious run as an NAIA golf power.

The all-sports titles, logically enough, went to some of the schools that had racked up single-sport championships. Saginaw Valley (MI) took first place back from Simon Fraser in 1984, and then gave way to Wayland Baptist in 1985. In 1986, long-time NAIA sports power Adams State reclaimed the honor it had last won in 1981.

❖

Women were carving out a place for themselves in the NAIA sports world alongside the men. In cross-country, Cindy Grant led Simon Fraser to a first-place finish in 1983, with Marquette (WI) runners-up. In 1984, paced by first-place finisher Katie Somers, Wisconsin-Eau Claire held off Portland (OR) to finish on top. In 1985, Portland moved up to the top spot, leaving Eau Claire in the dust. For the first time in the six years of competition, the top individual runner came from a school other than the winning team: Val Hilden of Pacific Lutheran.

Hawaii-Hilo annexed its third and fourth consecutive volleyball titles in 1983 and 1984 with Alofa Tagotaese nailing down MVP honors the first year for Sharon Peterson's Lady Vulcans. In 1985, two California teams squared off for the title, with St. Mary's College sweeping Biola for the championship.

In 1984, women began competing for a national soccer championship and St. Mary's brought home that title as well, blitzing Cardinal Newman (MO), 4-0. The next year, the finals were slated for Tacoma, but the weather was so bad that the game was moved indoors, where the women competed six on a side. Westmont (CA) thus eliminated Puget Sound's advantage in rainy-play experience and took the top spot with a 4-2 victory.

In women's basketball, Southwestern Oklahoma had moved from a 7-17 record in 1980-81 to an undefeated team and a national championship the next year, with new coach John Loftin recruiting and coaching exceptionally well. He brought in Kelli Litsch from a tiny school with only seven kids in her graduating class and she was the key to that first big season. The Lady Bulldogs repeated in 1983, and then fell in the quarterfinals of the expanded tournament in 1984, losing to eventual champion North Carolina-Asheville, 57-54. Mirroring the men's tournament, though playing in Cedar Rapids, Iowa, UNCA needed an overtime period to knock out Portland (OR), 72-70, to snare the title. Litsch and her Bulldogs were back with a vengeance in 1985, sweeping through the competition till they just pulled out a cliffhanger, 55-54, over Saginaw Valley in the final on an 18-foot jumper by Litsch, naturally. Litsch wound up her career with three national championships in four years, three tournament MVP awards, four first-team All-America selections, and two Academic All-American awards with a near 4.0 grade point average. Her graduation allowed the rest of the competition to catch up, and in 1986 Francis Marion (SC) took home the title with a 75-65 win over Wayland Baptist.

From an association viewpoint, the 1984 and 1985 tournaments were a financial disaster, losing around $80,000 each year paying the expenses of the expanded 16-team field in Cedar Rapids. The tourney moved back to Kansas City in 1986, but schools were going to have to bear a share of the costs of coming to the big show. This struck outspoken executive committee member Phyllis Holmes as a betrayal of the commitment to women's basketball, but also helps explain why it took many years before the women's numbers expanded to match the men's thirty-two teams.[34]

Three different indoor track and field powers triumphed at the indoor meets in Kansas City. In 1984, Prairie View A&M ousted defending champion Texas Southern, then finished second in 1985 and 1986 as Adams State and Wayland Baptist took home first-place honors.

Swimming honors were also passed around, with Wisconsin-Green Bay handily beating their state rivals from Eau Claire in 1984. The northwest fought it out in 1985 as Simon Fraser narrowly edged Central Washington, only to have their rivals move up to number one the following year with a solid win over Pacific Lutheran.

In gymnastics, Centenary (LA) narrowly edged Winona State (MN) in 1984, with Margot Todd Evans their big star. Winona turned the tables in 1985 and dropped Centenary to second place; Winona's Jean Schuler won the outstanding gymnast award. In 1985, Wisconsin-Oshkosh edged Minot State (ND) to become a first-time winner.

Top-seeded Emporia State (KS) successfully defended their softball title in 1984, winning a dramatic final game against Quincy, which had come up through the losers' bracket. In the final game, Quincy pitcher Amy Miller threw a no-hitter for seven innings, but her teammates failed to support her effort, and Emporia pushed across a run on two hits in the eighth to win, 1-0. Hornet ace Rhonda Clarke had only allowed one hit herself. Quincy came back in 1985 to beat a different Kansas team, Washburn, 4-2, in the championship game. In 1986, St. Mary's (TX), beaten 1-0 by Oklahoma City in an earlier game, gained revenge and a championship by beating the Oklahomans, 2-1, in the title game.

Tennis winners began with Arkansas-Little Rock, who beat out Texas-Permian Basin to win the 1984 title, then knocked off North Florida the next year to successfully defend their crown. North Florida moved up a notch in 1986 by taking their only tennis title.

Outdoor track and field continued to be dominated by Barbara Jacket's Prairie View A&M squad, which won its third, fourth, and fifth consecutive national championships.

The well-balanced Panther team included Deirdre Jackson, named outstanding performer at the 1985 meet, and LaVonda Luckett, who won the first of four consecutive 400-meter hurdle titles in 1984.

The award for the best overall program, the all-sports award went to Wisconsin-Milwaukee in both 1984 and 1985, even though the school's well-balanced program did not win a single championship in those two years. In 1986, Wayland Baptist (TX), with a title in indoor track and field and seconds in basketball and outdoor track and field, compiled the nation's top record.

11

The COP Takes Charge
1986-1990

The transition from the Harry Fritz era to the next phase in NAIA history did not take place without a degree of awkwardness. Concerned that Fritz might continue to interfere in the day-to-day operations of the NAIA staff, James Houdeshell of the NEC warned COP President Jeff Farris that Fritz's loosely defined responsibilities could make life difficult for the staff in the national office. Houdeshell hoped that Fritz would not be in the office causing trouble as Wally Schwartz and his co-workers tried to keep the ship afloat during the interregnum.

Farris responded that the NAIA was going to have to retain Fritz on the payroll until the end of July 1987, but that he was being kept from meddling in ongoing affairs. Reassuring the concerned Houdeshell, Farris assured him that Fritz would be working out of his home and had been asked to stay out of the office as much as possible. While he did come by occasionally, the "staff is getting some good things done."[1] Since the NAIA's finances were in a shambles, throwing away Fritz's $65,000 salary, and getting nothing in return, hardly seemed prudent. His assignment was to advise the COP, including reviewing personnel policies and developing a personnel manual, plus working up a list of potential contributors to enhance NAIA fundraising, a perennial concern.

The "reassignment" of Fritz had been announced in a press release on April 4. A follow-up statement on June 10 quoted Jefferson Farris, the chair of the COP who had become the de facto head of the association while the search for a new executive director proceeded. Even though the COP would not officially take over from the National Executive Committee until August 1, in the absence of an official executive director (Wally Schwartz was running the office on an interim basis), Farris emerged as the most audible voice of the NAIA. "Our immediate goals," he said, "are to establish an operating budget that reflects the sports program we want to run, within our means, and to select a successor to Harry Fritz as executive director."[2]

On July 6, the *Kansas City Star* editorialized its concern that the NAIA was "making noises about moving elsewhere." Calling on corporate support for the association, the paper noted that ESPN planned to televise the 50th anniversary tournament in the spring of 1987 if enough corporate sponsorships could be mustered. The NCAA also had its headquarters in the metropolitan area, but the *Star* saluted the NAIA as supporting sport for sport's sake, repeating the NAIA mantra that big-time sports had gotten out of hand at many institutions and that the small college association's team members were working toward academic degrees, not professional careers. The strong endorsement must have been heartening to the troubled NAIA.

The COP moved swiftly to deal with the drug problem that had become a national scourge and had not skipped over the NAIA. On July 11, the COP Administrative Committee formulated a new policy on substance abuse to be approved by the full COP and then the NEC. To be fully implemented by January 1, 1988, the new policy stressed education over punishment and allowed considerable institutional flexibility. It required each member school to develop a philosophy statement on substance abuse, including its educational and screening program.[3] Given the association's desire to maintain a higher moral level than its NCAA rival, the step was necessary if hardly the strongest imaginable.

When the COP convened in Kansas City on July 14, budgetary issues topped their agenda. Wally Schwartz presented a solid, thoughtful assessment of NAIA operations, including an insightful analysis of association finances that provided a firm basis for discussion and action. Leonard Campbell and Tom Feld, two members of the COP's Administrative Committee, presented a preliminary budget proposal based on Schwartz's work, estimating a balance of about $125,000 with which to start the new year on August 1. The group discussed at length a proposal to begin charging a registration fee for the national convention, a change that might produce an additional $30,000 in revenue each year. The practice of paying for meals at NAIA events and meetings would be eliminated, and though the numbers to generate a firm budget for 1986-87 still needed to be generated, the COP agreed that the 1987-88 budget must be a balanced one. A key part of a balanced budget would be a major overhaul of the association's dues structure, as the assembled presidents agreed that dues should pay for the NAIA's operation and that events should be self-supporting. One implication of the latter point was that the women's basketball tournament, which had been a big money loser, would be subsidized to a maximum of $30,000.

The presidents also set the wheels in motion for several other policy adjustments that would unfold over the next few years. Two major issues were higher academic standards, for which a new committee would be established, and limitations on numbers of games and scholarships, for which another committee would be set up. After approving the proposed drug policy and sending it to the NEC, the COP discussed the question of advertising or sponsorship by companies producing or selling tobacco or alcoholic products, but efforts to establish more restrictive policies failed. Finally, the touchy issue of exactly how the new governance structure was going to work elicited much discussion, especially the nature of the new relationship and functions of the COP and the NEC. It would take some time to iron out such details.[4] Farris sent out an enthusiastic summary of the meeting to COP members, especially informative for those who had not been in attendance. Terming the meeting "a big success," he noted the areas of concern to be addressed quickly and expressed optimism that his colleagues would catch the spirit of progress that those attending had experienced.[5]

With Fritz out and Wally Schwartz minding the store, the COP needed to complete the search for a new executive director, a task previously within the NEC's purview. Most of the Administrative Committee appears to have served as a search committee: Chairman Leonard Campbell (Southwest Oklahoma State), Tom Feld (Mt. Mercy College), Joe Struckle (Northwest Oklahoma State), Fred Young (Elon), and John Tomlinson (Mesa State). They did not have far to look. None of them wanted to take the job, but the chair of the COP, Jeff Farris of the University of Central Arkansas, was open to being persuaded. He had spent thirteen years leading UCA and had just completed a major strategic plan at the school, leaving him at 60 years of age not eager to start a new phase of the university's life. It seemed to be a natural move to take Farris, who had been the chair and key spokesman for the COP since its inception in 1985, and make him the executive director.[6] Though other candidates were considered, the other members of the Administrative Committee knew him well and felt they could work effectively with him. Other NAIA constituencies also strongly supported the calming, irenic Southern gentleman, seeing him as a figure who could pull people together. By the end of September, the virtually unanimous decision had been formalized.[7]

The new executive director had come up through the ranks. He had been involved with the NAIA as a player (for Arkansas State Teachers College in the 1946 national tournament), coach, faculty member, and university president at his alma mater, which had become the University of Central Arkansas, giving him insight into various key NAIA constituencies. Though perhaps a bit autocratic, he was a good administrator, a trait the reeling NAIA needed desperately. He had reached an age where he did not really need the job, enabling him to do what he thought was right without worrying about his long-term future. He liked the job, liked the people he was working with, and they reciprocated; Bill Patterson, who joined him from UCA to take charge of fundraising for the association in 1987, characterized him aptly as "one of the world's good people."[8] Wally Schwartz figured that he probably had the best sense of humor of any of the executive directors with whom he worked.[9]

Even before Farris formally took office, the COP announced two developments in publicity. The first, alluded to in the *Kansas City Star* editorial, was the signing of a deal with ESPN to televise the 50th anniversary men's basketball finals. The NAIA had to round up $250,000 in advertising to make it happen, but the boon to NAIA visibility made that work a labor of love, and the NAIA staff, working hand in hand with the Kansas City Area Chamber of Commerce, hustled that support before Farris came on board. After years of futilely chasing television coverage, this development seemed to augur only good for the future. Announcer Dick Vitale provided commentary and did a first-rate job learning the players and the ins and outs of the game.[10]

The experiment evidently succeeded, for in late 1987 the NAIA announced with great excitement the signing of a five-year deal with ESPN to televise the men's finals. Television, however, is a capricious mistress. For the 1989 championship, the post-1983 Thursday-to-Wednesday format was switched at ESPN's behest to a Tuesday through Monday schedule, with the championship game on Monday evening, where it better suited television's needs. In the transition, the consolation game for third place, which coaches had hoped to drop, was discontinued. A key factor in this television triumph was that ESPN's president, Bill Grimes, had been an NAIA basketball tournament player at West Virginia Wesleyan and had a special interest in building the NAIA/ESPN connection. Unfortunately, by the time the contract was up, Grimes had moved on to Unavision, the Spanish-language network, and no one else at ESPN had much interest in small college matters. The promise of increasing visibility through television turned out to be a will of the wisp.[11]

The other publicity change concerned *The NAIA News*. Beginning in late summer 1986, the stylish, color-picture laden bi-monthly was replaced by a five page, utilitarian publication appearing every two weeks. The new look was more functional, got the news out faster, provided more timely information to the members, no doubt saved money on postage on other information that could now be included in the magazine, and cost less to publish. In many ways, then, it was an improvement. Still, the new style cut back on lengthy coverage of championship events and offered a far less attractive format. Perhaps the austere look could be taken as symbolic of a more tightly run organization. In late 1990, an abortive attempt to launch a new colorful magazine entitled *Balance* (about student athletes balancing their two roles) foundered. Despite an impressive first issue featuring Kansas City Chiefs running back Christian Okoye, an Azusa Pacific alumnus, and attractive articles on current college athletes, *Balance* disappeared after two or three issues with hardly a trace.[12]

The most pressing order of business facing the new regime was to put the NAIA's financial affairs in order. In November, Wally Schwartz announced that the various associations within the broader body—for coaches, athletic directors, athletic trainers, and sports information directors—would henceforth have separate accounts for the funds generated by their dues, ending the rather haphazard accounting system that

Fritz had exploited to keep the NAIA afloat. The groups would have to develop formal budgets in order to get money disbursed, and they would then take responsibility for spending decisions on handbooks, awards, or other expenses.[13] This particular reform had a short life, as the COP developed a new, substantially higher dues schedule in January 1987 with the idea that institutional dues would now include appropriate memberships in the various associations. Also at that January meeting, the COP capped the creation of a budget by hiring the auditing firm of Schmidt, Cornish, and Smith to do an annual audit, something that had hitherto been impossible.

In a significant move to increase association revenue, the COP hired a director of development, interviewing 15 candidates before announcing the selection of Bill Patterson, who had been Farris's number two at UCA. His credentials were impressive: successful fund-raising at both private and public colleges, corporate experience, and a competitive nature. He assumed office on May 1, 1987, and by fall had established an associates program, designed to permit corporate sponsors to support the NAIA at different levels of commitment along the lines of college booster clubs. Funding could be used to help finance team trips to championships or to fund clinics or other programs.[14] In another move to try to ensure a stronger financial outlook, in October 1988 the COP established standing committees for the budget and development.

Because the NAIA budget was almost entirely derived from dues, running an office and championship program as advanced as those of the association's required increasing amounts of money. Long gone were the early days of Al Duer's tenure when $10 covered a school's obligation for the year. Farris believed the COP had to think big and jolt members with a touch of reality to escape the limitations of barebones budgets. In January 1987 the COP proposed a drastic increase in dues that was finally approved by the membership in April 1989, winning a 255-107 vote with 75 percent of member institutions voting. Under the new framework, to be phased in over three years, schools would wind up paying from $2250 to $3300 per year depending on their size. The new assessments provided a much more solid base for NAIA operations than had ever been the case before.[15]

Farris believed that the most important accomplishment on his watch concerned upgrading academic standards for NAIA student athletes. He argued that the steps the association took placed it head and shoulders above the NCAA, which made much smaller advances in the direction of academic respectability. At the March 1987 convention, members voted to disallow remedial courses in determining an athlete's academic load; only courses that contributed toward the athlete's graduation would count.

The task force on academic standards met on September 21-22, just in advance of a full COP meeting. Including representatives of athletic directors, coaches, the Eligibility Committee, and district chairs, it hammered out a consensus on higher standards. Recognizing that the NCAA had mounted a highly publicized campaign promoting its Proposition 48 on freshman eligibility, the task force, in effect, declined to re-invent the wheel and suggested that NAIA freshman athletes should also meet Proposition 48 standards. To be eligible for sports as a freshman, a student needed to meet two of the following three criteria: a score of 700 on the SAT or 16 on the ACT; a high school grade point average of 2.0; and graduation in the top half of one's high school class.

But that requirement, which was as far as the NCAA was prepared to go, struck the NAIA committee as only a starting point. Arguing that students needed to demonstrate academic seriousness and progress toward a degree, the COP group mandated that a student must be enrolled in at least 12 hours in the first semester to play, and have passed at least 12 hours to play in the second semester. Those not qualifying under Proposition 48 for freshman play would need to pass at least 24 hours their first year to play as sophomores. After that point, all student athletes would need to meet the 12- and 24-hour requirements each year, plus be certified by the faculty athletic representative as making "normal progress" toward a degree. In addition, they would need at least a 2.0 grade point average to be eligible to play during their junior year. Each institution would be required to file a report every summer on the previous year's grades, graduation rate, financial aid, and other matters.[16]

Convention approval of the proposals in March 1988 moved the NAIA to the forefront of the fight against weak academic performance by college athletes. Nevertheless, the NAIA continued to be frustrated by its relative invisibility in the shadow of the NCAA. The larger organization drew extensive national attention for adopting Proposition 48—after the NAIA had already done so. In the spring of 1989, the NCAA overwhelmingly rejected the NAIA's provisions for a minimum 2.0 grade point average by the junior year and "normal progress" toward a degree. In spite of that, much of the media and the academic community somehow continued to believe that the NCAA was more academically demanding than the NAIA. After all, that publicity about Proposition 48 showed how tough the NCAA was![17]

Trying to ascertain just how the public perceived college athletics, and particularly the NAIA, the COP's Marketing and Membership Committee undertook a study that they concluded in April 1989. Drawing on earlier public opinion surveys, they concluded that the public took a dim view of college athletics. Eighty-six percent in 1985 thought drug use was a problem in college sports, 44 percent felt intercollegiate athletics hurt the image of higher education, almost 70 percent believed college sports were overemphasized, and over 60 percent suspected cheating because of gambling on sports. Was the NAIA different? More likely, it simply didn't register with the American people. Surveying their own Kansas City opinion firm's employees, Valentine-Radford found that three-fourths of them admitted that they were not sure what the NAIA was—and this in the association's hometown. Only 22 percent thought the NAIA's academic standards were higher than those of the NCAA, and over three-fourths believed that aside from being smaller, NAIA institutions were basically the same as those in the NCAA. The national sports media were not much better informed. A survey of ten major media sources turned up none who could name the NAIA's executive director and only two (*Sports Illustrated* and the *Los Angeles Times*) who knew of the NAIA's greater commitment to academics. When asked the difference between the NAIA and the NCAA, they all cited smaller size, smaller athletic budgets, and a weaker level of performance. Academic standards did not register on their radar.[18]

The committee recommended creating a department of public relations, along with establishing a department of membership services to handle publications, ratings and statistics, awards, and so forth. Members of the COP should ratchet up their publicity efforts in their districts, and Farris should visit all the districts to rally the troops and generate publicity. Further, alumni should be rallied to the cause and corporate sponsors should be aware of the six to ten million NAIA alumni around the country.

In May 1989, in the wake of these recommendations and tightened academic standards by both the NAIA and NCAA, Farris, NCAA President Dick Schultz, and two others testified before the House of Representatives Subcommittee on Postsecondary Education investigating college athletics. Farris, whose statement appeared in *The NAIA News*, was dismayed by the disinterest the congressmen showed in his testimony. Discussion focused on what had gone on in the past and did not appear to be informed by any grasp of Proposition 48 or any NAIA upgrading of standards. The purpose of the hearings was unclear since no legislation was under consideration. All in all, Congress seemed even less informed than those believing the NCAA had tougher academic standards than the NAIA.[19]

Taking a different tack, in December 1987 the COP passed a resolution to require all NAIA member institutions to achieve full accreditation by their regional accrediting body within four years or lose their full NAIA membership. Not only would students be held accountable for their academic legitimacy, but NAIA colleges themselves would be as well.

Before it had even taken power in 1986, the COP had been discussing the need to impose limitations on sports programs. Length of season, number of games, distinctions between games and scrimmages, coaching contact days, and other issues raised serious questions about keeping a level playing field by regulating such matters. A COP task force met in Kansas City in June 1987 to develop some preliminary positions on what proved to be a very divisive issue. Schools proved reluctant to surrender their autonomy on program size and duration, and the committee not only failed to develop any unanimous recommendations, but also was unable to develop a strong consensus on what to recommend to the full COP.

At its September meeting, the COP suggested that the COP and NEC should together adopt recommendations to send to the members. To help formulate a policy, the NAIA would hold meetings in all districts to give members an opportunity to share their views and help shape legislation on limitations, academic standards, and divisions of play. By December 1987, the COP had unanimously approved a suggested set of limitations, but some members questioned whether the COP was, in fact, wandering rather far afield from its mandate to manage NAIA business and finance issues. This led Farris to send a memo to the COP and NEC outlining his understanding of the areas of responsibility of the two, and for the national office staff under him. The latter was to administer, not make, policy and interpret NAIA structure. The division of authority between the NEC and COP was, he admitted, less than crystal clear. The NEC was to "provide leadership in the championship events, all professional associations, eligibility and related matters, and those things directly connected with the competition aspects of the NAIA." The COP was to lead in the areas of budget and personnel. Academic issues were pervasive throughout the whole association and thus, he suggested, a common responsibility.[20] Given those definitions of responsibility, it appears that NEC members resisting COP encroachment on their turf had a valid concern.

By late December, the district meetings had taken place, grievances and suggestions had been aired, and the limitation proposals were ready to present to the membership at the convention in March along with the academic standards. Bob Wilson, chairing the basketball coaches organization, recalls that after his group had put in a lot of work, Farris told them that, in essence, the decision had already been made. The convention predictably approved the concept of limitations, which meant that the NEC was to draw upon further input from coaches and others and develop final wordings for formal passage at the 1989 convention. At that conclave, held in October in Memphis, delegates rejected a proposal to create yearlong eligibility for those student-athletes eligible at the start of the year, opting instead to retain the more stringent semester-by-semester requirement. They also approved limitations on the number of playing contests per season with accompanying interpretive regulations.[21] Again the NAIA had taken a principled stand.

Throughout this period, the question of increasing the number of sports split into divisions for championship play attracted a great deal of attention, consumed a lot of time, and ultimately raised enough objections to limit change. The division issue had begun with football back in 1967 and found an early resolution in that sport when it split in 1970. Not until 1979 did the idea of extending divisional play to other sports surface; in 1982, the convention approved a resolution to develop divisions for the 1983-84 school year, with four sports meriting consideration: men's and women's basketball, volleyball, and baseball. Men's soccer and softball lacked balance in divisions and were taken off the table. Then the 1983 convention overwhelmingly voted down divisions for a number of reasons: the threat to district organizational and competitive structures, financial repercussions, and poor understanding of the implications of the change for future competition.

In February 1987, NAIA President Roger Jenkinson reopened the issue, appointing a task force of nine to meet at the March convention, where an estimated 200 members turned out to participate in the discussion. That summer the NEC approved task force recommendations that the same rules should apply to all divisions, a school could choose its division by sport, and a minimum of 100 institutions would be necessary for a division. At the March 1988 convention, delegates approved divisions by a two to one margin and instructed the NEC to develop formal recommendations for the 1989 meeting. The details went to colleges sponsoring the four impacted sports in November and won their approval, but the following August the Executive Committee postponed implementation, saying women's basketball and volleyball would split in 1991-92 and men's basketball in 1992-93, with baseball put off until an indefinite future date. By the spring of 1990, Jeff Farris notified the NEC Divisions of Competition Committee that a consensus on the issue seemed elusive. Many opposed the planning of the shift rather than the concept itself, but some schools flatly said they would bolt from the NAIA if divisions were not adopted to give them a better chance to compete. Concerns about the impact of change on conferences and districts, plus travel costs, along with fuzzy criteria for placing schools in divisions seemed to create paralysis. In the end, only women's and men's basketball gained approval to divide their competition, and they did so beginning in the 1991-92 school year.[22]

While this discussion dragged on for over a decade, the original football split had run into problems. The football playoffs expanded to 16 teams in Division I and 16 more in Division II for 1987 and 1988, reaching their peak in those years. But the number of schools wishing to compete at the Division I level had declined to the point that in 1989 only eight teams were allowed to take part in their playoffs. In 1995, that number was slashed to four, and in 1997, reflecting a precipitous plunge in overall NAIA membership, divisions for football were abolished altogether and sixteen teams competed thereafter for one football championship. Whether basketball championships including 32 teams in each division for both men and women were overstocked as NAIA numbers declined was a question that would merit consideration in the new millennium.

Where the NAIA would be headquartered, the topic of the earlier-cited *Kansas City Star* 1986 editorial, became an increasingly discussed issue as the period unfolded. Other cities, hoping to lure the association away from Kansas City, constantly advanced offers of buildings, tax breaks, or other perks. The association's leaders frequently decried their low place on the Kansas City sports pecking order, with the NCAA, the Royals, the Chiefs, the Kings, and the Big Eight basketball tournament all seeming to attract more local attention. At the COP meeting in April 1990, one of the most ardent suitors, Canton, Ohio, was formally rejected by an 18-9 vote, with its smaller size and difficult air access offsetting its advantages. Then the COP voted 21-6 to stay in Kansas City—if the city kept its promises. Otherwise, the COP would actively pursue other options.[23]

Kansas City's grip on the NAIA did loosen in 1989. For several years before there had been talk of separating the annual convention from the men's basketball tournament, a move that could signify clearly that the association was about more than just basketball, and also dispel its perception as a Midwestern association. In 1989, the convention took place in Memphis in November, beginning a practice of alternating between the headquarters city and new locales while varying the time of the meeting.[24]

Women's progress in sports was uneven. In 1988, Phyllis Holmes became the first woman elected president of a co-educational athletic organization, another first for the NAIA in its finest pioneering mode. Holmes had served since 1967 at Greenville College, Illinois, as professor of physical education and women's athletic director. Though she was only the third woman to serve on the NEC, two resignations ahead of her set her up to take the reins. This NAIA first followed pioneering roles in integrating national sports championships in 1948, adding black colleges to association membership in 1953, and sponsoring women's national championships in a co-educational organization in 1980.[25]

A 1990 study of women in sport, however, reported a mixed record for women overall. The number of women's sports had increased from 5.61 per school (both NCAA and NAIA) to 7.24 since 1977, with basketball, volleyball, tennis, and cross-country the most popular sports. However, in 1972, women coached over 90 percent of women's teams. As men's and women's sports were integrated, men increasingly took over women's teams, so that by 1990 only 47.3 percent of women's teams had women as coaches. Even worse, the percentage of women's programs that were headed by women had dwindled to 15.9 percent, down from 90 percent in 1972. Women still held 32 percent of administrative jobs in women's programs.[26] The numbers reflected the ambiguous nature of progress. A similar phenomenon had struck professional baseball, when integration on the heels of Jackie Robinson's pioneering 1947 debut opened up organized ball to black athletes only to see more black athletes lose their jobs when the Negro leagues went out of business. A price women paid for integration into the male collegiate sports world was a decline in control over their own sports.

Holmes sought to assert a measure of control over a men's sport within the NAIA. She let loose a volley at men's soccer in a May 1989 column, decrying reports of drunken, rock-throwing fans, coaches verbally and physically abusing officials, and players fighting among themselves and hassling officials. She noted that schools were waiting for the NAIA to act rather than taking action themselves, and she called on them to be proactive and work to restore a level of civility to the sport. If soccer didn't clean up its act, she warned, it could possibly lose its championship competition.[27]

If soccer showed the worst side of the NAIA, student athletes showed perhaps the best. However, the NAIA's academic all-Americans, first established by baseball coaches in 1978 and then adopted by other sports, had to change their name after the 1986-87 school year. It seems the College Sports Information Directors Association had received a patent for exclusive use of that name. As a result, henceforth NAIA award-winners would be known as NAIA Scholar Athletes. Six hundred twelve athletes earned that honor the last year under the old name.[28]

With the establishment of tougher academic standards, limitations on seasons and games, stabilization of membership numbers, and progress on moving to divisions as solid accomplishments, Jeff Farris could afford to feel he had earned a well-deserved rest from his labors. At the fall convention in 1989, he surprised everyone by announcing that he was retiring at the end of the fiscal year on August 1. Chest pains and concern that he would not be able to effectively perform his duties led him to suggest that it was a good time to retire, for the NAIA was "on a roll now."[29]

But even as he laid plans for his departure, Farris recognized that the new governance structure he had helped launch suffered from serious defects that hindered the smooth working of the association. Revamping the NAIA's organization consumed much of his energy over his last year in office.

As reconfigured in 1986, the NAIA had two heads, with some question of just where the authority of each extended. The COP was clearly intended to function like a college board of trustees, but like some college boards, it tended to stray into the day-to-day functioning of the association, undermining the NEC's role. In addition, where the national office staff had related well to the athletic directors who made up the bulk of the NEC, they found the presidents a more difficult connection. Many athletic directors grew disenchanted with the NAIA, but once they had taken power, the presidents were not about to give it up.[30] Presidential rule, after all, was one more area in which the NAIA set the pace for the NCAA.

A look at the structure approved in 1986 raises the question of why the NEC had not been eliminated at that time. Evidently the original plan drawn up by Tom Feld had done that, for he recognized that a divided leadership could threaten smooth operations. Farris, however, sought to make the transition as smooth as possible and did not want to antagonize and alienate the NEC leaders any more than necessary, so the rival power center was retained. Within a year, Farris was regretting his softness and trying to clarify the less than crystal clear power division, sending the aforementioned memo to the COP and NEC members and repeating his basic vision in *The NAIA News* of September 12, 1987.[31]

In the fall of 1988, the COP set up a committee to revisit the governing structure, with Tom Feld again taking the lead. Some NEC members, including new president Phyllis Holmes, expressed frustration with what they perceived as the COP's attempt to pursue "top-down" policies such as the NCAA imposed, thus straying from the grass-roots governance that historically characterized the NAIA. Farris tried to pacify the increasingly restive athletic directors but met with little success. By April 1989, the COP had developed and approved Feld's new plan, and it appears to be another attempt to mollify the NEC, or at least athletic directors. It featured the COP, the athletic directors, and the faculty athletic representatives as equals, with a coordinating council drawing from the three to blend their perspectives. The COP would deal with finance and development, the athletic directors with competition, and the faculty athletic representatives with eligibility and academic standards. The proposed plan would include an executive director. The NEC asked for more time to consider the new look and won a delay in voting on it until the 1990 meeting. That turned out to be a serious tactical error.[32]

The COP had second thoughts about sharing power on an equal basis, and Farris led the writing of a new proposal, unanimously approved at the April 1990 COP meeting. The new arrangement had the membership at the top, the COP next on the power chart, then the CEO, with a National Coordinating Committee to advise him. Below him were three equal bodies: the athletic directors (ADs), the faculty athletic representatives (FARs), and the district chairs, with those three presiding over the various standing committees. The 1989 vision of the COP as one among equals had given way to the COP ruling without the constraints of an NEC at all.[33]

The NEC fought back with a proposal of its own. It looked similar in many ways to the COP design, but included a renamed NEC (the National Administrative Council) between the ADs, FARs, district chairs, and affiliated conferences below and the COP above, keeping to its college board oversight mission. During the spring and summer of 1990, *The NAIA News* carried articles describing the competing proposals with diagrams, debates, and the prospect of a knockdown, drag-out battle at the convention that fall. The presidents rallied their supporters, sending them talking points to persuade fellow CEOs to vote for the COP proposal, developed, COP chair Fred Young averred, with input from all the association's constituencies. Proponents of the proposal argued that it would give a much more meaningful role to the three groups represented below the COP and, rather than being an "us against them" contest, it would move all elements of the NAIA closer together.[34]

Tom Feld blasted the NEC proposal as undermining the executive director's administrative role in favor of the new Administrative Committee, perpetuating the very problems that necessitated a new body, and serving primarily to extend NEC power.[35] As the convention approached, Joe Struckle of the COP calculated that the original proposal would win handily, and when the NEC, following minor concessions in conference with the COP, withdrew its counter-proposal, the action suggested that it had come to a similar conclusion. Unopposed, the COP proposal sailed through the convention and the National Executive Committee, which had supplied the office of president of the NAIA since its inception, faded into history. The COP coup was complete.[36]

❖

Most athletes were likely oblivious to the politics of the NAIA, instead focusing on their world of academics and sports. In men's cross-country, the most focused individual during the 1986-1990 stretch had to be Rick Robirds of Adams State (CO). His team took the title each of the four years, a string marred only by in-state rival Western State tying the Indians in 1986. Robirds, meanwhile, captured the top spot in 1986, 1987, and 1989. But that was the end of the remarkable streak of cross-country wins for the school. Losing in 1990 and 1991, Adams State abandoned the NAIA.

In Division I football action, Carson-Newman (TN) outclassed the opposition, winning three of the four titles. In 1986, the Eagles shut down Cameron (OK), 17-0, on a muddy field, only to see the Aggies come back under similar conditions the next fall and turn the tables, 30-2. Carson-Newman rebounded in 1988 with a convincing 56-21 thrashing of Adams State in the title game behind Vernon Turner's 189 yards rushing and three touchdowns. They earned a repeat championship in 1989 by beating Emporia State (KS), 34-20, but despite playoff appearances the next three seasons, failed to capture another title and in 1993 they followed the Adams State example and left the NAIA to compete in the NCAA's Division II.

Division II football spread the honors around more than DI. In 1986 perennial power Linfield (OR) shut out Baker (KS) for the title, 17-0. The next year, hard-luck Baker lost in overtime in the semi-finals, after which Wisconsin-Stevens Point played to a 16-16 tie with Pacific Lutheran. When the Wisconsin school was determined to have played an ineligible athlete, it forfeited its entire schedule, but by the somewhat quirky NAIA calculation, PLU was still just co-champion with the other half deemed vacant. In 1988 the 1985 champion, Wisconsin-La Crosse, made it back to the title game, only to confront Westminster (PA) in a snowstorm and lose, 21-14, on a desperation 38-yard touchdown pass from Joe Micchia to Dave Foley as time ran out. In a rematch in 1989, Westminster unloaded a powerful offense on La Crosse and ran away with the game, 51-30.

In men's soccer, powerful Simon Fraser didn't surrender a goal in the 1986 playoffs until they ran into underdog Sangamon State (IL) in the finals. Bill Becher converted a penalty kick in the first half, and that was enough to permit the Prairie Stars to win, 1-0, and break the thirteen year domination of the sport by Quincy, West Virginia Wesleyan, and Simon Fraser. The following spring, the NAIA champs beat NCAA champion UCLA at the fourth annual World Collegiate Championship in Las Cruces, New Mexico, 3-1 on penalty kicks. They then lost the title game to the University of Dublin, 1-0, but beating UCLA made the tournament a big success for Sangamon and the NAIA. In 1987, Simon Fraser's Clansmen suffered a depressing rerun—they didn't give up a goal through the playoffs until the title match, when Boca Raton's Johnny Clare converted a header in sudden-death overtime to give the Floridians a 1-0 win and send the Canadians home disappointed again. In 1988, Sangamon State picked up its second championship with a 3-1 win over Alderson-Broaddus (WV), and West Virginia Wesleyan returned to its winning ways with a 1-0 triumph over Boca Raton in the 1989 final.

In men's basketball, where repeat champions were rare, four different schools copped titles in four years. Washburn (KS) captured its only basketball title ever in 1987 when the Ichabods edged West Virginia State, 79-77, in the final game. The 1988 tournament featured some of the most exciting games in the long history of the NAIA. Grand Canyon just made it to the title match with an overtime 99-96 quarterfinal win in over the College of Idaho and a 108-106 barnburner over Waynesburg (PA) in the semifinals. Meanwhile, Auburn-Montgomery nipped William Jewell (MO), 51-49, in the quarterfinals and won a comparative laugher, 74-70, over Charleston in the semifinals. Naturally, the final dragged the suspense into overtime before Grand Canyon eked out a thrilling 88-86 victory to grab the title. The wrap-up in 1989 continued the cliffhangers as East Central (OK) nipped Wisconsin-Eau Claire, 58-56, in one semifinal and St. Mary's (TX) edged Central Washington, 60-58, in the other. In the championship game, St. Mary's slipped by East Central, 61-58, leaving fans worn out

Profile: Philip Hutcheson
As his David Lipscomb team fell in the 1990 semifinals to eventual champion Birmingham-Southern after a record 41-win season, Hutcheson closed out a remarkable individual career, eclipsing Travis Grant's 18-year old collegiate record with 4106 career points. The 6'8" center won the Emil Liston Award (academic achievement) and the Frank Hesselroth Leadership Award (campus and community involvement) as a junior, made the GTE all-academic team with a 4.0 grade point average in political science, averaged near 30 points per game through his career without ever slipping into single digits in a game, and exemplifies the NAIA scholar-athlete ideal.

for the second consecutive year. In 1990, though Birmingham Southern won their semifinal game by only two points, they beat Wisconsin-Eau Claire almost handily, 88-80, to take home their first of two basketball crowns.

Swimming saw Central Washington successfully defend its title in 1987, but in 1988 Drury (MO) launched a seven-year stretch during which the school beat off all comers, with no one coming close through 1990. To top off the team honors, Cliff Cox (1988) and Tomas Eriksson (1989 and 1990) won outstanding swimmer awards for Drury.

In indoor track and field competition, Wayland Baptist ran its string of consecutive titles to five by winning in 1987, 1988, and 1989 before Adams State broke their streak with a win in 1990. Even changing head coaches from John Creer to Rick Beelby in 1989 didn't slow down the Texans. Curiously, Azusa Pacific, the perennial outdoor champion in the eighties, placed second all four years.

Central State (OK) continued to dominate wrestling competition, winning their fourth straight title in 1987, slipping to second behind Simon Fraser (BC) in 1988, and bouncing back to earn top honors again in 1989. At that point the institution bolted to the NCAA to compete in Division II, opening the field to Adams State to take the 1990 championship.

Baseball saw the Lewis-Clark (ID) dynasty in full bloom. After winning the title in 1984 and 1985, the Warriors had lost to Grand Canyon by a run in 1986. They left nothing to chance in 1987, scoring a record 105 runs in six games to please the home-town Lewiston fans, wrapping up their title with an 11-4 win over Emporia State. In 1988, they avenged their 1986 loss by beating Grand Canyon, 9-3, in the final game. The final victim in 1989 was St. Francis (IL), 5-2 losers, and in 1990 Auburn-Montgomery wound up in the runner-up spot as Lewis-Clark exploited their home-field advantage mercilessly, winning the final 9-4.

Tennis provided more drama, sharing the honors among four schools. In 1987, Auburn-Montgomery edged Charleston (SC) behind Jeff Skeldon. The next year, Lander (SC) beat out Texas-Tyler for the top spot, only to see the runners-up take top honors in 1989, with Ken Olivier leading Tyler over runner-up Auburn-Montgomery. In 1990, Elon (NC) took the title, with North Florida winding up in second place. Elon's Roland Thornquist won top player honors for the match.

In golf, Huntingdon (AL) bagged its third and fourth consecutive titles in 1987 and 1988 behind individual winners Joe Durant and David Schreyer. In 1989, Guilford (NC) ended the string, edging Huntingdon by three strokes to capture the top spot. In 1990, Texas Wesleyan beat intrastate and denominational rival Texas Lutheran for the championship, with Andy Fuller pacing the winning team with the best individual score.

Azusa Pacific cruised to three more outdoor track and field titles from 1987 to 1989, giving them a string of seven. Patrick Nwankwo and Ade Olukoju, two of the school's Nigerian connection, were named top performers in 1989 and 1990, but in the latter year APU saw its long winning streak come to an end in a close loss to Oklahoma Baptist. The eighties belonged to the Cougars.

❖

Women's cross-country featured four different winners in four years. In 1986, Wisconsin-Parkside came out on top, with Hillsdale's (MI) Gina Van Laar the individual champion. The next year, Leah Pells led Simon Fraser's winning team as the Canadians garnered their second title. In 1988, Pacific Lutheran beat out Adams State with Valerie Hilden setting the winning pace. Adams State moved up a notch in 1989 to match their men's team as champions that year.

Soccer provided much more in the way of dynasties. In 1986, St. Mary's (CA) knocked off Berry (GA), 3-0, to capture their second title in three years. The next year, Berry moved up to the top, tripping up Erskine (SC) in the final, 1-0. Pacific Lutheran moved into the elite class in 1988, beating Hardin-Simmons (TX), 2-0, to capture the Lutes' first title, led by the amazing Sonya Brandt, who hung up her spikes after scoring 130 goals as the first-ever four-year first team all-American. Even without Brandt, PLU came right back in 1989 to top Berry, 2-1, to earn back-to-back championships along with the first two of four coach-of-the-year awards for Colleen Hacker.

Hawaiian teams continued to dominate in volleyball competition. Brigham Young-Hawaii beat out Lewis and Clark (OR) to take the title in 1986, then repeated the following year over Western Oregon. Hawaii-Hilo kept the title out in mid-Pacific by frustrating Western Oregon again in 1988. Only in 1989 did Fresno Pacific (CA) overcome Hawaii Pacific and bring the championship back to the mainland.

Women's basketball ran into an Oklahoma monopoly even more dominant than Hawaii's hold on volleyball, as each of the four seasons saw one of the state's schools take the title. In 1987, a season in which some conferences and districts experimented with adding the three-point basket, Southwest Oklahoma captured the championship, defeating North Georgia in the final game, 60-58. In 1988, with the three-pointer officially part of the NAIA women's scene, Oklahoma City ran by Claflin (SC), 113-95, in the title game despite Miriam Walker-Samuels' 48-point effort for favored Claflin. Claflin came closer in 1989, but even Walker-Samuels' 49 points left her team one basket short of Southern Nazarene, 98-96, as the third team from the state took home top honors in three years. In 1990, the tournament moved to Jackson, Tennessee, where it was an instant hit and where it has remained ever since in a happy marriage of city and sport. Southwest Oklahoma, clearly the dominant team of the decade, won their fifth title in the ten years the women's championship had been held; this time they topped Arkansas-Monticello, 82-75, in the final game.

As in basketball, a few teams dominated swimming over these four years. Wisconsin-Eau Claire won the title in 1987, and then repeated in 1988 with Puget Sound coming in second. The two switched places in 1989 as Puget Sound won the first of two straight championships, topping Simon Fraser for first place in 1990. Annabel Bicknell of Simon Fraser earned the top swimmer award in both 1989 and 1990.

Prairie View A&M was the class of indoor track and field, but their efforts won them only one title, in 1987. The next three years they finished second, trailing Wayland Baptist by just 1.5 points in 1988 and Midland Lutheran (NE) by just 0.4 points in 1989. In 1990 Simon Fraser defeated all comers fairly handily with Alana Kripps winning top individual honors for the Clansmen.

The last winter sport, gymnastics, ran out of gas after the 1988 season. Winona State (MN) edged Centenary (LA) for first place in 1987, but Centenary bounced back to edge Ft. Hays State (KS) in the final national meet. The number of schools offering gymnastics as a sport had dwindled to a mere 16 when the NEC pulled the plug in April 1988.

Softball, on the other hand, was thriving, especially at Kearney State (NE). The Lady Lopers topped Francis Marion, 1-0, in the title match in 1987. They made it to the final six the next year, but Pacific Lutheran wound up winning a thriller, 2-0 in 10 innings over Minnesota-Duluth, to earn the championship. Kearney State made it to the final game in 1989, only to fall to Saginaw Valley (MI), 3-0. In 1990, two former winners matched up in the final, and Kearney State beat Pacific Lutheran, 6-3 in 8 innings, to snare its second title.

Flagler (FL) took all four women's tennis championships during the period on their way to five in a row. The runners-up were North Florida, Boca Raton, Grand Canyon, and Boca Raton again. It was a team effort, for not once in their five-year run did a Flagler player garner the outstanding player award. One player who did make her mark was Berit Bjork, a Swede playing for Arkansas-Little Rock. She was upset in the fifth round of singles in 1987, preventing her from capturing four straight titles in both singles and doubles.

Prairie View A&M, powerful indoors, was unstoppable in outdoor track and field. The Pantherettes breezed through the competition without any speed bumps. After a second place finish in the first year's meet in 1981, Prairie View won every year through 1990.

The NAIA-SIDA All-Sports awards for the period were won on the men's side by Central Washington in 1986-87, Grand Canyon and North Florida in a tie in 1987-88, and Adams State in both 1988-89 and 1989-90. The women's winners were Kearney State in 1986-87, then Pacific Lutheran for the next three years in an impressive run at the top.

12

Things Fall Apart
1990-1993

J eff Farris had planned to step down at the end of July 1990, but two factors combined to postpone his departure. First, the NAIA faced several pressing issues requiring action at the fall convention, and Farris felt some responsibility for seeing them through. Second, one COP choice for his replacement backed out over conflicts with his wife's career, and a second possibility was rejected by the Administrative Committee, reopening the search process.[1]

Five members of the COP—Fred Young, Lee Vickers, Ed Stevens, Joe Struckle, and Farris—whittled down a list of seven applicants to three finalists: Arthur DeRosier, President of Rocky Mountain College; John Friend, athletic director of Purdue-Calumet; and James Chasteen. Chasteen concurrently filled the presidencies of Athens State College and Calhoun State Community College in Alabama, the only person running two independent institutions of higher learning at that time. He had just finished a tour on the COP and knew the members well; when he saw that the search process was still open, he threw his name in the ring in early September. On the eve of the national convention in Kansas City, the three candidates were interviewed, and Chasteen won the nomination, with his term set to begin January 1, 1991. With the association's structural change came a change in his title. The executive director, reporting to the COP, would henceforth be the chief executive officer and president—the old president's position, elected by the membership as the head of the National Executive Committee, was abolished.[2]

The transition was the smoothest in NAIA history. The 1949 changeover from Emil Liston to Al Duer had been occasioned by Liston's sudden death, so the pioneer leader had not been able to appropriately brief his successor. The retirement of Duer in 1975 had brought a rather awkward transition to Harry Fritz, and the ouster of Fritz in 1986 had taken on the look of a comic opera when he resisted his "reassignment." This time the meticulous, well-organized, and contentedly retiring Farris prepared a thorough briefing notebook for Chasteen, outlining the current situation in the many areas of association concern. He appeared to be handing over a stable, healthy organization. That illusion did not last long.

Farris's transition notes for Chasteen afford a candid look at the state of the association as of December 1990 and provide insight into some of the issues that would trouble the organization during the new president's tenure. Interestingly, there is no sign of impending defections to the NCAA, which would be a defining mark of the Chasteen years.

Possibly the most exciting prospect Farris laid out was a new home for the NAIA. Negotiations were almost complete with the Jackson County Sports Authority to build a new headquarters building at the Truman Sports Complex, about six miles east of downtown Kansas City along I-70. The Royals and Chiefs had stadiums in the complex, and the location would enhance the NAIA's visibility. The plan called for the sale of bonds to finance the project, with neither the Sports Authority nor the NAIA needing to provide out-of-pocket money. Only two minor issues remained to be worked out: the size of the NAIA's nominal lease fee after the bonds were retired in 25 years, and the length of the lease, as Jackson County had leased the land to the Sports Authority for another 23 years; the NAIA wanted a 50-year lease. The annual cost to the NAIA was projected at around $155,000 to retire the bonds and operate the facility. It appeared to Farris that the whole matter should be worked out by February 1991.[3] When the COP rejected Canton's bid to lure the NAIA away from Kansas City, this prospect was one of the keys to keeping the association in its birthplace. Farris's optimistic portrait of the deal encouraged the new president, and when the deal fell apart, Chasteen's commitment to Kansas City suffered a devastating hit.

Farris warned Chasteen that the current budget was very tight. In fact, the NAIA ran two separate budgets, one for championship events and the other the general budget. The former paid for the events and, to the degree possible, paid teams' expenses to the championships. Football and basketball generated enough money to cover their events plus travel for their teams, and the surplus went to the general budget to fund the championship division, then to help fund team costs in the non-revenue generating sports championships. The dual system had been set up by the COP in 1988 to ensure that the championship revenues were not diverted to run the national office.

Limitations on financial aid to athletes, a concept approved in 1988, had been difficult to implement because defining financial aid proved terribly complex. After two years of discussions and surveys trying to clarify definitions and methodology, Farris admitted that progress was negligible. Just what should count as athletic aid and distinguishing that from monies available to all students were complicated issues, and not limited to NAIA schools. NCAA Division III colleges officially gave no athletic scholarships, yet they recruited athletes with euphemisms like "leadership grants," managing to appear pure while competing for athletes like other schools. Farris, uncharacteristically restrained, admitted, "I don't have much good advice for you."[4]

Establishing divisions for competition seemed relatively easy in comparison, yet that process had taken longer than anticipated. Basic guidelines required that at least half the member institutions had to participate in a sport for it to be eligible for divisions, with the expectation that at least 100 institutions would fit in each division. More subjectively, the divisions had to promote competitiveness and be financially sound. Men's and women's basketball were approved to split for the 1991-1992 school year. The initial placement put 235 schools in Division I men's basketball and 184 in Division II. Women were divided 199 and 194. For the first year, each Division I tournament would have 32 teams while the Division II tourneys would included 20.[5] Baseball and volleyball, the other prime prospects, never did divide. Declining membership, along with a lack of enthusiasm by the NAIA's baseball people, contributed to the limited realization of the push for further divisions.

Meanwhile, declining numbers had forced a reduction in Division I football playoffs from 16 teams to eight in 1989. When football had split in 1970, Division I schools were those that gave athletic scholarships, while the rest went Division II. But over time some schools and conferences had moved from Division I to Division II, and because the criteria for assignment were not clear-cut, the association had little basis to deny the shifts. But by 1989, only 52 schools in seven conferences were playing Division I football, while 105 schools in 12 conferences competed at the Division II level. The slippage continued as conferences like the Arkansas Intercollegiate, Oklahoma Intercollegiate, Central States, and West Virginia Intercollegiate bolted for the NCAA's Division II on Chasteen's watch. Thus, while basketball moved to divisions in 1992, football, the pioneer in the concept, returned to an undivided competition in 1997.

As noted previously, the NAIA has long sought to differentiate itself from the NCAA and professional sports by a greater commitment to sportsmanship and to the integration of athletics and academics. But in the late 1980s deteriorating standards of player, coach, and crowd behavior in American sports led to meetings of representatives of the NAIA, NCAA, NJCAA, the National Federation of High School Associations, and the NBA, NFL, NHL, and MLB. Though the idea of working together to enhance sportsmanship had not died, it had run into some major obstacles. First, the NAIA and high schools and junior colleges did not have the crowd problems experienced by the others, in large part because they didn't allow the sale of beer. The obvious solution, eliminating beer sales, was a non-starter since breweries owned several major league teams, and beer sales generated significant revenue for many other teams. As the limited possibilities for meaningful reform became evident, the heads of the various organizations lost interest and passed off the project to lower-level operatives. Farris advised Chasteen against personally investing himself in the effort.

Historically, the NAIA had prided itself on its district organization and the grass-roots approach to governance. Farris noted that the NEC had recommended and the membership approved a guideline that a district should have at least 10 member institutions. An alignment committee had met and rearranged some of the southeastern districts, then made their recommendation to the NEC. To the surprise of Farris and the national office, the people in Alabama, Mississippi, and Louisiana had not even been involved in the discussion, and Farris was embarrassed because he had written to them on the assumption that they were aware of the plans. The redistricting was due to take place in August 1991, but Farris urged some sort of reconsideration out of fairness to the affected schools. Hawaii presented its own distinct problems. Districts were to send a portion of their playoff revenues to the national office to help fund championships, but Hawaii always had to come to the mainland for bi- or tri-district playoffs and to play in championships not generating revenues. Because those schools had extremely high travel expenses, the COP had agreed to let the Hawaiians keep their district playoff revenues to cover some of their travel costs. As it happened, the NAIA's historic district structure was not long for the world, a topic to be treated in the next chapter.

Chasteen faced a challenge in implementing the new governance structure passed in the fall of 1990. The new National Coordinating Committee, comprised of two district chairs, two FARs, two athletic directors, and three at large members, needed a clear sense of its functions to work effectively. Farris informed the members of three areas of responsibility. They were to approve operational policies developed by the three councils (presidents, athletic directors, and FARs), see that they were understood by their various constituencies, and assure that all three were in accord. In other words, they were to function as a coordinating committee, as their name implied. Second, they were to recommend policy changes to the COP where appropriate, which meant that they had the power to initiate discussion of issues. Finally, they were to serve as the Appeals Committee on conduct and eligibility issues.

Chasteen faced other challenges as the new President. Where Jeff Farris had participated at almost every level of NAIA athletics and knew the territory, Chasteen lacked that sports background. He had, however, been a student, teacher, administrator, and college president in Alabama, as well as President of the National Junior College Presidents' Association. Farris had presided over the University of Central Arkansas, a major player in NAIA sports; Chasteen's Athens State was rather peripheral to the NAIA's inner circle, and the new President had never lived outside Alabama until his election. Chasteen had been a charter member of the COP and chaired the NAIA's

National Committee on Academic Standards. Both men got along well with the national office staff. Chasteen had great rapport with the folks in the office, managing by wandering, showing interest but in a non-directive way. He provided lots of positive reinforcement for the staff, creating a pleasant working environment. But he did not connect so well with the membership, partly due, no doubt, to his lack of a sports background. He lacked charisma and public presentation skills. Still, he exuded optimism, which clashed with what Bill Patterson, his Executive Vice-President, saw as the greater reality. Perhaps Chasteen's optimistic outlook blinded him to the seriousness of some of the problems confronting the organization.[6]

He may also have been a victim of bad timing. Membership had held steady during the Farris years, and Bill Patterson remembered a high level of commitment by college presidents during the late 1980s as the COP took control of the organization. Farris seemed to be able to motivate and inspire the COP members to play an active role. At meetings, they would gather in one of their rooms in the evening for drinks and sit up till all hours of the night discussing the NAIA and what needed to be done, sometimes with brutal frankness. As the years went by, however, presidents found other issues to occupy their time; as the NEC had feared, small-college presidents faced great pressures in the nineties, and when they left their COP meetings they focused on more immediate needs on their home campuses. Even at COP meetings, a new breed of president that had not been part of the 1986 coup began to emerge. They were fitness buffs. Instead of sitting up half the night discussing issues, they wanted seven hours of sleep and an early morning jog. As desirable as those goals are, they reflected a declining sense of ownership in the organization; in the nineties, many institutional defections came under presidents who were serving on the COP.[7] To some degree, this loss of cohesion mirrors similar declines in the sense of community in other areas of the fragmented modern world. Baseball old-timers lamented the decline of long rail trips where one talked baseball with teammates, reporters, and coaches, focusing their attention on the game; today cell phones, stock portfolios, less convivial plane flights, and individualism have undermined that camaraderie. But it may well be that where Jeff Farris was able to manage and motivate the COP, James Chasteen simply was not.

The COP met in Phoenix April 21-23, 1991, the first such gathering under the modified governance structure. Chasteen announced that he would be focusing on membership and resource development in the immediate future, an emphasis with disappointing results. The COP did finally fashion a tentative definition of athletic aid: "any scholarship, grant or other form of financial assistance, the terms of which require the recipient to participate in intercollegiate athletics at any NAIA member institution in order to be eligible to receive such assistance." With that definition in mind, the presidents set a limit of 33 football and 12 basketball full rides for Division I schools. Other sports also found their limits: baseball 12, golf 4, swimming and diving 8, track and field/cross country (combined) 10, track and field alone 7, softball 12, soccer 12, tennis 4, cross country alone 3, volleyball 12, and wrestling 6.[8] The COP held off on setting limits for Division II, and proposed limits of 12 for football and 3 for basketball went down to defeat at the September 1992 COP meeting. Chasteen was, tellingly, surprised that schools used athletic scholarships as enrollment boosters, reasoning that by giving a partial scholarship, the school would bring in the balance of the student-athlete's tuition and room and board and enhance the bottom line.[9] Finally, in April 1993, the COP approved limits of 12 and 5, paving the way for implementation in the fall of 1994.[10]

The group also had to respond to outside influences. Congress had passed the Student Right to Know and Campus Security Act of 1990, and it mandated reporting of graduation rates. Since the NAIA had already set in motion its own procedure, the COP agreed to adapt the association's plan to fit in with the government mandate; the biggest change was the government wanting six-year graduation rates rather than the NAIA's five. In addition, the COP brainstormed responses to the recent report of the Knight Foundation Commission on Intercollegiate Athletics. That report criticized many NCAA practices and led the NAIA's rival to begin moving toward presidential control and upgrading its academic eligibility standards, doing what the NAIA had already done. It also recommended certifying athletic programs to ensure their quality, something the NAIA was beginning to work on as well.[11] All in all, the NAIA's leadership had reason to be proud of their leadership in college sports at that point.

The annual convention in October 1991 took place in Portland, Oregon, with all activities under one roof. Out of that gathering came three task forces and an ad-hoc committee to work on an articulation agreement with two-year colleges. The task forces were: Enhancement and Involvement of Women in NAIA, chaired by Cathleen Real of Michigan's Siena Heights College (this group became the Gender Equity Committee in 1993); NAIA Membership, a crucial force chaired by Jim Williams of Auburn-Montgomery; and the NAIA's Future, a visionary group of ten under the direction of Joe Struckle of Northwestern Oklahoma State.

The Future Committee made its recommendations to the COP at the Kansas City meeting in February 1992, and the COP received the proposals with unanimous approval. First, affiliated conferences should be more fully integrated into the NAIA's governance structure, which would diminish the importance of the district, as conferences would play a significant role in the championship qualification procedure. In addition, the committee said that dual membership should remain an option for some schools as long as they adhered to NAIA rules and policies, with a one-sport exception for each gender to participate in NCAA championships without NAIA eligibility compliance. The NAIA should implement a self-study program to accredit or certify athletic programs, as the Knight report had urged the NCAA to do. The NAIA should also take action to ensure its commitment to the role of women and people of color in the association. The committee also affirmed divisions of competition, trying to attract state institutions into membership, and focusing on the association's core identity to strengthen its image. It seemed a good thing to have this proactive, forward-looking group playing an active role in the NAIA.[12]

In 1992, Bill Patterson negotiated a nice arrangement with ServiceMaster to introduce a ServiceMaster-NAIA Distinguished Graduate Program. Each month, *The NAIA News* would include a biographical sketch of one of ten nominees for the year, drawing on student-athletes who had distinguished themselves with their post-graduate accomplishments. The annual winner would be selected from that group by the NAIA's president, vice presidents, and director of communications and presented the award at the convention. Through the program, renewed for another three years in 1995, some $10,000 per year went into the scholarship funds of member institutions.[13]

The NAIA had led the way in women's rights in coed sports organizations, and with the task force established in 1991 the association had a chance to assess its progress in the area. The task force submitted a preliminary report to the COP in March 1992, and it took an upbeat approach. The NAIA's efforts to promote women's programs were deemed satisfactory, and considerable progress had been made over the decade since championship programs for women had been launched. They recommended a regular column on women's sports development in *The NAIA News*, but were told that the abbreviated News of that period had no room for additional columns. They proposed a "think tank" on women's issues, preferably not at the national convention; many schools sent only one representative to the annual meeting, normally the athletic director, who was usually male. NAIA member institutions should do a self-evaluation to measure their compliance with Title IX. They also pushed for hiring women at the national office and throughout the association.

These advocates for women could have presented a much less positive picture had they been so inclined. The Knight report had soundly criticized the NCAA for failing to implement Title IX mandates, a practice that had become common as enforcement and punishment had not followed noncompliance. The NAIA did not look very impressive, either. In 1990-91, 86.5 percent of monies prorated to national championship participating teams had gone to men, with women getting only the other 13.5 percent. The following year the numbers of women in NAIA college administrative positions was respectable, if hardly equal. Of 436 institutions, 59 had women athletic directors, 93 athletic trainers, 90 sports information directors, 60 faculty athletics representatives—and 46 had women as CEOs. But coaching was another matter. In all of men's sports, there were ten women serving as head coaches and three as assistants. But men played a hugely disproportionate role in women's sports. Of 367 women's basketball teams, 212 had men for head coaches and 155 had women, with another 114 women in assistant roles. Women coached only 17 out of 101 women's soccer teams. The best showings came in volleyball, where 222 out of 330 teams had women coaches, and softball, where 118 of 239 did.[14]

Despite these continuing inequities, women were getting to participate in growing numbers, especially in basketball. In 1990, 16 women's teams went to the national tournament in Jackson, Tennessee. In 1991, the number doubled to 32, and in 1992, with the splitting of men's and women's basketball into divisions, women sent 32 to Division I and another 20 to Division II. In terms of one of the NAIA's leading attractions, the possibility of competing for national championships, women in sport were flourishing. Jackson's embrace of the Division I tournament played a big role in getting basketball over the hump. While the sport had been a money loser in the mid-eighties, it had become the hot ticket in Jackson as almost 30,000 fans turned out for the weeklong championships in 1992, and city officials were talking about building a women's basketball hall of fame in town.[15]

While women's sports within the NAIA were experiencing spotty success, declining membership numbers were the most alarming and visible news in the association in the early nineties. From 465 members in the fall of 1990, membership dropped to 436, 409, and then dipped below the 400 mark to 389 in the fall of 1993. The loss of 76 members meant that fully *one-sixth* of the NAIA had evaporated in three years. The worst previous attrition had come in 1973, when the NCAA had split into three divisions and 45 of the NAIA's record high 558 members had decamped, a loss of about eight percent. But membership stabilized after that one-time event until the Fritz fade, another 10 percent drop from 519 in 1983 to 465 in 1986, when Jeff Farris came on board. The early nineties erosion was particularly alarming because there was no clear reason for a drop at that time.

Possible causes for the mass defections were numerous. Perhaps the tightened academic standards passed in 1988 had alienated some schools, and with a waiting period to get into the NCAA, the rush would have hit two years later. Raising the minimum SAT score to 740 in 1992 could have exacerbated this problem, though that increase merely aimed to bring the SAT minimum in line with that for the ACT exam. Possibly the financial aid limitations imposed in 1992 alienated some schools wishing to have more freedom. For some schools, the COP tightening controls on booster clubs in 1992 may have been the last straw. New NAIA policy mandated that any booster club funds were to be controlled by the institution, not the athletic department. In effect, all money facilitating the athletic program was to be administered by the institution, an attempt to avoid some of the abuses experienced by major NCAA programs with out-of-control boosters getting their schools in trouble for questionable "assistance."[16] Most crucial, of course, the NCAA was able to offer serious financial incentives. Though the rival association had been fully paying the way of Division II and Division III schools to regional and national championships for some years, the highly-publicized six-year $1 billion contract to televise the basketball final four signed in 1988 surely caught the attention of financially-strapped NAIA athletic directors and presidents.

A definite air of panic characterized the COP meeting in April 1992. The Membership Task Force made its first report, and it warned of a snowball effect. "Current trends in membership reflect a decline with some fear that the NAIA might dissolve. Such fear may be a contributor to the decline." In other words, to paraphrase Franklin Roosevelt, fear itself was much to be feared. The task force suggested that perhaps the NAIA was trying to be all things to all people and should clarify its identity. Planned membership might include, for example, all independent institutions, or all small institutions, or non-football schools, or non-scholarship colleges, or some other identifying characteristic that would make the association distinctive. That sort of brainstorming dovetails nicely with a reflective analysis by former NAIA President Carroll Land, who contends that dual membership may have been the root of much evil. If schools could be members of both the NAIA and the NCAA, how could the NAIA pretend to be distinctive? Land suggests, "We essentially sold our souls to try to save a 'cheating spouse,'" allowing dual members to play in NAIA championships but not requiring of them any significant commitment or loyalty. Had the NAIA told dual members to make their choice and bitten the bullet over whatever losses ensued, it might have produced a smaller but more committed membership.[17]

President Chasteen sat in on part of the meeting and prioritized his institutional recruitment efforts, to the committee's approval. First was retaining current members, then NCAA Division III institutions (some of which were dual members), then National Christian College Association schools, and finally NCAA Division II colleges. The committee concluded that the NAIA's philosophy of focusing on the balanced student-athlete should be the guiding principle of retention and recruiting efforts. Just how to go about the process seemed elusive, however. The degree of uneasiness felt by NAIA leaders was evident in the cover letter Bill Patterson sent to COP members summarizing the meeting. He encouraged them to open their communications to fellow presidents with some sort of "great things are happening at the NAIA" message, not to let their fears spread.[18]

A follow-up report from the task force in September 1992 was a bit more upbeat, though it is difficult to see why. Membership was down again, but they maintained that the NAIA was healthy at that point, reflecting a solid membership embracing the NAIA focus on the student-athlete. They did recommend at least a half time retention/recruitment person be hired or reassigned, and also that COP members hustle some new members and bear some of the burdens of keeping the association healthy. This optimism (or self-delusion) was reflected in a Chasteen letter to a newly elected COP member in early 1993, when he said, "The NAIA is probably in better shape financially than at any time in its history."[19]

Whether or not that claim was legitimate, two cornerstones of the NAIA's existence were overturned in 1993. The first was district organization, as we will see. The second was the association's 56-year connection with Kansas City. Following the 1989 meeting in Canton, the COP had narrowly voted to keep NAIA headquarters in Kansas City, but that vote was both close and contingent upon the historic home making good on its promises to help the association find a permanent location in the area. Chasteen, though not on the COP, had attended the Canton meeting as an observer, and thus he was aware that other cities were not only interested in enticing the NAIA to move, but willing to offer substantial economic incentives to relocate. The transition briefing paper Farris had prepared for the new CEO had indicated that Kansas Citians recognized the need to compete with new suitors, and Farris led Chasteen to believe that a new building at the Truman Sports Complex was just a few details away from being finalized. That promise turned out to be elusive.

By the spring of 1991, the minor details to be worked out for the new site had mushroomed to insurmountable size. The NAIA's vision of a nominal rental fee for the new building proved wildly overoptimistic, and the problems in reaching a settlement were exacerbated by divided authority among various Kansas City sports and governing bodies, none of which seemed to know what the others were saying or doing. Kansas City, the Chamber of Commerce, the Jackson County Sports Authority, the Sports Commission, the Visitors Bureau, and an ad-hoc backroom group all played roles in negotiations and reduced the chances of finding a solid long-term solution. And with the Truman Complex option evaporating, the NAIA faced a decision: the association's lease at the Midland Building in downtown Kansas City was up in the summer of 1991. Chasteen put a positive public face on the decision to renew the NAIA lease on their 8,000-square-foot space in the Midland Building, calling it the "best option" to meet "our immediate needs." Tellingly, though, instead of renewing the lease for a customary five years, the NAIA took out only a three-year lease. Kansas City's grip on the NAIA had become appreciably more tenuous.[20]

Basically, Chasteen recalls, Kansas City had the NAIA and could have kept the body in town, but simply blew it. Symptomatic of the city's problems, Chasteen had lunch with one leading local sports leader at the Kansas City Club, probably in 1992, and surprised him by saying that unless Kansas City got on the ball, the NAIA was likely to move. That got the attention of the local figure, who promised to take swift action to prevent the defection. But nothing happened.[21] Another blow to the city's hold on the NAIA came in the early nineties when Kemper Arena scheduled a Big Eight basketball game when the NAIA tournament had already been scheduled. The NAIA was forced to move its tournament back a week, reinforcing the perception that the association lacked clout in the local sports pecking order.[22] Chasteen maintained that he was not the primary force in promoting the move, and that he had grown to love Kansas City after living his whole life in Alabama, but he appears to have come to the conclusion that the long-time headquarters city was not just indifferent to the NAIA, but in fact hostile. And once such an idea gets in one's head, any supporting evidence becomes increasingly compelling.[23]

Meanwhile, Tulsa Mayor Rodger Randle initiated contact and proposed some attractive enticements if the NAIA would move to the Oklahoma community, located just 250 miles to the south. Discounted floor space and parking, country club memberships, and a supportive community were among the incentives to relocate. It didn't hurt that there was less competition for sports attention in Tulsa. Chasteen had never been to Tulsa, but Joe Struckle, head of the Future Committee and President of Northwest Oklahoma State, was a well-respected and articulate advocate for his state and described Tulsa as an up-and-coming city. Struckle had put Randle, an old hunting buddy, up to making the pitch to the NAIA.

Though the COP's leaders knew about the Tulsa bid, the NAIA staff was kept in the dark. Only Chasteen and top aide Bill Patterson were in on the negotiations. Adding to the level of secrecy, Carol Putnam was excluded from her normal function of arranging for Chasteen, Patterson, and Struckle to fly to Tulsa. On the eve of the annual convention, held in Kansas City in September 1992, those COP leaders flew to Oklahoma, held a press conference in Tulsa announcing the move, and then flew back to Kansas City, where the COP had convened prior to the annual convention. The COP then voted unanimously to accept Tulsa's bid and move the NAIA's headquarters to Oklahoma.

In a remarkable feat, the COP had conducted negotiations with Tulsa in utmost secrecy and sprang the move on the convention as a surprise. Chasteen attributed the secrecy to COP Chair Ed Stevens, President of George Fox College in Oregon, saying that playing things close to the vest was not his style. Nevertheless, rumors had begun to circulate at the convention that morning, and when Wally Schwartz, the senior NAIA staff member, found the CEO just before lunch and asked him about the stories, Chasteen put his arm around his shoulders and told him it was just a rumor. A few hours later the COP dropped the bombshell and Schwartz felt betrayed, souring him on the move and precipitating his retirement in 1995. The secret talks drove a wedge between Chasteen and the staff, and for some it poisoned the relationship.[24]

Ed Stevens announced the move to the public, and *The NAIA News* carried the story in the November 1992 issue. He asserted that the NAIA had not been seeking a new headquarters, but that Randle, the Metropolitan Tulsa Chamber of Commerce, and affiliated organizations had made a proposal that got the attention of the COP. (Unfortunately, Rodger Randle had resigned as mayor on July 31, 1992, to take an education position at the University Center at Tulsa. Susan Savage replaced him as mayor and served into 2002, and while her support for the NAIA was sufficient to carry through the transfer, it did not prove up to the task of making the city's relationship with the association an enduring one.)[25] Tulsa exceeded all the standards the COP had set a few years earlier for a possible new headquarters. In addition, *The New York Times* had rated Tulsa "America's Friendliest City," the city was rich in cultural diversity, and the NAIA would not be the low man on the local sports totem pole. The COP was clearly excited about the move.[26]

Who was responsible for the move? None of the NAIA leaders claimed that honor. Chasteen maintains that the COP was responsible. He told them when they approved the move that they would fly off from the convention and he would be left to clean up the mess in Kansas City. Wally Schwartz blamed Chasteen, his number two Bill Patterson, and Joe Struckle for the decision. Patterson noted that Struckle had tactfully held back in promoting the move, not wanting his Oklahoma connection to distort the process. Patterson agreed that he himself had played a major part in the negotiations with the Tulsans, for Chasteen was not a tough negotiator. Tom Feld on the COP had also played a key role, inducing Tulsa to up its offer to include an added $100,000 in moving costs and other considerations at a critical point in the negotiations. To the degree that the COP took the lead, Patterson guessed that they were responding to the obvious frustrations he and Chasteen were feeling with Kansas City. At any rate, once Chasteen had bought into the move, he carried the COP with him. There was plenty of credit (or blame, as it seemed later) to go around.[27] As President Kennedy said after the Bay of Pigs fiasco, success has a thousand fathers, but failure is an orphan.

The NAIA's headquarters might be moving, but the men's cross-country venue stayed in Kenosha, Wisconsin, where it had been since 1976 except for a foray to Salina, Kansas, in 1980. The new decade brought a new dominating power to the fore. Adams State had won 10 of the previous 11 titles, but in 1990 Lubbock Christian (TX) emerged, pushing the Indians into second place in 1990 and 1991 and right out of the NAIA after 1992. The new champions reeled off eight consecutive victories, all in fairly convincing fashion. The first four years of their reign James Bungei also took individual honors for his school.

In Division I football, Central State (OH) crushed Fort Hays State and Carson-Newman to get to the title match in 1990, where they took on Mesa State (CO), a narrow winner over Western New Mexico and Central Arkansas. Central State's Marauders then relegated Mesa State to their third runner-up finish, riding Ray Hill's 208 rushing yards to a 38-16 victory. Two of the 1990 teams were back in 1991's dramatic final. Central Arkansas, twice a co-champion after tying in the 1984 and 1985 title games, almost had a third tie, but finally won a see-saw battle over defending champion Central State, 19-16, on a dramatic Steve Strange field goal with seven seconds to play. Central State bounced back in 1992, eliminating Central Arkansas in the semifinal game and then nipping Gardner-Webb for the title by the same 19-16 score by which they had lost the previous year. The Marauders fought back from a 16-6 deficit in the fourth quarter and pulled out the game in the last minute after shutting down Gardner-Webb's NAIA total offense record-holding team.

In 1990, Division II football action, Peru State (NE) thwarted Westminster's bid for a third straight title with a 17-7 win, wrapping up a 12-0-1 season with the Bobcats' first national title. The next year Georgetown (KY) celebrated the centennial of its football program with its first-ever national championship, edging Pacific Lutheran in a battle of "class acts," 28-20. Both teams saluted the other's sportsmanship in a hard-fought but cleanly played game that modeled the NAIA ideal of athletic competition. In 1992, Georgetown lost in the first playoff round to Findlay (OH), and the Ohio smash-mouth offensive team barreled its way to its first national title since 1979, beating perennial power Linfield (OR) before a new NAIA Division II record crowd of 9,141 in Portland, 26-13.

West Virginia Wesleyan captured its second consecutive title and fourth in seven years in men's soccer in 1990, frustrating the College of Boca Raton again, this time by a 3-1 score. The losing Knights finally found the formula in 1991—they changed their name from Boca Raton to Lynn University, and rode a Lenin Steenkamp overtime penalty kick to a 2-1 win over Midwestern State (TX) and their second championship. The charm wore off in 1992, though, as Belhaven (MS) edged Lynn, 2-1, to capture their first title in four trips to the nationals.

In 1991, Oklahoma City won the final undivided men's basketball title, nipping Central Arkansas, 77-74, in the title game behind tourney MVP Eric Manuel. The next year featured the inauguration of divisional play in basketball, and for the first time ever, the two finalists returned to the Division I championship game. Oklahoma City came in undefeated, with a chance to match Central State (OH) in 1965 as the only undefeated champion. Central Arkansas sought revenge for their narrow loss in 1991, and after 40 minutes the two teams were dead even in a game viewed nationally on ESPN. The Chiefs then rode the hot overtime shooting of MVP Smoky McCovery to an 82-73 win and a successful defense of their title, giving Coach Darrel Johnson two titles, his perfect season, and a 72-3 record in his two years. In 1993 Hawaii Pacific captured the first Hawaiian national basketball championship at any level, beating top-seeded Oklahoma Baptist, 88-83, in the title game after squeaking through their previous two games by a total of four points.

The first Division II title game, like the first Division I game, went into overtime, suggesting that the hoped-for increase in competitiveness had triumphed. Grace College (IN) topped Northwestern (IA), 85-79, for first place, but the Cinderella story of the tourney was Dakota State, a 12-15 team that won four games in District twelve, then four at the nationals, including a win over top-ranked King College (TN), to make the semifinals, where the loss of their point guard to an emergency appendectomy finally stopped their improbable bid. In 1993, host Northwest Nazarene (ID) tried on the Cinderella mantle, only to fall in the semifinals to eventual champion Willamette (OR) in overtime. Willamette then knocked off top-seeded Northern State (SD) for the championship, 63-56.

Lubbock Christian edged Azusa Pacific for the 1991 indoor track and field title, dealing the Cougars their fifth straight second-place finish. Runner Mbarak Hussein won the first of two straight outstanding performer awards for the winners. The next year Adams State rode their distance runners to first place, once again leaving Azusa Pacific runners-up. In 1993, however, Central State (OH) beat out Lubbock Christian for top honors and ended APU's string.

Swimming power Drury (MO) won championships for the fourth, fifth, and sixth straight years despite a scare in 1991 when they edged Oral Roberts (OK) by only 1.5 points. They won handily over runners-up Simon Fraser and Puget Sound in 1992 and 1993. Coach Tom Reynolds' Panthers were paced in 1991 and 1992 by Kelly Kremer, who wound up his Drury years with eight individual titles.

Northern Montana's Skylights won the national wrestling championships in 1991 and 1992 and took second place in 1993, when Simon Fraser (BC) took three individual titles to bump the defending champions to second place. Justin Abdou won his fourth straight title for SFU at the 177-pound level to win outstanding performer recognition in 1993.

Lewis-Clark (ID) continued its domination in baseball in 1991, blanking Oral Roberts, 7-0, in the final game to cap a perfect 32-0 home record. The Warriors, who had ruled the sport since the nationals moved to their field in 1984, losing the title only once in eight years, showed that they could also win on the road, clobbering Mary Hardin-Baylor, 14-4, to take the 1992 title as the tournament moved to Des Moines, Iowa. Lewis-Clark hit a dry patch after that, and in 1993 St. Francis (IL) bested Southeastern Oklahoma in the championship game, 4-2. Paul Chovanec hurled the winning game and ran his record to 14-0 for the season, including five complete-game wins in the tournament. St. Francis was coached by Gordie Gillespie, who became the winningest coach in college baseball history with 1,347 wins more than offsetting 693 losses.

After finishing second in 1990 and ending their seven-year string of championships, Azusa Pacific was back on top in track and field in 1991, leaving Central State (OH) and Lubbock Christian (TX) far behind in a tie for second. The Cougars were paced by twin Nigerian freshmen sprinters Davidson and Osmond Ezinwa, with the former winning top performer honors in 1991 and 1992, when APU repeated as champion with Central State closing the gap in second place. In 1993, the

Marauders moved up a notch and beat out Prairie View A&M (TX) to win their lone track and field title.

In golf, North Florida had the best run over the three years, taking top honors over Oklahoma City in 1991, slipping to second behind Huntingdon (AL) in 1992, then moving back to the top spot over Huntingdon and Glenville State (WV) in 1993. Jamie Burns tied for the best individual score in 1992 and won it outright in 1993 to lead North Florida.

Lander (SC) won the tennis championship in 1991 and 1992, with BYU-Hawaii tying West Florida for second the first year and winning that position outright in 1992. Mobile (AL) took top honors in 1993, with North Florida and Auburn-Montgomery (AL) tying for second.

On the women's side of the sports ledger, perennial powers dominated soccer action. The 1990 game matched the previous year's finalists, but this time Berry College (GA) turned the tables on Pacific Lutheran (WA), winning 3-1 in overtime to avenge their overtime defeat in 1989. In the first season using a six-team pool format, Berry won its second title three years after its last crown. In 1991 Berry lost in pool play and Pacific Lutheran made it through to the title match, where they overwhelmed Missouri Valley (MO), 4-0, for the Lutes' third championship in four years. The Lutes came up just a bit short in 1992, though, as Lynn (FL) survived a first-half onslaught and scored on a header by Dorte Nielsen in the second to win, 1-0. Nielsen, the tournament MVP, scored five goals and racked up 11 points, both records.

In volleyball action, Hawaii Pacific knocked off Texas Wesleyan in the finals to complete the Lady Sea Warriors' ascent from third in 1988 and second in 1989. Hawaii continued to dominate the sport, as BYU-Hawaii swept IUPU-Indianapolis in 1991 to capture the national title. BYU-Hawaii kept the state's honor intact in 1992 by sweeping California Baptist in the finals. That victory gave Hawaii ten of the thirteen titles to date, leaving only three for California schools to divide among themselves.

In cross-country competition, Western State (CO) gained revenge on Adams State for the Indians' 1989 victory, turning the tables and racing to the 1990 title. Adams State regained the top spot in 1991, but couldn't hold on as Puget Sound (WA) launched a four-year string of championships in 1992.

Women's basketball, like men's, held only one championship in 1991, then split into two divisions. That last unified title, the first to feature a 32-team field, went to Fort Hays State (KS), when the Lady Tigers knocked off defending champion Southwestern Oklahoma, 57-53, behind star center and tournament MVP Annette Wiles' 20 points.

Arkansas Tech shot 66 percent from the field to blow out Wayland Baptist in the first Division I title game, 84-68, capping a 35-1 season with their 29th straight victory. Not so dominant the next season, Tech's Golden Suns reached the final game against the home-town Union University Lady Bulldogs in Jackson, Tennessee, and fought their way to a thrilling 76-75 win before 6,515 screaming local fans, finally capturing the game with a basket with only three ticks left on the clock.

Northern State (SD) grabbed the first Division II title with a solid 73-56 triumph over Tarleton State (TX), winning their four games by an average of 24.8 points. Barb Schmidt won tournament MVP honors with 20 points, including six straight three-pointers, in the final. The Wolves fell just short in their bid to repeat in 1993. Playing before big crowds in Monmouth, Oregon, Northern State lost the dramatic 71-68 final game to Northern Montana's Skylights, a District 12 rival that seemed to have a hex on the South Dakotans. Kristi Kincaid, a reserve for Northern Montana, won MVP honors.

Prairie View A&M (TX) continued its remarkable record in indoor track and field. Since the second year of national competition, 1982, the Pantherettes had finished first or second every season. In 1991 they nabbed their third title behind runner Barbara Smith, named the outstanding performer at the meet. In 1992 Simon Fraser (BC) edged Central State (OH) for first place, taking their second title in three years behind their dominating distance relay teams. Then Central State, after two consecutive second-place finishes, finally grabbed top honors in 1993 (as did their men's team) with six individual championships, leaving Wayland Baptist and Simon Fraser far behind.

In swimming and diving competition, Simon Fraser (BC) reversed the top two places of 1990 by edging Puget Sound for the 1991 title, led by freshman sprint-freestyler Sharon Wilson's three individual victories. In 1992, Drury (MO) won both men's and women's titles as the women began a three-year run of championships with Puget Sound finishing second each time. Each year from 1991 to 1994 multiple-event winner Lourette Hakansson of Drury earned recognition as the outstanding swimmer of the meet.

Spring sports featured softball, at which Hawaii Loa showed the greatest skill in 1991, as they cruised undefeated through the tournament, beating Puget Sound, 6-1, in the championship game. Pitcher Shannon Akau won MVP honors for the winners. The next year, Pacific Lutheran hammered out 42 runs in five games to overwhelm the field, beating Kennesaw State (GA) in the final, 3-2, in the Lutes' closest game. In 1993, West Florida bounced back from a morning 10-1 loss to Oklahoma City and shut down the Lady Chiefs, 4-2, in the deciding game. Tournament MVP Danelle Harvey, loser of the morning game, shook it off and won the "must-win" game.

Women's tennis crowned three different champions in three years. In 1991, Flagler (FL) won its fifth straight title, barely edging Auburn-Montgomery (AL), whose Saskia Hermans was named outstanding player. The next year the teams switched places, with the Alabama school coming out on top but Flagler's Helena Dahlstrom winning the first of two straight outstanding player awards. In 1993, Lynn University won the match, with Auburn-Montgomery dropping back to second. Over the span of twelve years after 1991, Auburn-Montgomery would win four firsts and six seconds as a perennial power.

Track and field provided continuity rather than mystery. In each of the three years Central State (OH) finished first and Simon Fraser (BC) wound up second. In 1991, Carolin Sterling won top performer honors with a 100-meter hurdle victory along with three relay wins. She took the award again in 1992 and performed well in 1993, when Central State teammate Deon Hemmings took home individual honors.

Putting together all of their sports accomplishments, the best of the best won the NAIA-SIDA All-Sports championships. In 1990-91 Lubbock Christian won men's honors handily, with Simon Fraser and Central State (OH) trailing distantly. Simon Fraser, however, did win the women's award, beating out Pacific Lutheran and Central State for the top position. In 1991-92, Adams State took the men's title, with Simon Fraser repeating as the women's winner. In 1992-93, Central State won men's honors, topping Simon Fraser and Lubbock Christian. Puget Sound nipped Central State for the women's title, with Simon Fraser winding up third. Times were good for schools in the northwest!

13

Going South
1993-1997

The move to Tulsa went fairly smoothly, with the new national office officially opening on August 2, 1993. Chasteen and a site selection committee had made several trips to Oklahoma before settling on Warren Place for the new headquarters and negotiating an acceptable arrangement for 8,700 square feet of space. Almost all of the staff relocated along with the national office; eager job aspirants were told that there were only four openings to fill. The veterans did not all fall in love with their new headquarters city, though, and several, including Wally Schwartz, drifted back to Kansas City over the next couple of years. In fact, by late 1995, only seven of the 27 employees in the office had more than two years experience. But the Tulsa staff took an active role in the community, volunteering in numerous civic organizations, from churches to the Chamber of Commerce to the United Way. In late 1996, Bill Patterson, one of its chief orchestrators, was still waxing eloquent about how great the move had been for the NAIA.[1]

A dramatic restructuring of the association affected most NAIA members much more than the relocated headquarters. After a half century of being organized into 32 districts, at the fall 1993 convention in Atlanta the membership jettisoned the district format in favor of a system of affiliated conferences and independents. Affiliated conference commissioners had launched the process at the Portland convention in late 1991, requesting the COP to assess the future of the NAIA and the role that affiliated conferences would play in that future. In February 1992, the Future Committee advocated integrating the conferences into the governing and championship structures in some way, leading the Council of Athletic Administrators to set up an ad hoc committee to develop a proposal for the CAA and the 1992 convention to consider. In August, the committee gathered and worked up a resolution and recommendations that the CAA accepted and took to the membership, which passed them at the tumultuous Kansas City convention after the bombshell of the Tulsa move had gone off.

In October 1992, the COP appointed a nine-person Committee on the Role of Affiliated Conferences, chaired by Bob Boerigter of Hastings College, Nebraska, to flesh out the recommendations and develop a plan to make the conferences a central part of NAIA operations. By the time the COP gathered for its April 1993 meeting in Tulsa, the committee had formulated a detailed map to achieve its goals, including placement of conferences and independents in nine regions (though the number of regions might vary by sport) and an outline of the route teams would take to the national tournaments. The COP unanimously approved the recommendations, sought a few refinements, and put it on the fall 1993 convention agenda in Atlanta. If approved, the proposal called for implementation for basketball immediately (1993-94) and for all other sports the following year.

To qualify as an affiliated conference, a league needed to have at least six NAIA-member institutions, a charter or constitution with appropriate officials, eligibility rules and standards at least as strict as the NAIA, and sponsor at least one men's and women's sport in fall, winter, and spring. Conferences would pay dues to the NAIA. At that point, the committee still envisioned retaining districts, though in a much-diminished role, but by the time the proposal came to the convention, the very few districts that would be able to play a role had become an anomaly and were eliminated.[2]

The proposal adopted by the COP in April 1993 included detailed listings of conferences for all sports. Since basketball would immediately implement the recommendations, it serves as a good example. Men's Division I basketball, with 193 colleges participating, included 16 automatic conference berths, nine regional berths for independents, and seven at-large slots to make up the 32 team field. The 16 conferences (with membership numbers) were:

Arkansas Intercollegiate (9)	Kentucky Intercollegiate (7)
Carolinas Intercollegiate (8)	Oklahoma Intercollegiate (6)
Chicagoland (7)	Sooner Athletic (6)
Eastern Intercollegiate (6)	Show-Me Collegiate (6)
Georgia Athletic (9)	Southern States (8)
Golden State Athletic (7)	Tennessee Collegiate (9)
Gulf Coast Athletic (9)	W. Virginia Intercollegiate (14)
Heart of Texas (6)	Wolverine-Hoosier (7)

Regional independents were grouped as Pacific Northwest (7), Pacific Northwest-Montana (5), Great Lakes (12), Far West (6), Far West-Hawaii (3), Southeast (7), Southwest (11), Midwest (10), and Northeast (8). There were some obvious inequities, but theoretically the at-large bids would even some of them out.

Men's Division II basketball encompassed 167 teams, 105 in 14 conferences, 62 in regional groupings meriting seven slots, with three at-large berths filling out the 24-team field. Conferences in Division II were:

Central Atlantic (9)	Midwest Classic (7)
Florida Sun (8)	Nebraska-Iowa (7)
Heart of America (9)	North Dakota Athletic (6)
Kansas Collegiate (9)	Northwest (7)
Lake Michigan (7)	South Dakota Intercollegiate (6)
Mayflower (7)	Tennessee-Virginia (11)
Mid-Central (6)	Texas Intercollegiate (6)

Division II had more equitable regional groupings for independents in seven regions—Pacific Northwest (9), Southwest (8), Midwest (10), Great Lakes (10), Great Lakes (7), Northeast (8), and Northeast (10)—but needed to work on creative naming.

Division I women were the only group with more independent than conference teams. A total of 164 teams—74 in conferences and 90 independents—meant only nine of the 32 slots would be automatic conference bids, 12 would go to regional champs, and 11 would be at-large bids. Their conferences were:

Arkansas Intercollegiate (9)	Gulf Coast Athletic (9)
Carolinas Intercollegiate (8)	Heart of Texas (6)
Eastern Intercollegiate (6)	Tennessee Collegiate (9)
Georgia Intercollegiate (7)	West Virginia
Golden State Athletic (6)	Intercollegiate (14)

Independents were organized into 12 regions, with some major inequities: Pacific Northwest (7), Pacific Northwest-Montana (5), Southwest (10), Southeast (7), Southwest-Oklahoma (12), Midwest (7), Midwest (8), Northeast (9), Great Lakes (10), Southeast (5), Southeast (6), and Far West (4). Eleven at-large bids would help level the playing field.

Division II women, in contrast to Division I, had the highest percentage of their schools in conferences. Of 170 schools, 115 would get 16 automatic bids as conference representatives, 55 independents would get seven regional slots, and a mere one at-large team would fill out the 24-team field.

Central Atlantic (8)	Mid-Ohio (6)
Cascade Collegiate (6)	Nebraska-Iowa (7)

Heart of America (9)	North Dakota Collegiate (6)
Kansas Collegiate (9)	Northwest (7)
Lake Michigan (7)	South Dakota Intercollegiate (6)
Mayflower (7)	Tennessee-Virginia (11)
Midwest Classic (6)	Texas Intercollegiate (6)
Mid-Central (6)	Wolverine-Hoosier (8)

The regional groupings of independents showed serious inequities: Southwest (7), Midwest (10), Southeast (5), Great Lakes (11), Great Lakes (7), Northeast (7), and Northeast (8), with that lone at-large slot available to reduce a sense of injustice.[3]

When the delegates convened in Atlanta in October 1993, the proposal had been refined. The four remaining districts had been eliminated and all districts would cease functioning after the 1993-94 competition. A Council of Affiliated Conferences (and Independents, by a friendly amendment—thus CACI) would replace the Council of District Chairs on the National Coordinating Committee, joining the Council of Athletic Administrators and Council of Faculty Athletic Representatives and three at-large members there. Representation on the CAA itself would be restructured to reflect the enhanced role of the affiliated conferences and the new regions. At the convention, the delegates overwhelmingly approved the proposed change, with 81.9 percent voting in favor of the radical break with association tradition.[4] Whether such a change would be interpreted as a healthy willingness to change with the times or as a sign of nervousness that the old ways were not working anymore, it significantly restructured the NAIA.

Along with the move to Tulsa and the restructuring, another optimistic note for the association concerned the budget. President Chasteen reported that a $122,000 budget surplus in 1992 had been surpassed by a $437,000 balance in 1993, an impressive turnaround from a $47,000 deficit in 1991. The good financial news put the NAIA in an expansive mood. Women's golf won approval as an invitational sport in 1993-94 and as a championship sport in 1994-95. Division II basketball for both men and women expanded from 20 to 24 teams, tying into the new regional structure, and women's soccer moved from a six to an eight-team playoff.

The flush mood passed. In October 1994, the COP asked the Council of Athletic Administrators to monitor the number of schools with wrestling and swimming and diving teams, which were dwindling. The CAA reduced the number of awards to reflect the smaller number of participants in those sports. More critically, the budget surplus evaporated, victim of reduced revenue from fall 1994 football and the men's basketball tourney in 1995. At the COP gathering in April 1995 in Tulsa, the presidents talked of cutting back basketball to 16 teams in each division and holding the tournaments in the same town. The two-division football structure would end following the 1995 playoffs as well. The chances of going to divisional play in volleyball, softball, and baseball, never overwhelming, evaporated in the face of potential increased costs. Back in the national office, at an Executive Cabinet meeting on April 19, Chasteen told his staff that the financial situation was critical and slashed travel and printing funds. Just two weeks earlier, he had insisted he sign all requisitions and instituted emergency procedures to cope with an anticipated $182,000 deficit.[5] Though the COP launched a National Corporate Advisory Board in October 1996 under the direction of Bob Terrell as a potential corporate fundraising body, the board never came close to matching the hopes surrounding its founding, and the optimism that had accompanied the move to Tulsa gave way to grave concern about the NAIA's health.[6]

A more immediate financial concern to member institutions concerned financial aid to student athletes. In 1994, the COP charged an ad hoc financial aid committee, chaired by David Stair of Evangel College (MO), to do three things. First, create a definition of financial aid for athletes that would include all institutionally controlled aid. Second, limit that aid in a way that would not reduce squad sizes for schools that depended on their numbers to keep enrollment healthy. Third, assure that limits would not restrict schools' ability to attract academically gifted student athletes. After wrestling with this mandate for two years, the ad hoc committee concluded that the task was well nigh impossible. Especially tricky, given the NAIA's emphasis on academics, was setting limits high enough to accommodate schools boosting their enrollment with athletes while still communicating to the public that academic concern.

Two additional problems confronted the ad hoc group. First, with all the changes that had occurred in NAIA operations over the past few years, a period of stability struck many members as highly desirable. Long-term planning was difficult if the rules changed every few years. Second, either changing the rule or keeping it the same had different institutions vowing to leave the NAIA, so the proposal was almost a lose-lose situation. Still, to include all institutional aid in the definition would make for a leveler playing field in each sport, along with making a clearer distinction between Division I and Division II in basketball by the number of scholarships accorded each.

The committee proposed a definition of institutional aid as "all aid institutionally managed or controlled exclusive of loans not controlled by the institutions, Pell grants, State Grants, and Government Work-study." It recommended aid ceilings roughly equivalent to existing levels if all institutional aid were included, starting with 38 scholarships in football, 15 in Division I basketball and eight in Division II. Most significant, it developed a brilliant concept to refocus emphasis on academic achievement by suggesting that only half of aid to students with grade point averages above 3.25 count and that no aid count against the ceiling for students with better than 3.5 grade point averages.[7]

The matter came to the COP for its decision at the April 1997 meeting. After a bit of tweaking with numbers, the concept developed by the committee passed the COP, though with rather higher floors than the original proposal. Continuing students with cumulative GPA of 3.6 or standing in the top 10 percent of their class would not have their aid counted against the ceiling, and students above 3.3 GPA or ranking in the top 25 percent would have only half of their aid count. This new arrangement offered a huge incentive to coaches to recruit true student-athletes in order to make their scholarship money go farther. The limits, by sport, were as follows: football 24, Division I basketball 11, Division II basketball 6, volleyball 8, track and field 12, cross country 5, swimming and diving 8, baseball 12, softball 10, golf 5, soccer 12, tennis 5, and wrestling 8.[8]

Meanwhile, the battle with the NCAA for schools' allegiance continued, with a new twist in 1995: so many schools moved to NCAA Division III that it had become the largest athletic association if the three NCAA divisions were counted separately. The NAIA was second, NCAA Division II third, and the highly publicized NCAA Division I the smallest. In 1995, the two lower-ranked NCAA divisions placed a moratorium on new members until they could figure out how to assimilate them. The NCAA News of May 27, 1996, offered the following headline: "Stronger NAIA eases threat of excessive growth in Division III." It noted that the NAIA had lost around 100 institutions over the past decade, citing accreditation standards, championship opportunities, and athletics philosophy as contributing factors. It quoted Bill Patterson's upbeat assessment of NAIA stability and his forecast that membership would hold around 365 for a few years, then likely increase. That assessment dovetailed with a Chasteen estimate in mid-1995, based on the best guesses of his staff and the NAIA councils, of membership remaining at least 350 for the next five years.[9]

That positive outlook seemed a bit optimistic, given almost 87 dual NAIA/NCAA members, many of whom were going through the four-year waiting phase before being able to become full NCAA members. (Meanwhile, ineligible for NCAA playoffs, they continued to compete for NAIA national honors, to the frustration of NAIA purists who saw such schools as traitors.) Louis Spry, who worked for the NAIA for a couple of years in the mid-sixties and went on to a long career with the NCAA, including chief financial officer, remembered that he visited many colleges and conference meetings pitching the NCAA, and he ran into Wally Schwartz, selling the NAIA, so often that they became good friends. Spry had retained a soft spot in his heart for the NAIA, noting that the NAIA's membership realized that there was no money and limited staff, so they appreciated what service they got from the national office. NCAA institutions, on the other hand, expected perfection from the well-paid national staff, putting it under unwelcome pressure. He was nostalgic for the grassroots, "mom and pop" NAIA operation. Chasteen liked to point out that the NCAA had more people in its enforcement office than the whole NAIA national staff, a condition encouraged by the NAIA's modest operating budget. As he recalls, "We didn't have any money on top of the table, much less under the table." In spite of Spry's sentimental feelings toward the NAIA, he believes that every conference he had wooed had eventually joined the NCAA.[10]

Some of the conference defections were more awkward than others. Almost all of the Arkansas schools, including Jeff Farris's University of Central Arkansas in 1993, left the NAIA during the nineties. With the departure of their chief football rivals, many Oklahoma schools, led by Northeastern Oklahoma, followed suit. Before they left, Joe Struckle and others wishing to stick with the NAIA had called Chasteen, seeking help in persuading their colleagues to remain. He promised a meeting in two months, but when it arrived he had no plan to offer them. Struckle stuck with the NAIA, realizing that modest-sized, 2000-student Northwestern Oklahoma could not afford to add more sports as mandated by the NCAA, and he convinced a few others to stay on board, but the bulk of the Oklahoma Intercollegiate Conference began the transition to the NCAA.[11] Because the trend since the 1980s had been for state universities to move to Division II, notably those in Wisconsin and Kansas, the NAIA was made up of roughly 80 percent smaller private institutions. The Oklahoma defections thus made some sense. More troublesome was the case of the Northwest Conference of Independent Colleges.

The NCIC—Lewis and Clark, Linfield, Pacific, Pacific Lutheran, Whitman, Whitworth, and Willamette—seemed a perfect fit for the NAIA. The conference had been around since the 1940s and members of the NAIA since 1959. The schools were small and kept athletics subordinate to their academic programs. But a majority of the institutions had new presidents on board (the average tenure for a small school president is only about three years), and many of them hailed from areas of the country where Division III was the accepted affiliation for small schools. At the conference meeting in November 1993 a proposal to bolt the NAIA for Division III was tabled by a 6-1 vote, providing time for proponents and critics of the shift to marshal and present their arguments. David Olson, Pacific Lutheran athletic director and former NAIA President, wrote a closely reasoned, balanced defense of the association that he sent to conference members. He noted the key role NCIC members had played in NAIA history, in particular in pushing for the affiliated conferences change in 1993. A shift to the NCAA would dramatically reduce NCIC opportunities for national competition, especially as the NCAA used power ratings rather than conference championships to choose competitors and Far West schools did not fare well in such choices. It would also hurt recruiting, as NAIA schools in the area could offer athletic scholarships and the NCIC could not. The financial benefits of the NCAA paying for national competition had to be weighed against the publicity gained by more frequent NAIA championship participation. For schools that rarely competed at the national level, that advantage disappeared completely. All in all, Olson strongly urged his colleagues to resist the siren call of the NCAA and stick with their longtime connection to the NAIA.[12]

The battle for the NCIC became heated at times during 1994. Whitworth's FAR, Bill Johnson, a strong NAIA supporter, quit his post when his president refused to meet with Bill Patterson on a lobbying visit. Linfield President Vivian Bull deferred to the judgment of Willamette's Jerry Hudson, who became the villain of the piece. Hudson served on the COP during 1994 even as he spearheaded the move to lead his conference out of the organization, with the COP finally expelling him after he voted to leave.[13] Chasteen denounced some of his posturing as pretentious and elitist.[14] Ed Stevens, President of independent George Fox College and 1992 COP President, felt pulled in all directions. Because of the affiliated conference measure, he had felt compelled to apply to join the NCIC, the only conference in the northwest. A new Cascade Conference was forming to take advantage of the affiliated conference advantage, but the NCIC had a history and prestige. Now Stevens was in the position of abandoning the NAIA if the NCIC did so, much to his sorrow. He lamented that the NCAA's money and power was destroying the NAIA, predicting that it would either go out of business or become solely an association of small, private schools.[15] Arleigh Dodson, commissioner of the NCIC, maintained that the conference had been NAIA all those years because there had been no Division III until 1973. The conference still didn't charge admission to games and focused on students, faculty, and alumni rather than marketing their games to the wider public. Now that members had expressed interest in competing nationally, it made sense to take advantage of the NCAA's ability to fund such trips. His key argument was that the NCIC schools, de-emphasizing athletics, fit best in an association that did not include athletic scholarships. By the end of 1994, the NCIC had made its choice: it applied for Division III provisional membership.

What could have been done? One thing would have been to get back defectors. In 1995, Chasteen wrote letters to Fred Young at Elon and Don Davis at Cameron suggesting that they take out dual membership and reclaim their NAIA heritage after having left a few years earlier. Neither took the bait.[16] In October 1996, the convention approved, with minimal discussion, a program to permit dual members eligibility exemptions for one sport, especially helpful to potential members in Canada.[17] The COP also sought to ease the way for repentant deserters to return to the NAIA fold, a desire NAIA leaders believed to be fairly widespread.[18] In addition, the COP developed a detailed timetable for recruiting new members, and also laid out its expectations for members of the COP, including being strong advocates of the association.[19] The COP and the national office also served as firefighters, countering rumors and misinformation as it surfaced. Chasteen was particularly exercised over an article in the May 3, 1996, *Chronicle of Higher Education*. The story focused on Division II and Division III restructuring plans, and mentioned in passing rumors that the NAIA might fold soon. That sort of suggestion contributed to what Bill Patterson called the "sinking ship syndrome," where schools applied to join the NCAA just in case, then had presidential ego involvement in carrying through even though the NAIA was alive and well.[20] Key leaders had no doubts about the organization's survival, but they were concerned about the erosion of membership and the NAIA's overall health.[21] Keeping membership numbers up, and with them morale, was a constant struggle.

As it turned out, leadership issues proved an even greater struggle, at least in the short run. With the change to an affiliated conference system in 1993, the COP shifted from representing the old 32 districts to representing the nine regions. Three would be elected from the five largest districts, two from the four smallest districts, making 23 elected, and the remaining nine were to be appointed by the administrative council, permitting adjustments to ensure balance, equity, and continuity. The COP then reelected Joe Struckle as chair for 1994.

In 1994, a new body emerged, the Leadership Council. Made up of the administrative council of the COP, the chair of the National Coordinating Committee, the chairs of the NCC's three councils (FARs, athletic directors, and affiliated conferences), President Chasteen, and representatives from the national office, the Leadership Council provided a forum for the open discussion of NAIA concerns and gave participants a healthy sense of empowerment in meetings roughly twice a year. Perhaps it empowered these leaders more than Chasteen had envisioned—in due course they came to the conclusion that he needed to be replaced.[22] Nevertheless, Chasteen betrayed his own concern with the way the NAIA's governance was functioning in a letter to Jim Houdeshell in mid-1995. He said, "The association voted overwhelmingly for the present organizational format and it is incumbent on each of us to make it work. . . . It will take time and patience to implement."[23] Clearly, something was awry.

At the fall 1995 COP meeting in Salt Lake City, James Bultman (Northwestern College, Iowa), chair of the Membership Retention and Recruitment Committee, handed out the results of a survey of current and departing NAIA institutions, with the information to be kept out of general circulation. It suggested that schools leaving the NAIA were most concerned with monetary and prestige issues, though they also expressed some unhappiness with the association's administration. Financial issues also ranked high among concerns of the ongoing members, but they expressed greater concern with the leadership of both the COP and Chasteen. This survey provided a foundation for a major marketing survey to be undertaken by Creative Resources, Inc., of Chattanooga, commissioned to prepare a detailed analysis by spring 1996.[24]

Perhaps in response to perceived criticism, Chasteen issued an executive report on November 1, 1995. He observed that COP membership had experienced a 90 percent turnover in three years, drastically reducing the members who had hired him and voted to move to Tulsa. He sought to clarify the functions of the national office, noting that it was divided into three components: the executive (primarily him), membership services, and championship services. Membership services dealt with membership retention and recruitment, sponsorships, publications, public relations, conventions, contracts with official status companies, and resource development. Championship services handled the 24 national championships, site selection for them, coaches' handbooks, rules and regulations, and sports information. His own responsibilities included day-to-day operation of the office, hiring and training its personnel, managing its finances, developing a balanced budget, assigning staff liaisons for championship events, organizing COP meetings and conventions, and traveling extensively. In essence, he seemed to be saying, he and his staff had extremely busy schedules and hardly merited the criticism directed at them.[25]

By the next COP meeting, at Grenelefe Golf and Tennis Resort in Haines City, Florida, on March 31 and April 1, 1996, Jim Bultman's Membership Committee had developed a strategic plan. The COP approved the plan and called for it to be dovetailed with the plan of action developed by Creative Resources, Inc. (CRI), also presented at the conference. The strategic plan examined the 225 institutions that left the NAIA over the past nine years. Of those, six had returned to the NAIA, 19 had joined NCAA Division I, 91 had gone Division II, and 60 had affiliated with Division III. Five had joined the National Christian College Athletic Association, and eight the National Small College Athletic Association. The remaining 36 had dropped athletics, closed their doors, or were unknown. Since 82.1 percent of the NAIA membership were independent with an average enrollment of 1,454, those who left that did not fit that profile were written off. The big question concerned the 151 who fit the NAIA profile (like the NCIC schools) and left anyway. Why did they leave?

One major reason, beyond those cited in the survey reported the previous fall, was the turnover of presidents. An average of 50 new presidents per year had taken over NAIA institutions in the past two years, most of them with NCAA backgrounds and a high comfort level with the NCAA. Though most of the association's monetary problems had existed prior to 1986, or even 1990, when the NEC played a major role in governance, the perception then was that the NEC was actively involved in running the NAIA and addressing its problems. As the NEC had warned back in 1986, college presidents had too many responsibilities to devote the attention to athletics that athletic directors did. The presidents also lacked the commitment to the association of their athletic people. Shockingly, of 97 institutions represented on the COP from 1985 to 1994, 20 had left the NAIA for the NCAA and 25 more had become dual members. The committee called for a concerted effort to seize the opportunity afforded by the NCAA's two-year moratorium on new members. There were 87 dual members and 73 new presidents who had not yet received a visit from the national office. The time was right for action—it was up to the NAIA to seize the moment![26]

The bombshell of the meeting, however, was the CRI report. The COP had authorized Creative Resources to undertake a marketing study for the NAIA. The agency had done a similar job for the new Mid-South All Sports Conference, and Georgetown College President William Crouch, new to the COP and part of that conference, promoted it as a capable outfit. The report surprised the Administrative Committee of the COP with its name (*NAIA Leadership 2000*) and the scope of its investigation: to "identify the organization's strengths, weaknesses, and general public image (both internal and external) with the intent of determining its current and future viability, organizational credibility, corporate visibility, and future marketability for the primary purpose of stemming attrition, retaining current members, and attracting new members."[27] It seemed, one observer later commented, more like a "get Chasteen" project than a marketing study, and perhaps that was Crouch's agenda.[28]

The study drew on Jim Bultman's membership satisfaction survey, Chasteen's executive report, the NAIA's staff's comparative study of the NAIA and NCAA, Cliff Hamlow's document "16 Positives of the NAIA," and an extensive series of interviews with representatives of member institutions, conferences, media, and others. The report hammered the NAIA's leadership, both the COP and its CEO, and claimed a "complete loss of confidence by the member schools." The COP had failed to establish a realistic, progressive vision for the NAIA, and in particular failed to convey the NAIA's mission to new presidents moving in from NCAA schools. More specifically, Chasteen had failed "to understand and be responsive to the needs of the membership." Some institutions blasted Chasteen for failing to interact with them personally, but many with whom he had interacted termed such interaction "exceedingly counterproductive." His credibility had evaporated among the membership, especially his continually maintaining that "all is well" in the face of obvious problems. He and the COP were both cited for failure to communicate crucial matters to the membership, most notably on the move to Tulsa. The report's alarmist tone peaked in its conclusion, which referred to the NAIA's position in a football metaphor: "fourth and long, and the clock is ticking down."[29]

The Administrative Committee was stunned and aghast. It gathered up the copies of the report and had them destroyed. Chair Ken Bootsma then instructed the CRI's Archie Ellis to make some changes before a more sanitized version was admitted to the record and distributed to the full COP. In particular, the new report deleted "complete" from loss of confidence in the leadership and "exceedingly" in assessing the counter productivity of Chasteen's interactions with member institutions. Strong recommendations that the organization return to Kansas City were stricken, along with several references to a new or incoming CEO, which seemed rather presumptuous.[30] The COP then offered Chasteen no suggestions on improving his performance and he returned to his job in Tulsa, though he did receive a copy of Bootsma's memo and knew that his situation had become somewhat tenuous.

On June 16-18, 1996, the Leadership Council met in Albuquerque for its regular session, and the Administrative Committee allowed Chasteen to resign, buying out the remaining two and a half years of his contract to smooth his exit. Bill Patterson, his top aide, had to negotiate the severance arrangement as Chasteen had a rolling three-year contract and the COP brass had not figured out such details; Patterson didn't think the membership would have been too happy about the package had they known.[31]

The loss of membership probably most upset the COP. The leadership felt that Chasteen needed to have a better grasp of what schools were at risk, and though there were too many institutions for him to visit himself, *someone* should have been on top of problems and flagged risky members. Chasteen's defense was that by the time he was aware of departures, they were pretty much a done deal; once a president's mind was made up, there was no point in fighting a losing battle. He felt one had to pick one's fights carefully. But his officious manner tended to alienate presidents (who were a bit inclined that way themselves). He was always James, not Jim, and would "blow a gasket" if anyone used the familiar term on him. His staff recognized that Chasteen's sugarcoating of issues was just that. Ideally, he would have moved effectively to bring reality up to the sugarcoated level, but they felt he seemed paralyzed by the stresses and more inclined to just let things slide.[32]

After initially resisting the idea, Bill Patterson accepted the position as interim CEO while the search for a new head took place. To assist him, Greg Feris, chair of the CAA and athletic director of Wayland Baptist University in Texas, took a leave from his home school duties for the first half of 1997 to work on crucial member retention issues as a special advisor to Patterson. The interim president gave a rousing speech at the national convention on October 15, 1996, setting forth a number of goals for the association. He accentuated the positive—the NAIA's commitment to academics and doing the right thing—and enjoined the membership to seize the next two years to hang onto the 79 dual-member institutions that would be eligible to join the NCAA over that period. He reaffirmed his belief that the NAIA would survive, but acknowledged that it might be a different kind of organization in the future. At any rate, the staff was hard at work getting things up to speed for a new president.[33]

The Leadership Council took on the added task of searching for Chasteen's successor. Sheila Stearns, chancellor of Western Montana College, took over for Ken Bootsma as chair of the COP in mid-1996, becoming the first woman to hold that post. She and Georgetown's Bill Crouch co-chaired the Search Committee. On one thing they agreed: it should not be a college president, but someone who could bridge the COP/athletic director divide and market the NAIA effectively. The committee met in Dallas on September 3-4 and selected two finalists for the position, a pace suggesting an expedited process to get the association moving forward in a hurry. The two candidates, former California Angel President Richard Brown and Bob Terrell, a man near retirement age, were brought in to Tulsa to meet with the staff, and the reaction there and from telephoned references was negative enough that the two were dropped from consideration and the searchers went back to square one.[34]

After a lengthy process, the association finally settled on Steve Baker as the new President/CEO. A former major league pitcher of modest accomplishment (7-16, 5.13) over four seasons, Baker was a youthful and vigorous 41-year-old, bringing a new level of energy to the top spot. He had worked the past seven years as vice president of market development for Major League Baseball International, overseeing European operations. Over a period of several months the Search Committee got to know Baker and he researched the NAIA, about which he had only a modest understanding despite having received his bachelor's degree from an NAIA-member, the University of Denver. He attended the COP meeting in April 1997 in Tulsa and took an active part in business there while splitting his time between his New York responsibilities and his new NAIA job. On May 5 he officially became the sixth CEO in the sixty-year history of the body.

In men's fall sports, cross-country continued to fall under the sway of Lubbock Christian. The Chaparrals of 1993 defeated the top NCAA team, Arkansas, and went on to capture their fourth straight NAIA title, led by four-time winner James Bungei. In 1994 and 1995 Lubbock won again, this time paced by Simeon Sawe. In 1996, the Chaparral spell was broken. Yes, the team won a seventh straight crown, but Life's Silah Misoi set the 8000 meter record of 23:14 to take first-place individual honors and Life (GA) took their second of three consecutive second-place team finishes. A power shift was in the making.

Division I football continued as an eight-team playoff in 1993 and 1994. The first year East Central Oklahoma knocked off Glenville State (WV) in a high-scoring final, 49-35. In 1994, Northeastern State kept the title in state in a defensive battle, nipping Arkansas-Pine Bluff for the championship, 13-12, after trailing 10-0 on the losers' home field. Matt Weber passed for a season-high 173 yards on nine completions to spark the win. In 1995 another perennial Division I power, Central State (OH) stymied Northeastern Oklahoma's bid for a repeat, 37-7. One of only four teams in the contracted division playoffs, the Marauders were paced by Antonio Davis, who passed for four touchdowns and 240 yards to cop most valuable player honors. The final Division I title went back to the Sooner state, as Southwestern Oklahoma State edged Montana Tech, 33-31, on a late safety.

In Division II football, Pacific Lutheran (WA) unveiled a scoring juggernaut for the 1993 playoffs, blasting their way to 198 points in the four games, culminating their run with a 50-20 blowout of Westminster (PA). The air went out of the Lutes' offensive balloon the next season and Westminster turned the tables with a 27-7 triumph, capturing their sixth national title in the school's 100th year of football. The classy teams combined for a mere six penalties. In 1994, quarterback Jon Kitna set a new NAIA record for career total offense but could manage only a tie for his Central Washington Wildcats, 21-21 against the Findlay (OH) Oilers. In a gracious post-game interview, Findlay coach Dick Strahm said, "if a tie is like kissing a sister, then this is a pretty good looking sister." In 1996, senior quarterback Kurtiss Riggs passed for 431 yards and five touchdowns to lead Sioux Falls (SD) to a 14-0 record and its first national championship in a 47-25 trouncing of Western Washington.

Soccer got off to a rousing start as sixth-seeded Sangamon State (IL) upset heavily favored Lynn University, 4-3, in overtime. The Knights had gone 20-0, outscored their opponents 115-5, and were coming off a runner-up finish the previous year. They wound up in the same spot despite outshooting the Prairie Stars, 24-11. In 1994, for the first time using a World Cup-style draw to put teams into pools, West Virginia Wesleyan came out on top, beating Lynn in the semifinal match and then beating Mobile (AL), 4-2, for the title in front of MVP goalkeeper Bjorn Kohl. The next year, Lindsey Wilson College (KY), emulating Sangamon State two years earlier, overcame a sixth seeding and fought its way to a 2-1 win over Midwestern State (TX) in the title game. In 1996, the Blue Raiders showed they were not a flash in the pan, winning all four games by a combined 14-1 score, including a rousing 5-0 final over Birmingham Southern (AL).

Division I basketball highlighted the men's winter sports schedule. Fifth seeded Oklahoma City survived an 86-85 cliffhanger over Oklahoma Baptist in the semifinals, then topped Life (GA) in the 1994 title game, the first held in Tulsa, 99-81. In 1995, Birmingham Southern's Panthers dodged the tight games and won all five of its games by double digit margins averaging 24 points, culminating in a 92-76 championship game over Pfeiffer (NC) behind MVP James Cason's 27 points and 10 rebounds. The 1996 game saw Oklahoma City's Chiefs return to the winner's circle for the fourth time in the nineties, beating top-seeded Georgetown (KY) in the final, 86-80. Georgetown was playing without Coach Jim Reid, who was in the hospital and died soon after the tournament. In 1997, Life returned to the title game, this time as the top seed against another Oklahoma team, Oklahoma Baptist. The Running Eagles beat the local favorites, 73-64, to cap a brilliant 37-1 season. The Point Park Panthers (PA) were the Cinderella team of the tourney that year, advancing to the semifinals before the team without a gym finally succumbed to Oklahoma Baptist.

In 1994, Eureka College (IL), captured the Division II basketball title with a 98-85 win over Northern State (SD), with Chris Peterson leading the team in scoring through their title run. In 1995, the Division II field was expanded from 24 to 32 teams and hometown fans in Nampa, Idaho, came out in record numbers, over 31,000, to watch their Northwest Nazarene team fall in overtime to Bethel (IN) and star Mark Galloway, 103-95, to climax a high-scoring tournament. Fans were treated to another overtime thriller in 1996, this time seeing nearby Albertson College beat out Whitworth (WA), 81-72, as tournament MVP Damon Archibald poured in 29 points. In 1997, the two finalists managed to settle matters in regulation time, a rarity in Division II finals, but only when Randy Romer sank a 12-footer with three seconds left to give the Pilots of Bethel (IN) their second title in three years, 95-94, over Siena Heights (MI).

In men's swimming and diving competition, Drury (MO) wrapped up its seventh consecutive title in 1994, beating out Puget Sound (WA) for the second year in a row. In 1995, Puget Sound won its first national championship ever, edging Simon Fraser

(BC) in the final event to reward a dazed coach Chris Myhre. Puget Sound apparently liked being on top, for they repeated as titlists in 1996 behind top swimmer Marc Kincaid, leaving Whitworth (WA) in their wake, and again in 1997, with Simon Fraser back in the runner-up position.

Profile: Ila Borders
She was not the first woman to play college baseball. Jodi Haller pitched in two games for the NAIA's St. Vincent's (PA) and Julie Croteau played three seasons for St. Mary's (MD) in the NCAA. But when Ila began her career at Southern California College on 15 February 1994 with a complete game 12-1 win over Claremont, she became a phenomenon. She compiled a 2-4, 2.92 record as a freshman starter, but slipped to 1-7, 7.20 as a sophomore, and 1-1, 5.18 in middle relief as a junior. She also remembers being hit by pitches in all 11 of her at bats—men weren't too happy at her pursuing her dreams at their expense. She transferred to Whittier College for her senior year and wound up with an 8-17, 5.17 record in college. She then signed with the St. Paul Saints and became the first woman to play in a men's professional league. Her four-year pro career took her from St. Paul to Duluth-Superior to Madison to Zion before she retired in 2000, with her 1-0, 1.67 1999 season at Madison her finest. She was abused like Jackie Robinson, but with a 72 mph fast ball and 58 mph curve, lacked his skills. Nevertheless, like his, her uniform and glove are in the Hall of Fame in Cooperstown.

Indoor track and field competition had a repeat winner in 1994 as Central State (OH) edged perennial runner-up Azusa Pacific. The next year, Lubbock Christian, paced by distance runner and top meet performer Julius Randich, kept the Cougars in second place and won their second indoor title. In 1996, Azusa Pacific finally broke through; after eight second-place finishes, APU defeated Oklahoma Baptist to take the title. In 1997, Life (GA) edged California Baptist, with Kenya's James Njoroge of Taylor (IN), winner of the 800 meter and mile runs, earning his second consecutive top performer award.

In wrestling, Southern Oregon and Western Montana tied for first in 1994, just nipping Mary (ND). Findlay (OH) won handily in 1995, but in 1996 Missouri Valley began a two-year run at the top, both years leaving Mary in second place.

Baseball featured four different winners in four years as St. Francis had finally broken Lewis-Clark State's monopoly in 1993. Kennesaw State (GA) edged Southeastern Oklahoma, 2-0, in the title game in 1994 with pitcher Todd Kirby garnering MVP honors. In 1995, Bellevue (NE) fought off an opening loss and rode shortstop Nic DeLuca's four homers to the title, beating Cumberland (TN) in the final game, 8-5, for their first national championship in any sport. Lewis-Clark State returned to the top in 1996, blowing out St. Ambrose (IA), 9-0, in the final to cap off a 15-game season-ending winning streak with its ninth national title. Newcomer Brewton-Parker (GA) topped that the next year by running off 31 straight wins to end the season, the final an 8-4 win over Bellevue to give the Barons their first championship.

Outdoor track and field saw perennial champion Azusa Pacific, runners up most years in indoor competition, win their tenth and eleventh titles in thirteen years in 1994 and 1995 before the magic ran out and they slipped to second behind Lubbock Christian in 1996. In 1997, a new dynasty was born as Life (GA) won its first of four straight championships.

Men's tennis found Texas-Tyler on top in 1994 as Marco Sitepu led his team to its first title since 1989. In 1995, Auburn-Montgomery (AL) began a two-year turn as champion, paced by Brazilian Gustavo Silva in 1996. Mobile (AL) kept the title in state in 1997, dropping Auburn-Montgomery to second place behind Fernando Ibarrola's play.

Golf was truly a team sport, as none of the individual winners (Henrik Nystrom, Lynn, 1994; Steve Armstrong, Pfeiffer (NC), 1995; Steve Galko, Texas Wesleyan, 1996; and Keith Hoard, Spring Hill (AL), 1997) was able to lead his school to the team title. Huntingdon (AL) won its sixth team title in ten years in 1994, but Texas Wesleyan nipped West Florida by one stroke to win the 1995 championship. Lynn (FL) duplicated that narrow margin in 1996, edging Berry (GA) for first place. Mobile (AL) beat Huntingdon handily in 1997, replicating their tennis results.

Eight teams faced off in women's soccer in 1993 and they matched up well, with six of the seven games being decided by one goal and three going to overtime, including the title game. In that match, Berry (GA) earned its third national title with a 1-0 win over Lynn (FL), firing away at all-tournament goalkeeper Joyce Parson with four shots hitting the crossbar in overtime before Tracy Moll finally got one into the goal. That year also marked the appearance of the first all-female team of referees at the nationals. In 1994 Lynn was back in the final, this time taking on Park (MO), which had beaten out Berry in pool play. Lynn was ready, taking a 3-1 win for its second championship in three years. The Knights returned for a 12-team playoff the next year, joining Berry and Pacific Lutheran (WA) as the only three-time champions in women's soccer when they soundly defeated Lindenwood (MO), 4-1, in the title match. Lynn would not be seeking a fourth title, though, as the school moved to NCAA Division II play when the year ended. In 1996, two at-large entries made it through pool play, expanded to 16 teams for the first time, before clashing in the title match. Simon Fraser (BC) won its first title with a 3-2 win over Mobile (AL)—in five overtimes. Paula Seabrook booted in the winning goal in the 160th minute of play to climax the longest final match in the tournament's history.

In 1993, Andrea Egans led Puget Sound (WA) to the women's volleyball championship, sweeping Hawaii-Hilo in the final and achieving the only win by a school other than BYU-Hawaii in a seven-year span. The Seasiders were back on top in 1994, sweeping Western Oregon in the final as Daniela Carneiro earned MVP honors. In 1995, BYU-Hawaii won again, beating Puget Sound's Loggers, 3-1, for the title behind Anik Valiengo. In 1996, Pt. Loma (CA) was the sweep victim as the Seasiders won their third straight title.

Puget Sound had better fortune in cross-country. In 1993, the team successfully defended its 1992 title, and the Loggers continued their dynasty with victories in 1994 and 1995 before finally falling to second behind Simon Fraser (BC) in 1996. That year, Cari Rampersad won her third straight title in the 5000-meter race; the Simon Fraser runner was the only woman at that time to have won more than once.

Division I women's basketball was dominated by Southern Nazarene University (OK), which swept to an unprecedented four straight titles. In 1994, the team wrapped up a perfect 34-0 season by blitzing David Lipscomb, 97-74, in the final game with JoAnna Bailey taking MVP honors. The Lady Redskins defended their title the next season despite a tournament record 35.4 points per game by Southeastern Oklahoma's Crystal Robinson. In the final, SNU edged Southeastern, 78-77, to finish the season 30-2. During the regular season top-ranked Southeastern beat SNU in both 1995 and 1996, but in the 1996 tournament the Lady Redskins overcame another Crystal Robinson MVP performance, including 34 points in the final, to win a second-straight nail-biter, this time by an 80-79 score. In 1997 SNU was back again, beating Union (TN) in the final, 78-73. The win gave SNU its fifth title, fourth in a row, and made seniors Gayla Smith and Astou Ndiaye, the tournament MVP, only the third and fourth college players, male or female, ever to win national titles in each year of their eligibility.

Division II basketball provided a bit more variety. Northern State (SD), the 1992 champion in the inaugural year for Division II competition and the runner-up in 1993, retook the title in 1994 with a 48-45 win over Western Oregon. Despite returning just one starter, Western Oregon was back in the championship game in 1995 and beat Cascade Conference rival Northwest Nazarene (ID), 75-67, in the first 32-team field for

Division II. Sandie Graves paced the winners with 27 points in the title game. Graves was back in 1996 and led Western Oregon's top-seeded Wolves to a repeat title, knocking off Huron (SD), 80-77, in the final. Northwest Nazarene took its first title in 1997, led by the play of MVP Erica Walton, beating Black Hills State (SD), 64-46, in the championship game, and giving the new Cascade Conference three straight titles.

A few schools dominated women's indoor track and field competition. In 1994, Wayland Baptist (TX) topped Central State (OH) for first place, paced by distance runner Rosa Ibarra. Southern-New Orleans (LA) beat out Central State in 1995, but in 1996 the Ohio school recaptured the title it had last won in 1993, edging Wayland Baptist for first place. The following year, Southern-New Orleans rebounded to win its second crown in three years.

Drury captured its third consecutive swimming and diving title in 1994, with Lourette Hakansson and Nida Zuhal sharing individual honors. After that the Northwest took over. In 1995, Simon Fraser (BC) returned to the top, beating out Puget Sound (WA) behind freshman Diana Ureche, who won the first of four consecutive outstanding swimmer awards. The top two schools flip-flopped in 1996, with Puget Sound winning the meet, but SFU was back on top in 1997, leaving the Loggers in their wake.

Oklahoma City swept all four softball titles during this period. In 1994 their leadoff hitter, Tracy Mosely, was named MVP as the Chiefs downed Athens State (AL), 3-1, in the final game. Pitching ace Tammy Braithwaite stopped Puget Sound in the 1995 championship game, 3-1. Shawnee State (OH) forced a final game in 1996 by edging the Chiefs, 1-0, but Oklahoma City blasted the upstarts, 9-0, when the chips were down and nabbed their unprecedented third-straight title. A parallel story unfolded in 1997 when Athens State beat the defending champs, 3-2, to force a final game. Oklahoma City romped in that one, 12-0, with an exhausted Lady Bear team collapsing in their seventh game in two days.

In outdoor track and field competition, Central State (OH) won its fourth straight title in 1994, paced by hurdler Catherine Pomales, with Doane (NE) winding up second. Southern-New Orleans nipped Central State in 1995, then the Ohio crew bounced back to win handily over Azusa Pacific in 1996. Southern-New Orleans regained the top spot in 1997, with Mary (ND) taking second place.

Women's tennis was dominated by teams from the Sun Belt. In 1994, Mobile (AL) knocked off in-state rival Auburn-Montgomery for the title. The next two years saw Mobile slip to second place as Lynn (FL) won both years, led by Petra Stankova in 1995. In 1997, BYU-Hawaii won its first tennis title, beating out perennial power Auburn-Montgomery behind the strong play of Teresa Stromberg.

In 1995, the NAIA launched a new sport, women's golf, as a championship event, and Lynn (FL) grabbed the first team trophy, along with individual honors, captured by Josefin Stalvant. Zoe Grembeek paced a repeat win in 1996 before Lynn bolted for the NCAA. In 1997, Tri-State (IN) took team honors, while Hanna Krehling of Spring Hill (AL) won the individual title.

❖

The most impressive on-the-field awards went to the schools with the best all-around programs. The NAIA-SIDA All-Sports awards in 1994 went to Puget Sound (WA) in the women's category, with Simon Fraser (BC) trailing in second place. Azusa Pacific (CA) edged out Central State (OH) and Simon Fraser in the men's competition. In 1995, Puget Sound repeated as women's winner, with Lynn (FL) and Simon Fraser next in line. Lubbock Christian took the men's award that year, far in front of Azusa Pacific. In 1996 Simon Fraser nipped Lynn for the women's title, while Findlay (OH) beat out Lubbock Christian (TX) and Azusa Pacific for the men's honors. In 1997, Simon Fraser completely dominated the women's competition and Life (GA) even more overwhelmingly outpaced the men's field.

In 1996, the NAIA was added to the prestigious Sears Directors' Cup awards, which gave a Waterford Crystal trophy to the top sports programs in NCAA Divisions I, II, and III, and the NAIA. Because it weighed both men's and women's sports, it provided an incentive for schools to upgrade their women's programs. Pacific Lutheran (WA) won the 1996 NAIA award, after which Simon Fraser (BC), playing off its strong women's programs, began a string of five consecutive titles. The fact that SFU had the largest enrollment of any NAIA school might have contributed to its dominance.

14

Revitalization
1997-2001

The new NAIA President hit the ground running when he finally took the reins on May 5, 1997. He had been building up momentum in the half year before his formal induction, displaying what would become a recognizable character trait: he studied matters at great length before reaching a conclusion. He had spent a good deal of time investigating the NAIA to determine its viability and prospects. He had shared some of his early ideas with the Leadership Council, and his deliberate pace slowed what had seemed a rather breakneck rush to get a new CEO in place. His debut at the April 1997 COP meeting in Tulsa showed that he was totally engaged and familiar with the NAIA. He and the association had needed to develop a comfort level with each other that had been unnecessary in any previous transition, all of which had involved insiders moving into the top position.

Perhaps that was the key to Baker's success in boosting NAIA morale. He was an outsider, not associated with either the college presidents or the athletic directors. Whatever the protestations of common purpose those two groups mouthed, tension between them had lurked near the surface of NAIA affairs since the COP coup in 1986. The elimination of the NEC in 1990 had, it seemed, completed the triumph of the presidents, but the victory seemed increasingly pyrrhic as morale and numbers declined under Chasteen. The selection of Baker gave athletic directors a palpable sense that, while he was not one of them, neither was he one of the presidents. A neutral CEO facilitated a more harmonious working relationship between the rival power centers that boded well for the association.

Baker had caught the attention of the Leadership Council in part because they had determined that a marketer, not a president, would best suit the NAIA's needs. He had played professional baseball from 1976 to 1986, and then returned to college to earn his bachelor's degree in business administration from the University of Denver in 1989. While there he coached the baseball team, though he failed to internalize any sense of the NAIA at that NAIA college. He went on to earn an MBA in management from the J. L. Kellogg Graduate School of Management at Northwestern University in 1990, which paved the way for seven years as a vice president for Major League Baseball, moving from game development to market development to market development in Europe. Once the NAIA presidency surfaced as a possibility, he found himself intrigued by the association's commitment to the student-athlete as a viable combination. He also found the national office staff and the COP to be impressive and committed to the NAIA's mission.

After having spoken with many NAIA presidents, Baker developed an action plan for a new CEO and submitted it to the Search Committee in early December 1996. He set forth his perceptions of NAIA problems as reflected in his conversations. Lack of visibility for the NAIA and its championship events headed the list of concerns, followed by poor communication between the national office and both member institutions and the public. It did appear that the COP was willing to follow a vibrant new leader with a solid strategic plan. While presidents had a clear sense of what the NAIA was about, along with a great deal of pride in the association, Baker argued that goals such as a "positive message," a "powerful mission statement," and a "new vision," while admirable, would not solve the NAIA's problems. As he saw it, words were nice, but success required a solid plan with concrete actions spelled out.

Baker cited several areas to be addressed by a new CEO, including greater visibility for both the NAIA and the CEO, better communication with the presidents and the public, better service to member institutions to improve retention, an aggressive marketing campaign, a restructuring of the national office to reflect current needs, and enthusiastic leadership. Of particular note, he cited the history and value system of the NAIA as key strengths that had a unique ability to "tug at the heart" in a compelling way that would appeal to potential corporate partners.[1]

Once on board, Baker moved to demand more of the office staff and make it proactive rather than reactive to market forces. Chasteen, he recalled staff telling him, had been happy with an 8:30 to 5:00 day; he was popular with the staff but perhaps too easy to work for. Baker avoided any "Black Monday" massacre, instead allowing those not committed to his more demanding regimen to gradually eliminate themselves. By the fall of 1998, he had brought in some solid new people, including Lori Heeter, Dawn Harmon, Natalie Cronkhite, and Jim Carr, and had developed a leaner staff (down from 26 or 27 to the low 20s) who were happy and productive.[2] He bought out Bill Patterson's contract, and the top aide to Farris and Chasteen admitted that he was ready to move on.[3] Baker had to make some adjustments of his own. He had been accustomed to major league perquisites, and it took some coaching for him to realize that planning plane trips carefully to exploit lower fares was an important part of financial management at the NAIA—flying first class on the spur of the moment was not the NAIA way. He also needed to soften his sometimes brusque manner and learn to let subordinates know they were appreciated—he demanded a lot of himself and expected no less from anyone else, and he learned to recognize the importance of acknowledging others' contributions.[4] Baker was a natural optimist and a visionary, but he was also a flexible pragmatist. He was open to trying new things, but if they didn't work out, he would shift gears and move in a new direction. His sense of direction invigorated those who worked around him, infusing them with a sense of common purpose.

That resiliency stood Baker in good stead as he moved to implement new marketing ideas. He recognized that the NAIA's biggest problem was a lack of visibility, and much of his energy was spent in trying to overcome that handicap. During his first four years in office, he sought through NAIA Properties to get member college bookstores to include NAIA items in their inventories, he tried to get NAIA television into dining commons and other campus common areas, he sought to build up a board of well-heeled backers to be NAIA advocates, he pushed to increase emphasis on regional organization and marketing, and he oversaw the launching of the Champions of Character initiative. Aside from modifying the NAIA's regional structure, first established in 1993 and under the NAIA's control, only the Champions of Character program succeeded.

NAIA Properties, a trademark management and merchandising program, ran into an economic fact of life trying to market NAIA items in campus bookstores: colleges had outsourced the running of the bookstores to profit-oriented outside companies that failed to see the marketing potential for NAIA materials. They also feared reduced profit margins if they bought into the NAIA. While students snapped up t-shirts, sweatshirts, and countless other things carrying the school's name, the companies believed that students' loyalty toward and identity with their schools was not transferable to the NAIA. Given Baker's own lack of awareness of the NAIA at the University of Denver, he could not have been too surprised.

The College TV Network (CTN) was another idea that died aborning. Launched with great fanfare in October 1997, the plan envisioned piping in customized music videos and advertising to common areas of campuses. With advertisers lining up to place their products before the lucrative college crowd, Baker envisioned NAIA revenues of up to $2 million over ten years. But the bulk of the NAIA campuses had a Christian affiliation, and though there existed a great supply of Christian music, relatively few videos existed. The lack of materials resulted in a one-day loop, which quickly bored the young audience. Efforts to develop new Christian videos resulted in inappropriate or poor quality products, and after a year only 25 colleges had signed up. CTN fizzled and was bought up by MTV in 2003.[5]

The Corporate Advisory Board, set up by the COP and spearheaded by Robert Terrell, held its first meeting in March 1998, but found it difficult to gain traction. Despite good intentions, the board met infrequently, and by 2001 it was moribund. Even though Baker did occasionally brief members, the hoped-for influx of money and increased visibility simply did not materialize. The board (and its modest success) paralleled similar contemporaneous efforts by some of the NAIA's financially shaky tuition-driven colleges.

It was proving difficult to market the NAIA to outside parties. Baker found more fertile ground within the organization to plant what became his mantra: "Don't run from change. Embrace it."[6] He moved the NAIA into the electronic age by launching a web page on May 15, 1997. He went farther in October 1998 when, following a recommendation by Creative Resources, he transformed *The NAIA News* from a monthly magazine of news and photos to an on-line news service with more timely weekly updates. In time those became daily updates, as Dawn Harmon took charge of the sports information duties and embraced the potential of the Internet. The electronic format saved the association between $70,000 and $80,000 per year in production costs, yet the change was bittersweet—NAIA news became available almost instantaneously, but the historical record the old magazine had provided was lost.

In an additional attempt to improve constituent communication and encourage life-long allegiance to the NAIA, some of the body's leading figures set up a new alumni association in October 2000. Forty-three long-time NAIA stalwarts contributed $1000 each as founding members, with Cliff Hamlow, Carroll Land, Jim Houdeshell, Joe Struckle, Dennis Spellman, and Larry Lady serving as the Executive Committee. Setting as its goal to help the national office in whatever way possible, its first major project was to finance the recapturing of the association's history with this book. Increasing membership and developing further projects lie in the future.

Another in-house project that involved rallying the true believers rather than having to sell the NAIA to the outside world was regional enhancement. Though not part of Baker's 1996 agenda, this decentralizing tendency became a key to his thinking. Once the idea had been unanimously endorsed at the fall 1997 convention in Kansas City by the Council of Athletic Conferences and Independents, Baker set up a regional enhancement task force. As he saw it, the new focus would allow the national office to provide better member service, market the NAIA on a more accessible regional level rather than a national level, and potentially reduce costs for national championship play.[7]

The 14-member task force, chaired by staff member Lynn Adams, developed a grid embodying three options for a restructuring, each with from seven to nine regions. These options, which envisioned a regional director from NAIA staff residing in each region, went to the COP's Administrative Committee on October 8, 1998, for its consideration. In the following months, Baker visited many member institutions, talked about NAIA issues, and listened attentively to the feedback. One clear message he got was that the nine regions were too large for effective interaction. Thus, at the spring 1999 COP meeting, the CEO suggested a fourth option calling for expansion to 14 regions, and after extended discussion the COP approved that proposal with its attendant marketing plan. The COP then called on the Council of Athletic Administrators to review the proposal at their June meeting, develop plans for qualification, and try to restrict the amount of team participation in regional play. In the meantime, the national office would form two regional teams, one with three and one with four regional directors, to provide service to member institutions.[8] The idea for on-location staff members never materialized. Yet by 2000, the regional emphasis meant that COP members represented not their college but their regions, while much of the NAIA's governance was being done by Regional Management Committees. Decentralization seemed to be working on an administrative level.

However, attempts to limit participation in the nationals ran afoul of vigorous protests from cross country and track and field coaches and their associations. They successfully resisted eliminating the right of membership entry in national meets, arguing that such a restriction would wreak havoc on cold-weather schools. They cited Greg Larson of Doane College, a track athlete who never met the automatic standard in his event, yet won two individual national titles and was a six-time All-American. His induction into the NAIA Hall of Fame vindicated coaches and athletic directors exercising discretion about entering deserving athletes who met provisional standards but fell just short of automatic qualification, or, as they put it, functioning as professionals.[9] Other pressure from below has raised the number of participation in the national competition in several sports from 16 schools (14 regional champions, an at-large selection, and a host college) to 20 (allowing five at-large berths). The attempt to limit national teams has worked best in baseball, with seven super-regional winners (two regions combined) and the host team making up an eight-team tournament. Basketball, track and field, swimming and diving, and wrestling bypass regional competition and go directly to the national level.

Baker recognized that halting the decline in membership was crucial to the NAIA's health. Chasteen had met informally with his NCAA counterpart, Cedric Dempsey, to seek mutually beneficial solutions to the hemorrhaging NAIA member list. The NCAA's Division III had been growing so fast it was having difficulty assimilating the additional members. An NAIA collapse would swamp the NCAA with a flood of schools, so a temporary resolution of the numbers crisis gave both sides a respite; in 1995 the NCAA imposed a two-year moratorium on new members. The two chiefs also considered a possible NCAA subsidy to help keep the NAIA afloat, but tepid support from the NCAA's ranks, as well as potential anti-trust issues, shot down that humiliating possibility.[10]

The numbers did hold from 1997 until 2002, an encouraging indication of Baker's re-energizing the association. From 344 members in 1997-98, of which 70 were dual members and thus mostly expected to move to the NCAA when their probation time was up, membership declined only to 332 by 2001-02. By 2000, the NAIA seemed to have regained its self-confidence. In April, pursuant to a resolution from the Golden State Athletic Conference, the COP resolved that dual members, who had to that point been able to compete for NAIA championships while they awaited NCAA admission, would no longer be able to participate in NAIA title competitions. No longer would the NAIA allow itself to be used in such a manner. Further distancing the association from the popular perception, "if you can't be in the NCAA, you can always play NAIA ball," in March 2001 the COP established a $1500 application fee to join the NAIA and instituted more rigorous screening of applicants to determine their viability for NAIA competition—it would no longer be an easy alternative.

To market the NAIA effectively, Baker recognized, meant that the association had to have a recognizable distinctiveness. In his 1996 proposal to the Search Committee, Baker had noted that the NAIA's value system enabled it to "tug at the heart." That became the cornerstone of a new initiative to promote character in NAIA sports. Oddly, considering that the NAIA considered its values to be a distinctive, the association had been a charter member of the Citizenship Through Sports Alliance in 1996, with first Bill Patterson and then Steve Baker serving on its board of directors. The alliance included Major League Baseball, the National Football League, the National Basketball Association, the National Hockey League, the Women's NBA, the U.S. Olympic Committee, the NCAA, the NJCAA, and the NFSHSA. Members decried the deterioration of America's sports culture and behavior and sought to bring back self-respect and respect for others to the sports scene. Within that context, the NAIA established the Dr. LeRoy Walker Sportsmanship Award and presented it to the first winner, Rebecca Whittle of Wayland Baptist University, at a Sports Alliance summit in June 1999.

The irony is that the NAIA sought to distinguish itself from most of the other groups in the alliance as more pure. It seemed a bit like an incumbent president running against that crowd in Washington—he was very much a part of what he was running against. At any rate, in October 1998 Baker set up a Leadership Committee with representation from the various councils, charging it to create a distinctive sportsmanship initiative for the NAIA and its members.[11] A year later the committee had developed the Walker award and was working to incorporate gender and racial sensitivity into its character-building program.[12]

At the spring 2000 COP meeting, Baker laid out the Champions of Character concept for discussion, eliciting some soul-searching over whether the NAIA was really practicing what it preached. New Director of Development Rob Miller, former head of the small National Christian College Association, came aboard in March and took charge of the program. He met with a new Character Committee in Tulsa that summer and assembled the first components of the program, then presented an overview of the initiative for convention delegates in Portland, Oregon, that fall. The Cascade Conference volunteered to test the program at its schools during the 2000-01 school year, incorporating evaluations of sportsmanship by players, coaches, and fans while seeking to educate those constituencies and raise standards. By the spring of 2001 Miller had asked all member institutions to either designate a Campus Character Representative or have the athletic director serve in that capacity. Campuses across the country began to see increasing promotion of the five core values of character: integrity, respect, responsibility, servant leadership, and sportsmanship. The NAIA had launched a distinguishing campaign to distance itself from many of the problems besetting organized sport in the country. This was not mere lip service, either—community support for the Champions of Character initiative was to be one of the key components in assessing suitors to entice the NAIA away from Tulsa.

The COP dealt with a number of nuts and bolts issues as the millennium neared its end. In March 2000, following years of thought, the presidents mandated that all member institutions would have to join a catastrophic insurance program. The NCAA had long provided its members with free catastrophic insurance coverage, though with a $65,000 deductible—that had been an incentive for some schools leaving the NAIA. The NAIA policy, which the national office negotiated with Mutual of Omaha, would cost each school $1200 but have a much lower $25,000 deductible. The requirement went into effect for the 2000-01 school year.[13]

Baker presented a proposal at the Chicago COP meeting in spring 1999 to move the NAIA away from its historic dues assessment based on enrollment and toward a flat fee. No doubt stimulated by a serious cash-flow problem that year, Baker argued that invoicing schools by full time equivalent (FTE) enrollment was an imperfect science since FTE fluctuated, and, more importantly, that the NAIA had always assumed that smaller enrollments meant fewer sports sponsored, an assumption that had not been borne out when scrutinized. The COP concluded that, beginning in 2000-01, a three-year adjustment would move dues to a flat $4000 per school (which became $4400, as it happened). This contrasted unfavorably with a $900 fee for NCAA Division II and Division III institutions, but Baker expressed his hope that that the NAIA assessment would decrease as alternative revenue sources were tapped.[14]

At the April 1999 COP meeting, Paul Mills (Bartlesville Wesleyan, OK) called on the group to consider allowing five seasons of competition for student athletes. The COP, after preliminary discussion, referred the matter to the National Coordinating Committee, which had the national office prepare a detailed study of the pros and cons of such a move. Due to different ways of computing graduations rates (How does one count transfers in and out? Does one count back from degree recipients or forward from entering freshman classes?), and very slow government provision of data they collect, the numbers are only suggestive. Less than one third of entering freshmen appear to graduate within four years, with a comparable number doing so after five years. In other words, while in the sixties a four-year college career was fairly normal, that was no longer the case. Perhaps athletic eligibility should reflect that reality.[15]

Several arguments favored the proposal. Many academic programs require five years to complete, particularly teacher education. With the heavy time commitment required by athletics, onerous academic loads are not desirable. Other activities such as music and theater, as well as financial aid, are often open to students beyond the four-year standard. The change would no doubt lead to more athletes graduating, a major consideration in the debate on some campuses. Finally, the change would give students a greater opportunity to compete.

The downside centered on perception. Without a solid public relations strategy, the public would perceive that the NAIA was using and abusing marginal students, just the opposite of the sort of image the Champions of Character initiative sought to promote. Further, such public perceptions might be partially accurate—some good students who might graduate in four years could be pressured to delay commencement to permit them to compete in a fifth season. Though the issue continued to evoke discussion in subsequent years, including endorsement by the councils of FARs and Athletic Conferences and Independents, the momentum was killed when the COP voted, 14-10, against the principle at their spring 2000 meeting.[16]

Another issue discussed at that meeting concerned dual affiliation. The Administrative Committee questioned whether permitting NAIA institutions to also belong to the NCAA was a desirable policy to continue. Jeff Struckle did a rigorous study of the problem, noting that the association had encouraged dual membership in the crunch years after 1993 because it seemed like a way to hang on to members that otherwise might simply move to the NCAA. It had been, he thought, a policy for desperate times. With membership numbers stable, and with toughened requirements to join the NAIA, he recommended banning dual membership. The major reason, again, was perception. The NAIA had been promoting dual membership to keep its numbers up, but dual members were widely, if inaccurately, perceived to be in the process of moving to the NCAA following a probation period of four years. Some schools were considering leaving the NAIA because they feared for its viability, so the dual memberships created a sort of catch-22: high numbers created the impression of questionable survivability, so more schools joined the NCAA as a hedge against NAIA disintegration, creating an increased sense of vulnerability, and so forth. Thus his recommendation to end dual membership, even though he calculated that around 34 of 60 dual members would leave earlier than they might otherwise with attendant loss of revenue to the NAIA. The COP approved the proposal with five reservations, allowing for NAIA loyalists in areas with limited NAIA options in some sports and other "legitimate" dual members to continue. The proposal then came before the whole convention in Portland in the fall of 2000 in the form of a constitutional amendment. Needing two thirds to pass, it fell three votes short at 132-70, with Regions I and II rallying in defense of dual memberships as a way to ensure that schools could transition *into* the NAIA.[17]

Women's issues were an ongoing concern for many in the NAIA. The Gender Equity Committee, set up in the mid-1990s with representatives from the various councils, began in 1997 to sponsor symposia at the national conventions. The first attracted almost 40 female student-athletes from around the country to learn about opportunities in athletic administration. Athletic directors seeking to hire female administrators had found it difficult to locate such individuals—the symposia were designed to make women aware of career opportunities and deepen the pool of possible female applicants for appropriate jobs. One student from a dual-member institution said she believed the NAIA was doing more to promote women in athletics than the NCAA.[18]

A dissenting voice came from Lisa Hutchens of Union University and Barbara Townsend of the University of Memphis, who published "Gender Equity in Collegiate Sports: The Role of Athletic Associations" in *Initiatives* in the spring of 1998. They decried the NCAA's failure to live up to Title IX standards and noted that the NAIA on paper supported gender equity, but had not demonstrated any proactive commitment to date beyond its symposia. Despite NAIA members reporting on scholarship programs, for example, the national office had not tallied the results and thus had no summary data available. They also noted that the NAIA had not implemented any bylaws to enforce Title IX compliance. In fact, the departure of Sheila Stearns left a COP void on the Gender Equity Committee in 1999. When Rick Artman (Siena Heights, MI) filled that vacancy in 2000, he verbalized his disappointment at the lack of purpose and structure of the committee, prompting Jim Carr to promise more aggressive staff work to provide direction for the committee.[19]

Whether basketball should continue with two divisions of play provoked some debate in 2001. The American Mideast Conference Presidents Council unanimously recommended a return to the one-division format that had been in effect until 1992. Among other arguments for their proposal, having one men's and one women's tournament would be more marketable and reduce friction within conferences and regions over their appropriate level. Most important, the declining number of Division I schools meant that the ratio of teams to national tournament participants, while it had remained steady in Division II men and women around 5.66 to 1, had slipped from 6.94 (men) and 5.84 (women) to 3.59 and 3.41 in Division I, which was far out of line with any other NAIA sport. The AMC recommended a 64-team tourney for each gender, with the first 32 games to be on members' courts and the final 32 teams then playing off for the national title in the city where the national headquarters were located. They also suggested that scholarships be set at eight, a compromise between Division II's six and Division I's eleven.

The Council of Athletic Administrators, also noting the declining ratios, developed their own proposal, suggesting a reduction in tournament size from 32 to 24 teams while retaining two divisions. They sent out questionnaires to coaches and athletic directors (plus a few presidents and conference commissioners) for feedback, and were swamped with resistance. The coaches favored keeping 32 teams by a twelve-to-one margin, indicative of their interests, while the ADs, who had to fund the trips, still favored the larger field by a three-to-one ratio.

The presidents had been cool to moving to one division in 2000, fearing that a number of Division II teams that were very competitive at that level would no longer be so if lumped in with Division I schools.[20] The possibility of losing some of those schools to NCAA Division III cooled any enthusiasm for the change. It is almost always more popular to add rather than subtract championship opportunities. A year later, responding to the AMC proposal, the COP voted to study the scholarship issue inherent in a possible switch to one division, backing away from the broader question of the change itself. In March 2002 the presidents essentially dropped the idea altogether.[21]

Underlying all the other issues confronting the NAIA was the Tulsa question. The Creative Resources study of the NAIA in 1996 found that the move from Kansas City to Tulsa, despite winning approval from member institutions, had severely damaging side effects. Chasteen and a select few around him had made the decision to move, perhaps for good reasons, but the membership never felt it had been a part of the decision or that the leaders had communicated well with them. Kansas and Missouri presidents, the survey found, had been adamantly opposed to the move, though they stifled their objections. In the long run, whatever gains might have accrued from the transfer had been overwhelmed by the loss of good will and support over the way the affair had been handled. Aside from the geographic change, the move had cut off 55 years of tradition and history, a difficult loss to offset.[22]

The NAIA had signed a five-year agreement with Tulsa running from 1993 to 1998. The key Oklahomans who had negotiated the deal and found a way to make it work had, unfortunately, shortly departed from their positions as mayor, city councilman, and head of the Chamber of Commerce. Other events had conspired to undermine the relationship. In 1995, a fire had damaged the Mabee Center on the eve of the basketball tournament and got headlines; although the venue was quite satisfactory for play, fans stayed away in droves and the NAIA lost $85,000 on the under-attended tourney. More critical, many of Oklahoma's NAIA schools, including Northeastern, Southeastern, Southwestern, and Panhandle State had followed earlier defectors Cameron and Central State out of the association, robbing the basketball tournament of much of its local appeal.

Baker had taken office determined to cultivate good relations with Tulsa's key leaders, but found that his busy travel schedule reduced the time available for such bridge building. His sometimes brusque manner did not endear him to Mayor Susan Savage or the head of the Chamber of Commerce, and by the spring of 1998 the CEO had concluded that while the NAIA had bought into Tulsa forever, the city did not feel any great commitment beyond the letter of the five-year agreement. As he tried to negotiate an extension of the NAIA's agreement with the city, he gradually came to the recognition that while the NAIA had been an institution in Kansas City, in Tulsa it lacked that historic connection. As he noted, when the basketball tournament was in Kansas City, it was Kansas City's tournament; in Tulsa, it was the NAIA's tournament.[23]

Baker reported to the COP in April 1998 that with the end of the five-year lease, the NAIA's unsubsidized rate per square foot would jump from $9.50 to $13.50. While the mayor was supportive of the NAIA, she felt the city had fulfilled its obligations to the association and that further subsidies were not going to happen. "In general," he concluded, "there is a feeling of malaise in Tulsa about the NAIA." Kansas City, Lexington, Kentucky, and Oklahoma City had expressed interest in hosting the Division I men's basketball tournament, and beyond extending its stay in Tulsa through 2001, the NAIA had no binding ties to the city.[24]

The following year, Baker noted that attendance at the Division I men's tournament had again fallen just short of 32,000, a far cry from the sixties in Kemper Arena a decade before. He did acknowledge the lack of Oklahoma teams in the final four, seeming almost defensive about the modest total. He included a copy of an article in the Tulsa *World* featuring Larry Ferguson, a state legislator. Ferguson decried the "chilly reception" the NAIA had received, citing the departure of so many Oklahoma schools from the association, along with the suggestion that the NAIA had boosted the economy of Tulsa by an estimated $65 million in six years. But the article went on to quote Northeastern State athletic director Gil Cloud saying there was no way he'd return to the NAIA after investing four years to become an active NCAA Division II member.[25] By the fall of 1999, Baker continued to feel he had not gotten a strong statement of support from the mayor or an aggressive Tulsa Sports Commission effort to generate stronger local support. He went so far as to refer to "our plight" here in Oklahoma.[26]

Tulsa's hold on the NAIA began unraveling quickly in 2000. Mayor Savage responded to a Steve Baker letter requesting talks to improve the NAIA's lot by phoning and complaining of being "blind-sided" and "slapped in the face."[27] When a meeting did finally materialize on March 17, Savage was conspicuous by her absence, and despite the presence of a number of heavy hitters from the Tulsa community, that seems to have been the last straw for Baker. Though the Tulsans talked of a downtown revitalization and the NAIA's place in it, the CEO appears to have felt that such prospects were too speculative. On April 1, citing Tulsa's uncooperative and unenthusiastic spirit, he recommended to the COP that they seek requests for proposals (RFPs) from cities that had expressed interest in the NAIA, including Tulsa. With memories of the 1993 surprise move in mind, COP chair Barry Dorsey (Rio Grande College) promised to keep the COP apprised of developments.[28]

In August, the Relocation Committee met and narrowed the 19 solid proposals down to a final group of five: Cleveland, Ohio; Fort Wayne, Indiana; Lexington, Kentucky; Olathe, Kansas, and St. Charles County, Missouri. The committee spent the next six months visiting the five finalists and developing in considerable detail the potential relationship with each. By the end of the year, Lexington and Cleveland had fallen by the wayside, leaving three finalists as the new year dawned. Baker proved a tough and resourceful negotiator, once again demonstrating his penchant for taking as much time as necessary to get the decision right.

Meanwhile, the Tulsa *World* excoriated the NAIA in a caustic editorial ("Adios") on September 11, 2000. Criticizing the association for whining about a lack of support, the paper claimed the local media and business community had bent over backwards to promote the NAIA. "It's just a tough sell to get folks out to watch short guys from colleges they've never heard of play basketball." Denouncing the NAIA's attempts to work out a new deal as extortion, the angry editor suggested purchasing a tent to make future moves easier.

So what were Baker and his committee looking for? They listed seven minimum qualifications: an easily accessible international airport, five NAIA schools within 100 miles, infrastructure and proven support for athletics, commitment to the NAIA's vision and amateur athletics, facilities, a basketball arena, and a hotel and transportation infrastructure. As the committee sought refined proposals, they focused on four areas: championships (ability and willingness to host some NAIA nationals), character initiative (coordination with school districts was critical), sites and facilities, and the financial package an applicant could assemble. Both St. Charles County (O'Fallon is about 35 miles west of St. Louis) and Ft. Wayne possessed one-site facilities to cover most needs. Both promised buildings or adequate space and millions of dollars in financial incentives. Both offers were very impressive.

Despite the attractiveness of the other two finalists, the committee decided on Olathe as the new NAIA home. The city is 20 miles southwest of Kansas City on

Interstate 35, and thus it had the built-in advantage of representing a return to the association's roots. COP members Bob Brower (Point Loma Nazarene) and Roger Parrott (Belhaven) had both worked at MidAmerica Nazarene University in Olathe and lobbied for the city. Olathe agreed to host one national championship each sport season, with the Chamber of Commerce (President Frank Taylor a key player), the Kansas City Sports Commission, and the Olathe School District to work hand-in-hand with the NAIA. Perhaps the critical ace in Olathe's hand was the city's billing as a city of character and the enthusiasm of Patricia All of the school district for embracing the Champions of Character initiative. The Honeywell Corporation agreed to donate at least 10,000 square feet of office space (valued at over $16,500 per month) until the NAIA could complete its permanent national office building, which would also house the Hall of Fame and Character in Sport displays. Olathe offered additional financial and philosophical incentives that clinched the deal, and on March 7, in a conference call, the COP unanimously endorsed the Olathe selection.[29] The NAIA was coming home.

No doubt blissfully unaware of such esoteric matters as the move to Olathe, NAIA scholar athletes continued their pursuits in their own competitive venues. Men's fall sports began with cross-country, with Life (GA) ending three years of frustration behind Lubbock Christian, which dropped its program, and began a string of four straight titles of its own. Sammy Nyamong took individual honors in 1997, after which Kenyan Silah Misoi, who set the NAIA record in 1996, took top honors in 1998 and 1999.

Football began life without divisions in 1997, and Findlay (OH) rode a 60-yard touchdown run by quarterback Bo Hurley, the national player of the year, to a 14-7 victory over Willamette (OR). The runners-up had made history earlier in the season when Liz Heaston, a member of the women's soccer team, had kicked two extra points to bail out an injury-ridden football team, thus becoming the first female football player in collegiate history. In 1998, Azusa Pacific (CA) won its first football title with a come-from-behind 17-14 win over Olivet Nazarene (IL) behind national player-of-the-year Jack Williams' 108 yards rushing. In 1999, Eddie Eviston, quarterbacking Georgetown (KY) and capturing the first of three consecutive player-of-the-year awards, fell just short of the national title when Georgetown lost the championship game to Northwestern Oklahoma, 34-26, failing to hold a 20-7 lead. In a 2000 rematch, Georgetown avenged that defeat by shutting out the Oklahomans, 20-0.

In men's soccer, Seattle (WA), paced by MVP Tom Hardy, nipped Rockhurst (MO) in double overtime, 2-1, to capture its first national championship in 1997. Coach Pete Fewing was equally proud of the tournament sportsmanship trophy his Chieftans earned. Lindsey Wilson (KY) rebounded in 1998 and won its third title in four years, beating Illinois-Springfield, 2-1, in the title game. National player-of-the-year Orlando

Bueso scored the winning goal and ran the Blue Raiders' record to a perfect 25-0-0. Showing a fondness for 2-1 victories, Lindsey Wilson took the next two national championships, edging Mobile (AL) in 1999 and Auburn Montgomery in overtime in 2000 by the same score. Graeme Abel and Shawn Lee won tournament MVP honors for Lindsey Wilson those two years.

Division I men's basketball saw Georgetown (KY) capture its first crown after sixteen trips to the tournament. The fourth-seeded Tigers won all of their games by double-digit margins and stopped Southern Nazarene (OK) in the 1998 final, 83-68, paced by MVP Will Carlton. The next year, unseeded Life (GA) nabbed its second title in three years by overcoming a 26-point deficit to beat Mobile (AL), 63-60, on an off-balance 25-foot Corey Evans shot with two seconds left on the clock. In 2000, Life earned top seeding and lived up to it, though they again relied on a shot in the last few seconds to nip Georgetown, 61-59. In 2001 Faulkner (AL) edged Science and Arts (OK), 63-59, for their first championship.

In Division II basketball, Bethel (IN) rode star Rico Swanson's hot hand to their third title in four years in 1998, beating Oregon Tech, 89-87, in a thrilling title game. In 1999, despite losing a bumper senior class, Bethel almost won another title, but Cornerstone (MI), the top seed, edged the defending champs, 113-109 in overtime. Tourney MVP Mike Long hit 35 for the winners in the highest-scoring game in tournament history. In 2000, eight-seeded Embry-Riddle handled Ozarks (MO), 75-63, to win their first title, but a new cast was on hand in 2001, as Northwestern (IA) edged MidAmerica Nazarene (KS) for the championship, 82-78. The winners, runners-up in 1992, nabbed their first title while the Pioneers lost in their first championship game.

Indoor track and field competition produced four different winning teams during these four years. Lindenwood (MO) edged out Azusa Pacific, back in their traditional runner-up slot, in 1998. The following year Cal Baptist knocked Lindenwood down to second place with their first national title. Life (GA) won handily in 2000, and McKendree (IL) beat out Azusa Pacific in 2001, though the Cougars' pentathalon star Bryan Clay earned outstanding performer honors.

Swimming and diving honors went to the traditional NAIA winners. With Drury's departure, Puget Sound (WA) had won three straight titles, but Simon Fraser (BC) reasserted itself in 1998 and reeled off four consecutive championships, with Cal Baptist taking second in 2000 and 2001. Graham Duthie of Simon Fraser took outstanding swimmer honors in three of the four years.

Montana State-Northern dominated wrestling competition, winning the 1998, 1999, and 2000 meets by a wide margin before Southern Oregon and Missouri Valley passed them by in 2001. Turk Lords won four straight titles for the Montanans and won the Gorrarian award in 2001.

Spring sports action was concentrated in Tulsa in 1998 and West Palm Beach, Florida, in 1999 as the NAIA experimented with a "spring games" concept, bringing all the sports together in one venue for an Olympic-like festival. Disappointing attendance in Tulsa and logistical problems in Florida put an end to the experiment after two years.

Idaho schools dominated baseball action even with the competition far from home in 1998 and 1999. Albertson took the title in 1998 with a 6-3 win over unsung Indiana Tech, riding five unearned runs to the title. Lewis-Clark (ID) regained the top spot in 1999, winning its tenth title with a 7-2 win over the Cyclones after Albertson had forced a final game with a 2-1 win. When the tournament returned to their home turf in Lewiston in 2000, Lewis-Clark pounded Dallas Baptist, 10-1, for their eleventh title. In 2001, though, Birmingham-Southern (AL), led by MVP third-baseman Connor Robertson, came through the losers' bracket and beat the Warriors 10-3 and 8-3 to win the championship.

Men's tennis was swept all four years by Oklahoma City, led by two-time outstanding player Egberto Caldas. Runners-up were Mobile (AL), Auburn-Montgomery (AL) twice, and Georgia Southwestern State. Oklahoma City had never won a title before this remarkable run.

Men's golf featured a more varied winner's circle, as Berry (GA) won by one stroke over Texas Wesleyan in 1998, Texas Wesleyan moved up to the top spot in 1999, Malone (OH) beat out Berry in 2000, and Oklahoma City took top honors in 2001.

Men's outdoor track and field competition saw Life (GA) dominate. In 1998 they repeated as champions by a narrow margin over Southern-New Orleans, but in 1999 and 2000 they found no serious challengers as they ran their string of titles to four. In 2001, Azusa Pacific finally broke the streak, decisively pushing Life to a distant second place.

In women's cross-country, Simon Fraser, paced by Heather deGeest in both 1997 and 1998, overwhelmed the field to win their second and third consecutive titles. In 1999, though, Malone (OH) moved up from second place to capture the crown, far ahead of runner-up Spring Arbor (MI). In 2000, the Lutherans held sway. Concordia of California beat out Concordia of Nebraska for their first title, and the Nebraskans' first of three consecutive second-place finishes.

Revenge was sweet in women's soccer, as Mobile (AL), loser to Simon Fraser (BC) in five overtimes in 1996, beat the Clan, 2-1, in overtime after playing to a scoreless tie in regulation time in the 1997 final. The next fall, Azusa Pacific won the title in their first trip to the nationals, once again sending Simon Fraser home on the short end of a 2-1 score in the final as Kendra Payne tallied one goal and assisted on the other. In 1999, Katie Gardemoer led Westmont (CA) to a 3-0 win over Transylvania (KY) for a second straight Golden State Athletic Conference title. In 2000 Simon Fraser, reprising its five-overtime win of 1996, edged Lindenwood (MO), 1-0, in a sudden-death fifth overtime.

In volleyball action, BYU-Hawaii capped a perfect 25-0 season with a clean sweep of its games in the nationals, leaving Biola (CA) outclassed in the 1997 title match for its fourth consecutive championship. Columbia (MO) took the next two finals, beating out Northwest Nazarene (ID) and Fresno Pacific (CA) in 1998 and 1999 and freeing the volleyball crown from the monopoly of Pacific states. In 2000 Dickinson State (ND) dethroned Columbia in a hard-fought final match to interrupt their string of victories.

Women's Division I basketball fans in Jackson, Tennessee, exulted in 1998 when hometown Union College broke Southern Nazarene's four-year stranglehold on the title with a nail-biting 73-70 win in the final game, avenging a five point loss to the Lady Redskins the year before and helping ease the pain of a one-point loss to Arkansas Tech in the 1993 championship. In 1999 Union lost in the quarterfinals, Southern Nazarene in the semifinals, and Oklahoma City ran away from Simon Fraser (BC) in the championship game, 72-55, paced by MVP Patty Cantella. A rematch of the finalists in 2000 produced the same result: Oklahoma City beat Simon Fraser, 64-55. In 2001, the Lady Chiefs managed a "three-peat," beating Auburn-Montgomery (AL) in the final game, 69-52. Southern Nazarene was hanging in there, though, making it at least to the semifinals every year since their four titles in a row.

In Division II women's basketball action, unheralded Walsh (OH) knocked off another unseeded team, Mary Hardin-Baylor (TX), 73-66, in 1998 to become the first unseeded team to win a Division II title. No upsets in 1999, though—top ranked Shawnee State (OH), led by player-of-the-year Erica Hayes' 34 points, easily handled St. Francis (IN), 80-65, for the championship. In 2000, it was upset time again as 15th seed Mary (ND) beat Northwestern (IA), 59-49, to grab the title. A more seasoned Northwestern team returned to the final the next year and parlayed the play of repeat MVP Jennifer Recker to a 77-50 thumping of Albertson in the title match.

Women's swimming and diving competition was intense as Puget Sound (WA) just nipped Simon Fraser (BC) in 1998 and 1999, but when the Loggers bolted to NCAA Division III the Canadian team handily beat Cal Baptist in 2000 and 2001 behind outstanding swimmer Lisa Huffman.

Women's indoor track and field saw a dynasty emerge after Simon Fraser (BC) edged Mary (ND) in 1998. The next three years McKendree (IL), led by sprinter Agne Visockaite, beat out Mary, then Life (GA) twice to capture all three crowns, the first coming in only the third year of the school's program under coach Gary White.

In softball, Simon Fraser (BC) knocked out Oklahoma City, denying the Chiefs a fifth straight title, but the error-prone Clan gave away too many runs and lost twice to new titlist Western Washington, who took the 1998 title with a 5-1 win. Simon Fraser still had Oklahoma City's number the next season, but this time two wins over the Chiefs, including a 7-3 final, gave the Canadians the championship and ace pitcher Kathy Iggulden an MVP award. In 2000, Oklahoma City and Azusa Pacific knocked Simon Fraser out of the tournament, after which the Chiefs regained their title with a 5-1 win. The Chiefs were back in 2001, reestablishing their dominance under coach Phil McSpadden, who won his sixth national title in 14 seasons, in 13 of which he took his team to the nationals, with a 5-3 win over old nemesis Simon Fraser.

BYU-Hawaii repeated as women's tennis champion in 1998, beating out Auburn-Montgomery (AL) for the top spot. The next year AUM moved up a notch and tied Brenau (GA) for first place in the last championship with the winner determined by total points. Beginning in 2000, the top two teams determined the winner in a head-to-head match, and AUM took advantage of the new format with victories over Brenau in 2000 and 2001.

Track and field featured a variety of winners. In 1998, Simon Fraser (BC) beat out Mary (ND) for the top spot, though Jamie Mulske of Mary won her second-straight top performer award. McKendree (IL) decisively beat Life (GA) in 1999 with hurdler/pentathlete Neisha Thompson the outstanding athlete, but Life turned the tables in 2000. In 2001, Doane (NE) tied Life for first place, garnering their first title.

Women's golf saluted four winners in four years. In 1998, Mobile (AL) took top honors, with Southern Nazarene (OK) replacing them as champions in 1999. In 2000 Mary Hardin-Baylor (TX) won their first crown, led by individual champion Denise Thiele, followed by another first-time winner in 2001, British Columbia.

15

Back to the Future
2001-2004

The move back to the Kansas City area coincided with the launching of the new Champions of Character initiative. The combination of Olathe, a "city of character," with the NAIA, focusing on character as its distinctive quality, provided some thematic consistency as the association sought to reconnect to its roots. Steve Baker promoted character as the NAIA "brand," distinguishing it from other sports organizations even as it worked to spread its message.

Bruce Brown, a dynamite inspirational speaker with background in Seattle sports from junior high to the pros, wowed the crowd at the fall 2000 convention with his talks on the potential of sports as a character builder. He worked with Rob Miller as a "special presenter" thereafter, sharing his two key messages with receptive audiences: building character through sport and redefining the term athlete using the five core values of Champions of Character. In 2002, Miller finally got Brown on board full time and added Kelly Noonan as an assistant in development, giving the character effort a critical mass.

The major thrusts of the Champions of Character program were, first, to member institutions. By March 2002, 114 colleges had bought into the initiative and Miller was pushing for 100 percent participation. A year later, the number of participating institutions had risen to 193. Those subscribing to the movement sought to educate fans, coaches, and players about how to integrate character into their participation in sports. Coaches met with their teams to instruct them on their expectations and players signed pledges to try to live up to the higher ideals. Public address announcements before games focused on one of the five core values, and athletic directors and campus character representatives sought to keep all elements of the sports program aware. Champions of Character banner were hung in gyms and displays around campuses focused on individual values. Reports from campuses suggested that the initiative was, in fact, having a positive effect on the culture of athletics.

Phase II in implementing the Champions of Character initiative involves designing a certification process whereby college campuses can become "program centers" to train their coaches and athletes to spread the message of character in sports. Doing so on a mass scale is clearly beyond the capabilities of the small NAIA national office staff, but with some 5000 coaches and athletic directors and far more athletes on almost 300 campuses, NAIA trainers can use the multiplier effect to certify those people. Making the training simple and keeping time and monetary costs to a minimum was a project for a Champions of Character task force in the summer of 2004. It appeared likely that a few colleges would pioneer the "program center" concept and become resource centers for other member institutions. It is even possible that the Champions of Character initiative could spin off and become independent of the NAIA, though that seems unlikely. Character is such a key element of the NAIA's mission that the focus on it seems an altogether appropriate component of NAIA activities.[1]

The third, and most crucial, thrust of the Champions of Character was outreach to younger athletes, and it has already begun on the NAIA's home turf. During the 2002-03 school year, the Olathe school district and youth sports programs got intensive hands-on attention from NAIA representatives who met with players, parents, coaches, and officials to gauge their attitudes and develop strategies to improve the culture of youth sports. The Olathe "external" character outreach became a model for other colleges to use in their communities. Nearby colleges, including Baker, Avila, and Ottawa, provided older athletes to work with youngsters throughout the Kansas City metropolitan area. In October 2003 the NAIA made a new Champions of Character outreach kit available to all member institutions, and by the following spring 75 colleges had ordered the kit. At that point, fan behavior—which seemed to be deteriorating nationally—was set as the next key focus for the Champions of Character initiative.[2]

While Baker and NAIA insiders maintained that better service to member institutions and promotion of character were signs of a healthy, reinvigorated organization, neutral observers found membership numbers an easy shortcut to assessing the NAIA's health. During the NCAA moratorium on new additions, the numbers held up well—from the fall of 2000 to the fall of 2001, nine members left and 13 joined, giving a rare up tick in numbers from 328 to 332. But with 25 dual members awaiting admission to the NCAA, Baker recognized that the stability of his tenure was shortly to end. Despite a compliment from Transylvania athletic director Brian Austin that Baker had gotten the NAIA to think outside the box, his school moved to NCAA Division III.[3] The numbers for fall 2002 declined dramatically as only three new members joined but 28 departed. Thirteen had completed Division II provisional status and moved to the NCAA, while another five joined Division III. More surprising, seven either closed their doors or dropped their athletic programs altogether, the latter including Life (GA), which had made nine straight trips to the Division I men's basketball tournament and won it three times.[4] The NAIA was fighting not only the NCAA, but also a national recession and financial hard times.

In combating the NCAA, the NAIA was equipped with both subjective and objective criteria. Subjectively, according to the Creative Resources study in 1997, people in the NAIA pictured the NCAA's Division I as "professional," Division II as valuing athletics more highly than academics, and Division III as least true to its athletic de-emphasis mission. Supposedly offering no athletic scholarships, DIII schools finessed the system by, for example, offering all athletes a "leadership scholarship" or some other award.[5]

Jeff Struckle had drawn up a more objective contrast between the NAIA, Division II, and Division III in the mid-90s and updated it in 2000 and 2004. His comparison document provided prospective defectors or recruits with solid data upon which to base their decision. For example, membership in the NAIA cost $4,400 per year, while the two NCAA divisions charged only $900. But average dues per conference more than offset that, running $3,178 for the NAIA but $13,747 for Division II and $8,330 for DIII. It cost $1,500 to apply for NAIA membership, but $12,000 for DIII and $14,000 for DII. The NAIA had a one-year wait to join, while the NCAA had just added a one-year exploratory year (which gave the NAIA an opportunity to try to dissuade defectors) plus four years of provisional status. Other basic comparative data as of February 2004 were as follows:

	NAIA	DII	DIII
Member institutions	299	282	430
Percentage private	82%	44%	80%
Average enrollment	1,866	4,117	2,278
Championships	23	25	27
Average number sports	10.96	13.8	16.5
Average athletic budget	$1.4m	$3.2 m	$1.5m
Top 25 in NACDA Director's Cup	$2.5m	$5.1m	2.5m[6]

One former NAIA college president recalled that the public institutions of the Division II type resented the more "church-oriented" NAIA, as did some of the more nominally church-related institutions. There may well be at least the hint of a fault line between the NAIA and the NCAA on religious grounds.[7]

Following the great defection of 2002, NAIA numbers continued to decline, though just to 299 in 2003 and an estimated 290 in 2004, losses attributable to school closures or athletic cutbacks as well as NCAA attraction. Still, to reduce the attractiveness of their rival to NAIA schools, the association voted in 2002 to prohibit dual members transitioning to the NCAA to participate in NAIA championships during their provisional NCAA period. No longer could such schools exploit NAIA generosity of spirit. A further attempt to eliminate dual membership altogether (it had dwindled to a handful of schools with special needs, not plans to defect) was blocked by the two California conferences in 2002. On the other hand, former members desiring to rejoin the NAIA would have their one-year waiting period waived if they dropped the NCAA flat.

The NAIA was not sitting back and accepting stable numbers as satisfactory, but aggressively pursued likely prospects to join the association. In March 2003, Baker listed six categories of schools that he was targeting. First were historically black colleges and universities, which had largely defected from the NAIA but, aside from struggling to survive as institutions, had found it difficult to compete in the NCAA. Second were Division II schools facing budget cuts from strapped state governments. A third group were Division III schools that recognized the possibilities for generating enrollment hikes through athletic scholarships. A fourth category was to create new conferences or entice entire conferences to jump from the NCAA to the NAIA. These options had merit because NAIA conferences tended to seek stability for their members rather than recruiting new schools, and joining the NAIA as an independent did not appeal to many prospects. Fifth were colleges just developing athletic programs. Finally, Baker saw possibilities for growth in Canada and Mexico.[8]

Canada offered especially intriguing possibilities. Lakehead University (ON) had been the first Canadian school to join, back in 1967, but for many years Simon Fraser University (BC) had been the only Canadian member of the NAIA. President Gordon Shrum had naively envisioned a football program that could compete for a spot in the Rose Bowl when the school opened in 1965, but astutely hired Lorne Davies as athletic director. Despite a modest budget, Davies worked wonders. By the time Davies retired after 30 years in 1995, SFU had grown to be the largest institution in the NAIA with almost 15,000 students. Competing in the NAIA gave him a recruiting edge north of the border, as did his offering athletic scholarships when no other Canadian school did. Besides slowing the athlete drain to the United States and working to eliminate the negative connotations of "jock," Davies built a very competitive institution, particularly in swimming and men's soccer. Simon Fraser won the Sears Director's Cup for the NAIA from 1997 through 2001, meaning it had the top sports program in the association.[9]

The University of British Columbia, the University of Alberta, and the University of Victoria joined Simon Fraser in the NAIA between 1999 and 2001. They are part of the Canada West Conference, which would like to give freshman athletic scholarships, a policy opposed by Canadian Interuniversity Sport. There is a chance the whole conference might jump to the NAIA; the Canadian association is rethinking its position on athletics and may cut back on its offerings, which would make the NAIA even more appealing.[10]

On a more mundane level, the low rate of presidential participation in some NAIA affairs moved Baker to speak out at the March 2002 COP gathering. As streamlined for 2004, a convention normally runs two and a half days, with the Council of Athletics Administrators convening a day early to get through their extensive agenda. The convention itself includes meetings of CACI (Council of Affiliated Conferences and Independents), FARs, some conferences, and the strengthened Region Management Committees, along with seminars for Champions of Character and Career Opportunities. The groups caucus together to discuss proposed Constitution and by-laws changes after a "state of the NAIA" address by President Baker. Finally, all delegates join for the general business meeting, at which proposals are voted up or down. The terrorist attacks of September 11 had postponed the fall 2001 convention until March 2002, and the already-scheduled September 2002 conclave took place on schedule. But the positive March 2002 experience inspired the NAIA to wait 18 months before holding another convention, as the old practice of combining the convention with the Division I men's basketball tournament reestablished its appeal.

Baker called on presidents to play a larger role in the conventions, noting that only 40 to 60 usually attended. Not surprisingly, some athletic directors still believed, as they had back in 1986, that their presidents did not really understand athletics in spite of making progress since they took over the NAIA. A committee set up to address the problem opted for the carrot, not the stick, and pushed for measures to make attendance at the conventions more meaningful for presidents. By including more sessions directly targeted at CEOs and shortening the convention by a day (shortage of time was the most frequent excuse for presidential non-attendance), they hoped to boost attendance appreciably at the 2004 gathering.[11] The previous convention, in September 2002, had drawn only 32 presidents, and the national office sought a 100 percent increase in 2004. A few last-minute cancellations held the number to 45, but highly positive feedback on forums designed especially for presidents augured well for the future. By that time Baker's efforts to promote increased presidential involvement in conference matters had upped the number of conferences with an active presidential role to 20 of the NAIA's 27 conferences. In a related effort to increase presidential effectiveness, the COP moved in March 2002 to increase the term of their chair from one to two years. Jim Dennis (McKendree) in 2003 and 2004 was the first to serve the longer stretch and Loren Gresham (Southern Nazarene) was elected to begin serving his two years in January 2005.

Baker raised another issue in 2002: gender and racial opportunities. Some observers had criticized the NAIA as a "lily-white" organization, which seemed an affront to the association's record as a pioneer in moving black athletes and colleges into the sports mainstream. As the CEO noted, many of the historically black colleges were closing their doors, while most of the rest had succumbed to the siren song of the NCAA, where they were having difficulty competing. As noted earlier, he made those schools a prime target for NAIA recruiting efforts. The Gender Equity Committee's goal was educational rather than policy-making. Its symposia at the annual conventions attracted women students with some interest in careers in athletic administration, and the committee held its sole yearly meeting at the convention, but it had no means or motivation to track progress in hiring women. Baker noted a decline in hiring women as coaches without having an explanation, though it seemed that an increase in competitiveness, expanded recruiting duties, and competing time claims from families were likely factors.[12]

The fifth year of competition surfaced again at the 2002 convention. Proponents argued that the average time to graduate had risen to approximately four-and-a-half years for all students and a bit longer for athletes, so an additional year of competition merely reflected the new reality. It also made it more likely that athletes losing their athletic scholarships after four years would be able to complete their degrees. It would simplify eligibility determinations by eliminating red-shirting and hardship retrieval of seasons lost to injury or other factors. Critics stressed that private schools would lose a major marketing tool—that their students, unlike those at many public institutions, were graduating in four years. Despite the strong arguments on its behalf, the measure went down to a narrow defeat, suggesting that the concept still had legs. In a related matter, at the 2004 convention delegates approved clarification of rules allowing students to continue in a fifth-year teacher education program at their undergraduate college or pursue a second major there following graduation and be able to participate in intercollegiate athletics if they had eligibility remaining.

President Baker suggested to the COP at their spring 2004 conference that while the NAIA had done a solid job of promoting and running athletic events and was fast building its character component, it had not done as good a job on the academic side of its mission. He urged attention to increasing NAIA student-athlete graduation rates as the chief indicator of success in the academic area. Coincidentally, a congruent measure to slightly de-emphasize athletics in the interest of academics came to the convention floor at the March convention that year. The Council of Athletic Administrators had commissioned a survey of athletic directors in the fall of 2002 to get some solid data on the number of classes students were missing for various athletic seasons. The CAA had then drawn up a list of proposed cuts in the number of games permitted in different sports. After some debate over whether the whole slate of limitations should be implemented or if each sport should be treated separately, the whole slate was approved. The limitations were as follows, effective August 2005:

Sport	Old	New
Baseball	65 total contests	55 contests
Basketball	32 games, dates	30 games
Cross-Country	10 meets	8
Football	11 games (15 contests)	11 contests
Golf	20 matches/tournaments	14
Soccer	20 games	18
Softball	30 dates	28
Swimming/Diving	15 meets	12
Tennis	30 matches/tournaments	24 m/t/scrim.
Indoor Track	12 meets	10
Outdoor Track	12 meets	10 (12 if no indoor)
Volleyball	30 dates	28
Wrestling	25 dates	20[13]

International students had intermittently attracted attention in the NAIA as a problem, and in 2002 the association established an International Student-Athlete Task Force to address pertinent issues. Most serious, during the 2002-03 school year the Legislative Services department spent a great deal of time investigating reports that many NAIA international and domestic tennis players had received cash awards for their tennis play in Europe and thus should have lost their amateur standing within the NAIA. The inquiry led to 53 players being found in violation of the policy and stimulated efforts to provide a level playing field, particularly in tennis. Though brief consideration was given to a proposal to limit international students to 25 percent of any sport's roster, that would have penalized legitimate foreign students attracted by academic opportunity in the United States. Instead the committee developed a recommendation, approved by the convention in March 2004, which charged a season of competition for any year in which an athlete had received compensation, including payment for expenses, after high school graduation or the equivalent. The rule takes effect for new matriculants after August 1, 2005. The stated purpose for the policy is to reduce competitive advantage a student might gain by experience outside college competition.[14]

Seemingly bucking the academic inclination that led to shortened seasons, the NAIA in 2003 decided that the 24-week practice and play limit could be interrupted three times rather than twice, loosing the reins on coaches adept at gaming the limitation. Then in 2004, they went another step in that direction by narrowly approving a Golden State Athletic Conference proposal to deregulate summer play, practice, or scheduling. Another GSAC proposal approved by the convention reestablished 12 units as a full semester of enrollment, bringing the association back to its original standard after years of tinkering down to nine, then six units. The change brought the NAIA into alignment with junior colleges, the NCAA, and federal financial aid standards.[15]

On the ground, the move to Olathe got off to a great start. The office space provided by Honeywell suited the NAIA's needs very well. Fourteen of the 21 staff people relocated to Olathe from Tulsa, including the "best and the brightest" of them.[16] Olathe was the fastest-growing community in Kansas, and the future looked bright, with fundraising and pledged support solid. Then came September 11, 2001; the terrorist attacks on the United States further undermined the nation's economic confidence, already at a low ebb. Fundraising, never easy for the NAIA in the best of times, hit a wall. Baker estimated it would take $6,000,000 to break ground on the new headquarters building, which was to house an NAIA Hall of Fame and a Champions of Character center with conference facilities. Though the association closed on land for the new building in June 2003, getting the Cedar Creek property for around one-third market value, the capital campaign stalled around $3 million in cash and in-kind contributions. Where the initial estimate was that the NAIA would use the Honeywell facilities for about 18 months after the mid-2001 move, by fall 2002 Baker was estimating November 2004 for occupancy and a year later had architects scaling back the building to a less expensive plan and groundbreaking still in the indefinite future.[17] By then it had become clear that the planned Conference Center for the Champions of Character was probably not necessary since activities were likely to be in the field rather than at headquarters. New plans called for a building in the 12,000 to 15,000 square foot range. Fortunately, Honeywell seemed in no hurry to reclaim the NAIA's space, relieving a good deal of potential pressure for a quick groundbreaking.[18]

The NAIA was also disappointed in some of the sports arrangements in Olathe. The Olathe District Athletic Complex proved sub par for the national track and field tournaments held there in 2002 and 2003, and the hoped-for upgrade at the new College Boulevard Athletic Complex faded as the school board dropped plans for a track.[19] The national track meet had to be relocated to Louisville for 2004, though Olathe hoped to reclaim it with upgrades of the ODAC track.

On the other hand, the move back to the Kansas City area rejuvenated the men's Division I basketball tournament. It returned to a welcoming Municipal Auditorium, where it had been until the 1975 move to Kemper Arena. During its eight years in Tulsa, the tournament had drawn an average of 30,439 fans, with only the first two years topping 36,000 and the final two, with the honeymoon over, failing to top 24,000. Back "home" in downtown Kansas City, the tourney averaged 37,479 in its first three years.

Only six NAIA tournaments generated money for the association: football, the four basketball tourneys, and baseball, which benefited from the splendid promotional efforts of host Lewis-Clark State. Football drew over 5,000 each year to the title match in Hardin County, Tennessee. Division II men's basketball, hosted by the College of the Ozarks in Missouri, ranged in attendance between 18,000 and 25,000. The Division I women's tournament in Jackson, Tennessee, had peaked over 41,000 in 1997 and

1998, but had dropped to the low twenties by 2003 as local favorites Union and Freed-Hardeman faded from contention. The biggest draw was Division II women's basketball, which had been gaining support every year in Sioux City, Iowa, and hit an impressive 46,104 in 2004. Baseball usually drew in the mid-30,000 range in its Idaho venue. Many of the other sports barely cover the costs of NAIA staff on hand to assist in administering them.

Further potential exposure comes on television. In 2003-04, the NAIA began a five-year contract with CSTV (College Sports Television) to broadcast the football and four basketball championship games. The association shares production costs with CSTV, but as viewership increases and advertisers get on board, CSTV could become a revenue source. CSTV was originally only available on the DirecTV satellite service, and there only as part of a premium sports package, but by 2004 some cable services were picking it up and within a couple of years it could be part of some basic cable or satellite packages.[20]

Televised or not, the sports action continued on the field. Men's cross-country saw Life (GA) complete its run of three seconds and four firsts with a victory over Malone (OH) in 2001. The course at Wisconsin-Parkside, which hosted the meet from 1981 through 2002, when the institution dropped its NAIA affiliation, was dedicated in 2001 to longtime NAIA supporter Wayne Dannehl. In 2002, Minot State (ND) won its first of two consecutive titles, beating out Eastern Oregon in Wisconsin and then Black Hills State (SD) in Louisville in 2003, with Jerry Ziak of the University of British Columbia taking first place that year.

The men's soccer competition featured an odd twist in 2001. Top-seeded Lindsey Wilson (KY) beat Auburn-Montgomery, 4-0, for the championship, but the runners-up managed the unusual distinction of having tied their first three games and won each on penalty kicks to reach the final. In 2002, Mobile (AL) edged Park (MO), 2-1, in the title game, with Park vacating the second spot due to an ineligible player. The Rio Grande (OH) Redmen, who had not lost a regular season game since 2000, beat Fresno Pacific (CA), 1-0, to cap a 24-0-1 season with the 2003 title as the field expanded to 20 teams.

Eddie Eviston led Georgetown to a repeat title in football, topping Sioux Falls (SD), 49-27, in 2001 in front of a crowd of 6,750. Carroll (MT) captured the championship the next two years, ruining Georgetown's bid for a three-peat in 2002, 28-7, behind junior quarterback Rob Latrielle's 264 yards passing and three touchdowns. Sophomore QB Tyler Emmert improved on that in 2003, capping a 15-0 season by passing for 344 yards and three touchdowns as the Fighting Saints topped Northwestern Oklahoma, 41-28, in a wild offensive battle.

Division I men's basketball returned to Municipal Auditorium and racked up its best attendance since 1992, when the tournament last appeared at Kemper Arena. Unseeded Science and Arts (OK) knocked off fifth-seeded Oklahoma Baptist, 96-79, behind tournament MVP Michael Williamson for the title. The next year, Concordia (CA) won its first title, nipping Mountain State (WV) in overtime, 88-84, after the losers had toppled top seed Georgetown in the semis. Mountain State avenged its defeat in 2004, completing a splendid 37-1 season by edging Concordia in a title rematch, 74-70, with Zach Moss the leading scorer and MVP.

For two years, Division II basketball followed the script as top seeds took first place. In 2002, Evangel (MO) won its first title after being top-ranked all season, filling the gym at nearby College of the Ozarks as they beat Robert Morris (IL) handily, 84-61. In 2003 Northwestern (IA) survived a second-round scare and romped through the field to uphold its number one seeding, beating Bethany (KS) in the final game, 77-57. Brandon Woudstra was named MVP, reprising his award with the 2001 champs, and also took player of the year honors. In 2004, though, Oregon Tech upset all the experts. Seeded 16th, the team became the lowest seed ever to win the tournament, beating Bellevue (NE) in the title match, 81-72. Oregon Tech also garnered the MVP award (Kevin Baker), coach of the year (Dan Miles), and the team sportsmanship award—truly a season to remember.

Men's swimming and diving saw a new winner in 2002 as Seattle beat out Cal Baptist for first place. The next year Cal Baptist, with repeat outstanding swimmer Felix Sutanto leading the team, finished second again, with Simon Fraser (BC) back in their accustomed top spot. The two finished in the same ranking in 2004 as Simon Fraser won a record sixteenth swimming title.

Azusa Pacific (CA) dominated indoor track and field competition as the Cougars won all three titles. Runners-up were Doane (NE) in 2002, MidAmerica Nazarene (KS) in 2003, and Lindenwood (MO) in 2004. Bryan Clay of APU was a co-winner (with Cumberland's Anthony Kabara) of the outstanding performer award in 2002, but then Spring Arbor's David Rotich took that honor the next two years.

In wrestling action, Lindenwood won its first ever title in 2002, narrowly defeating host Montana-Northern in front of around 7,000 fans. Missouri Valley edged in-state rival Lindenwood for the 2003 crown. In 2004 Montana-Northern, led by repeat Gorrarian Award-winner Emmett Willson, beat out Menlo (CA) for first place.

Lewis-Clark State (ID) continued its domination of NAIA baseball competition. In 2002, they knocked off Oklahoma City in the final, 12-8, and they came right back the next year to beat the top-seeded Stars on consecutive days, 6-5 and 7-5, to nail down their 13th title. Pitcher Marc Kaiser earned MVP honors with two victories. In 2004 their luck ran out—two one-run defeats eliminated them, opening the door for Cumberland

(TN) to win its first title. Led by MVP first-baseman Donnie Burkhalter's .350 average and eight RBIs, Cumberland left Oklahoma City in the runner-up spot for an unprecedented third straight year, 10-3.

Men's track and field featured a familiar champion in 2002 as Azusa Pacific (CA) successfully defended its title, edging Life (GA) in Olathe. The 2003 title went to Lindenwood (MO), which beat out Dickinson State (ND), while John Ngure of Huntington (IN) was named outstanding performer for his victories in the 10,000-meter and marathon races. In 2004, Dickinson's Blue Hawks topped Lindenwood to win their first title ever. Decathlon and javelin winner Ben Bagdanof of Fresno Pacific (CA) earned the top performer award.

Oklahoma City continued to dominate men's golf competition, nipping Berry (GA) in 2002 as Tyrone Van Aswegen of the Stars took individual honors. Paced by Nicholas Allain, Oklahoma City beat out Berry again in 2003, leaving the runners-up in that position for the fifth time in ten years (they did win one title as well). In 2004, the Stars won their fourth straight title, leaving Johnson and Wales (FL) ten strokes back. Chad Wensel of The Master's (CA) prevented Allain from winning back-to-back honors.

In tennis matches, three teams dominated. In 2002, Auburn-Montgomery broke Oklahoma City's stranglehold of four straight titles, beating the Stars, 5-0, with the losers vacating their second place finish due to an ineligible player. The next year Oklahoma City was back on top, beating Azusa Pacific in the final, 5-1, though Sam Fletcher of the Cougars won top player honors. APU wound up second again in 2004 as Auburn-Montgomery regained first place with a 5-0 victory.

On the women's side of the ledger, three different schools won cross-country honors. In 2001, Cedarville (OH) beat out Concordia (NE), which finished second for the second of three consecutive years. The 2002 winners hailed from Northwest College (WA), though both years Emilie Mondor of Simon Fraser (BC) was the individual champion. The Clan got back on top in 2003, edging Northwest, while Mirriam Kaumba of Oklahoma Baptist had the meet's fastest time.

Westmont (CA) dominated soccer. In 2001, the Warriors gave up only one goal (in an overtime 2-1 win over Lindsey Wilson) in the tournament, beating Oklahoma City in the final, 1-0. The next year, they beat Azusa Pacific, a conference rival, 2-1 for the title. The Sullivan twins, Karin and Kristi, paced the Westmont squad, with Karin the 2001 MVP and Kristi both MVP and player of the year in 2002. In 2003, Westmont hosted the tournament and became the first host to triumph, beating Lindsey Wilson in an unprecedented seven overtimes, 2-1, capturing a record third straight title, and earning Karin Sullivan another MVP award.

Volleyball had more variety in its finals. In 2001 Columbia (MO) knocked off National American (SD) with Kenny Moreno of the winners taking MVP honors. The next year, National American overcame Elele Ekadeli, MVP and player of the year from Houston Baptist, and swept the Texans in the final. Fresno Pacific grabbed the 2003 championship with a 3-1 win over Columbia, the Sunbirds' second title and first since 1989.

It was all Oklahoma in Division I basketball. In 2002, Jhudy Gonzalez led Oklahoma City to an 82-73 win over rival Southern Nazarene, with Jadrea Seeey of OCU the player of the year. SNU turned the tables in 2003 with a nail-biting 71-70 win in the title game; Sasha Seriogina won the MVP award and TaKesha Watson was named player of the year. SNU was back in 2004, trumping Oklahoma City again, this time 77-61. The two schools split the big awards, with Ndeye Ndiaye of SNU taking the MVP and TaKesha Watson of OCU repeating as the player of the year.

Division II basketball also had a double winner. Hastings (NE) knocked off Cornerstone (MI), 73-69, in 2002, then parlayed their top seeding in 2003 into a repeat when they beat Dakota Wesleyan, 59-53. Their star, Elizabeth Herbek, won both MVP and player of the year awards. Host Morningside (IA) beat Cedarville (OH), 87-74, in 2004 for the Mustangs' first title behind the play of MVP Megan Cloud and player of the year Brittany Carper.

Swimming and diving was more predictable. Simon Fraser (BC) won three more titles to run their string to five in a row. In 2002, they beat out Seattle and Cal Baptist in a very competitive three-way competition, but Seattle fell by the wayside and the Clan topped Cal Baptist in 2003 and 2004 in meets that the two schools dominated. The 2004 title was the tenth for Simon Fraser's women's teams.

Traditional powers also dominated indoor track and field. Azusa Pacific lost in 2002 as McKendree (IL), led by sprinter Agne Visockaite, took their fourth title in a row. Then the Cougars took charge and won handily the next two years, leaving Doane (NE) a distant second in 2003 and Simon Fraser (BC) far behind in 2004. Vivian Chukwuemeka led an impressive cast of APU stars.

The softball tournaments featured three consecutive sudden death finals. In 2002, Point Loma (CA), led by shortstop and player of the year Cheryl Bolding, beat Oklahoma City, 1-0, to force a final game, then came up short, 2-1, as the Stars grabbed their third title in a row and seventh in nine years behind MVP pitcher Lindsey Voss. The next year, Mobile (AL) edged Simon Fraser (BC), 2-1, to force a final game, and like Point Loma came up just a bit short—the Clan won the final game and the championship, 3-1, behind MVP Erin Thomas. In 2004, the Thomas (GA) Night Hawks edged Simon Fraser, 5-4, to force a final game, and this time the underdog pulled out their second win in a row, beating the Clan, 5-4, once again as SFU committed multiple errors.

In tennis action, the perennial powers continued their winning ways. Auburn-Montgomery had won three straight titles, including a tie with Brenau (GA) in 1999, before Brenau beat them, 5-2, in 2002. The next year, Northwood (FL) kept the Alabamans in second place, taking the title match, 5-3. In 2004, however, Auburn-Montgomery moved back to its accustomed perch at the top of the heap, sweeping Azusa Pacific, 5-0.

On the golf course, Southern Nazarene won its second title in four years by beating out Nova Southeastern (FL) in 2002. Itzel Nieto of Lindenwood (MO) won the individual title. Northwood's golfers matched their tennis players by knocking off Oklahoma City by five strokes for the title in 2003, with Dana Langdon of Brescia (KY) racking up the best individual score. In 2004 the University of British Columbia set a tournament record by shooting 1249, beating Oklahoma City by five strokes. Despite UBC's heroics, the individual star was Nicole Wildes, a sophomore from Berry (GA), whose 293 (+5) obliterated the old record of 303 for the tournament.

Azusa Pacific (CA) continued its track and field domination. After Doane (NE) held them to second place in 2002, the Cougars topped Lindenwood in 2003 and 2004, and with their indoor victories both years had a record four straight titles. Vivian Chukwuemeka ran her NAIA title tally to eleven with her shot put and discus exploits.

The most impressive athletic achievement for an NAIA school is to win the NACDA Directors' Cup, emblematic of the outstanding overall athletic program. In 2002, Oklahoma City had the cup in its grasp, but eligibility violations cost it points and Lindenwood (MO) edged the Chiefs for first place, with Simon Fraser taking third, Azusa Pacific finishing fourth and Malone (OH) fifth. Lindenwood successfully defended its title in 2003, followed by Simon Fraser, Azusa Pacific, Mary (ND), and Oklahoma City. In 2004, Simon Fraser reclaimed the top spot, followed by Azusa Pacific, Lindenwood, Oklahoma City, and two North Dakota schools tied for fifth: Dickinson State and Mary.

What does the future hold for the NAIA? There appears to be a measure of stability in the association's sports championships. The number of colleges sponsoring the different sports varies, but with a few obvious exceptions, the numbers are healthy. The question of continuing to divide the basketball competition into two divisions is likely to linger, especially if the number of Division I schools continues to decline. Wrestling and swimming and diving are the sports whose numbers are most alarming—their future as national championship events is in jeopardy, especially since the NCAA rebuffed overtures to combine both associations for these small competitions. A motion to discontinue sports offered by less than 10 percent of member institutions was tabled at the June 2003 meeting of the Council of Athletics Administrators, but the proposal indicated the thinking of some association leaders.[21] The number of schools sponsoring sports, by season, in 2003-04:

Fall		Winter		Spring	
Cross-Country M	193	DI M bkb	102	Baseball	211
Cross-country W	202	DII M bkb	165	Golf M	175
Football	96	DI W bkb	99	Golf W	116
Soccer M	211	DII W bkb	167	Softball	209
Soccer W	215	Indoor T&F M	111	T&F M	139
Volleyball	253	Indoor T&F W	113	T&F W	142
		Swim/Diving M	15	Tennis M	113
		Swim/Diving W	17	Tennis W	131
		Wrestling	24		

Unfortunately, the fate of the NAIA does not rest entirely in its own hands. Remember the image of the NCAA as the United States and the NAIA as Canada—what the bigger organization does affects the smaller one dramatically. Rumors of the top 64 NCAA schools breaking away and forming a new organization, one that would not have to share its huge television revenues with the rest of its less fortunate fellows, fuel speculation about the potential impact of such a move on the NAIA. Many Division II schools might find the NAIA more attractive without the DI subsidies they now enjoy. The June 2004 expansion of the Bowl Championship Series to include two more schools has laid to rest for the time being a threatened lawsuit by Tulane University, but the possibility of a split will not go away. At the other end of the NCAA spectrum, if Division III schools eliminate red-shirting and disguised athletic scholarships, rumored possibilities as DIII continually reevaluates its policies, a number of those colleges might find the NAIA more appealing. If neither of those eventualities comes to pass, the NAIA will need to continue its hard work recruiting potential members that fit the association's ideals.

President Baker anticipates a possible summer 2004 restructuring of the NAIA's national office to focus on two key functions. First, he has brought on board Greg Glore as Director of Development to raise funds, and Mike Campbell to concentrate on corporate sponsorships as Director of Marketing. The second function is member services, which the CEO wants to *exceed* constituent expectations. Personnel changes could accompany the new structure.

For the NAIA to have a successful future, it needs to continue to stamp the character brand on its institutions and on the public's perceptions of them. To a large degree, this action is within the association's own power, though it will require more successful fundraising. Second, the NAIA must build its headquarters building in Olathe and establish a solid presence there. Getting its headquarters built would lend an aura of permanence to the association that would help curb negativism. Finally, the NAIA must stabilize its membership numbers. Steve Baker projects modest growth to 300 institutions in 2005 and 306 in 2006, though such projections have proven over-optimistic in the past. That sort of reversal of recent trends is essential to counter the outsider image of the NAIA as a dying organization. Much of its future depends upon perception, and stability in location and size is a critical element in strengthening the NAIA's image. Fortunately, around 95 percent of the NAIA's members are in affiliated conferences; those schools have a base in the association that makes them much less likely to defect than the less-well-connected independents.

Dual memberships are largely a thing of the past. Current NAIA members are more solidly committed to the association than has been the case in many years. A modest-sized organization of small colleges with common goals, competing with comparable schools, has proven to be a viable concept. Those who bleed NAIA blue and have bought into the ideals of the association share the vision of college athletics articulated by Al Duer many years ago. Sports should be an integrated, appropriately-emphasized, and character-building element of a college's overall institutional mission. That vision is alive and well in the 21st century.

NAIA Membership by Year
1942 through 2004

Year	Members	Year	Members
1942-43	110	1974-75	513
1942-44	n.a.	1975-76	509
1944-45	116	1976-77	513
1945-46	137	1977-78	509
1946-47	179	1978-79	512
1947-48	225	1979-80	512
1948-49	260	1980-81	519
1949-50	309	1981-82	515
1950-51	314	1982-83	527
1951-52	370	1983-84	519
1952-53	425	1984-85	498
1953-54	419	1985-86	471
1954-55	435	1986-87	465
1955-56	437	1987-88	472
1956-57	444	1988-89	479
1957-58	443[1]	1989-90	474
1958-59	n.a.	1990-91	465
1959-60	456	1991-92	436
1960-61	456	1992-93	409
1961-62	450	1993-94	389
1962-63	452	1994-95	390
1963-64	447	1995-96	364[3]
1964-65	470	1996-97	362
1965-66	470	1997-98	344
1966-67	517	1998-99	333
1967-68	523	1999-2000	330
1967-69	546	2000-01	328[4]
1969-70	553	2001-02	332
1970-71	548	2002-03	307
1971-72	561	2003-04	299
1972-73	557	2004-05	292
1973-74	558[2]		

[1] NCAA adds College Division
[2] NCAA splits into three divisions
[3] NCAA 2-year moratorium on new members
[4] NCAA 2-year moratorium on new members

NAIA Member Institutions Since 1959

NAIA membership records are limited prior to 1967. The first complete list is for the 1959-60 school year, but a gap ensues until 1964-65, followed by another gap until 1967-68, after which the record is complete. For this roster, I have assumed that schools that belonged to the NAIA before and after a gap were members during the intervening years, though that was likely not always the case. For schools that joined or dropped out during gaps, the exact year is impossible to determine, so I just give credit for the years for which we do have data. The result, unfortunately, lacks precision, but it is as accurate as possible at this point. A few schools have no dates associated with them, suggesting that their membership fell entirely during the gaps.

Many colleges have changed their names since 1959. I have listed them, where I know of the change, under their current name, with the former name in parentheses. Other schools will be listed under both old and new names with their separate dates of membership, simply because I am unaware of the institutional continuity.

Current members are rendered in bold type.

John R. M. Wilson
January 2004

Abilene Christian, TX 1973-82
Adams State, CO 1959-92
Adelphi, NY 1959-70
Adelphi Suffolk, NY 1964-68
Adrian, MI 1959-60
Agnes Scott, GA 1982-93
Alabama A&M 1959-73
Alabama Christian 1982-85
Alabama State-Florence 1959-65
Alabama State-Livingston 1959-60
Alabama State-Montgomery 1959-84
Alabama State-Troy 1959-60
Alabama-Huntsville 1973-87
Alabama-Montevallo 1967-69
Alaska 1959-73
Alaska Methodist 1967-73
Alaska-Anchorage 1975-77
Alaska-Fairbanks 1973-82
Alaska-Juneau 1984-87
Alaska-Pacific 1986-90

Alaska-Southeast 1988-90
Albany State, GA 1959-75
Alberta 1999—
Albertson, ID 1992—
Albuquerque, NM 1967-72
Alcorn A&M/State, MS 1959-84
Alderson-Broadus, WV 1959-95
Alice Lloyd, KY 1981—
Allen, SC 1959-87, 1993—
Allentown, PA 1982-89
Alliance, PA 1964-87
Alliant International, CA
  (US International), 1969-79, 994—
Alma, MI 1959-78
Alvernia, PA 1981-93
Ambassador, CA 1976-78, 1991-97
American Christian, OK 1974-76
American International, MA 1959-60
Anderson, IN 1959-92
Anderson, SC 1993-99

Angelo State, TX 1967-82
Appalachian State, NC 1959-70
Aquinas, MI 1967—
Arizona State 1959-65
Arkansas 1959-94
Arkansas A&M 1959-73
Arkansas Baptist 1980-82, 1990-92
Arkansas State 1959-75
Arkansas Tech 1959-98
Arkansas-Little Rock 1964-75, 1983-91
Arkansas-Monticello 1959-60, 1971-95
Arkansas-Pine Bluff 1964-98
Armstrong State, GA 1967-74, 1979-86
Aroostook State, ME 1969-70
Asbury, KY 1972—
Ashland, OH 1959-68
Assumption, MA 1959-60
Athens State, AL 1964-2004
Atlanta Baptist, GA 1970-73
Atlanta Christian, GA 2001-03
Atlantic Christian, NC 1959-90
Atlantic Union, MA 1988-2001
Auburn-Montgomery, AL 1975—
Augsburg, MN 1959-83
Augusta, GA 1967-74, 1982-86
Augustana, IL 1967-75
Aurora, CO 1967-68, 1971-72
Aurora, IL 1959-65, 1968-84
Austin, TX 1959-88
Austin Peay State, TN 1959-60
Avila, MO 1976—
Azusa Pacific, CA 1967—

Babson, MA 1968-75
Bacone, OK 2001—
Baker, KS 1959—
Baldwin-Wallace, OH 1959-60
Ball State, IN 1959-60
Baptist, SC 1970-76, 1982-83
Baptist Bible, MO 1974-87
Baptist Bible, PA 1977-84
Barat, IL 1989-2004
Barber-Scotia, NC 1967—
Bard, NY 1981-94
Barrington, RI 1964-75, 1977-85
Barton, NC 1990-95
Beaver, PA 1981-93
Belhaven, MS 1964—
Bellarmine, KY 1976-78
Bellevue, NE 1969—
Belmont, TN 1959-98

Belmont Abbey, NC 1959-95
Beloit, WI 1959-60
Bemidji State, MN 1959-91
Benedict, SC 1959-80, 1987-2002
Benedictine (St. Benedict's), KS 1970—
Benedictine Heights, OK 1959-60
Bentley, MA 1969-73
Berea, KY 1959—
Berry, GA 1959—
Bethany, CA 1988—
Bethany, KS 1959—
Bethany, WV 1959-75
Bethel, IN 1967—
Bethel, KS 1959—
Bethel, MN 1959-84
Bethel, TN 1959—
Bethune-Cookman, FL 1959-73
Biola, CA 1964—
Birmingham Southern, AL 1970- 2001
Bishop, TX 1959-84
Black Hills State, SD 1959—
Blackburn, IL 1959-78
Bloomfield, NJ 1959-2001
Blue Mountain, MS 1982—**Bluefield**, VA 1986—
Bluefield State, WV 1959-95
Bluffton, OH 1959-91
Boca Raton, FL 1977-78, 1983-92
Boise State, ID 1968-70
Boston State, MA 1959-74
Bowie State, MD 1971-84
Brandeis, ME 1982-84
Brenau, GA 1982—
Brescia, KY 1986—
Brevard, NC 1999—
Brewton Parker, GA 1987—
Briar Cliff, IA 1967—
Bridgeport, CT 1959-60
Bridgewater State, MA 1959-77
Bristol, TN 1979-81, 1985-88
British Columbia, 1999—
Brockport State, NY 1970-71
Bryan, TN 1971-86, 1988—
Bryant, RI 1967-75
Buena Vista, IA 1959-76
Buffalo, NY 1967-69
BYU-Hawaii 1974-98

C.W. Post, NY 1959-60, 1987-90
Cabrini, PA 1978-88
Caldwell, NJ 1982-2002
Calgary, AB 2001-03

California Baptist (Los Angeles Baptist) 1967–
California Lutheran, 1964-91
California Maritime 1996–
California State, Dominguez Hills 1970-79
California State, Fullerton, 1964-65
California State, Hayward 1998–
California State, Monterey Bay 1996-2004
California State, San Marcos 1998-
California State, Stanislaus 1969-70, 1973-74
California Tech 1959-60, 1967-84
California Western 1959-69
California, Riverside 1964-68
California, San Diego 1959-60, 1967-84
California, Santa Barbara 1959-60
California, Santa Cruz 2001-03
Calumet, IN 2000–
Calvary Bible, MO 1967-74
Calvin, MI 1959-60
Cameron, OK 1970-74, 1976-89
Campbell, NC 1967-77, 1982-86
Campbellsville, KY 1967–
Capitol, MD 1989-92
Cardinal Newman, MO 1982-85
Cardinal Stritch, WI 1985–
Carlow, PA 1982–
Carroll, MT 1959–
Carroll, WI 1959-68, 1972-81
Carson-Newman, TN 1959-93
Carthage, IL 1959-60
Carthage, WI 1964-76
Cascade, OR 1964-68
Cascade, OR 2003–
Castleton State, VT 1964-2001
Catawba, NC 1959-93
Cedar Crest, PA 1987-91
Cedarville, OH 1959–
Centenary, LA 1982-92
Centenary, NJ 1989-90, 1992-94
Central, IA 1959-71
Central, MO 1959-60
Central Arkansas 1975-93
Central Bible, MO 1977-87
Central Christian, KS 2002–
Central Connecticut State 1964-65
Central Methodist, MO 1964–
Central Michigan 1959-65
Central State, OH 1959-85, 1987-03
Central State, OK 1959-89
Central Washington 1959-2001
Chadron State, NE 1959-92
Chaminade, HI 1979-89
Chapman, CA 1959-60, 1982-83

Charleston, SC 1959-60, 1967-89, 1994-95
Charleston, WV 1979-94
Chatham, PA 1988-89
Chicago State, IL 1964-88
Chico State, CA 1959-60
Christian Brothers, TN 1959-98
Christian Heritage, CA 1987–
Christopher Newport, VA 1972-74
Church, HI 1970-74
Claflin, SC 1959–
Claremont-Harvey Mudd, CA 1964-78
Clark, GA 1959-73
Clarke, IA 1986-97
Clayton State, GA 1970-75, 1978-99
Clinch Valley, VA 1976-83, 1985-86
Coastal Carolina, SC 1978-95
Coker, SC 1978-95
Colorado Christian (Colorado Baptist) 1987-90
Colorado School of Mines 1959-92
Colorado State 1959-60
Colorado-Colorado Springs 1967-71
Columbia, GA 1986-92
Columbia, MO 1974–
Columbia, SC 1982-83, 1985–
Columbia Christian, OR 1972-75, 1980-92
Columbia Union, MD 1987-97
Columbus, GA 1969-74, 1983-89
Concord, WV 1959-95
Concordia, CA (Christ College Irvine) 1986–
Concordia, IL 1969-83
Concordia, IN 1964-76
Concordia, MI 1980-81, 1989–
Concordia, MN 1959-2002
Concordia, NE 1959–
Concordia, NY 1981-86
Concordia, OR 1979–
Concordia, TX 1983-85, 1995-99
Concordia, WI 1982-97
Concordia Lutheran, TX 1982-83, 1985-95
Connecticut 1959-60
Converse, SC 1982-83, 1985-94,
Coppin State, MD 1967-84
Cornerstone, MI 1994–
Corpus Christi, TX 1959-71
Covenant, GA 1987–
Covenant, TN 1968-87
Creighton, NE 1959-60
Crown, MN 1999–
Culver-Stockton, MO 1959–
Cumberland, KY 1967–
Cumberland, TN 1964-65, 1983–
Curry, MA 1959-60, 1973-75

Daemen, NY 1978-82, 1987—
Dakota State, SD 1969—
Dakota Wesleyan, SD 1959—
Dallas, TX 1964-96
Dallas Baptist, TX 1968-2002
Dana, NE 1959—
Danbury State, CT 1959-65
Daniel Payne, AL 1973-75
Davenport, MI 2003—
David N. Myers, OH 2004—
Davidson, NC 1982-86
Davis & Elkins, WV 1959-95
DC Teachers (Washington, DC) 1967-68, 1971-75
Defiance, OH 1959-91
Delaware State 1959-79
Delaware Valley, PA 1964-65
Delta State, MS 1959-60, 1970-75
Denver, CO 1976-90
DePauw, IN 1982-91
Detroit, MI 1967-73, 1976-82
Detroit Business, MI 1964-65, 1973-75, 1982-95
Detroit Tech, MI 1959-78
DeVry, GA 1983-85, 1990-92
Dickinson State, ND 1959—
Dillard, LA 1959—
District of Columbia 1980-83
Doane, NE 1959—
Dominican, CA 1987—
Dominican, IL 1997-2002
Dominican, NY 1974-2002
Dominican, WI 1967-72
Dordt, IA 1972—
Dowling, NY 1968-82
Drew, NJ 1969-73
Drury, MO 1959-94
Dubuque, IA 1959-76
Dyke, OH 1974-93

Earlham, IN 1959-89
East Carolina, NC 1959-60
East Central Oklahoma State 1959-2003
East Tennessee State 1959-60
East Texas Baptist 1959-99
East Texas State 1959-84
Eastern, PA 1972-91
Eastern Baptist, PA 1964-72
Eastern Connecticut State 1967-75
Eastern Illinois 1959-72
Eastern Mennonite, PA 1971-75
Eastern Michigan 1959-71
Eastern Montana 1959-81

Eastern Nazarene, MA 1967-75, 1979-91
Eastern New Mexico, 1959-85
Eastern Oregon 1959—
Eastern Washington 1959-80
Edgewood College, WI 1987-95
Edward Waters, FL 1964—
Eisenhower, NY 1970-81
Elizabeth City State, NC 1959-78
Elizabethtown, PA 1959-60
Ellendale State, ND 1964-65
Elmhurst, IL 1959-80
Elmira, NY 1971-75
Elon, NC 1959-92
Embry-Riddle, AZ 1990—
Embry-Riddle, FL 1967-77, 1987—
Emmanuel, GA 1994—
Emory & Henry, VA 1967-70
Emporia, KS 1959-74
Emporia State, KS 1959-92
Erskine, SC 1959-92
Eureka, IL 1959-95
Evangel, MO 1967—
Evergreen State, WA 1979—

Fairleigh Dickinson, NJ 1959-60
Fairmont State, WV 1959-95
Faulkner, AL 1985—
Fayetteville State, NC 1959-82
Federal City, DC 1969-74
Felician, NJ 1995-2002
Ferris State, MI 1959-81
Findlay, OH 1959-2000
Fisher, MA 2001—
Fisk, TN 1959-75
Fitchburg State, MA 1964-71
Five Towns, NY 2001-02
Flagler, FL 1976—
Florence State, AL 1967-74
Florida A&M 1959-72, 1978-79
Florida Atlantic 1975-83
Florida Gulf Coast 2001-02
Florida Memorial 1959—
Florida Tech 1967-74, 1978-86
Fontbonne, MO 1987-91
Fort Hays State, KS 1959-92
Fort Lauderdale, FL 1980-83
Fort Lewis, CO 1964-86, 1987-92
Fort Valley State, GA 1959-77
Fort Wayne Bible, IN 1967-77
Francis Marion, SC 1972-92
Franciscan, IA 2003—

Franklin, IN 1959-92
Franklin, OH 1982-85
Franklin Pierce, NH 1974-88
Frederick, VA 1967-68
Fredonia, NY 1967-77
Freed-Hardeman, TN 1976—
Fresno Pacific, CA 1967—
Friends, KS 1959—
Friendship, SC 1979-82
Furman, SC 1983-84

Gallaudet, DC 1959-60, 1973-75
Gannon, PA 1959-73
Gardner-Webb, NC 1969-93
General Beadle State, SD 1959-69
Geneva, PA 1959—
George Fox, OR 1964-99
George Mason, VA 1967-79
George Williams, IL 1967-84
Georgetown, KY 1959—
Georgia, 1959-60, 1972-91
Georgia Southern, 1964-69
Georgia Southwestern, 1968—
Georgian Court, NJ 1982-2002
Glassboro State, NJ 1959-72
Glenville State, WV 1959-95
Golden Gate, CA
Goldey-Beacom, DE 1990-2003
Gonzaga, WA 1959-60, 1982-86
Gordon, MA 1964-75, 1977-89
Gorham State, ME 1959-71
Goshen, IN 1967—
Grace, IN 1964—
Graceland, IA 1959—
Grambling, LA 1959-77
Grand Canyon, AZ 1964-91, 2003-04
Grand Rapids Baptist, MI 1986-94
Grand Valley State, MI 1967-81
Grand View, IA 1979—
Great Falls, MT 1967-85, 2000—
Green Mountain, VT 1983-2003
Greensboro, NC 1967-74
Greenville, IL 1959-95
Guilford, NC 1959-91
Gustavus-Adolphus, MN 1959-84
Gwynedd Mercy, PA 1990-93

Hamline, MN 1959-83
Hampton Institute, VA 1959-85
Hannibal-LaGrange, MO 1985—
Hanover, IN 1959-93

Harding, AR 1959-97
Hardin-Simmons, TX 1964-65, 1982-97
Harris Stowe State, MO (Harris Teachers) 1969—
Haskell Indian, KS 2000—
Hastings, NE 1959—
Hawaii 1959-60
Hawaii-Hilo 1976-94
Hawaii-Loa 1983-92
Hawaii-Pacific 1979-98
Hawthorne, NH 1972-88
Henderson State, AR 1959-94
Hendrix, AR 1959-92
High Point, NC 1959-95
Hillsdale, MI 1959-98
Hillyer, CN 1959-60
Hiram Scott, NE 1967-71
Holy Family, PA
Holy Names, CA 1987—
Hope International, CA (Pacific Christian) 1971-76, 1983-84, 1994—
Houghton, NY 1969—
Houston Baptist, TX 1967-69, 1989—
Howard, AL 1959-65
Howard, DC 1959-68, 1971-73
Howard Payne, TX 1959-83
Humbolt State, CA 1959-65
Huntingdon, AL 1964—
Huntington, IN 1959—
Husson, ME 1964-2004
Huston-Tillitson, TX 1959—

Idaho 1959-90, 1991-92
Idaho State 1959-60
Illinois Benedictine 1971-81
Illinois State-Normal 1959-65
Illinois Tech 1970-81, 1985—
Illinois Wesleyan 1959-82
Illinois-Jacksonville 1959-81
Illinois-Springfield 1995—
Incarnate Word, TX 1986-99
Indiana Central 1959-72
Indiana Northwest 1998—
Indiana Purdue-Fort Wayne 1981-83
Indiana Purdue-Indianapolis 1978-95
Indiana Southbend 1987—
Indiana Southeast 1977—
Indiana State 1959-65, 1970-76
Indiana Tech 1964—
Indiana Wesleyan (Marion) 1968-85, 1987—
Iona, NJ 1959-60
Iowa Wesleyan 1959—

Jackson State, MS 1959-82
Jacksonville, FL
Jacksonvillle State, AL 1964-81
Jamestown, ND 1959—
Jarvis Christian, TX 1970-91, 1995—
Jersey City State, NJ 1959-71
John Brown, AR 1964—
John F. Kennedy, NE 1968-75
John Jay Criminal Justice, NY 1973-75
John Wesley, MI 1972-77
Johnson & Wales, CO 2003—
Johnson & Wales, FL 2001—
Johnson & Wales, SC 1996-2004
Johnson C. Smith, NC 1959-83
Johnson State, VT 1973-2002
Judson, AL 1982-89
Judson, IL 1967—
Judson Baptist, OR 1981-83

Kalamazoo, MI 1959-60
Kansas State 1959-60, 1970-77
Kansas State Teachers 1959-60, 1970-73
Kansas Wesleyan 1959—
Kearney State, NE 1959-90
Keene State, NH 1969-82
Kendall, IL 1997-2004
Kennesaw State, GA 1983-94
Kentucky State 1959-84, 1987-88
Kentucky Wesleyan 1959-60, 2003—
Keuka, NY 1985-87
King, TN 1971—
King's, NY 1959-95
Knoxville, TN 1959-77, 1990-91, 1999—

La Sierra, CA 1996-99
LaGrange, GA 1959-2002
Lake Erie, OH 1987-96
Lake Forest, IL 1959-76
Lake Superior, MI 1967-81
Lakehead, ON 1967-78
Lakeland, WI 1959-70, 1971-95
Lamar State, TX 1959-60
Lambuth, TN 1959-65, 1972—
Lander, SC 1969-92
Lane, TN 1959-72
Langston, OK 1959-85, 1987—
LaRoche, PA 1977-95
Laval, QE 2003—
LaVerne, CA 1959-82
Lawrence Tech, MI 1959-80
Lea, MN 1967-71

Lee, TN 1974—
Lees-McRae, NC 1991-95
LeMoyne-Owen, TN 1959-82
Lenoir-Rhyne, NC 1959-93
LeTourneau, TX 1959-93
Lewis & Clark, OR 1959-98
Lewis, IL 1959-80
Lewis-Clark State, ID 1967—
Liberty Baptist, VA 1975-84
Life, GA 1989-2002
Life Bible, CA 1967-69
Limestone, SC 1974-98
Lincoln, MO 1959-65, 1999-2001
Lincoln, PA 1959-87
Lincoln Memorial, TN 1959-91
Lindenwood, MO 1980—
Lindsey Wilson, KY 1986—
Linfield, OR 1959-98
Lipscomb, TN (David Lipscomb) 1959-2001
Livingston, AL 1967-77
Livingstone, NC 1964-84
Loras, IA 1959-60, 1967-86
Louisiana 1959-60, 1969-2000
Louisiana State-Shreveport 1992—
Louisiana Tech 1959-60
Loyola, LA 1990—
Lubbock Christian, TX 1970—
Luther, IA 1959-60
Lycoming, PN 1959-60
Lynchburg, VA 1967-74
Lyndon State, VT 1959—
Lynn, FL (Boca Raton) 1977-78, 1983-95
Lyon, AR 1994—

Macalester, MN 1959-83
Mackinac, MI 1967-69
MacMurray, IL 1959-65, 1974-78
Madonna, MI 1988—
Maine-Augusta 1985-93
Maine Maritime Academy 1968-89
Maine-Farmington 1967-2003
Maine-Fort Kent 1973—
Maine-Machias 1970—
Maine-Presque Isle 1970-2004
Malone, OH 1964—
Manchester, IN 1959-92
Mankato, MN 1959-60, 1978-81
Marian, IN 1964—
Marian, WI 1981-97
Marist, NY 1967-73
Marquette, WI 1982-85

Mars Hill, NC 1967-93
Martin Luther, MN 1998-2004
Martin Methodist, TN 1994–
Mary, ND 1970–
Mary Hardin-Baylor, TX 1978-2000
Mary Holmes, MS 1969-70
Marycrest, IA 1976-91
Maryland State-Frostburg 1959-71, 1973-76
Maryland State-Princess Anne 1959-70
Maryland State-Towson 1959-60
Maryland-Baltimore County 1972-74
Maryland-Eastern Shore 1970-81
Marymount, KS 1970-89
Massachusetts Pharm and Science 1992-93
Master's, CA 1985–
Mayville State, ND 1959–
McKendree, IL 1959–
McMurry, TX 1959-97
McNeese State, LA 1959-68, 1970-71
McPherson, KS 1959–
Medaille, NY 1975-78
Menlo, CA 1988-89, 1998–
Mercer, GA 1959-87
Mercy, MI 1982-87
Mercyhurst, PN 1970-81
Mesa, CO 1975-92
Messiah, PA 1967-74, 1976-81
Methodist, NC 1967-75
Metropolitan State, CO 1968-87
Michigan Lutheran, 1964-70
Michigan Tech 1971-72
Michigan-Dearborn 1979–
MidAmerica Nazarene, KS 1970–
Mid-Continent, KY 2001–
Middle Tennessee State 1959-60
Midland, NE 1959-65, 1971-72
Midland Lutheran, NE 1967–
Midway, KY 1990–
Midwestern, TX 1959-97
Miles, AL 1959-73
Milligan, TN 1959–
Millikin, IL 1959-75
Mills, CA 1999–
Millsaps, MS 1973-74
Milton, WI 1959-82
Milwaukee School of Engineering, WI 1974-93
Minnesota-Crookston 1994-99
Minnesota-Duluth 1959-76, 1979-94
Minnesota-Morris 1964-95
Minot State, ND 1959–
Misericordia, PA 1981-92

Mississippi 1973-75
Mississippi Industrial 1981-82
Mississippi Valley State 1964-86
Mississippi Vocational 1959-60
Missouri Baptist 1978–
Missouri Southern 1968-89
Missouri Valley 1959–
Missouri Western 1969-89
Missouri-Kansas City 1959-87
Missouri-Saint Louis 1967-71
Mobile, AL 1985–
Monmouth, IL 1959-60
Monmouth, NJ 1964-78
Montana State, **Northern** (Northern Montana) 1959–
Montana Tech (Montana School of Mines 1959–
Montana-Western (Western Montana) 1959–
Montclair State, NJ 1959-68
Montevallo, AL 1969-97
Montreat, NC 1993–
Moorhead State, MN 1959-95
Morehouse, GA 1959-70
Morgan State, MD 1959-64
Morningside, IA 1959-89, 2001
Morris, SC 1964–
Morris Brown, GA 1959-72
Morris Harvey, WV 1959-79
Mount Aloysius, PA 1997-2001
Mount Angel, OR 1967-70
Mount Marty, SD 1970–
Mount Mary, WI 1984-85
Mount Mercy, IA 1978-85, 1987–
Mount Olive, NC 1985-95
Mount Saint Clare, IA 1987-2003
Mount Saint Joseph, OH 1985-98
Mount Saint Mary, NY 1983-87
Mount Saint Mary's, CA 1985-95
Mount Saint Paul, WI 1968-70
Mount Senario, WI 1975-79, 1994-2002
Mount Vernon Nazarene, OH 1974–
Mountain State, WV (College of West Virginia) 1995–
Mundelein, IL 1989-91

Nasson, ME 1968-83
National, SD 1983-91, 1995-97
National American, SD (National) 1983-91, 1995–
National College of Education, IL 1982-90
National-Louis, IL 1990-91
Nazareth, MI 1981-82

Nazareth, NY 1977-83
Nebraska Wesleyan 1959-60, 1982—
Neumann, PA 1986-93
Newman, KS 1973—
Nevada 1959-60
New Bedford Tech, MA 1959-60
New England, ME 1979-99
New England, NH 1968-72, 1974-89
New Hampshire 1967-71, 1973-79
New Haven, CT 1964-71
New Mexico Highlands 1959-92
New Mexico Western 1959-60
New Paltz State, NY 1971-73
New York State 1959-65
New York Tech 1967-71
Newark Engineering, NJ 1964-74
Newark State, NJ 1964-72
Newberry, SC 1959-92
Newman, KS 1973—
Nicholls State, LA 1964-75
Nichols Business, MA 1964-65
Norfolk State, VA 1964-69, 1971-84
North Adams State, MA 1967-73
North Carolina 1959-65, 1968-70
North Carolina A&T 1959-74
North Carolina Central 1970-84, 1986-88
North Carolina Wesleyan 1967-74
North Carolina-Asheville 1967-85
North Carolina-Charlotte 1967-69
North Carolina-Greensboro 1968-74
North Carolina-Wilmington 1967-77
North Central, IL 1959-73
North Dakota State 1959-60
North Dakota-Ellendale 1967-70
North Florida 1982-93
North Georgia 1959-68, 1972—
North Greenvillle, SC 1995-2002
North Park, IL 1964-72
Northeast Louisiana State 1959-71
Northeastern Illinois 1967-89
Northeastern Oklahoma State 1959-98
Northern Arizona 1970-71
Northern Illinois 1959-60
Northern Kentucky 1972-75
Northern Michigan 1964-68, 1982-85
Northern State, SD 1959-95
Northland, WI 1959—
Northwest, WA 1986-89, 1996—
Northwest Nazarene, ID 1959-2002
Northwestern, IA 1964—
Northwestern, MN 1964-65, 1995—

Northwestern, WI 1970-71, 1986-90
Northwestern Louisiana State 1959-77
Northwestern Oklahoma State 1959—
Northwood, IN 1967-74
Northwood, FL 1990—
Northwood, MI 1967-93
Northwood, TX 1967-74, 1987—
Notre Dame de Namur, CA 1980-83, 1993-94, 1998—
Notre Dame, FL
Notre Dame, NH 1992-02
Notre Dame, OH 1988—
Nova, FL 1985-02
Nyack, NY (Nyack Missionary) 1964-2003

Oakland, MI 1974-76
Oakland City, IN 1959-92
Occidental, CA 1959-78
Oglethorpe, GA 1959-60, 1974-78
Ohio Dominican 1970—
Ohio Northern 1959-71
Ohio Valley 1995-99
Oklahoma Baptist 1959—
Oklahoma Christian 1967—
Oklahoma City 1985—
Oklahoma Liberal Arts 1973-74
Oklahoma Panhandle (Panhandle A&M, Panhandle State), 1959-97
Oklahoma Wesleyan (Bartlesville Wesleyan) 1977—
Olivet, MI 1959-60
Olivet Nazarene, IL 1959-60, 1969—
Omaha, NE 1959-73
Oral Roberts, OK 1967-71
Oregon College of Education 1959-81
Oregon Tech 1964—
Ottawa, KS 1959—
Ottawa, ON 2002-03
Ouachita Baptist, AR 1959-97
Our Lady of the Lake, TX 1979-85
Owosso, MI 1970-73
Ozarks, AR 1959-97
Ozarks, MO 1967—

Pace, NY 1959-71
Pacific, OR 1959-99, 2001-02
Pacific Lutheran, WA 1959-98
Pacific Union, CA 1995—
Paine, GA 1964-85
Palm Beach Atlantic, FL 1973-76, 1988-2003
Pan American, TX 1959-65, 1982-85

Park, MO 1964–
Parsons, IA 1959-60, 1972-73
Patten, CA 1994–
Paterson State, NJ 1959-71
Paul Quinn, TX 1959-60, 1967-90, 1998–
Pembroke State, NC 1959-92
Penn State-Behrend 1972-85
Penn State-Bloomsburg 1964-71
Penn State-California 1959-79
Penn State-Capitol 1979-87
Penn State-Cheyney 1959-65
Penn State-Clarion 1959-83
Penn State-East Stroudsburg 1959-65
Penn State-Edinboro 1959-82
Penn State-Harrisburg 1987-93
Penn State-Indiana 1959-82
Penn State-Kutztown 1964-65
Penn State-Lock Haven 1959-72
Penn State-Mansfield 1959-71, 1973-74
Penn State-Middletown
Penn State-Millersville 1959-71, 1973-76
Penn State-Shippensburg 1959-68
Penn State-Slippery Rock 1959-65, 1968-78
Pepperdine, CA 1959-60
Pershing, NE 1962-71
Peru State, NE 1959–
Pfeiffer, NC 1959-95
Philadelphia Bible, PA 1964-74, 1983-84
Philadelphia Pharmacy and Sciences, PA 1969-98
Philadelphia Textile Institute, PA 1959-60
Philadelphia Textiles and Sciences, PA 1964-65
Philander Smith, AR 1959-93
Phillips, MS 1982-86
Phillips, OK 1959-99
Piedmont, GA 1959-99
Pikeville, KY 1959–
Pittsburg State, KS 1964-70, 1977-89
Pittsburgh-Bradford, PA 1980-97
Pittsburgh-Johnstown, PA 1975-82
Platteville State, WI
Plattsburgh State, NY 1959-74
Plymouth State, NH 1973-75
Point Loma Nazarene, CA (Pasadena) 1959–
Point Park, PA 1967–
Pomona, CA 1964-78
Portland, OR 1959-60, 1982-86
Portland State, OR 1959-65
Portland-Gorham, ME 1971-78
Prairie View A&M, TX 1959-97
Pratt Institute, NY 1959-73
Presbyterian, SC 1959-93
Presentation, SD 1995–

Principia, IL 1959-60, 1967-74
Puget Sound, WA 1959-65, 1982-99
Purdue-Calumet, IN 1969–
Purdue-North Central, IN 1999–

Quincy, IL 1959-86, 1999–
Quinnipiac, CT 1959-73, 2002-03

Racine, WI 1972-74
Radford, VA 1979-82
Redlands, CA 1959-82
Regina, SK 2004–
Regis, CO 1959-60, 1970-90
Reinhardt, GA 1999–
Rhode Island 1964-75
Richmond Professional, VA 1964-68
Ricker, ME 1967-78
Rider, NJ 1959-65
Rio Grande, OH 1959-91, 1992–
Robert Morris, IL 1995–
Roberts Wesleyan, NY 1964-86, 1995–
Rockford, IL 1959-83
Rockhurst, MO 1959-92
Rockmont, CO 1978-84
Rocky Mountain, MT 1959–
Roger Williams, RI 1969-85
Rollins, FL 1959-60
Roosevelt, IL 1972-76, 1982-91
Rosary, IL 1982-97
Rose Tech, IN 1964-71
Rose-Hulman, IN 1971-74
Rosemont, PA 1984-85
Rust, MS 1964-82
Rutgers, NJ 1968-82
Rutgers-South Jersey 1970-72, 1973-77

Sacramento State, CA 1959-65
Sacred Heart, KS 1969-73
Saginaw Valley, MI 1970-89
Saint Ambrose, IA 1959-2001, 2002–
Saint Andrews, NC 1964-74, 1987-95, 2001-02
Saint Anselm's, NH 1959-60
Saint Augustine's, NC 1959-85
Saint Benedict's, IN 1967-69
Saint Bernard, AL 1959-76
Saint Cloud, MN 1959-69, 1970-72, 1978-81
Saint Edward's, TX 1959-99
Saint Francis, IL 1971-72, 1973–
Saint Francis, IN 1967–
Saint Francis, ME 1968-79
Saint Francis, NY 1959-60
Saint Francis, PA 1959-68

Saint Gregory's, OK 1997—
Saint John Fisher, NY 1974-82
Saint John's, KS 1981-87
Saint John's, MN 1959-84
Saint Joseph, NY 1987-95
Saint Joseph, VT 1975—
Saint Joseph's, IN 1959-60
Saint Joseph's, ME 1971-2002
Saint Joseph's, NM 1959-65
Saint Louis Pharmacy, MO 1993—
Saint Martin's, WA 1959-2001
Saint Mary, KS 1989—
Saint Mary, NE 1982—
Saint Mary of the Plains, KS 1964-92
Saint Mary of the Woods, IN 1986-90
Saint Mary's, CA 1979-86
Saint Mary's, IN 1982-90
Saint Mary's, MD 1968-79
Saint Mary's, MI 1978-92
Saint Mary's, MN 1959-83
Saint Mary's, TX 1959-99
Saint Michael's, NM 1959-65, 1982-83
Saint Norbert, WI 1959-81
Saint Olaf, MN 1974-82
Saint Paul's, VA 1959-60, 1980-81
Saint Peter's, NJ 1959-60
Saint Procopius, IL 1969-71
Saint Rose, NY 1982-91
Saint Scholastica, MN 1973-83, 1987—
Saint Thomas, FL 1988—
Saint Thomas, MN 1959-84, 1986-87
Saint Thomas, TX 1978-85
Saint Thomas Aquinas, NY 1973-85, 1987-2000
Saint Vincent, PA 1964—
Saint Xavier, IL 1970—
Salem, WV 1959-95
Salem State, MA 1964-74
Salisbury State, MD 1967-74
Sam Houston State, TX 1959-82
Samford, AL 1967-68, 1969-71
San Diego State, CA 1959-60
Sangamon State, IL 1977-95
Santa Fe, NM 1967-89, 2001—
Savannah Art & Design, GA 1987-92
Savannah State, GA 1959-73
Schreiner, TX 1984-2002
Science & Arts, OK 1974—
Sciences, PA 1998—
Seattle, WA 1980-2002
Seattle Pacific, WA 1959-60, 1982-91, 1993-94
Selma, AL 1990-96
Seton Hill, PA 1984—

Shaw, MI 1959-60, 1970-83
Shaw, NC 1964-65, 1969-85
Shawnee, OH
Shawnee State, OH 1987—
Sheldon Jackson, AK 1985-93
Shenandoah, VA 1970-76
Shepherd, WV 1959-95
Shimer, IL 1964-68
Shorter, GA 1959—
Si Tanka/Huron, SD (Huron) 1959—
Siena Heights, MI 1972—
Simon Fraser, BC 1968—
Simpson, CA 1959-60, 1971-73, 1996—
Simpson, IA 1964-71, 1973-76
Sioux Falls, SD 1959—
Skidmore, NY 1981-85
South Carolina
South Carolina State 1959-78
South Carolina-Aiken 1976-91
South Carolina-Spartanburg 1976-90
South Dakota Mines/Tech 1959-73, 1982-83,
    1987-89, 2003—
South Dakota State 1959-60
South Dakota Tech 1973-87, 1989-94
South Dakota-Springfield 1971-84
Southampton, NY 1964-73
Southeastern, LA 1959-60, 1967-75
Southeastern, DC 1978-82
Southeastern Mass Tech-Dartmouth 1967-75
Southeastern Mass Tech-Fall River 1964-65
Southeastern Mass Tech-New Bedford 1964-65
Southeastern Oklahoma State 1959-99
Southern, LA 1959-65, 1968-70, 1972-73,
    1976-77
Southern A&M, LA 1967-68, 1970-72
Southern Arkansas 1970-71, 1976-96
Southern Baptist, AR 1989-90
Southern Baton Rouge, LA 1973-82
Southern Benedictine, AL 1976-79
Southern Colorado 1964-91
Southern Connecticut State 1959-65
Southern Illinois 1959-60
Southern Maine 1978-85
Southern Nazarene, OK (Bethany Nazarene)
    1969—
Southern New Orleans, LA 1972—
Southern Oregon 1959-82, 1990-92, 1997—
Southern State, AR 1959-76
Southern State, SD 1959-71
Southern Tech, GA 1978—
Southern Utah 1964-88
Southern Vermont 1980-81, 1986-89

Southern Virginia 1998–
Southern Wesleyan, SC (Central Wesleyan) 1974–
Southwest, NM 1985–
Southwest Baptist, MO 1967-87
Southwest State, MN 1970-94
Southwest Texas State 1959-82
Southwestern, KS 1959–
Southwestern, TX 1959-93
Southwestern Adventist, TX 1994-2002
Southwestern Assemblies of God, TX 1997–
Southwestern Louisiana 1959-70
Southwestern Oklahoma State 1959-98
Spalding, KY 1993–
Spring Arbor, MI 1964–
Spring Garden, PA 1971-84
Spring Hill, AL 1959-60, 1971–
Stanislaus State, CA 1970-73
State N&I, ND 1959-60
State, NY 1969-71
Stephen F. Austin, TX 1959-82
Sterling, KS 1959–
Stetson, FL 1959-65
Steubenville, OH 1959-65, 1974-81
Stillman, AL 1959-82
Stonehill, MA 1959-65
Sue Bennett, KY 1992-98
Sul Ross State, TX 1959-80, 1982-97
SUNY Delhi, NY 2001–
SUNY Tech, NY 1980-83
Susquehanna, PA 1959-60

Tabor, KS 1959–
Talladega, AL 1967-2003
Tampa, FL 1959-71
Tarkio, MO 1959-91
Tarleton State, TX 1964-95
Taylor, IN 1959–
Tech Delhi, NY 2003–
Teikyo Marycrest, IA 1991-96
Teikyo Post, CT 1990-2002
Teikyo Westmar, IA 1990-95
Tennessee A&I State 1959-70
Tennessee Temple 1979-80, 1986-87
Tennessee Wesleyan 1964–
Tennessee-Martin 1959-60, 1971-72
Texas A&I 1959-82
Texas A&M International 2002–
Texas College 1959-92, 1999–
Texas Lutheran 1959-2000
Texas Southern 1959-85
Texas Wesleyan 1959-99, 2002–

Texas-Dallas 1977-82, 1994-99
Texas-Permian Basin 1982-88, 1995–
Texas-Tyler 1983-97
Thomas, GA 1994–
Thomas, ME 1968-2003
Thomas More, KY 1968-90
Tiffin, OH 1972–
Tift, GA 1982-87
Toccoa Falls, GA 1981-84
Tougaloo, MS 1964–
Tougalou Southern Christian, MS 1959-60
Transylvania, KY 1959-65, 1976-2004
Trenton State, NJ 1959-65, 1967-72
Trevecca Nazarene, TN 1972–
Trinity International, IL 1969-85, 1989–
Trinity, TX 1959-60, 1978-82
Trinity, VT 1982-91
Trinity Christian, IL 1988–
Trinity Western, BC 1982-83
Tri-State, IN 1967-2004
Troy State, AL 1964-78
Tusculum, TN 1968-69, 1974-99
Tuskegee Institute, AL 1959-71

Union, KY 1959–
Union, TN 1971–
Unity, ME 1969-93
Upper Iowa, 1959-75
Upsala, NJ 1959-60
Urbana, OH 1967–
Ursuline, OH 2000–

Valdosta State, GA 1959-74
Valley City State, ND 1959–
Valley Forge Christian, PA 1982-83
Valparaiso, IN 1959-60
Vanguard (Southern California) 1965–
Victoria, BC 2001–
Villa Madonna, KY 1959-68
Villa Maria, PA 1981-85
Virginia Commonwealth 1968-71
Virginia Intermont 1988–
Virginia State 1959-83
Virginia Union 1959-73, 1976-78
Virginia Wesleyan 1970-74
Virginia-Wise 2000–
Viterbo, WI 1987–
Voorhees, SC 1967–

Waldorf, IA 2003–
Walsh, OH 1969–
Warner Pacific, OR 1964-92, 1999–

Warner Southern, FL 1989–
Warren Wilson, NC 1974-79, 1985-86, 1990-92
Wartburg, IA 1959-75
Washburn, KS 1959-90
Wassuk, NV 1986-87
Wayland, TX 1959-65
Wayland Baptist, TX 1967–
Wayne State, NE 1959-91
Waynesburg, PA 1959-90
Webber, FL 1984-86, 1988–
West Coast Christian, CA 1984-87
West Florida 1970-76, 1980-96
West Georgia 1964-74, 1979-80, 1982-83
West Liberty State, WV 1959-95
West Virginia State 1959-97
West Virginia Tech 1959-95
West Virginia Wesleyan 1959-95
Westbrook, ME 1992-96
Western Baptist, OR 1970–
Western Carolina, NC 1959-72
Western Connecticut 1967-77, 1982-83
Western Illinois 1959-71
Western New England, MA 1967-90
Western New Mexico 1964-96
Western Oregon 1981-2001
Western State, CO 1959-60, 1976-92
Western Washington 1959-98
Westmar, IA 1959-90, 1995-98
Westminster, MO 1959-92, 1997-98
Westminster, PA 1959-97
Westminster, UT 1959-65, 1968-79, 1983–
Westmont, CA 1959–
Wheeling, WV 1964-95
Whitman, WA 1959-99
Whittier, CA 1959-79
Whitworth, WA 1959-98
Wilberforce, OH 1959-82, 1990–
Wiley, TX 1964-91, 1994–
Willamette, OR 1959-98
William and Mary, VA 1982-84

William Carey, MS 1959–
William Jennings Bryan, TN 1982-83, 1986-88
William Jewell, MO 1959–
William Penn, IA 1959-76, 2001–
William Woods, MO 1981–
Williams Baptist, AR 1990–
Willimantic State, CT 1964-65
Wilmington, DE 1959-60, 1970-2003
Wilmington, OH 1964-91
Wilson, PA 1985-91
Windham, VT 1973-78
Windsor, ON 1998–
Wingate, NC 1978-93
Winona State, MN 1959-94
Winston-Salem State, NC 1959-85
Winthrop, SC 1975-83
Wisconsin Lutheran 1989-97
Wisconsin-Eau Claire 1959-93
Wisconsin-Green Bay 1969-76, 1982-90
Wisconsin-LaCrosse 1959-91
Wisconsin-Milwaukee 1982-83, 1985-89
Wisconsin-Oshkosh 1964-83, 1985-90
Wisconsin-Parkside 1969-95, 1997-2002
Wisconsin-Platteville 1959-90
Wisconsin-River Falls 1959-92
Wisconsin-Stevens Point 1959-93
Wisconsin-Stout 1959-91
Wisconsin-Superior 1959-90
Wisconsin-Whitewater 1959-80
Wofford, SC 1959-88
Woodbury, CA 1969-70
Worcester, MA 1972-74

Xavier, LA 1959-60, 1969–

Yankton, SD 1959-85
York, NE 1970-71, 1993–
York, PA 1969-75
Youngstown, OH 1959-60

Glossary of Acronyms

AAHPERD	American Alliance for Health, Physical Education, Recreation, and Dance
AAU	Amateur Athletic Union
ADA	Athletic Directors Association
AIAW	Association of Intercollegiate Athletics for Women
CAA	Council of Athletics Administrators
CACI	Council of Affiliated Conferences and Independents
CIS	Canadian Interuniversity Sport
COP	Council of Presidents
CRI	Creative Resources, Inc.
FAR	Faculty Athletic Representative
FIBA	Foundation of International Basketball
GSAC	Golden State Athletic Conference
NAIA	National Association of Intercollegiate Athletics
NAIAC	National Association of Intercollegiate Athletic Coaches
NAIB	National Association of Intercollegiate Basketball
NASC	National Athletics Steering Committee
NASPE	National Association for Sport and Physical Education
NCAA	National Collegiate Athletic Association
NCC	National Coordinating Committee
NCCAA	National Christian College Athletic Association
NCIC	Northwest Conference of Independent Colleges
NEC	National Executive Committee
NFSHSAA	National Federation of State High School Athletics Associations
NIT	National Invitational Tournament
NJCAA	National Junior College Athletic Association
PAC	Presidents Advisory Committee
SID	Sports Information Director
USOC	United States Olympic Committee

Endnotes

Chapter 1

1   Kevin Henry, "The Beginnings of the Nation's Oldest College Basketball Hoops Fest," *NAIA News*, February 1994, 10.

2   Jack Falla, NCAA: *The Voice of College Sports* (Mission, Kansas: NCAA, 1981), 28.

3   "The History of Basketball," *Baker World of Sports*, n.d. (c. 1971), 16.

4   Francis Lentz Hoover, *A History of the National Association of Intercollegiate Athletics* (unpublished doctoral dissertation, Indiana University, 1958), 33. Unless otherwise noted, most of the material in the first three chapters of this volume has been taken from Hoover's dissertation, copies of which are on file in the NAIA archives.

5   Eugene Kean, "Baker Founder of the N.A.I.A.," *Baker World of Sports*, n.d. (c. 1971), 12-14.

6   Henry, "The Beginnings of the Nation's Oldest College Basketball Hoops Fest," 11.

7   Hoover, *History*, 50.

8   Mark E. Dean, *A History of Intercollegiate Athletics at Indiana State Teachers College* (unpublished dissertation, Indiana University, 1955), passim.

9   It is interesting to note that probably the best history of the *NCAA, Jack Falla's NCAA: The Voice of College Sports* (1982), has only one citation of the NAIA in its index. One is reminded of Canada's relationship with the United States. While a history of the United States might largely ignore its less populous neighbor to the north, Canadian history cannot neglect the giant force bordering it. Think of the NAIA as Canada.

10   Falla, *NCAA*, 57.

11   *Ibid.*, 61, 76.

12   Theodore W. Forbes, *The National Association of Intercollegiate Athletics Since 1942* (unpublished doctoral dissertation, Columbia University, 1955), 202.

13   Henry, "The Beginning of the Nation's Oldest College Basketball Hoops Fest," 11.

14   *Ibid.*, 12.

Chapter 2

1   Milton S. Katz and John B. McLendon, Jr., *Breaking Through: The NAIA and the Integration of Intercollegiate Athleticism Post World War II America* (privately published, 1988), 9. Copies of this excellent booklet can be found in the NAIA archives.

2   *Ibid.* 10.

3   *Ibid.*, 10-11.

4   John Arnold interview, 2 October 2003.

5   Katz and McLendon, *Breaking Through*, 11.

6   *Ibid.*, 12.

7   *Ibid.*, 13.

8   Dick Mackey, "The NAIA: An Unbelievable Basketball Tournament That Tests Endurance of Fans, Players," *Kansas City Star*, 10 March 1970, 6B.

9   *NAIA News*, February-March 1985, 4.

10   Bill Schroeder clipping, 28 June 1977, Al Duer file, NAIA.

11   Carroll Land interview, 1 July 2003.

12   Mackey, "The NAIA," 6B.

13   Earl V. Pullias, "Goals for the Church Related Liberal Arts College: The 70s and Beyond," in Carroll Land files, Point Loma Nazarene University.

14   Falla, *NCAA: The Voice of College Sports*, 132-134.

15   Hoover, *History*, 87-88.

Chapter 3

1   *NAIA News*, December-January 1984-85, 8.

2   Katz and McLendon, *Breaking Through*, 14.

3   *Ibid.*

4   *Ibid.*, 14-15.

5   *Ibid.*, 15-16.

6   *NAIA News*, April-May 1980, 5-6.

7   Katz and McLendon, *Breaking Through*, 17.

8   *Ibid.*, 18.

9   *Ibid.*, 18-19.

10   *Ibid*, 19-20.

11   *Ibid.*, 22.

12   *Ibid.*, 23, 30.

13   Falla, *NCAA*, 135.

14   Katz and McLendon, *Breaking Through*, 26-27.

15   *Ibid.*, 27.

16   Carroll Land interview, 1 July 2003.

Chapter 4

1   Carroll Braxton Land, *A History of the National Association of Intercollegiate Athletics* (unpublished dissertation, University of Southern California, 1977), 34. Most of the material in Chapters Four through Seven has been drawn from Land's thorough treatment, especially uncited information.

2   *Ibid.*, 53-54, 94.

3   Katz and McLendon, *Breaking Through*, 28.

4   Land, *History*, 66.

5   *NAIA News*, Spring 1960, 8.

6   *Ibid.*, 7.

7   *NAIA News*, Winter 1961, 3.

8   Land, *History*, 75.

9   Land, *History*, 103.

10   Katz and McLendon, *Breaking Through*, 26, 24.

Chapter 5

1   John Brooks, "A Clean Break with the Past," *American Heritage* (August 1970), in John R. M. Wilson, ed., *Shaping the American Character* (Lanham, Md.: University Press of America, 1980), 307ff.

2   Land, *History*, 134.

3   *Ibid.*, 162.

4   Falla, *NCAA*, 86.

5   *Ibid.*, 87.

6   Land, *History*, 166-168.

Chapter 6

1   Land, *History*, 194.

2   Land, *History*, 209-210.

3   *NAIA News*, Spring 1969, 21.

4   *NAIA News*, Fall 1969, 3.

5   Land, *History*, 251.

6   *NAIA News*, Fall 1971, 19, 22.

Chapter 7

1   Land, *History*, 272.

2   Bill Richardson, "Al Duer Symbolic of N.A.I.A.," *Kansas City Star*, 4 March 1971, 15.

3   Wally Schwartz interview, 4 September 2003.

4   *Ibid.*

5   *NAIA News*, Fall 1971, 6.

6   Land, *History*, 275.

7   *NAIA News*, Fall 1971, 3. By way of a personal disclaimer, while on the faculty at Mid-America Nazarene College, I was faculty advisor for our club soccer team from 1977 through 1982, when it became a varsity sport. I also played on the team, as did occasional other faculty and even a few "townies." The athletic department exercised no control that I recall, and I was never aware that there were NAIA guidelines under which we should operate . . . and which we clearly violated.

8   Paul S. Boyer, ed., *The Oxford Companion to United States History* (New York: Oxford University Press, 2001), 740.

9   Erin Van Winkle, "Educational Amendments of 1972: Partnership at Bayfield Elementary School," 8 November 2000, at http://extendedcampus.fortlewis.edu/tedweb/bayfield/BayVanWinkle.html.

10   This was not the first women's tournament. The Division for Girls and Women's Sports of AAHPERD began offering national championships in 1966 and by 1972 had seven of them: golf, gymnastics, track and field, badminton, swimming and diving, volleyball, and basketball. The birth of the AIAW reduced this option to irrelevance. (Lisa C. Hutchens and Barbara K. Townsend, "Gender Equity in Collegiate Sports: The Role of Athletic Associations," *Initiatives* (Spring 1998), 1-17.)

11   Land, *History*, 286.

12   *Ibid.*, 286-287.

13   Wally Schwartz interview, 4 September 2003.

14   Falla, *NCAA*, 181, 232-233.

15   Bill Patterson interview, 11 September 2003.

16   *NAIA News*, Spring 1974, 3.

17   Wally Schwartz interview, 4 September 2003.

Chapter 8

1   Land, *History*, 363-365.

2   *NAIA News*, November-December 1978, 15, 18.

3   Louis Spry interview, 4 February 2004.

4   *NAIA News*, Winter 1975, 3.

5   Land, *History*, 338-340.

6   1976 Annual Convention transcript, 33, 132.

7   Land, *History*, 340-341.

8   1977 National Convention transcript, 14-15.

9   1979 National Convention transcript, 12, 7-8.

10   *Ibid.*, 13.

11   *Ibid.*, 9-10.

12   *NAIA News*, April-May 1984, 4.

13   1979 National Convention transcript,, 14.

14   1977 National Convention transcript, 124-138; *NAIA News*, Summer 1977, 18.

15   977 National Convention transcript, 53-59.

16   *NAIA News*, Fall 1977, 14.

17   *NAIA News*, July-August 1986, 2.

18   1977 Annual Convention transcript, 28.

19   Carroll Land interview, 1 July 2003.

20   *NAIA News*, November-December 1978, 3.

21   1979 National Convention transcript, 13, 28-41.

22   Dave Olson recalled overhearing an ill-informed convention delegate refer to the ambiguously-named but very male Carroll Land and his supporters as "a bunch of lesbians." (David Olson interview, 22 December 2003.)

23   *NAIA News*, April-May 1979, 3.

24   *NAIA News*, August-September 1978, 3.

Chapter 9

1   Celeste Ulrich, "Outlooks is Bright in New Frontiers of Women's Athletics," *Coaching: Women's Athletics*, September-October 1980, reprinted in *NAIA News*, December-January 1981-82, 3.

2   *Ibid.*, 4.

3   *Ibid*; Hutchens and Townsend, "Gender Equity in Collegiate Sports," 1-17.

4   Falla, *NCAA*, 182.

5   1980 National Convention transcript, 31-53; Land to author, 3 December 2003.

6   John Crowl, "NAIA to Reserve Leadership Positions for Women," *Chronicle of Higher Education*, 28 March 1984.

7   *NAIA News*, June-July 1980, 3.

8   Falla, *NCAA*, 172-174.

9   *NAIA News*, April-May 1983, 3.

10   *NAIA News*, December-January 1981-82, 28.

11   John Crowl, "NAIA Delegates Reject Creation of Divisions in 4 Sports," *Chronicle of Higher Education*, March 1983, 18.

12   *NAIA News*, April-May 1983, 3; October-November 1983, 8.

13   *NAIA News*, December-January 1979-80, 16-18.

14   *NAIA News*, February-March 1981, 18.

15   *NAIA News*, August-September 1981, 7; February-March 1982, 10-13.

16   *NAIA News*, August-September 1982, 3-5.

17   *NAIA News*, February-March 1983, 6-7.

18   1980 Annual Convention transcript, 88.

19   *NAIA News*, October-November 1981, 6.

20   NAIA Annual Meeting Minutes, 17 March 1983, 2.

21   1980 National Convention transcript, 80, 66.

22   *NAIA News*, February-March 1981, 7.

23   *Ibid.*, 4-6, 18.

24   *NAIA News*, December-January 1981-82, 3; Carroll Land interview, 1 July 2003.

25   *NAIA News*, February-March 1982, 13-15.

26   Wally Schwartz interview, 4 September 2003.

27   Wally Schwartz interview, 2 March 2004.

28   Wally Schwartz interview, 4 September 2003.

Chapter 10

1   Fritz to Executive Committee, 21 June 1983, NEC files, NAIA.

2   *NAIA News*, April-May 1984, 4.

3   John A. Crowl, "NAIA to Reserve Leadership Positions for Women; 'Eligibility Fee' Rejected," *Chronicle of Higher Education*, 28 March 1984; *NAIA News*, February-March 1984, 4.

4   *NAIA News*, October-November 1984, 2.

5   *NAIA News*, December-January 1984-85, 2-7.

6   NAIA Executive Committee minutes, 15-20 March 1984.

7   *Ibid*.

8   Jefferson Farris interview, 11 September 2003.

9   Fritz to National Executive Committee, May 1985, NEC files, NAIA.

10 Minutes of NAIA Summer 1985 Meeting, 12 July 1985, NEC files, NAIA.

11 David Olson interview, 22 December 2003.

12 Minutes of NEC, 14-15 September 1985, NEC files, NAIA.

13 Olson to NEC, 14 November 1985, NEC files, NAIA.

14 Olson to Fritz, 21 January 1986, Olson file, NAIA.

15 *NAIA News*, January-February 1986, 4-5.

16 Charles S. Farrell, "Small College Sports-Governing Body to Vote on Plan for Presidents to Control Organization," *Chronicle of Higher Education*, 12 February 1986, 31-32.

17 Jefferson Farris interview, 11 September 2003.

18 Farris to Charles Morris, et al, 10 January 1986, COP files, NAIA.

19 Bill Patterson and Jefferson Farris interviews, 11 September 2003; Carroll Land interviews, 1 July 2003, 27 March 2004.

20 Wally Schwartz interview, 4 September 2003; Wayne Kraiss interview, 25 Sept. 2003.

21 David Olson interview, 22 December 2003.

22 *Ibid*.

23 Jefferson Farris interview, 11 September 2003; Wayne Kraiss interview, 25 September 2003; *NAIA News*, May-June 1986, 2.

24 Schwartz to NEC, 6 May 1986, NEC files, NAIA; Jefferson Farris interview, 11 September 2003.

25 Crowl, "NAIA to Reserve Leadership Positions for Women," *Chronicle of Higher Education*, 28 March 1984.

26 Olson to Selected NAIA leaders, 8 August 1985, NEC files, NAIA.

27 Minutes of NEC meeting, July 1984, NEC files, NAIA.

28 *NAIA News*, February-March 1984, 4; Minutes of NEC, 13 March 1986, NEC files, NAIA.

29 *NAIA News*, June-July 1984, 4-5.

30 Fritz to NEC, 25 October 1983, 28 August 1984, NEC files, NAIA; *NAIA News*, August-September 1984, 5-6.

31 *NAIA News*, November-December 1985, 3.

32 *NAIA News*, March-April 1986, 4.

33 *NAIA News*, December-January 1984-85, 23.

34 NEC minutes, July 1985.

Chapter 11

1   Farris to Houdeshell, 9 June 1986, COP Files, NAIA.

2   NAIA press release, 10 June 1986, COP Files, NAIA.

3   NAIA policy paper, 11 July 1986, COP Files, NAIA.

4   Minutes of July 1986 COP Meeting, COP Files, NAIA.

5   Farris to NAIA COP, 22 July 1986, COP Files, NAIA.

6   Jeff Farris interview, 11 September 2003.

7   Tom Feld interview, 29 January 2004.

8   Jefferson Farris interview, 11 September 2003; Bill Patterson interview, 11 September 2003.

9   Wally Schwartz interview, 4 September 2003.

10 Jefferson Farris interview, 11 September 2003; Bill Patterson interview, 11 September 2003.

11 Farris memo, 18 March 1987, COP File, NAIA.

12 *NAIA News*, 9 November 1990, 1.

13 *NAIA News*, 18 November 1986, 1.

14 *NAIA News*, 10 March 1987, 1; 3 November 1987, 1.

15 Minutes, COP meeting, 1-3 April 1989, COP Files, NAIA.

16 Report, Academic Standards Committee, 21-22 September 1987,

17 Tom Feld to District 15 CEOs, 4 April 1989, COP Files, NAIA.

18 Marketing and Membership Committee Report, 2 April 1989, COP files, NAIA.

19 *NAIA News*, 20 June 1989, 1-2.

20 Farris to COP and NEC, 19 October 1987, COP File, NAIA.

21 *NAIA News*, Convention Wrap-up, October 1989, 1.

22 Chronological Review of Divisions of Competition Proposal," NEC files, NAIA; Farris to Divisions for Competition Ad-Hoc Committee, 7 March 1990, NEC files, NAIA.

23 COP Minutes, 23-25 April 1990, COP files, NAIA.

24 *NAIA News*, 26 March 1987, 1, 5; 26 July 1988, 1.

25 *NAIA News*, 16 August 1988, 1, 6.

26 *NAIA News*, 25 June 1990, 2.

27 *NAIA News*, 23 May 1989, 3.

28 *NAIA News*, 28 July 1987, 2.

29 *NAIA News*, Convention wrap-up (October 1989), 1, 2.

30 Wayne Kraiss interview, 25 September 2003; David Olson interview, 22 December 2003.

31 Tom Feld interview, 29 January 2004.

32 *NAIA News*, 12 September 1989, 4.

33 *NAIA News*, 27 August 1990, 4.

34 Wayne Dannehl and Jim Houdeshell to NAIA leaders, 29 June 1990, NEC files, NAIA; Fred Young to NAIA Presidents, Athletic Directors, and Faculty Athletic Representatives, 14 May 1990, COP files, NAIA; Joe Struckle to COP, 29 May 1990, COP files, NAIA.

35 Feld to COP, 6 August 1990, COP files, NAIA.

36 Joe Struckle to COP, 15 August 1990, COP files, NAIA.

Chapter 12

1 Joe Struckle interview, 11 March 2004; Carol Putnam interview, 12 March 2004; William Patterson interview, 11 September 2003.

2 James Chasteen interview, 2 October 2003; *NAIA News*, 12 October 1990.

3 Transition notes, 20 December 1990, COP files, NAIA.

4 *Ibid.*

5 *NAIA News*, 15 February 1991, 4.

6 Carol Putnam interview, 11 September 2003; Bill Patterson interview, 11 September 2003; James Chasteen interview, 2 October 2003; Carroll Land to author, 13 February 2004, in author's possession.

7 Bill Patterson interview, 11 September 2003.

8 *NAIA News*, May 1992, 8.

9 James Chasteen interview, 2 October 2003.

10 John E. Moore, Jr., to District 16 Presidents, 25 April 1991, COP files, NAIA; *NAIA News*, May 1993, 12.

11 *Ibid.*

12 *NAIA News*, April 1992, 3; Future of the NAIA Committee Meeting Minutes, 25-27 February 1992, COP files, NAIA.

13 *NAIA News*, November 1995, 4.

14 Preliminary Report from the Task Force on Enhancement and Involvement of Women in NAIA, March 1992, COP files, NAIA.

15 *NAIA News*, March 1993, 3.

16 Council of Presidents, approved policies, n.d. (early 1992?), COP files, NAIA.

17 Membership Task Force Report, 12 April 1992, COP files, NAIA; Land to author, 13 February 2004.

18 Membership Task Force Report, 12 April 1992; Patterson to COP, 24 April 1992, COP files, NAIA.

19 Membership Committee Report, September 1992, COP files, NAIA; Chasteen to Ivory Nelson, 11 January 1993, COP files, NAIA.

20 *NAIA News*, 5 August 1991, 1.

21 James Chasteen interview, 2 October 2003.

22 Tom Feld interview, 9 March 2004; Joe Struckle interview, 11 March 2004.

23 *Ibid.*; Wayne Kraiss interview, 25 September 2003.

24 *Ibid.*; Wally Schwartz interview, 4 September 2003; Carol Putnam interview, 11 September 2003; Steve Baker interview, 9 September 2003.

25 Joe Struckle interview, 11 March 2004.

26 *NAIA News*, November 1992, 8.

27   Interviews with Chasteen, Patterson, Schwartz, Struckle, Kraiss, Land, and Feld.

Chapter 13

1   Bill Patterson to job applicants, 14 May 1993, NAIA; Chasteen Executive Report, 1 November 1995, COP files, NAIA.

2   *NAIA News*, May 1993, 8, 9, 11.

3   Report of the Committee on the Role of Affiliate Conferences, 18 April 1993, COP files, NAIA, 11-14.

4   *NAIA News*, November 1993, 10.

5   COP minutes, April 1995, COP files, NAIA; Executive Cabinet minutes, 4 April, 19 April 1995, Executive Cabinet file, NAIA.

6   COP minutes, October 1996, COP files, NAIA; Steve Baker interview, 9 September 2003.

7   Ad Hoc Financial Aid Committee report, 13 March 1996, COP files, NAIA.

8   COP minutes, April 1997, COP files, NAIA.

9   *NCAA News*, 27 May 1996; Chasteen to Orville C. Walz, 17 August 1995, Chasteen Reading File, NAIA.

10   Louis Spry interview, 4 February 2004; James Chasteen interview, 2 October 2003.

11   Steve Baker interview, 9 September 2003; Joe Struckle interview, 11 March 2004; Bill Patterson interview, 11 September 2003.

12   "NCIC and National Affiliation Issues," April 1994, in Patterson reading file, NAIA.

13   Bill Patterson interview, 11 September 2003.

14   James Chasteen interview, 2 October 2003.

15   Stevens to Ken Bootsma, 8 November 1994, NCIC file, NAIA.

16   Chasteen to Davis, 18 April 1995; Chasteen to Young, 8 May 1995, Chasteen reading file, NAIA.

17   COP minutes, October 1996, COP files, NAIA.

18   NAIA Membership Committee minutes, 5 April 1997, COP files, NAIA; Joe Struckle interview, 11 March 2004.

19   Documents in COP files, 1994, NAIA.

20   Bill Patterson interview, 11 September 2003.

21   Joe Struckle interview, 11 March 2004; Tom Feld interview, 9 March 2004.

22   Cliff Hamlow interview, 6 April 2004.

23   Chasteen to Houdeshell, 6 July 1995, Chasteen reading file, NAIA.

24   COP minutes, 23-27 September 1995, COP files, NAIA.

25   Executive Report, 1 November 1995, COP files, NAIA.

26   Membership development strategic plan, COP agenda book, March 1996, NAIA.

27   Creative Resources, Inc. "NAIA Leadership 2000," 2.

28   Bill Patterson interview, 11 September 2003.

29   "NAIA Leadership 2000," 10-14, 50.

30   Bootsma to Administrative Committee, 11 April 1996, Baker reading file, NAIA.

31   Bill Patterson interview, 11 September 2003.

32   Wayne Kraiss interview, 25 September 2003; Steve Baker interview, 9 September 2003.

33   Patterson to staff, 12 November 1996, COP files, NAIA; "Report of the Interim Chief Executive Officer to the Membership," insert to *NAIA News*, November 1996.

34   *NAIA News*, August 1996, 3; Carol Putnam interviews, 12 March 2004, 26 April 2004; Cliff Hamlow interview, 6 April 2004; Bill Patterson interview, 11 September 2003.

Chapter 14

1   Baker to search committee, 3 December 1996, COP Correspondence file, NAIA.

2   Steve Baker interview, 9 September 2003.

3   Bill Patterson interview, 11 September 2003.

4   Carol Putnam interview, 11 September 2003.

5   Steve Baker interview, 9 September 2003.

6   *NAIA News*, August 1998, 3.

7   Baker to NAIA Presidents, 4 November 1998, COP Correspondence file, NAIA.

8   Baker to COP, 4 May 1999, COP Correspondence file, NAIA.

9   Jim Helmer to COP and CAA, 7 June 1999, COP Correspondence file, NAIA.

10   Baker interview, 9 September 2003; Cedric Dempsey interview, 21 Nov. 2004.

11   President's Report to October 1998 COP Meeting, COP file, NAIA.

12   President's Report to October 1999 COP Meeting, COP file, NAIA.

13 COP Minutes, 31 March-1 April 2000, COP file, NAIA.

14 COP Minutes, 9-10 April 1999, COP file, NAIA.

15 Jim Carr and Robert Rhoads to COP, 6 March 2000, COP file, NAIA.

16 Report of the NCC to the COP re Fifth Year Eligibility, March 2000, COP file, NAIA; COP Minutes, 31 March-1 April 2000, COP file, NAIA.

17 Struckle to Steve Baker, 1 March 2000, COP file, NAIA.

18 *NAIA News*, November 1997, 8.

19 COP Minutes, 24-26 September 2000, COP file, NAIA.

20 Baker to COP, 14 April 2000, COP correspondence file, NAIA.

21 COP Minutes, 30-31 March 2001, 17-19 March 2002, COP file, NAIA.

22 Creative Resources, "NAIA Leadership 2000," revised ed., April 1996, NAIA, pp. 13-14.

23 Steve Baker interview, 9 September 2003; Bill Patterson interview, 11 September 2003.

24 President/CEO report to COP, April 1998, COP Agenda Book, NAIA.

25 Tulsa *World*, 2 April 1999.

26 President/CEO report to COP, October 1999, COP Agenda Book, NAIA.

27 Baker to Barry Dorsey, et al, 19 January 2000, COP correspondence file, NAIA.

28 COP Minutes, 1 April 2000, COP files, NAIA.

29 Baker to Relocation Committee, 22 Feb. 2001, COP file, NAIA; COP Minutes, 7 March 2001, COP file, NAIA.

Chapter 15

1 Interviews with Steve Baker and Bob Wilson, 14 June 2004.

2 CEO report to COP, March 2004, COP Agenda Book, NAIA.

3 "NAIA on the Move," *Athletic Management*, June-July 2001, 9-10.

4 Report of the CEO to COP, 14 September 2002, COP Agenda Book, NAIA.

5 Ron Prettyman interview, 15 December 2003.

6 NAIA-NCAA Comparison Document Summary, February 2004, NAIA.

7 Wayne Kraiss interview, 25 September 2003.

8 CEO reports to COP, March 2003, September 2003, COP Agenda Book, NAIA.

9 "No Rose Bowl, but . . . ," *NAIA News*, Summer 1995, 8-9; Jeff Struckle interview, 8 September 2003; "O Canada," *NAIA News*, September 1997, 3-5.

10 Jeff Struckle interview, 8 September 2003.

11 CEO Report to COP, March 2002, COP Agenda Book, NAIA.

12 CEO Report to COP, March 2002, COP Agenda Book, NAIA; Lori Thomas phone conversation, 9 June 2004.

13 COP Agenda Book, March 2004, NAIA.

14 Bylaws amendment #1, COP Agenda Book, March 2004, NAIA.

15 Bylaws amendment #4, COP Agenda Book, March 2004, NAIA.

16 Baker to Dallas Baptist University President, 22 June 2001, Baker Reading File, NAIA.

17 COP minutes, 28 September 2003, COP file, NAIA.

18 Steve Baker interview, 14 June 2004.

19 Steve Baker interviews, 9 September 2003, 14 June 2004.

20 Steve Baker interview, 14 June 2004.

21 CAA Minutes, 11 June 2003, COP Agenda Book, September 2003, NAIA.

Index

About the Author

John R. M. Wilson was born in Vancouver, British Columbia, in 1944 and grew up in Santa Barbara, California. He played sophomore baseball at Santa Barbara High School and soon realized that his dream of playing in the big leagues was not going to happen. A 1964 graduate of University of California at Santa Barbara, Wilson earned his Ph.D. in history from Northwestern University in 1971.

Since 1966, Wilson has taught at three NAIA schools: Minot State College (ND) from 1966 to 1974, Mid-America Nazarene College (KS) from 1976 to 1989, and Southern California College/Vanguard University since 1989. At Vanguard, he has chaired the Athletic Committee since 1990, served as Champions of Character representative since 2001, and been a player/coach of the faculty/staff intramural softball team since 1991. A professor of history at Vanguard, Wilson teaches a class on baseball history.

Additionally, Wilson is the author of *Turbulence Aloft: The Civil Aeronautics Administration Amid Wars and Rumors of Wars, 1938-1953* (1979), *A New Research Guide in History* (1986), *Herbert Hoover and the Armed Forces* (1993), and the editor of *Forging the American Character* (4th ed., 2003). Most recently, Wilson has written some twenty baseball-related biographies for Oxford's *American National Biography*. Wilson has been married 37 years to the former Mary Ahlberg, with whom he has two daughters and five grandchildren.